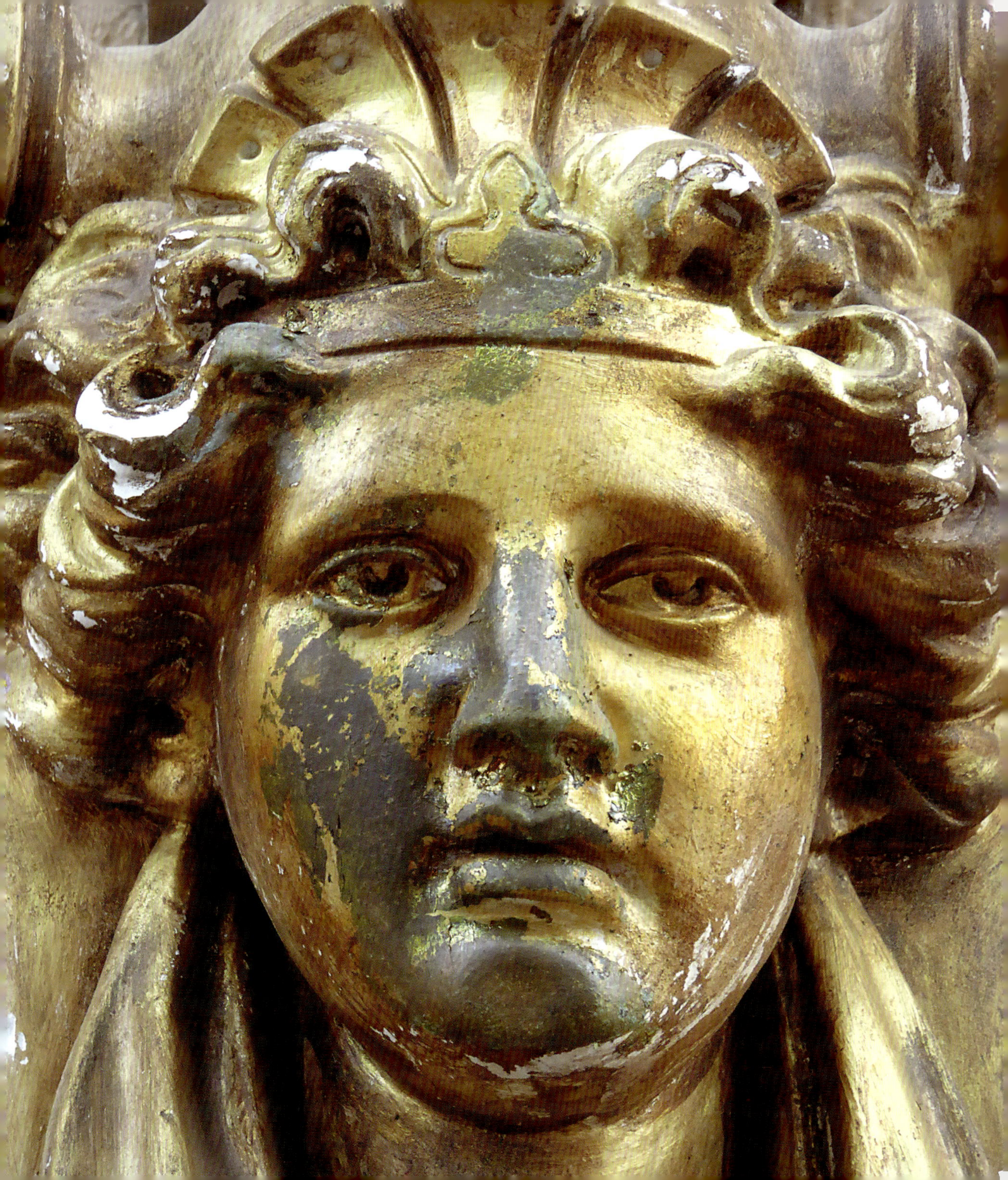

ATHENS UNVEILED

ANNA A. ANGELIDAKIS

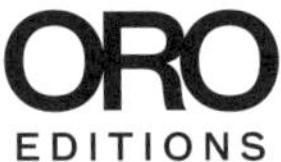

Publishers of Architecture, Art, and Design
Gordon Goff: Publisher

www.oroeditions.com
info@oroeditions.com

Published by ORO Editions

Photography and book design: Anna Angelidakis
Photo Editor: TJ Gemignani
Text: Anna Angelidakis
ORO Project Coordinator: Kirby Anderson
Headline typeface: "Monad," designed by Yasin Yalçın

10 9 8 7 6 5 4 3 2 1 First Edition

Library of Congress data available upon request. World Rights: Available

ISBN: 978-1-957183-03-9s

Color Separations and Printing: ORO Group Ltd.
Printed in China.

International Distribution: www.oroeditions.com/distribution

ORO Editions makes a continuous effort to minimize the overall carbon footprint of its publications. As part of this goal, ORO Editions, in association with Global ReLeaf, arranges to plant trees to replace those used in the manufacturing of the paper produced for its books. Global ReLeaf is an international campaign run by American Forests, one of the world's oldest nonprofit conservation organizations. Global ReLeaf is American Forests' education and action program that helps individuals, organizations, agencies, and corporations improve the local and global environment by planting and caring for trees.

ATHENS UNVEILED

A PORTRAIT OF LATE 19TH-CENTURY ATHENS THROUGH HER STREETS AND NEIGHBORHOODS

ANNA A. ANGELIDAKIS

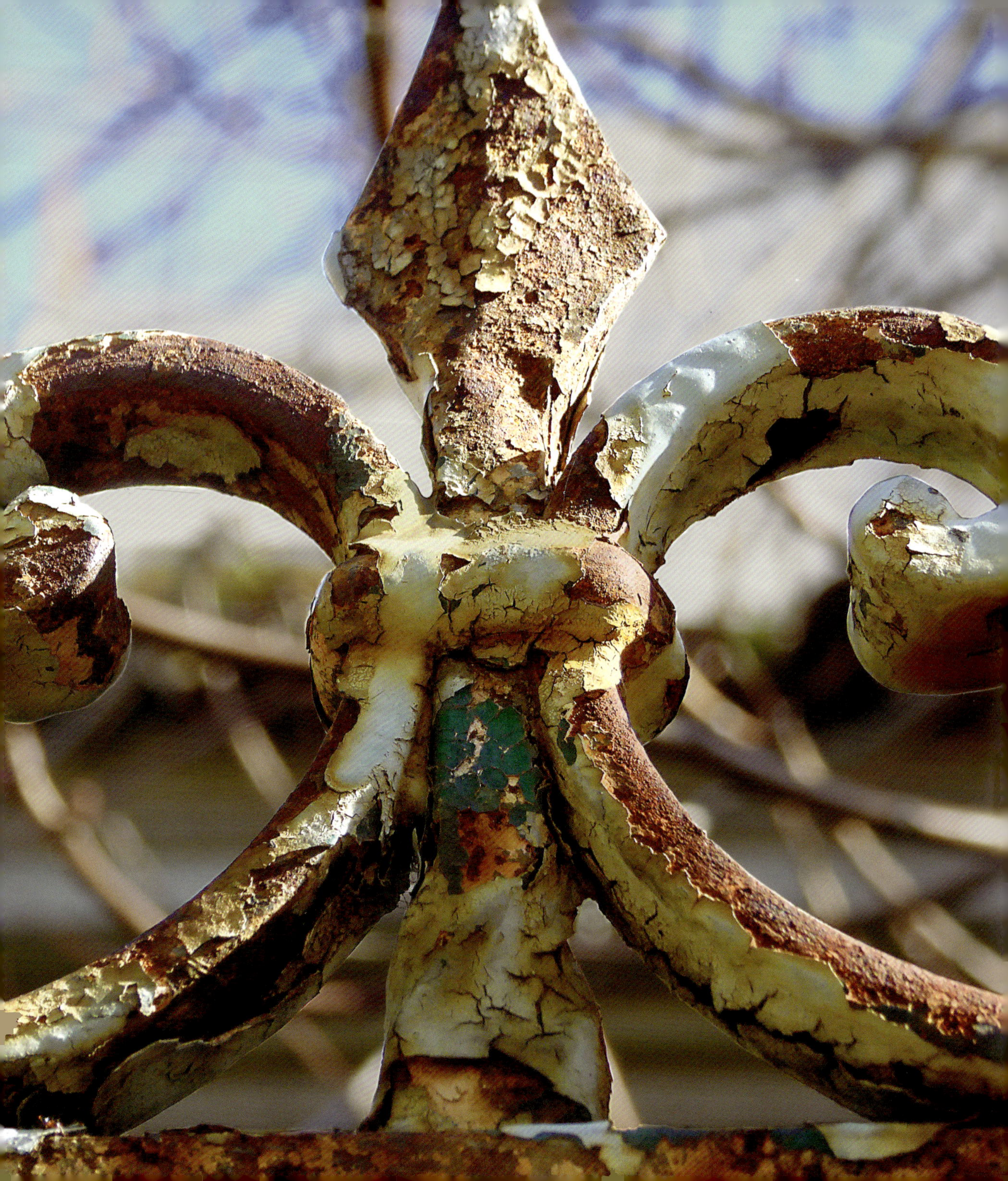

CONTENTS

Opposite: *Detail of rusty gate, Athens*

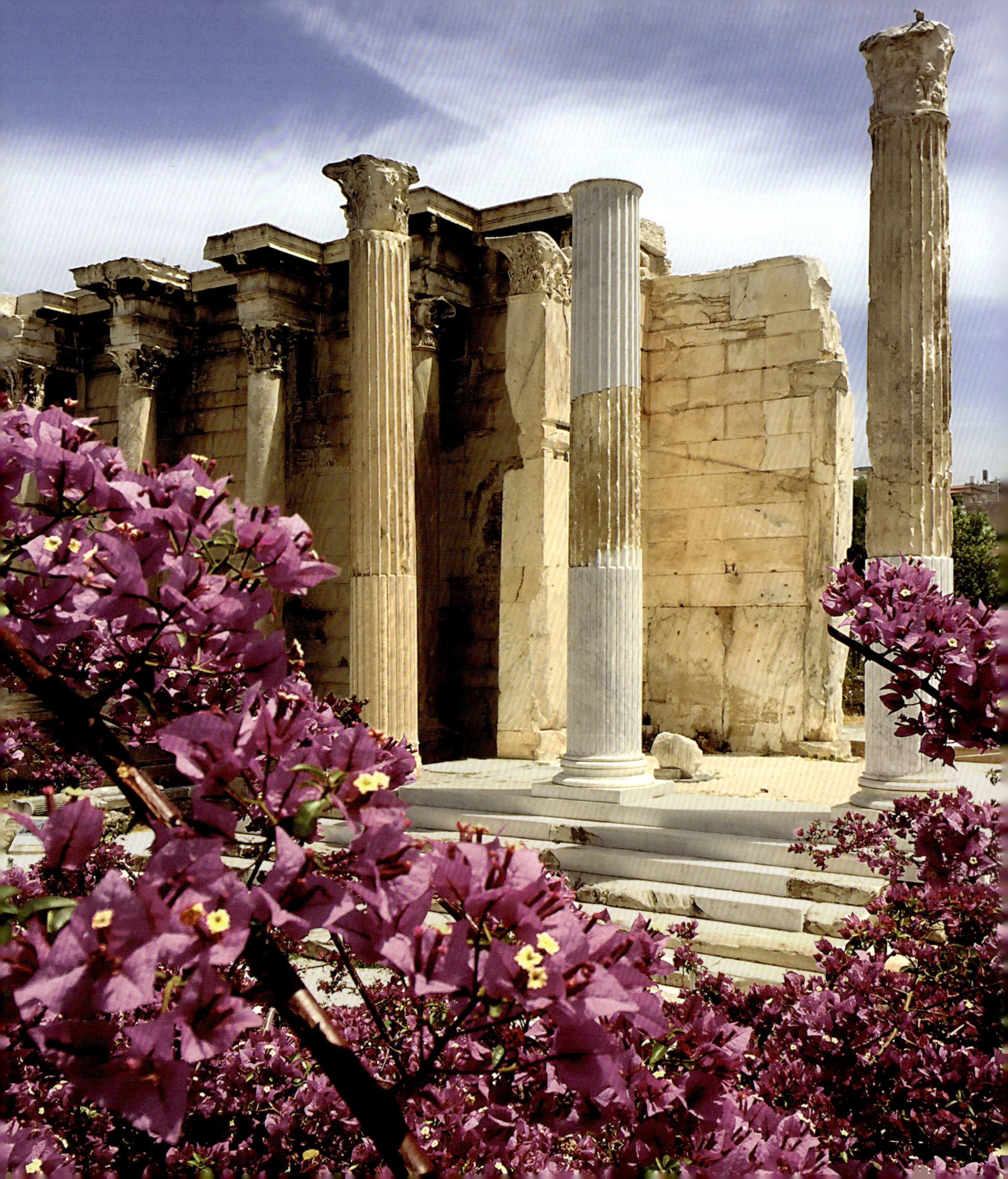

INTRODUCTION

Nineteenth-century Athens, early spring. An eerie silence spreads over the valley as if all movement has frozen in space. The moon climbs higher, playing hide and seek with the fast-moving clouds. Perched above the goddess' highest pediment, the moon sees it all: the small hamlets clustered around the ancient rock, the windswept paths and the broken columns, remnants of a past glory.

A gust of wind surges from the east, rising a cloud of dust. The old shepherd wraps his cape closer to himself unable to sleep. A group of young urchins hovers behind a pile of rubble, waiting for an unsuspecting straggler. Maybe, tonight, they'll get lucky; maybe the King's guards will stagger by, drunker than ever, making them an easy prey to rob.

Why would anyone wish to live in this godforsaken place? A place where the stench rises depending upon how the wind blows, where animals and people sleep together for warmth. Nobody speaks of the old glory, because no one remembers it, and those who do, avert their faces. Ruins, ruins, and more ruins. Hunger and disease.

Opposite: *Hadrian's Library, Monastiraki Square, Athens*

INTRODUCTION

In darkly lit cafés, the tavern owners fill the jugs for one more round. The wine tastes bitter but it blurs the worries. How is this land to forge ahead? Who is to care for them and their children? What is there to hope for?

A man finds solace in the hands of a prostitute, a widow selling her body for a piece of bread to feed her children, but it's fleeting like everything else. In a cold room, a young poet scribbles down verses, dreaming of a new Greece. He's burning with fever and coughs up blood on his straw mattress. "Just pray; God is merciful," the local priest tells him.

What is one to do? What is one to say? How to endure? Yet, despite the glumness, the clouds suddenly part and a starry lit sky blankets the valley. The wind shifts again, releasing an intoxicating scent from a tangerine tree. There's magic in this land. The moment that all seems lost, hope sprouts again like a beam of moonlight making everything possible.

In another part of town, a carriage stops in front of a towering mansion with ornate windowsills and balcony rails decorated with exotic birds and flowers. Marble figureheads observe the guests with impervious gazes bored at their banality.

Opposite: *Timeless travelers, Athens*

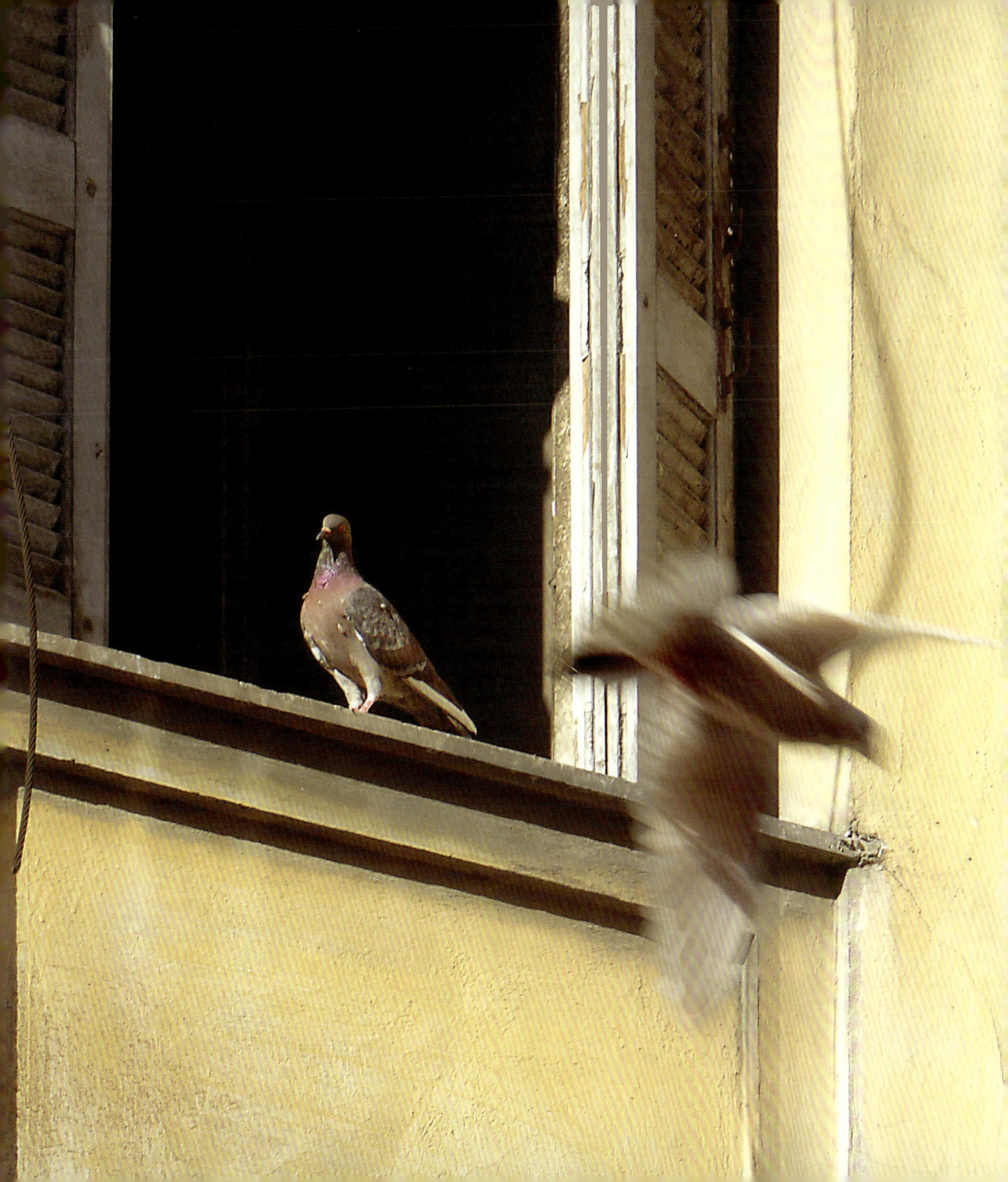

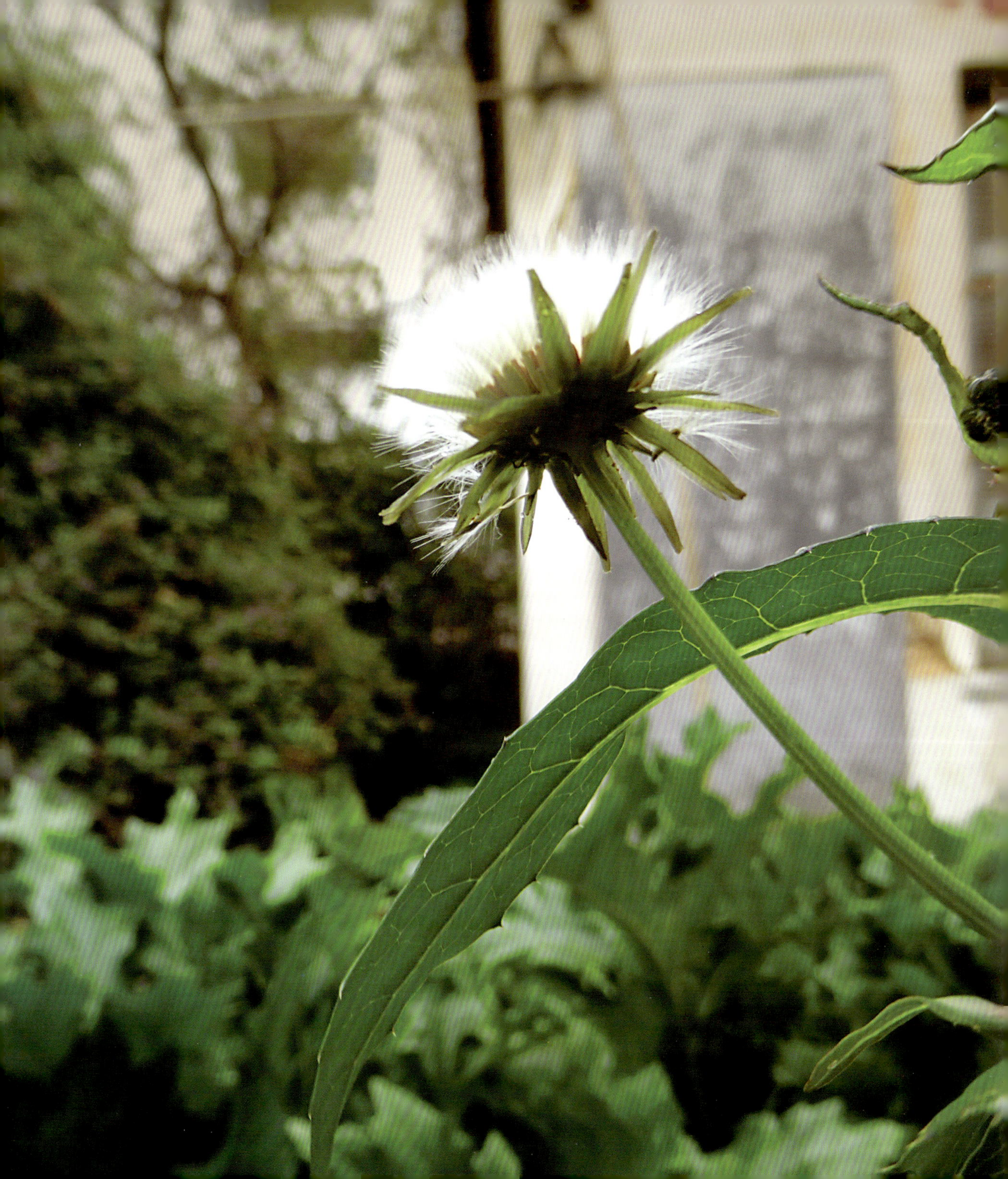

INTRODUCTION

The guests, dressed in their finest clothes, have arrived for yet another dance. Women in exquisite silk dresses, low-cut necklines and sparkling necklaces, are escorted by men in black top hats. The women giggle as local coolies lift them up from their carriages and drop them at the gated door, so as not to dirty their satin shoes.

Music trickles from the open windows and couples waltz under crystal chandeliers. The hostess flaunts her French and German at her guests, the only acceptable languages of the aristocracy. At the end of the hall, a group of men gather around a marble fireplace, the roaring flames illuminating their waxed mustaches.

They smoke pipes lit by servants, and sip expensive wines from Bavaria and France. They are the new rulers, laughing and exchanging broken ancient words, a sign of their finest education. These are the king's ambassadors, the selected ones, eager to civilize this savage nation. British, French, Bavarians, and Russians, watching each other like hawks, hungry to claim a part of this newly founded nation and add their names to history.

Opposite: *Flower blooming amidst ruins, Athens*

INTRODUCTION

Still, away from it all, a new vision is taking form; marble is cut from the Pentelikon Mountain and hand-hewn stone is brought in from Piraeus. Plans are drawn, roads are constructed, and grand buildings erected. Workers and artisans from the islands flock to the city to work side by side with famed architects, sculptors, and painters. Wealthy Greek merchants and businessmen who lived abroad have returned, pouring their wealth into rivaling the ancient city. Nothing is to be spared. Magnificent buildings are raised, and wide boulevards are carved out of the hills. Palm trees are planted and grand fountains sculpted. Universities, libraries and hospitals are built, and so the new capital slowly emerges.

Writing about late nineteenth-century Athens presents many challenges, primarily involving how to do justice to this complex nascent period of the Greek nation. I'm not a historian nor a scholar, so I speak out of no authority. Instinct and my love for Athens are my guides, the city I was born and raised in. No matter the many places in which I've lived, Athens has remained my compass. For the longest of time, my interest was rooted in classical Athens. Walking around the city was like stepping back into antiquity and catching a glimpse of something greater.

Opposite: *Terracotta flower pot with blooming geraniums, Plaka, Athens*

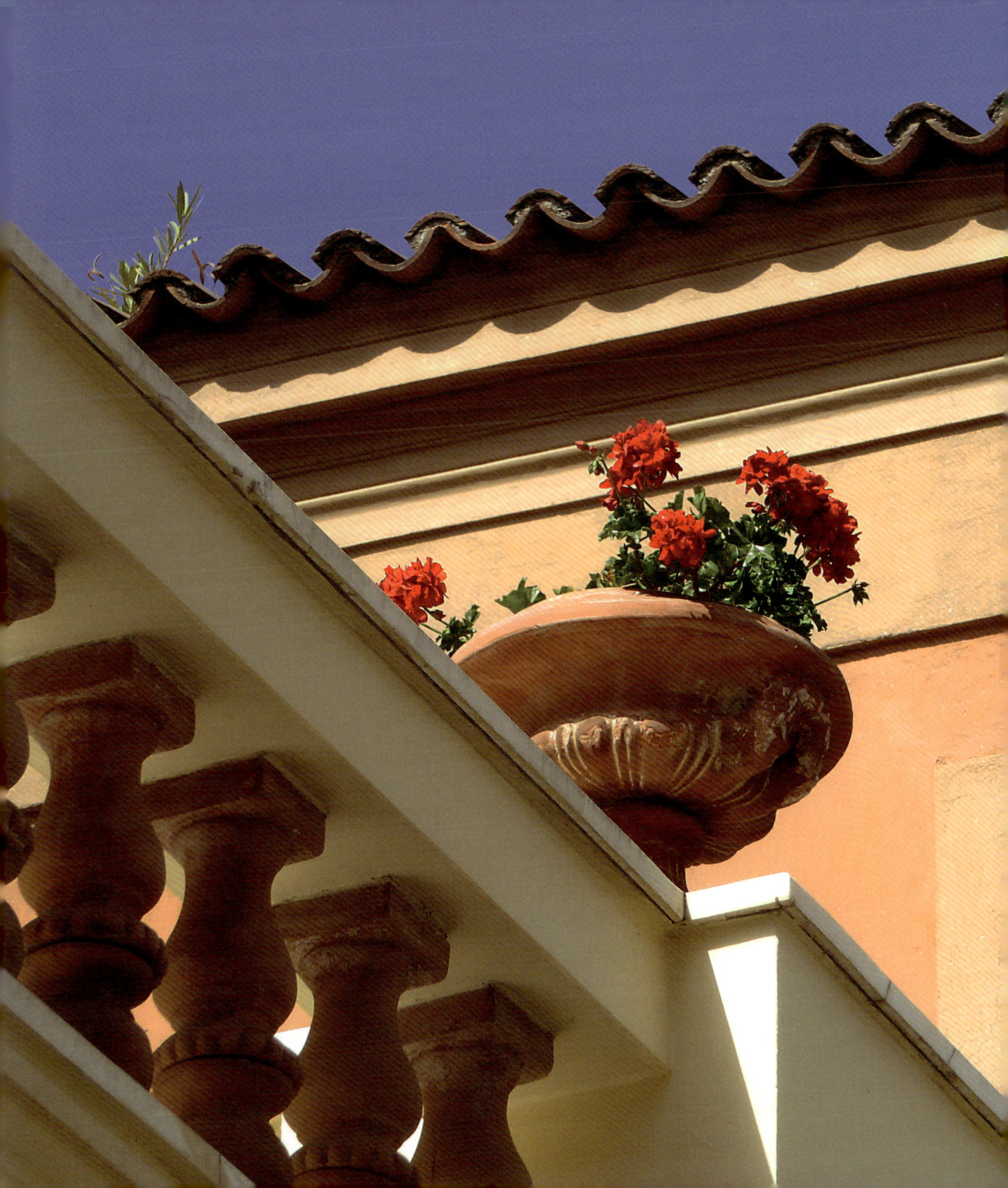

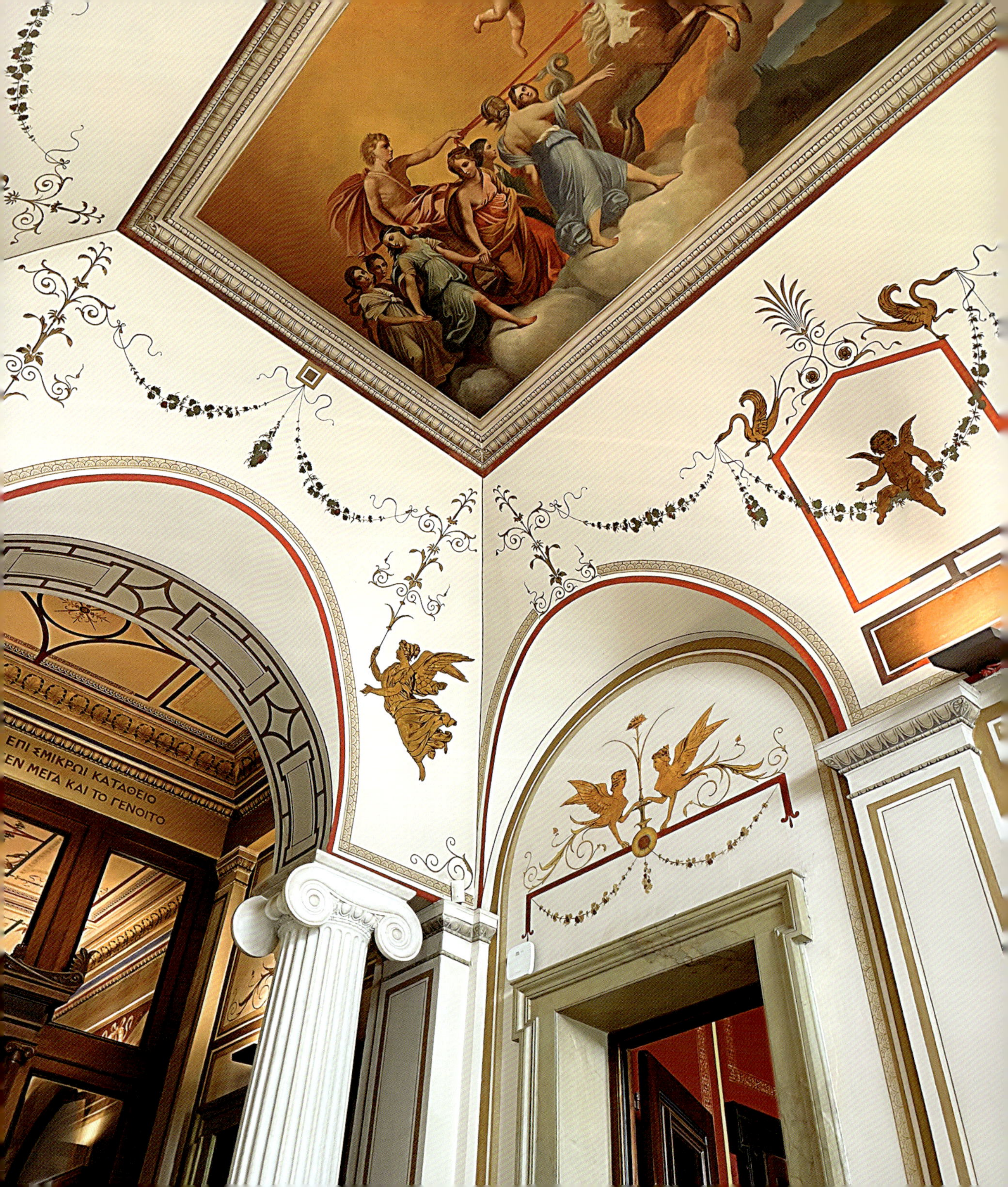
ΕΠΙ ΣΜΙΚΡΩΙ ΚΑΤΑΘΕΙΟ
ΕΝ ΜΕΓΑ ΚΑΙ ΤΟ ΓΕΝΟΙΤΟ

INTRODUCTION

It was upon my return from New York to Athens in 2020 that my perspective shifted. Covid was already taking its toll; the lock down was so severe, we were hardly allowed to leave our homes except to buy food, medicine, and to exercise. Since all the museums and archaeological sites were closed, I began walking parallel to the rail lines, moving from neighborhood to neighborhood. One street led to another, revealing an Athens that I hardly knew.

The Athens I discovered, was tired and in need of mending. Behind the luster of the ancient sites and tourist destinations, rows of half demolished and decaying mansions spoke of another glory, their inhabitants long forgotten. Alleys scented with herbs and spices from the Middle East and cheap Chinese clothing stores spoke of a universality, where Greeks and immigrants live side by side.

This antithesis between ancient Greece and nineteenth-century Athens drew me in with a profound force. I wanted to "see" again and process this information that had always been present, but I had failed to notice.

Opposite: *Numismatic Museum of Athens–Iliou Melathron, Athens*

INTRODUCTION

Athens Unveiled pays homage to the people, streets, and neighborhoods of late nineteenth-century Athens, where some of the finest neoclassical buildings stand next to abandoned mansions, brothels, and old factories. Where shoppers still bargain over the price of clothes and produce on the old streets of commerce, and where young poets compose lyrics and poetry, bringing life and all of its beauty into sharp focus.

Athens Unveiled is divided into five sections: 1. Neoclassical Athens 2. Forgotten Glory 3. The Heart of Commerce 4. Neighborhoods of Ill Repute 5. A League of Their Own.

Choosing what to include in this book often seemed like an impossible task. There was so much visual and historical information to draw from, in the end, I decided to follow my instinct and include what spoke to me on a personal level. The rest I leave to the reader, to go out and explore this city of beauty and contradictions and add their own visions and observations to this very humble list.

Opposite: *Abandoned courtyard, Psyrri, Athens*

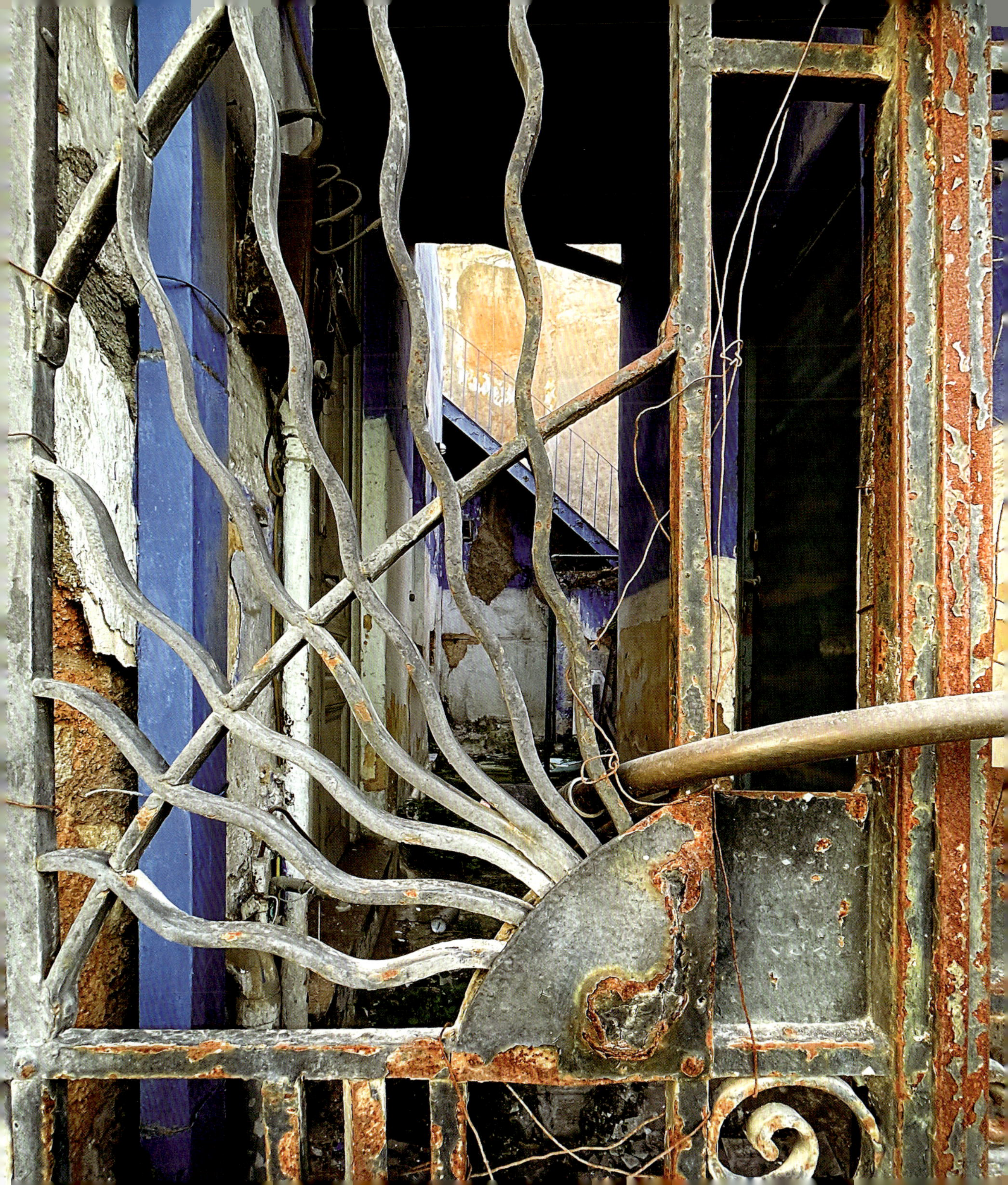

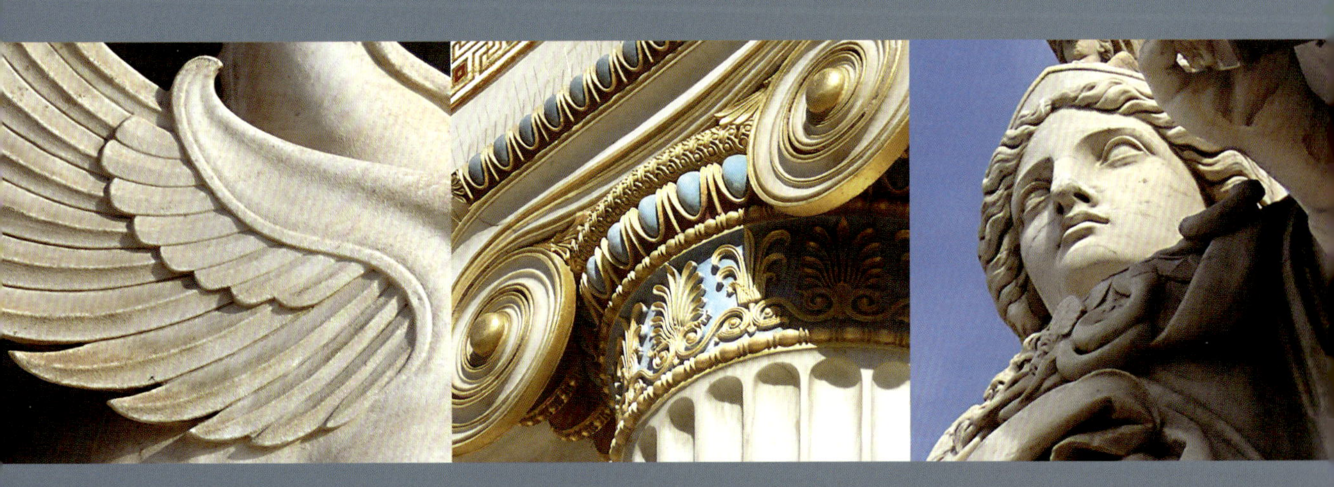

ATHENIAN RENAISSANCE

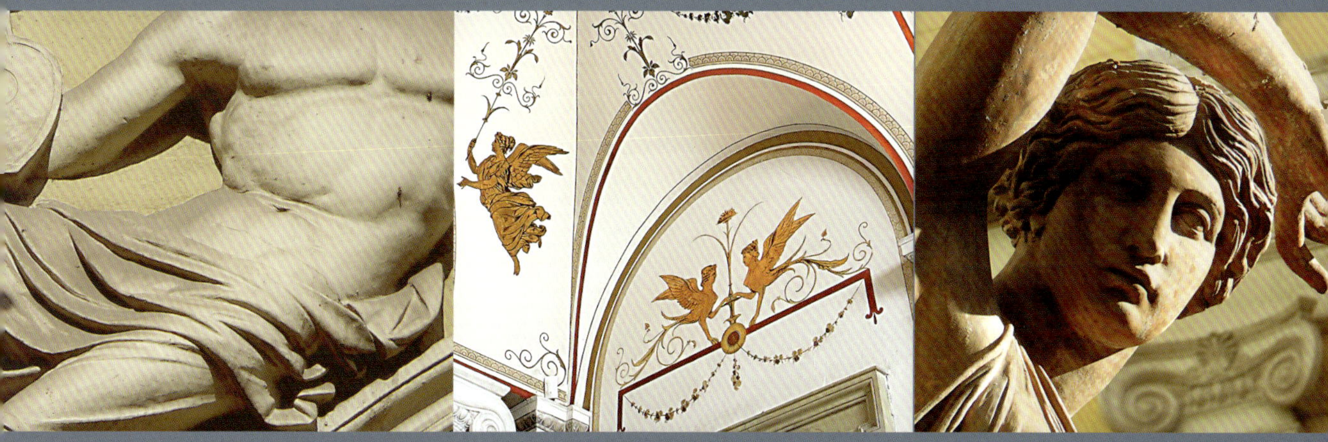

Stairways leading to the stars, sapphire blues and terracotta reds blending with cypress greens and golds, cast iron cupids and nymphs perched on balconies, embracing. Architects, painters, and sculptors drawing and redrawing plans, eager to recapture the glory of the city that once was. The city that will always be. Athens.

Neoclassical architecture emerged in Europe in the 1750s as a reaction to the Baroque and Rococo styles. The discovery of the archaeological ruins in Pompeii and Herculaneum inspired architects to resurrect the building styles of ancient Greece and Rome. Grandeur of scale, simplicity of geometric forms, and dramatic use of columns, often in the Doric style, are a few of the characteristics of this revival.

Following the establishment of the Greek kingdom in 1832, King Otto invited an elite of architects and artisans, primarily from Bavaria and Denmark, to build a capital equal to those of other European countries. Architects such as Friedrich von Gärtner, Leo von Klenze, Theophil Hansen, Hans Christian Hansen, Wilhelm von Weiler, and Ludwig Lange, are only a few that partook in this neoclassical revival.

INTRODUCTION

Yet, it's Ernst Ziller's work that marked Athens in the most profound way. He designed, built, and supervised more than five hundred public and private buildings, not only in Athens but also around Greece. He is rightfully considered one of the most influential architects of his time.

Ziller formalized the connection between Renaissance and antiquity in the most masterful ways. While his teacher, Theophil Hansen, mostly worked in Vienna and Copenhagen, Ziller lived and breathed the Greek air. Surrounded by brilliant sunlight and archaeological treasures, he adjusted his style to work harmoniously with the proportions and the needs of Athens.

Themes drawn from nature and mythology, bold colors and forms, elegant Caryatids figures are his signature style. He was the first to bring artificial ventilation and central heating to Greece and decorated his buildings with cast iron balconies and designs.

While there are many neoclassical buildings to admire throughout Athens, my hope is to draw attention to some of the lesser known buildings that deserve equal attention.

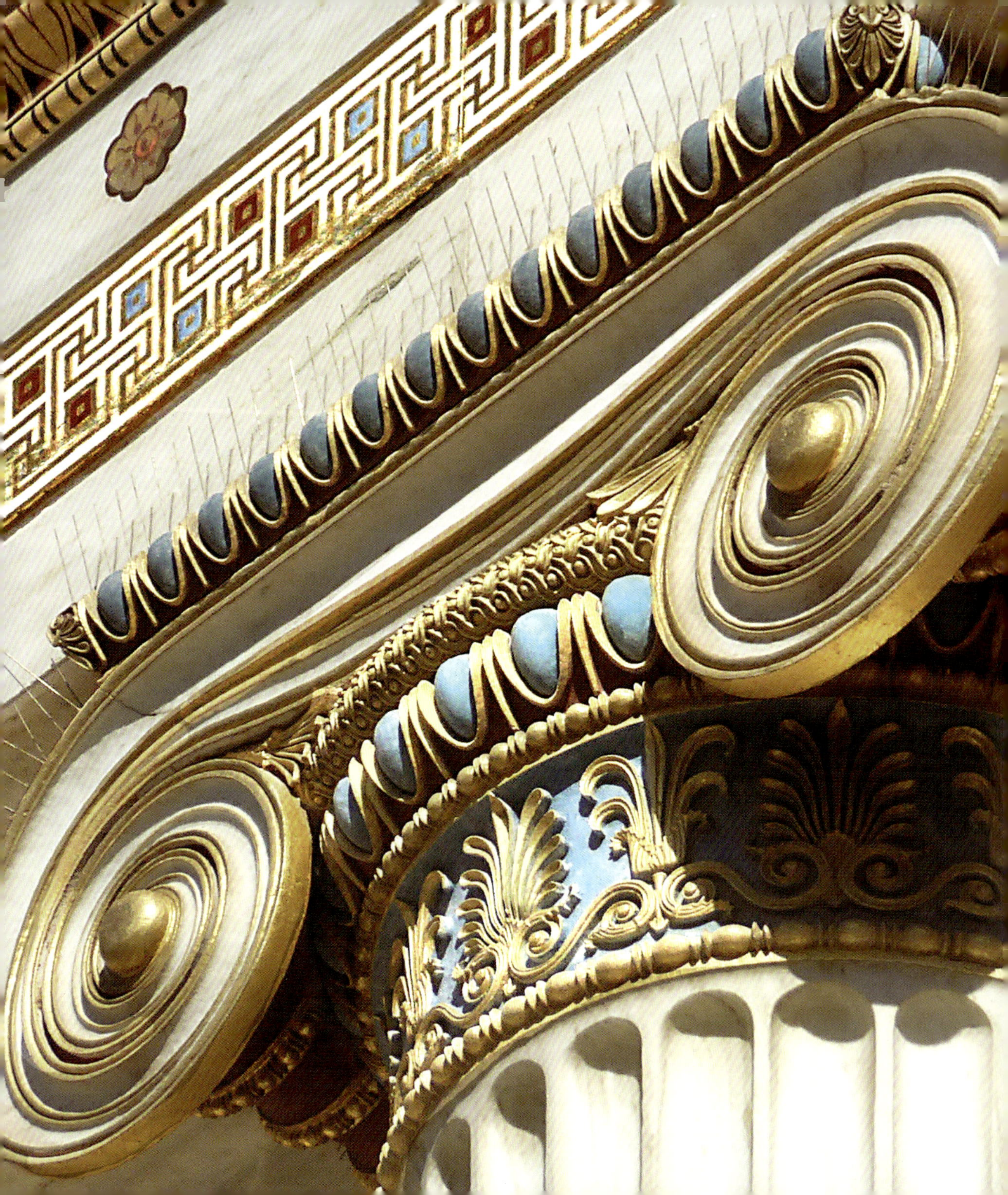

ATHENIAN TRILOGY

October evening on Panepistimiou Street. Saffron colors flood the sky, caressing Athena's statue. The shadows grow longer, illuminating Plato's pondering eyes and Socrates' brow. The grounds empty out, as night descends, unveiling Athens' magic.

The "Athenian Trilogy," as The Academy, The University of Athens, and The National Library are known, is the finest example of neoclassical architecture in Athens. Visited by hundreds of visitors every year, the buildings are hardly "seen." Their sheer size often overshadows the details and artistry that went into the sculptures and paintings, works of true ingenuity.

The University of Athens

The University of Athens, also known as the Panepistimio, was the first building commissioned by King Otto I to represent his vision for the new capital. Designed by Christian Hansen, its exterior follows traditional classical lines and geometric shapes. A lavish forty-five meter mural designed by Carl Rahl and painted by Eduard Lebiedzki speaks of an opulent world inspired by the greatest palaces of Vienna.

The Athenian Trilogy, *28 Panepistimiou Street; height of nineteenth-century architecture*

ATHENIAN TRILOGY

Benefactors, such as Simon Sinas, Ioannis Dombolis, and other revolutionary generals, played an equally important role by contributing large sums of money to the building's completion. It was in front of the university that General Theodoros Kolokotronis pronounced the prophetic words, "This house," meaning the university, "will devour the other house," meaning the palace.

The National Library of Athens / Vallianeio Megaron

The National Library of Athens, also known as Vallianeio Megaron, was funded by the brothers Panagis, Marinos, and Andreas Vallianos. Designed by Theophil Hansen and Ernst Ziller, its purpose was to gather and safeguard all the written intellectual property of Greece. The library, built with Pentelic marble, follows the Doric style of architecture with simple lines and unadorned columns, creating a powerful contrast with the Renaissance-style staircase that leads to its entrance.

In 2017, the collection of over two million books, manuscripts, and periodicals was relocated to the Stavros Niarchos Foundation Cultural Center and is accessible as an open archive.

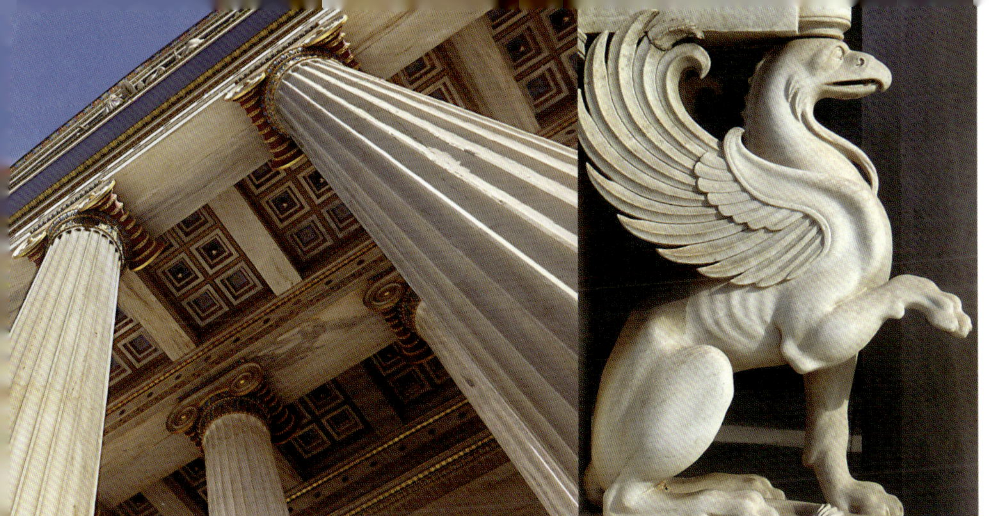

Top: *Ionic columns leading to the entrance of The Academy by sculptor Malakate; architectural designs by Theophil Hansen and Ernst Ziller*

Top right: *The National Library of Athens, Vallianeio Megaron, detail of Sphinx on stairway; architectural designs by Theophil Hansen and Ernst Ziller*

Right: *Statue of goddess Athena by sculptor Leonidas Drosis located at the front steps of The Athens Academy*

Following pages: *Eros figures and goddess Athena depicted as patroness of arts and science by sculptor Franz Melnitzky*

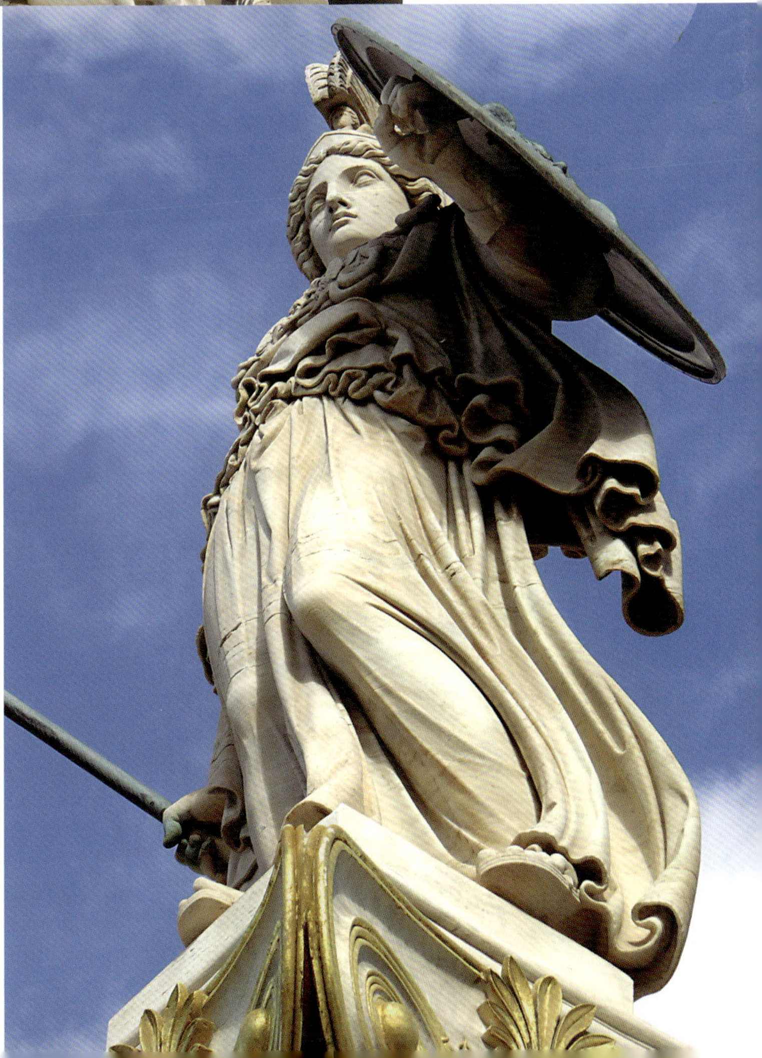

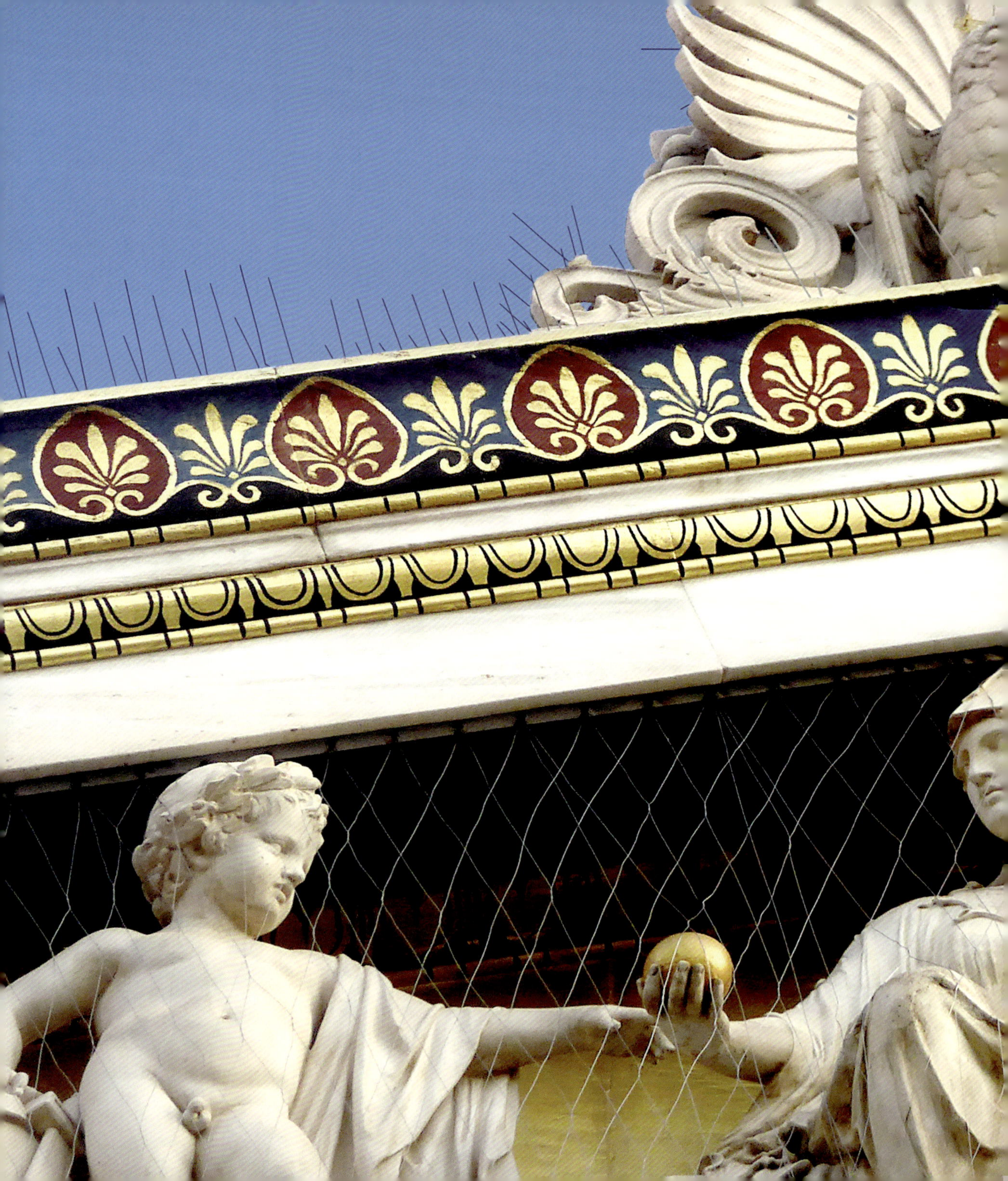

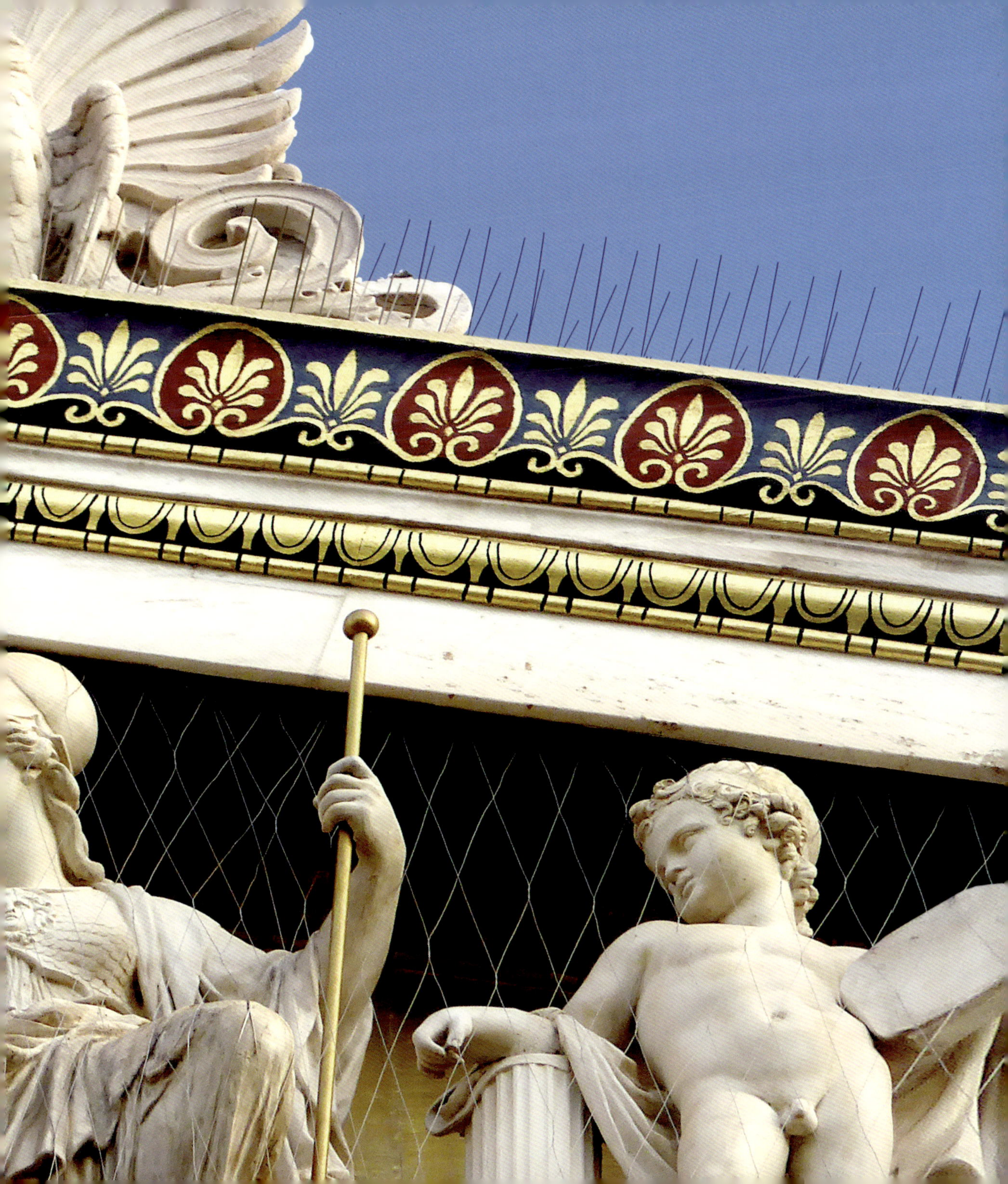

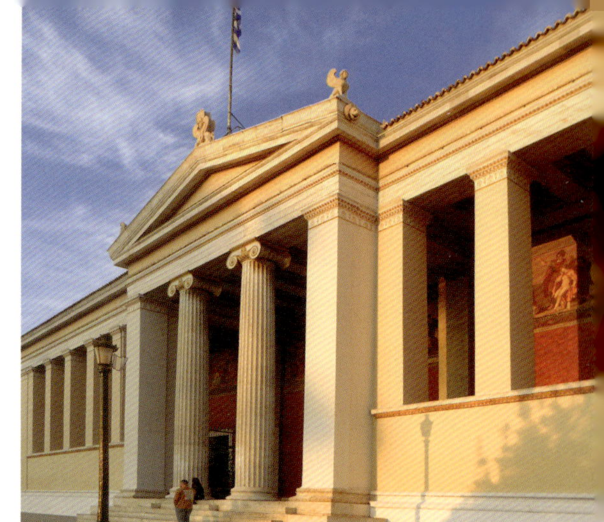

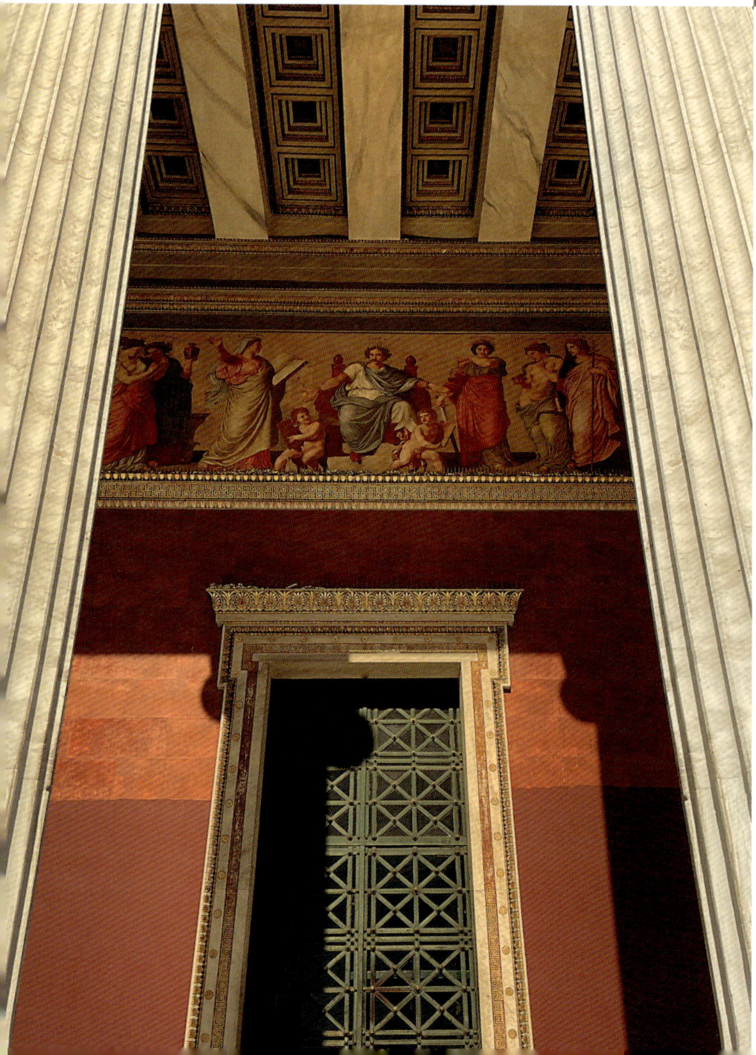

Top: *Sunset at the steps of the National and Kapodistrian University of Athens; architectural design by Christian Hansen*

Left: *The National and Kapodistrian University of Athens; mural detail depicting King Otto flanked by Science and Philosophy; mural design by Karl Rahl, painted by Edward Lembersky*

The Academy of Athens

The Academy is the collective work of some of the most extraordinary architects, sculptors, and painters of the period. Theophil Hansen and Ernst Ziller drew the plans and supervised the construction. Sculptor Leonidas Drosis was responsible for the multi-figure pediment representing Athena's birth, the statutes of Apollo and Athena, as well as the seated marble figures of Plato and Sophocles.

The columns leading to the entrance were carved by the sculptor Malakates from the island of Tinos, and the eight smaller pediments, depicting Athena as the patroness of shipping, agricultural arts, and science, are the terracotta work of Austrian sculptor Franz Melnitzky. Painter Christian Griepenkerl undertook the challenging task of decorating its interior inspired by Aeschylus' "Prometheus Bound."

The National Library is closed to the public, but don't let that deter you. There's plenty of beauty to enchant you.

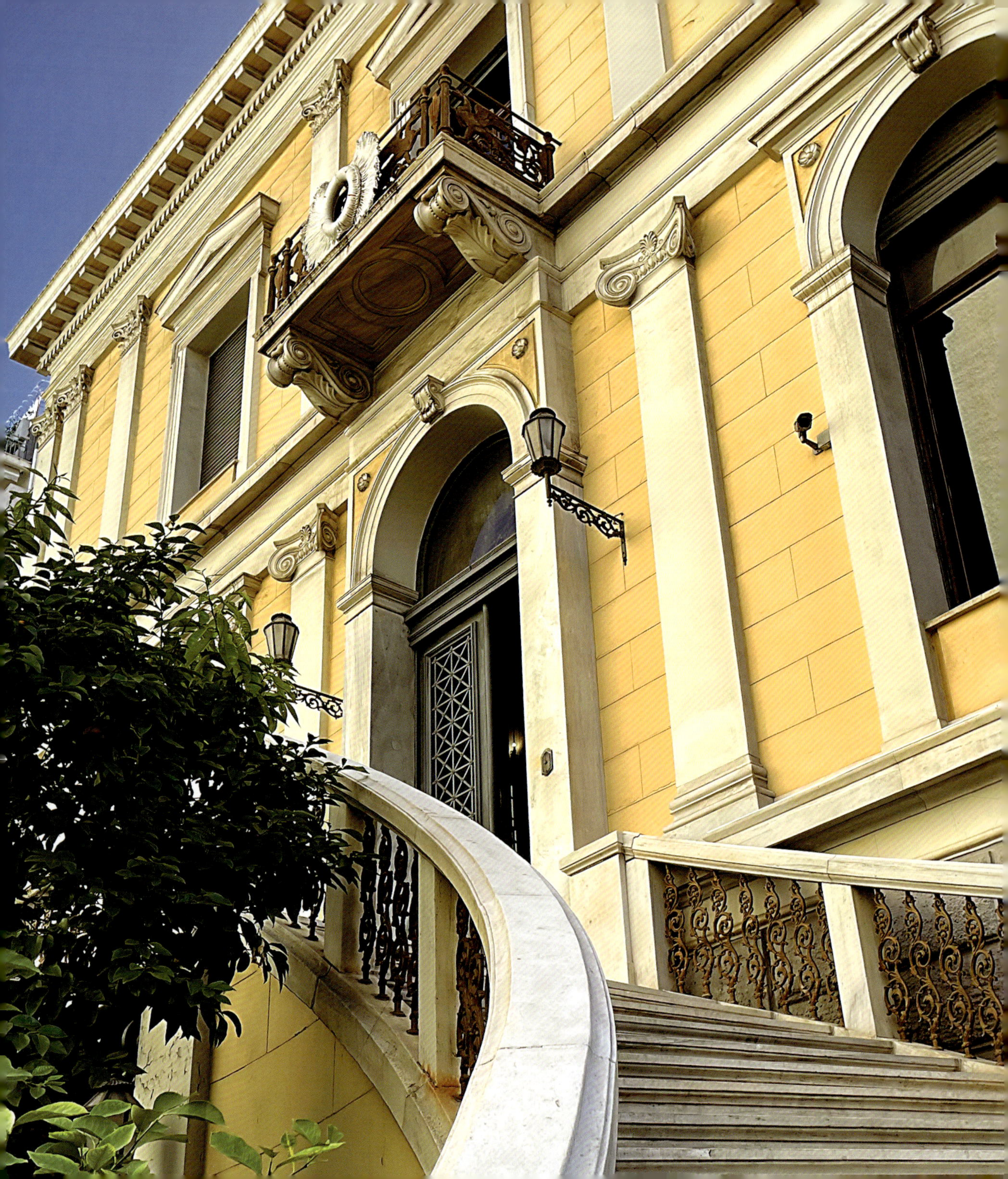

NUMISMATIC MUSEUM ILIOU MELATHRON

Opulent, with a double circular staircase flanked by Ionic columns leading to a cast iron entrance, the Numismatic Museum is one of the finest examples of nineteenth-century neoclassical architecture. Designed by Ernst Ziller between 1878-1880 for Heinrich Schliemann as his private residence, the building reflects the grandeur and wealth of the newly established capital.

Also known as "Iliou Melathron," the Palace of Ilion, the mansion was commissioned to represent Schliemann's highest ideals and accomplishments with themes drawn from classical literature, mythological, and allegorical scenes. Magnificent rooms, painted by the famed Slovenian painter Jurij Šubic, are inspired by Pompeii's frescoes. Ancient quotes illustrated on the walls, marble fireplaces, and mosaic floors created by famed mosaic families from Livorno, speak of the mythical grandeur that Schliemann always imagined.

Each room, with its radiant color combinations, takes one's breath away. Just when one thinks that he's seen it all, another doorway appears, leading to an even more opulent room.

Numismatic Museum of Athens–Iliou Melathron, *Eleftheriou Venizelou 12; www.nummus.gr; Hours: Tuesday to Sunday: 8:30 a.m. – 3:00 p.m.; Monday: Closed*

NUMISMATIC MUSEUM—ILIOU MELATHRON

Guided by Ziller's sense of balance, nothing feels forced or unnecessary. Dance halls, libraries, children's playrooms, and lavish bedrooms speak of an affluence that few could imagine.

The garden, a quiet oasis in the heart of the city, offers a glimpse of what it must have been for the Schliemann family to walk around the grounds, amidst intoxicating colors and scents. Today, clay statues of gods and goddesses flaunt their beauty in the most unabashed way, as guests enjoy a light meal at the museum's café.

The original twenty-six nude figures surrounding the garden quickly drew the ire of respectful Athenian society, which demanded their removal. In response, Schliemann ordered the statues to be covered with fabrics, making their sight even more "scandalous" than before.

Another design element inside the building is the display of tetragammadions (swastikas), appearing not only on the floors but also as a part of the iron work that surrounds the building. In Sanskrit, the swastika design means "well-being."

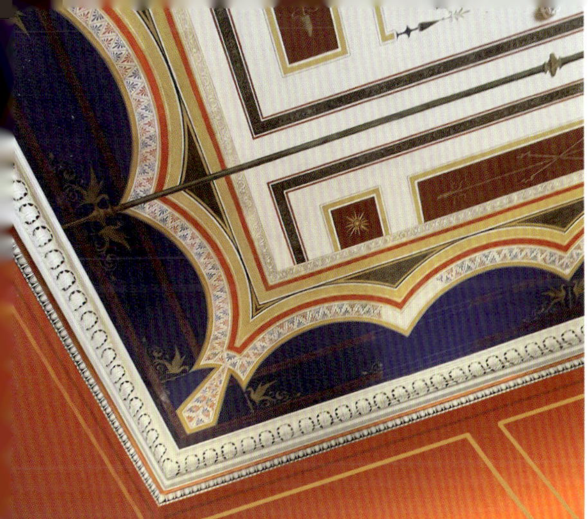

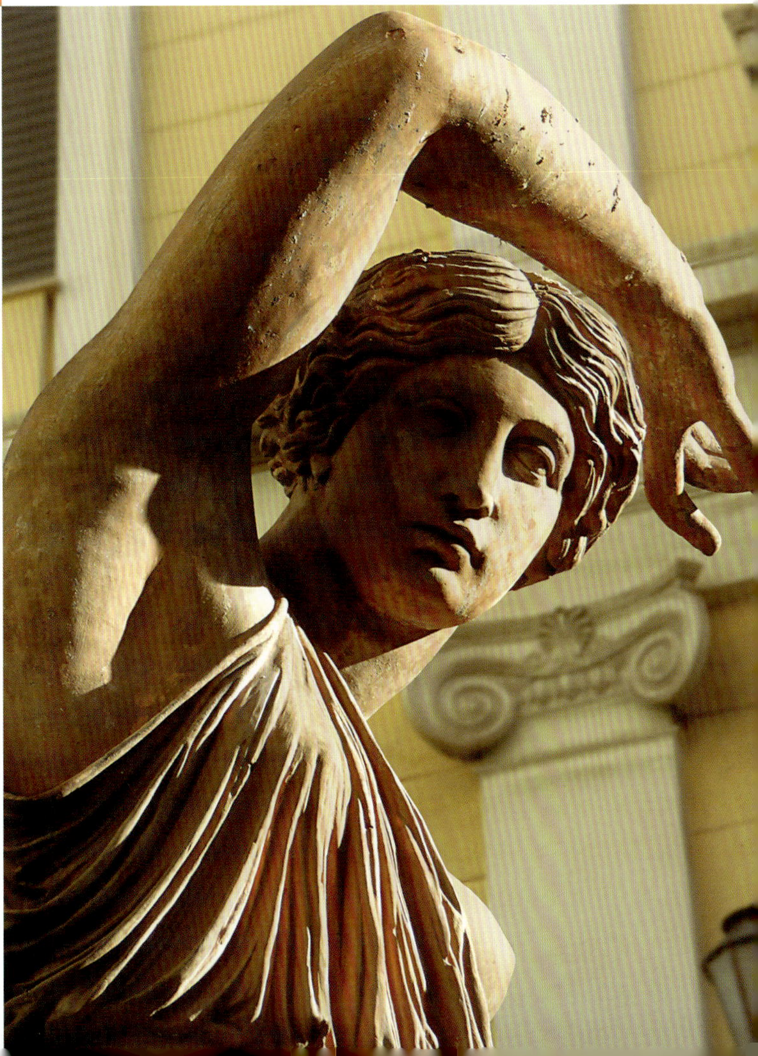

Top: *Ceiling detail, architectural design by Ernst Ziller for Heinrich Schliemann*

Right: *Museum's grounds, statue of goddess Artemis*

Following pages: *Interior room with coin collection, ceiling and frescoes painted by Jurij Šubic with ancient quotes on the walls*

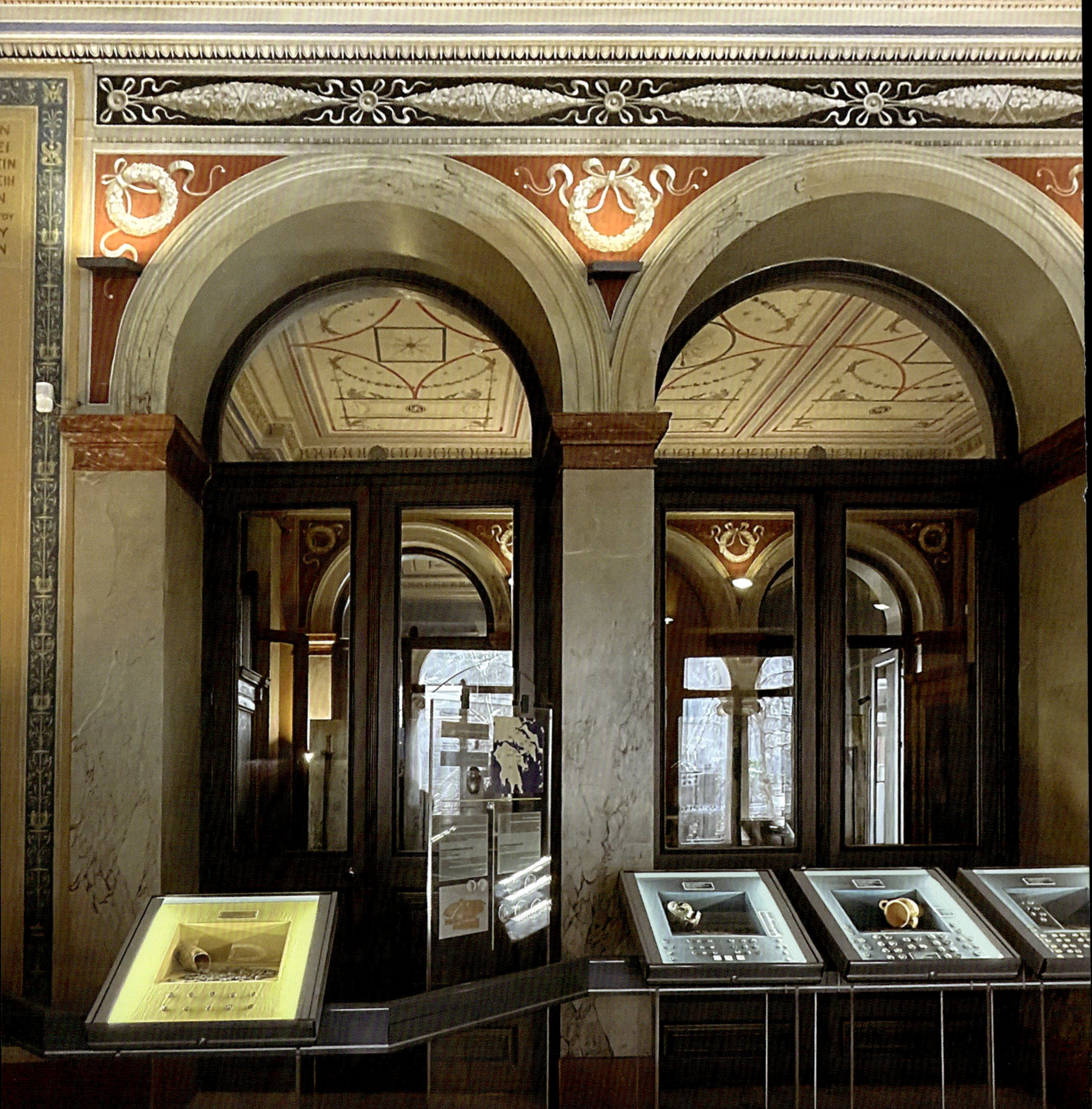

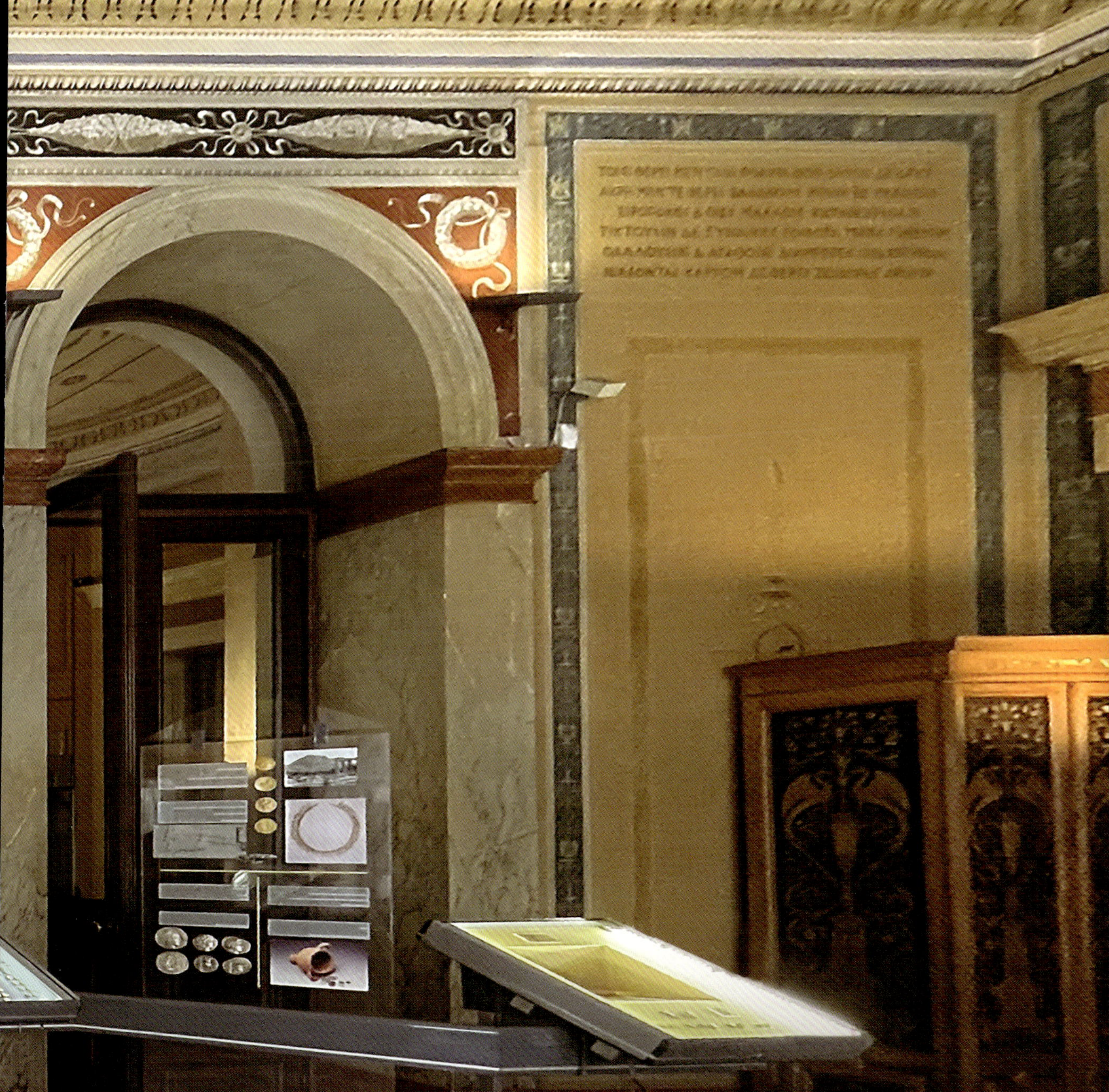

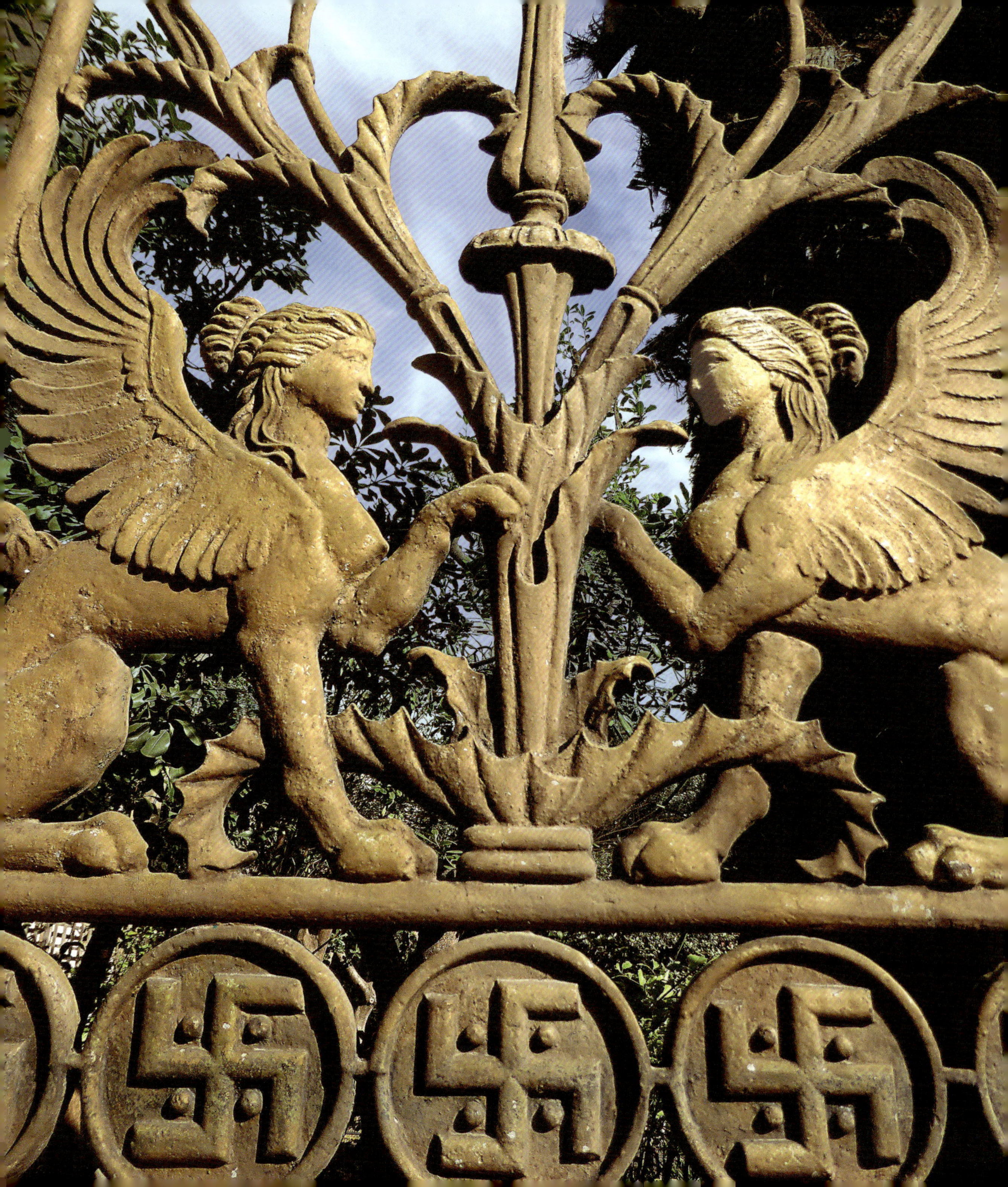

NUMISMATIC MUSEUM—ILIOU MELATHRON

A millennium before Hitler appropriated it, swastikas were used by Hindus, Buddhists, Jains, Greeks, Celts, Christians, and Native Americans. Swastika designs were also found in Troy dating back 4,000 years, so it was natural for Ziller to incorporate them in his designs.

The Iliou Melathron was famed for its Thursday dances, where all of Athenian aristocracy was present. Sophia Schliemann, a quintessential hostess, drew a list of guests from the most important families. An invitation meant that one had reached the pinnacle of Athenian society. After Schliemann's death, his wife stopped entertaining and accepted visitors only in the blue room, among them the Prime Minister of Greece, Eleftherios Venizelos.

The museum houses a collection of over 500,000 coins, medals, gems, weights, stamps, and related artifacts from 1400 B.C. to modern times. Don't let the numbers intimidate you. The displays showcase only what's necessary, allowing the visitor to admire some of the most exquisite coins, but also highlighting the grandeur of the house.

Opposite: *Iron gate with facing winged sphinxes and "tetragammadion" designs symbolizing well-being, inspired from designs found at the excavations of Troy*

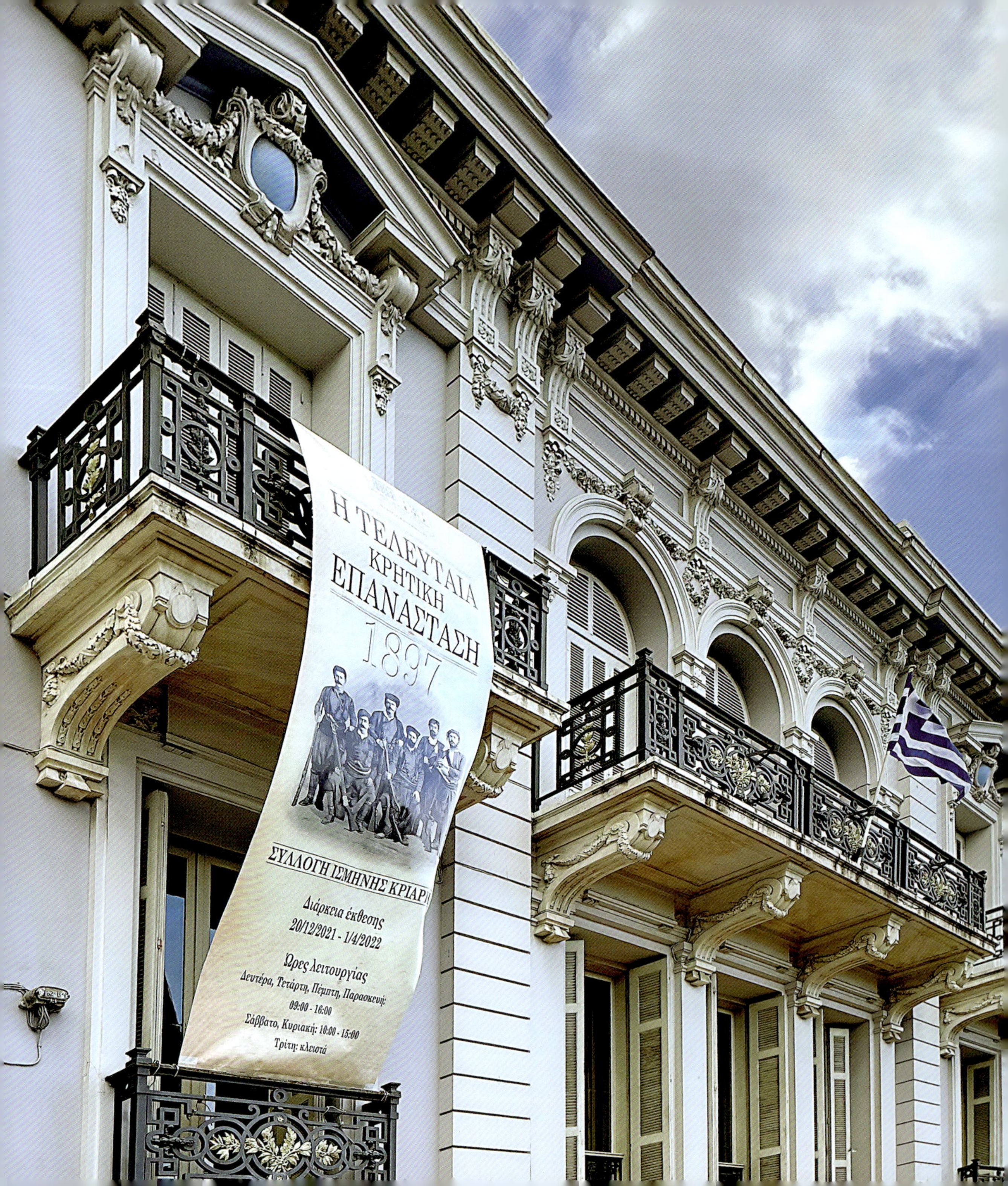
Η ΤΕΛΕΥΤΑΙΑ
ΚΡΗΤΙΚΗ
ΕΠΑΝΑΣΤΑΣΗ
1897
ΣΥΛΛΟΓΗ ΙΣΜΗΝΗΣ ΚΡΙΑΡ
Διάρκεια έκθεσης
20/12/2021 - 1/4/2022
Ώρες λειτουργίας
Δευτέρα, Τετάρτη, Πέμπτη, Παρασκευή:
09:00 - 16:00
Σάββατο, Κυριακή: 10:00 - 15:00
Τρίτη: κλειστά

MUSEUM OF THE CITY OF ATHENS VOUROS-EUTAXIAS FOUNDATION

Infused in light, regal, and yet discreet. These are the impressions that come to mind when you first see the Museum of the City of Athens. Gracefully standing on Paparrigopoulou Street, away from the cacophony of the roaring motorcycles and car horns, the building draws you in with its quiet grandeur. Entering the grounds is like stepping into another time, a serene world where rooms were lit by candlelight and dinner was served on bone china plates.

However, there was nothing serene about this world when Athens struggled to form her new identity, and the nation's future was decided on the flip of a coin. King Otto I and his wife, Amalia, had just arrived, shrouded in the veil of their youthfulness and naively believing that this was going to be just another adventure.

Not that the young king lacked ideals, but the task was much greater than his abilities, and his alliances were conflicted. The Greek people welcomed him and Otto returned their affection with sincerity, but soon all sides were to become disillusioned.

Museum of the City of Athens – Vouros Eutaxias Foundation, 5-7 Paparrigopoulou Street, Klavthmonos Square, Athens; www.athenscitymuseum.gr; Hours: Monday, Wednesday, Thursday, Friday: 9:00 a.m. – 4:00 p.m., Saturday, Sunday: 10:00 a.m. – 3:00 p.m.; Tuesday: Closed

MUSEUM OF THE CITY OF ATHENS VOUROS-EUTAXIAS FOUNDATION

Unable to control the influences of the "Great Powers" of England, France, and Russia, and miscalculating the political clout of the Greek revolutionary generals, Otto found himself isolated. Declaring himself a monarch did little to alleviate the conflict, and after thirty years of a turbulent reign, he was exiled.

In 1836, while waiting for the construction of the official palace on Syntagma Square, the couple moved to the mansion of Stamatios Dekozis-Vouros, a wealthy banker from Chios Island. It's hard to imagine how young Otto perceived his new quarters in comparison to his upbringing, but it's fair to assume that everything must have looked simplistic, if not provincial.

It's the simplicity of this building, however, and its elegance, that makes it stand out from the rest. Dim corridors lead into carefully tended rooms, where paintings and various artifacts bathe in diffused light. A simple throne, raised on a small platform, hardly denotes a kingly palace, but it's the intimacy of the rooms and the silence that allows one to be immersed in the period.

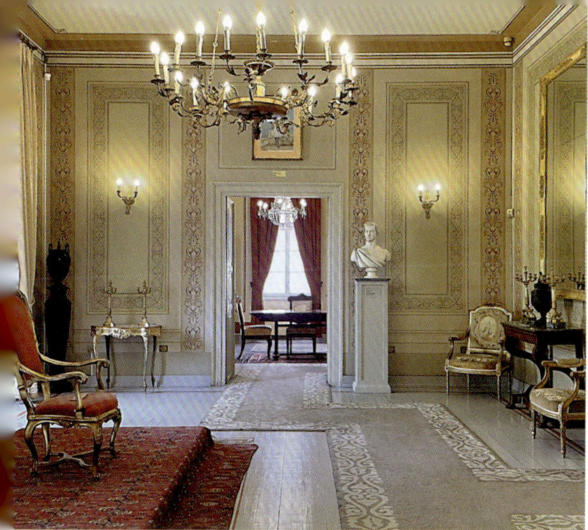

Previous page: *Museum of the City of Athens – Vouros-Eutaxias Foundation; designed by Gustav-Adolf and Joseph Hoffer*

Top: *King Otto's reception room; original throne can be found at the National Historic Museum*

Right: *Desk facing Klavthmonos Square; Kiki and Sotirios Papastratos Rooms*

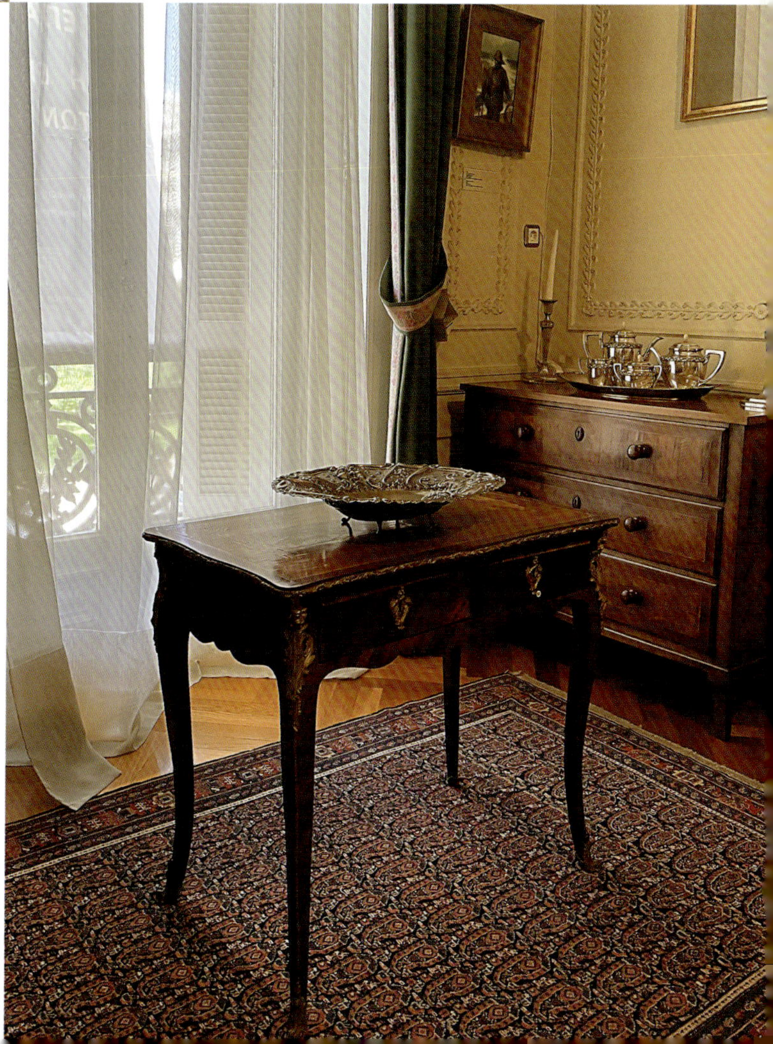

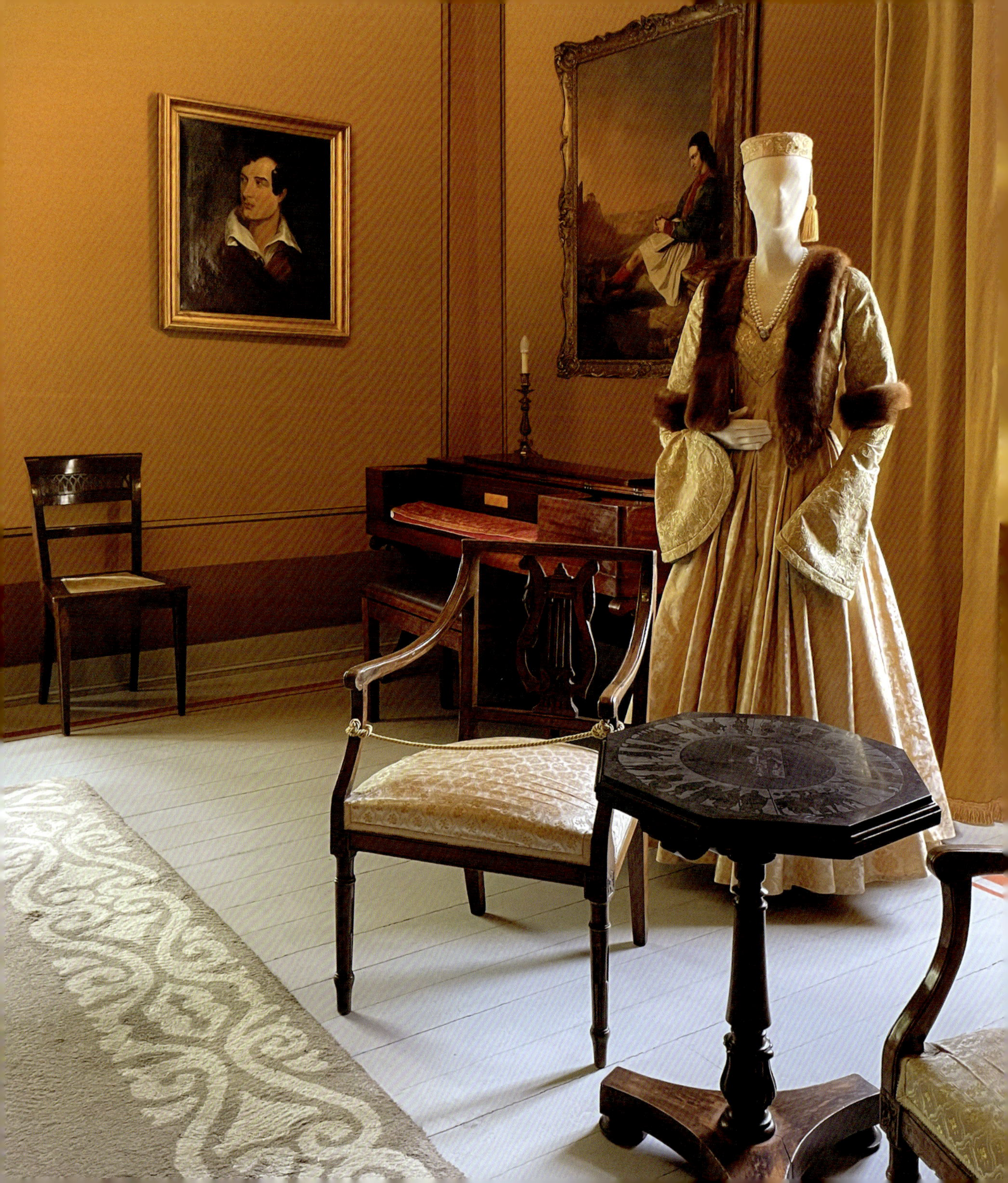

MUSEUM OF THE CITY OF ATHENS VOUROS-EUTAXIAS FOUNDATION

The construction of the building was awarded to the German architect Gustav-Adolf Lueders and Hungarian architect Joseph Hoffer. Designed in the early Renaissance style, it offers a representational view of early Athenian classicism. In 1859, a second house, adjacent to the first, was added to host the members of the Dekozi-Vouros family, including the founder of the museum, politician and arts patron Lambros Eftaxias.

On the ground floor, paintings, gravures, and engraved sculptures present the history of Athens from the Turkish rule to this day. The Athens City Museum features a library of rare books and hosts approximately 40,000 items, ranging from antiquity to the twenty-first century.

A garden extends from the back of the museum where Queen Amalia planted a palm tree that still stands on the grounds. A small café under a shaded trellis offers respite from the heat and allows one to ponder this fascinating part of Greek history that is so often ignored.

Opposite: *Mannequin in Queen Amalia's attire; painting right: Lord Byron, in the background the Acropolis, by Sir Charles Lock EastLake; painting left: Lord Byron, Anonymous*

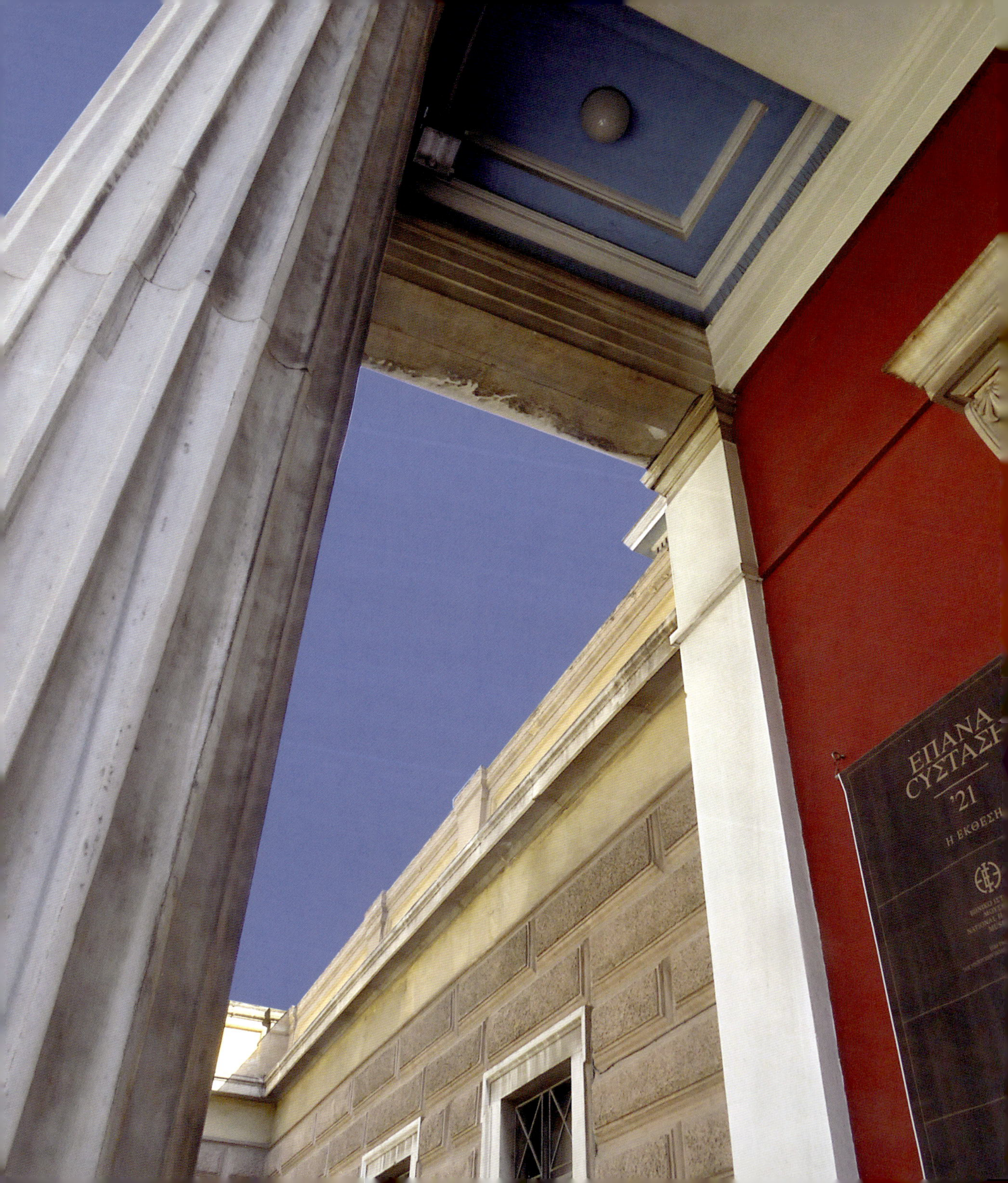
ΕΠΑΝΑ
ϹΥΣΤΑΣ
'21
Η ΕΚΘΕΣΗ

NATIONAL HISTORICAL MUSEUM

The year is 1883. Meet Mrs. Kostaina standing at the steps of the parliament, her shapely body barely fitting into her tight dress. Her professions are many and her skills uncountable. "Begging with dignity" is her motto, and when asked, she describes herself as a saleswoman. The Athenians love her and give her the nickname "Psorokostaina," "Penniless Kostaina," a nickname that eventually will be allegorically equated with the troubled state of Greece.

A little further away, meet Mr. Sakoules, named after the torn bags, "sakoules," that he always drags behind him. He demands that people "financially help him," and when rejected, he spreads his bile with curses and the now famous quote, "I can't believe that so many Athenians are unable to feed a lazy man."

And there is the widow Rozou, dressed in the style of famed Charlotte Corday, who murdered her husband, French revolutionary leader, Marat. Displaying a boisterous hat made from feathers and waiving an umbrella from the parliament's balcony, she's a force to reckon with.

National Historical Museum, Old Parliament Building, *Kolokotronis Square and Stadiou Streets, Athens; nhmuseum.gr; Hours: 8:30 a.m. – 2:30 p.m.*

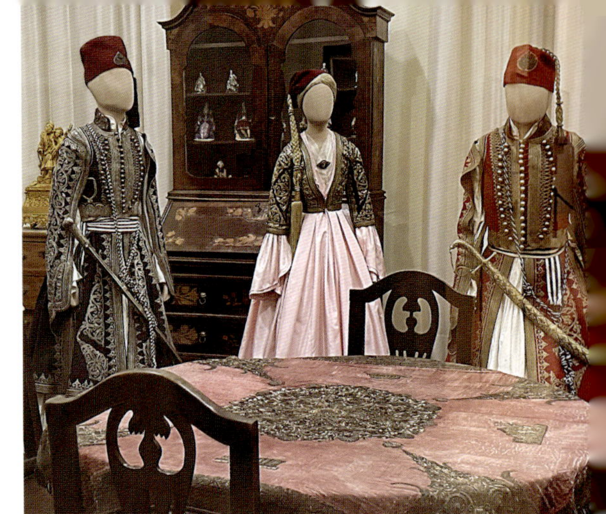

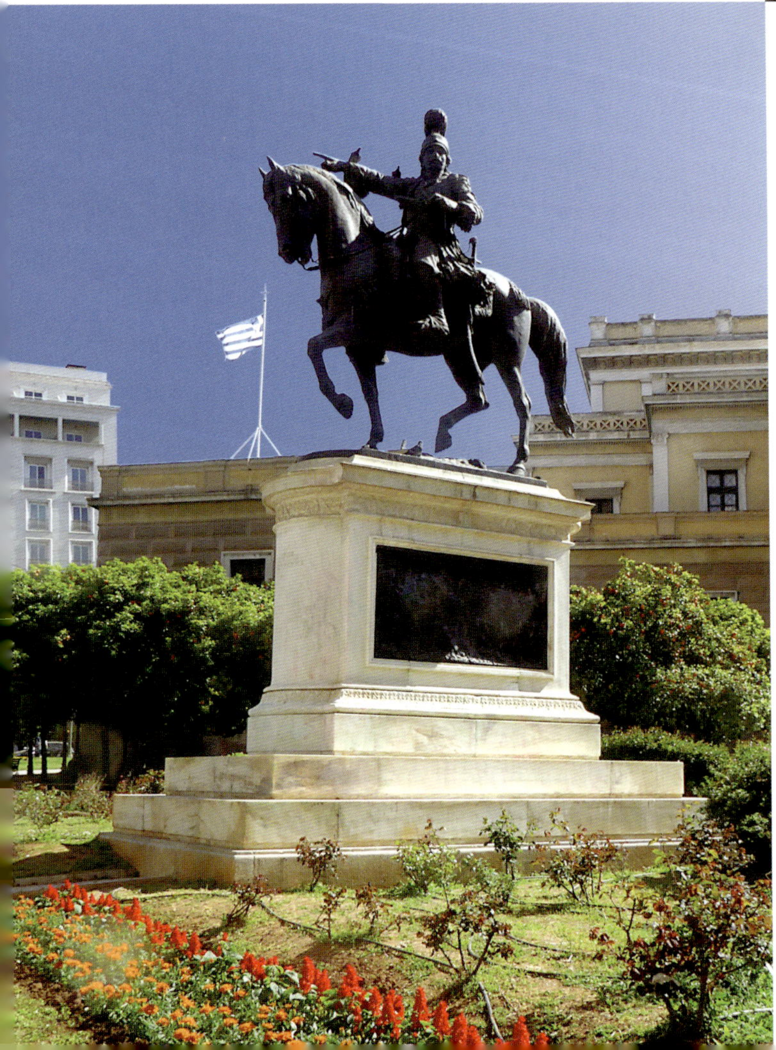

Top: *Traditional Greek costumes set in affluent nineteenth-century dining room*

Left: *Equestrian statue of General Theodoros Kolokotronis, sculpted by Lazaros Sohos with material from the melted cannons of Palamidi Castle*

NATIONAL HISTORICAL MUSEUM

The National Historical Museum, also known as the "Old Parliament," is deeply interwoven with the political, economic, and social life of Greece. Construction of the building began in 1858 at the request of Queen Amalia, based on plans by French architect François Boulanger. In 1863, after Otto's exile, the plans were modified by architect Panagiotis Kalkos.

The parliament's sessions were often open to the public. The participants watched from the galleries and voiced their disapproval by heckling or hissing. Stomping their feet was another response to unpopular propositions or legislation which often led to the sessions breaking down.

However, it was not only the public, but also the deputies themselves, who sometimes exacerbated the situation. Since canes were almost always an accessory of men's fashion, the parliamentarians often used theirs as weapons against the audience or one other.

On the outside, thugs hired by the opposing parties started arguments, and it was not uncommon for the square to be turned into a boxing ring.

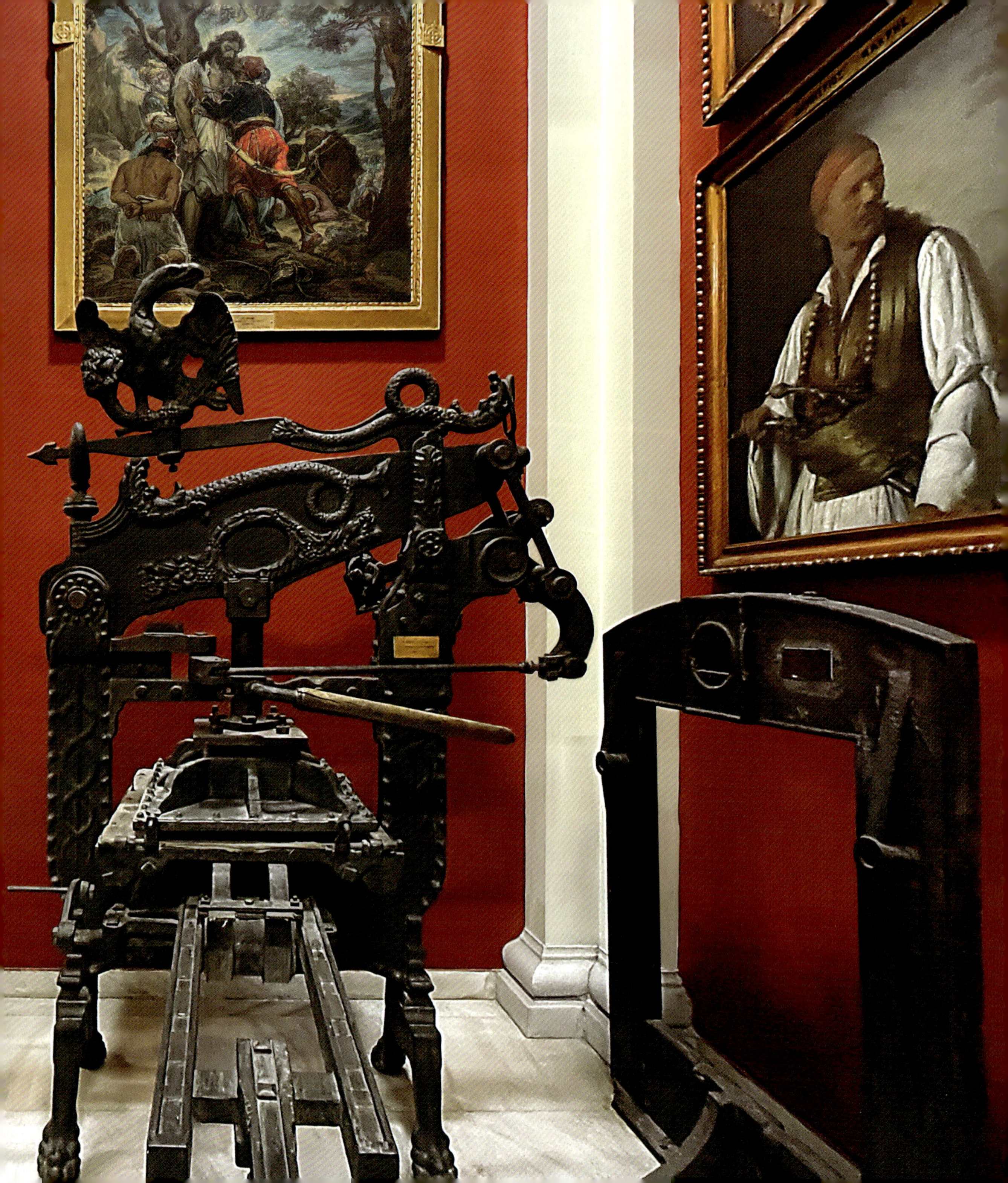

NATIONAL HISTORICAL MUSEUM

In 1935 the parliament was moved to Syntagma Square, where it remains to this day. The old parliament was decreed by Prime Minister Eleftherios Venizelos to the Historical and Ethnological Society of Greece to establish The National Historical Museum.

The National Historical Museum is not a place to miss. Standing gracefully amidst a tangerine grove, it hosts a treasure trove of artifacts dating back to the fall of Constantinople in 1453 up to The Second World War. It's the spirit of the Greek Revolution and the establishment of the modern Greek nation, however, that is mostly captured within its walls.

Paintings, manuscripts, weaponry, military uniforms, and regional costumes are only a few of the items displayed. Every room speaks of a humble yet prideful nation, the realization reaching a crescendo at the great parliamentary hall, with its crystal chandeliers and exquisite architecture.

It's here in this hall that one grows quiet, as if not to disturb the old revolutionary generals whose spirits still pulsate within the grounds.

Opposite: *Printing press, brought to Greece in 1829 by Philhellene and publisher, Amboise Didot*

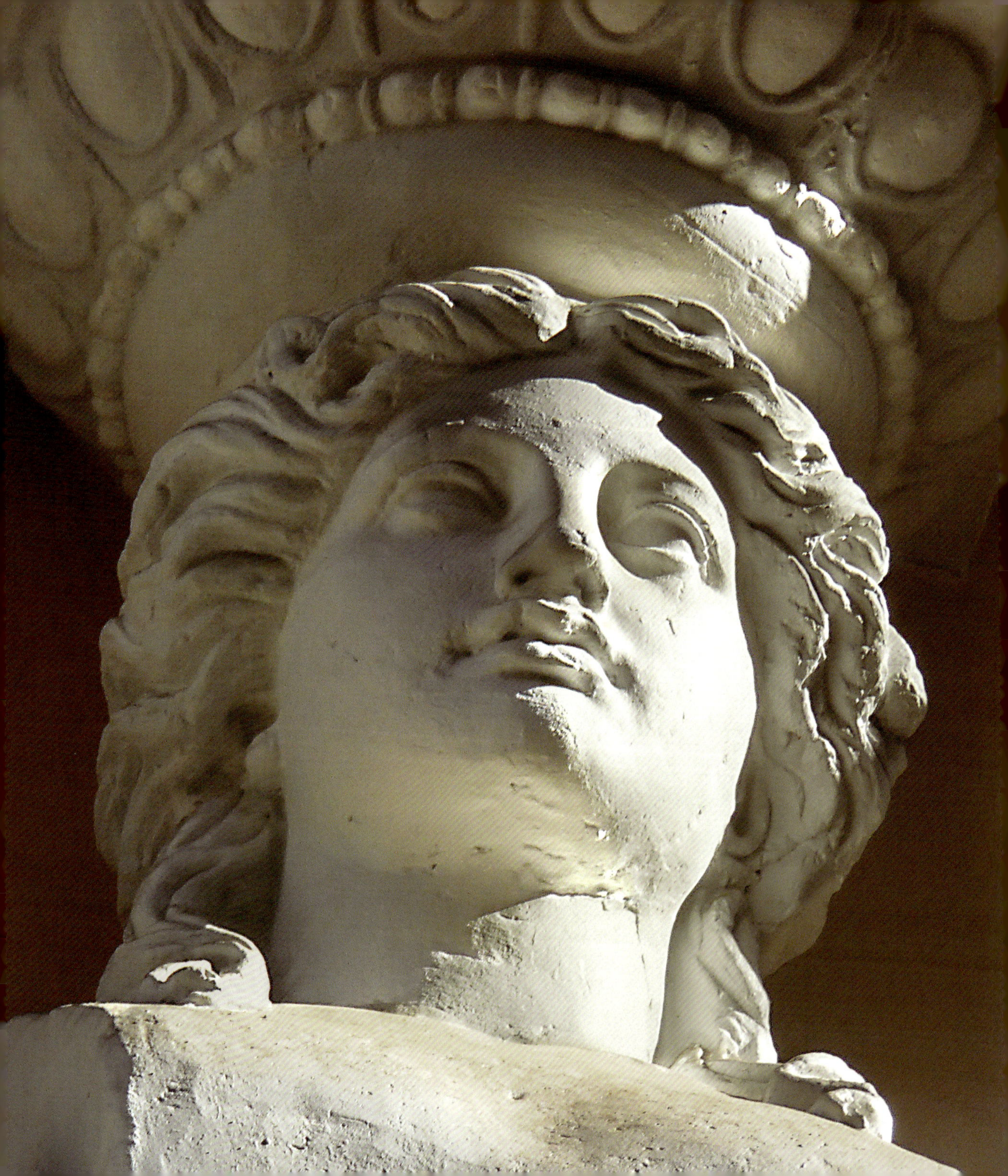

LOVERDOS MUSEUM ZILLER MANSION

A brisk spring day. A man nimbly skips over a pile of stones, spreading a set of plans on the dusty ground. He looks around, taking it all in. In his mind the structure is already completed: the symmetrical walls, the high ceiling rooms, the elegant forms, and the Caryatids' heads watching the city like sentinels. Other architects have preceded him, but he's unmatchable, his piecing blue eyes breaking through the clouds, seeing beyond the obvious and the mundane, almost reaching the gods.

At another place in town, a second man dips his pen into an ink well, his brooding dark eyes immersed in piles of paperwork. From the open window, a waft of lemon blossoms brings him to a halt. His gaze wanders upwards towards the icon of the Virgin Mary holding a lily. He's a banker, a man of numbers, who has traveled the world and made a fortune, but his love for this land always pulls him back, and he's here to honor it.

The first man, Ernst Ziller, is ethereal, drawing his inspiration from classicism. The second one, Dionysios Loverdos, is earthbound, drawing

---

Loverdos Museum – Ziller Mansion, *6 Mavromichali Street, Athens; loverdosmuseum-bma.gr; Hours: Monday: 8:30 a.m. – 3:30 p.m., Tuesday: Closed, Wednesday to Sunday: 8:30 a.m. – 3:30 p.m.*

LOVERDOS MUSEUM—ZILLER MANSION

his inspiration from the Byzantine world and Greek history. Both share the same vision: to see Greece shine again in all her brilliance.

The museum is a place not to be missed. Designed by Ziller as his private residence, it encapsulates his architectural genius. He and his wife, Sofia Dourou, spent some of the happiest years of their lives in this home, but Ziller was an artist, not a businessman. After investing in several unsuccessful real estate projects, his business was brought crashing to the ground, forcing him to lose his entire fortune, including this house.

In 1912 Dionysios Loverdos purchased the building, converting it for his private Byzantine collection. In 1980 a fire erupted, destroying the building. Luckily, the largest part of Loverdos' collection had already been moved to the Byzantine Museum for restoration, so it was saved.

Following a painstaking renovation, the museum opened its doors to the public in 2021 and now stands as one of the finest examples of neoclassical architecture. Entering the building, one feels as if they have walked into a sacred place.

Opposite: *Green room I.4; icon above fireplace: Christ Ecce Homo, eighteenth-century*

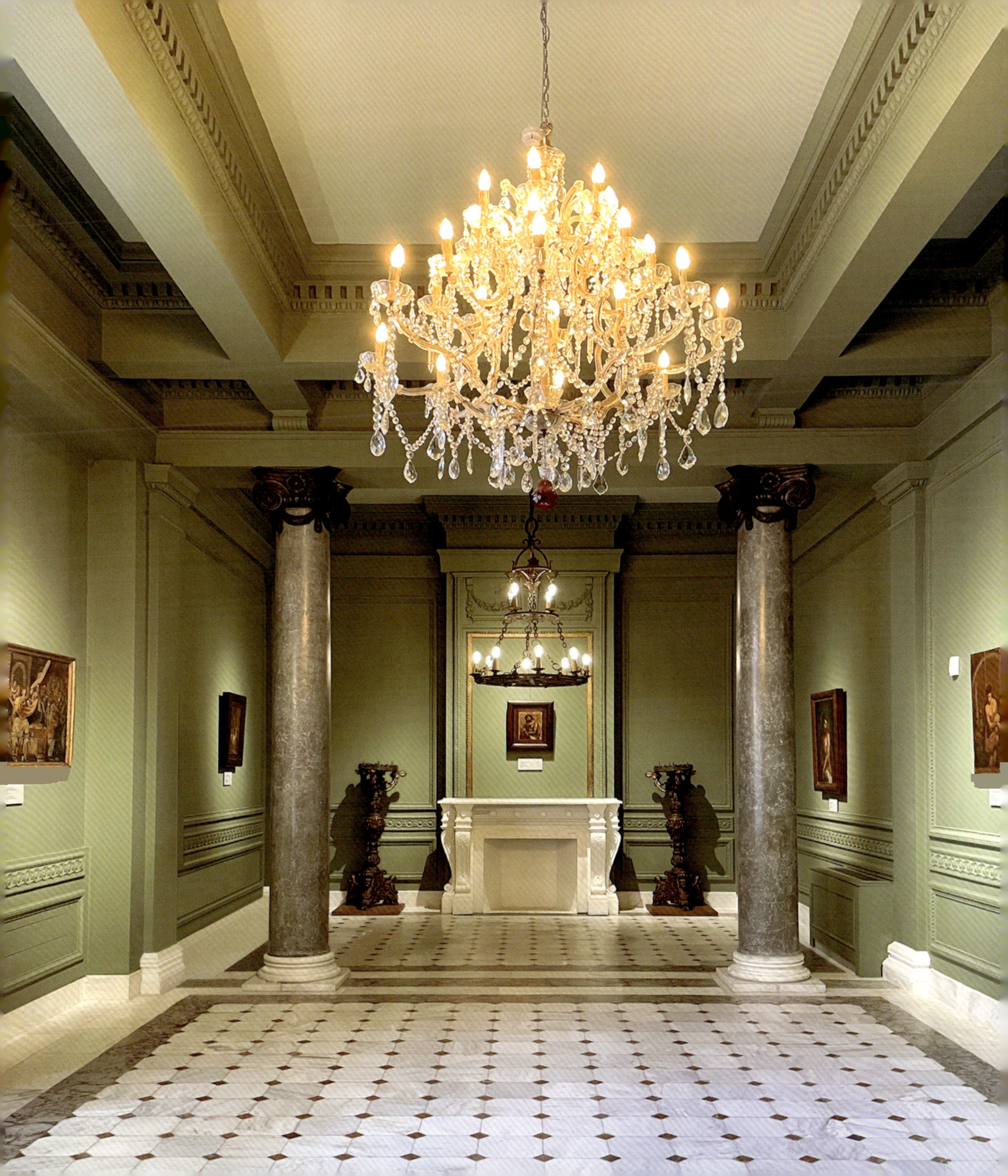

LOVERDOS MUSEUM—ZILLER MANSION

The rooms, each one more majestic than the next, with high ceilings, winged nymphs and griffins painted by Slovenian painter Jurij Šubic, speak of unsurpassed beauty. Priceless icons from the Cretan and Ionian schools of iconography are quietly displayed, their rich colors accentuated by deep orange terracotta walls.

When one thinks that the dream is over, other doorways appear, leading to other rooms and finally into the ballroom, a striking space painted in sage green, with tiled floors, where some of the most powerful icons of the collection are exhibited. It's in this room I felt that the two men's spirits meet, one with his love for all things classical and the other with his deep faith and passion for his country. A small courtyard, with a brilliantly set Byzantine chapel, adds to an already unsurpassed experience.

Excellence meeting excellence. Step in and share the magic. You'll be forever transformed.

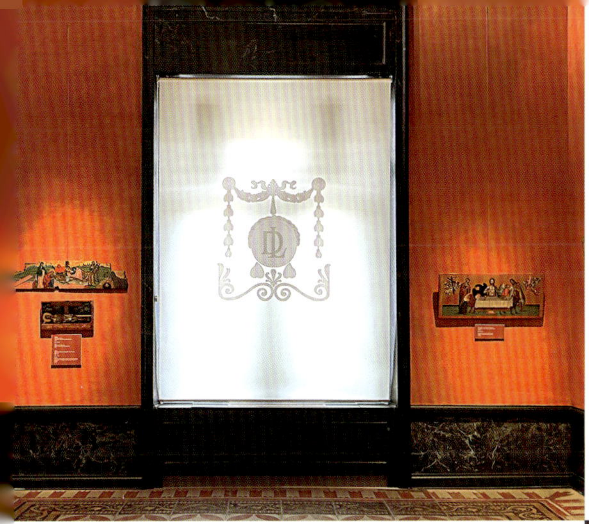

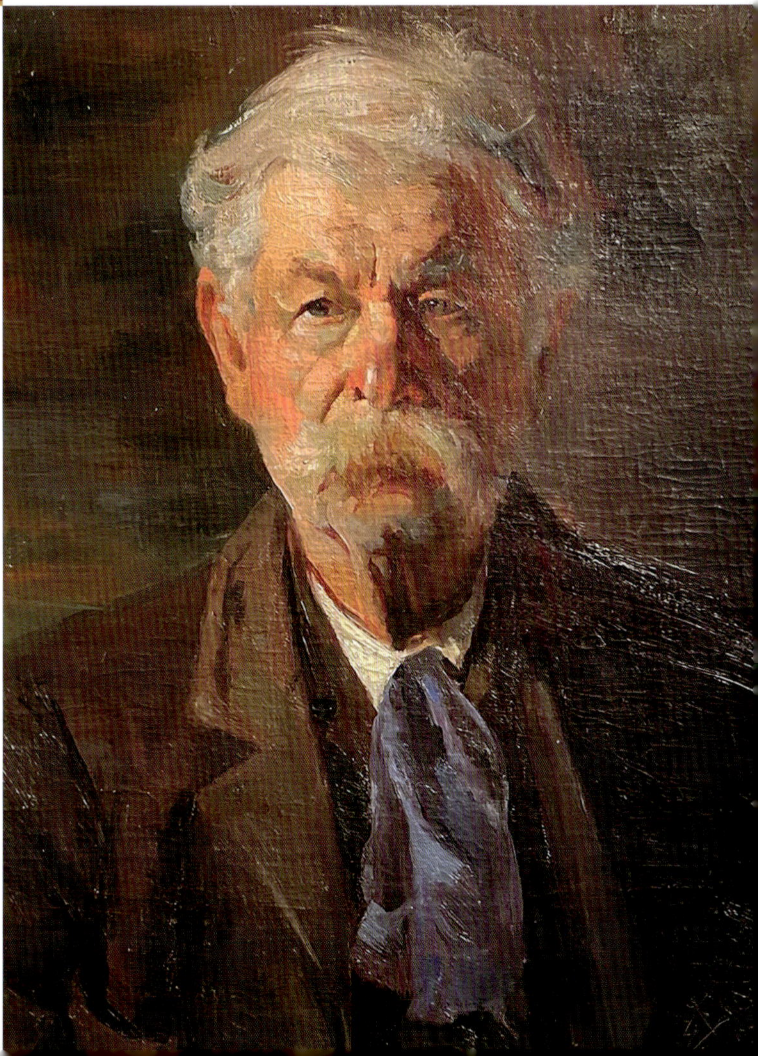

Top: *General view of room I.3 with Dionysios Loverdos' monogram on window; icon on the right: Allegory of Holy Communion, by Konstantinos Kontarinis, eighteenth-century; icon left top: Lamentation of Christ, by Eustathios Mavrogiannis, 1823; icon left bottom: Christ Epitaphios, eighteenth-century*

Right: *Portrait of Ernst Ziller by Stratis Gavalas, 1904; loan from the National Gallery – Alexandros Soutsos Museum*

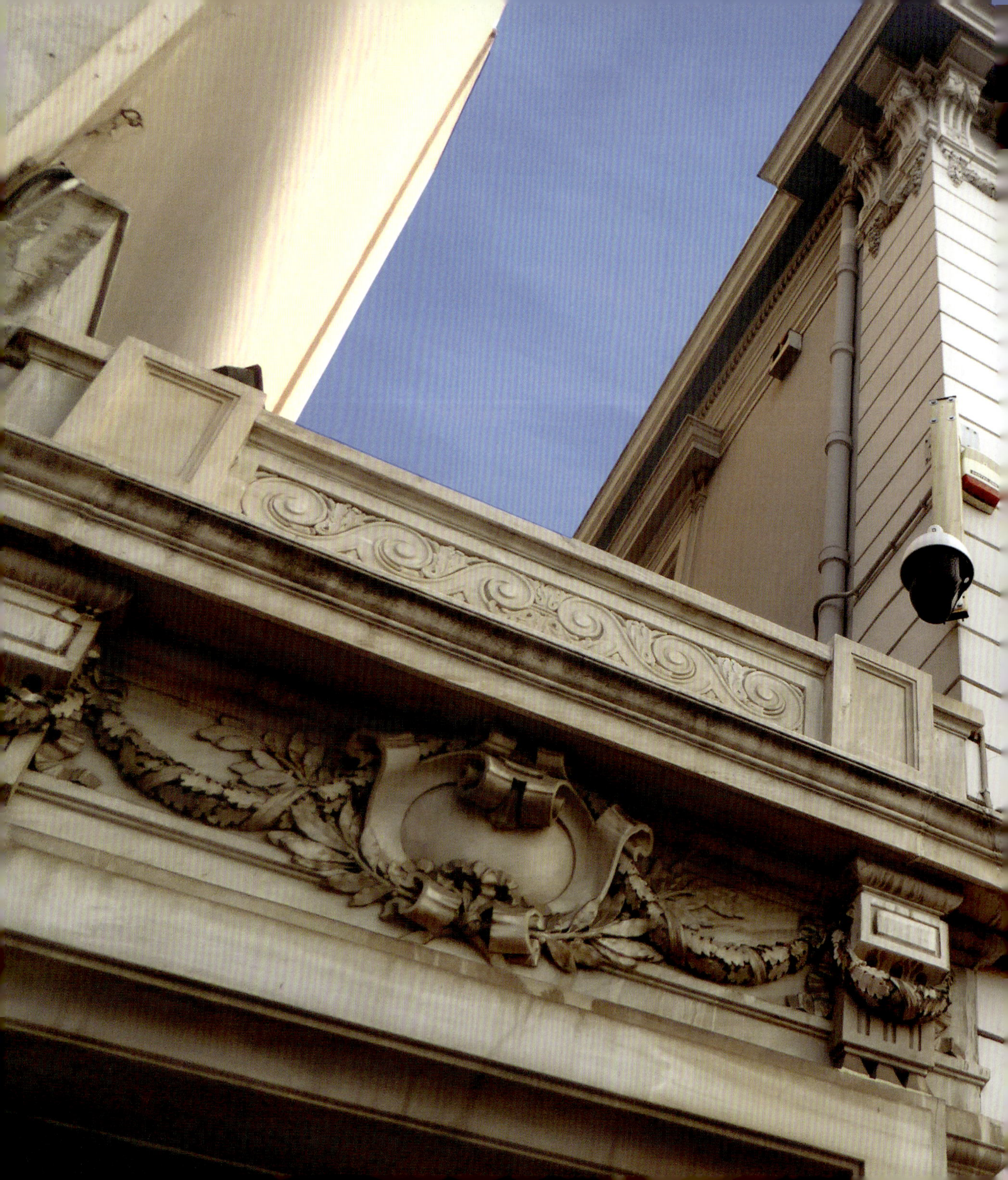

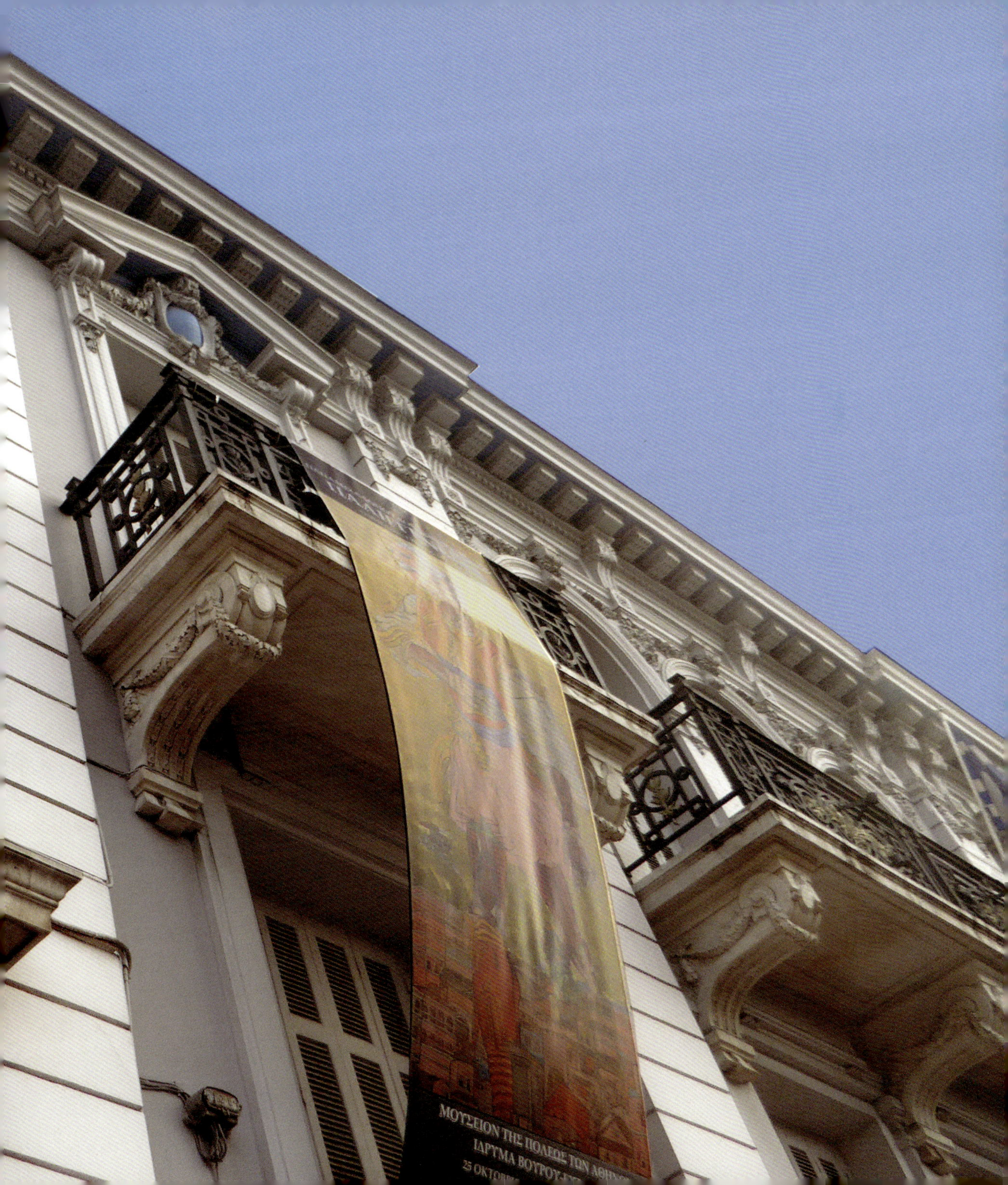
ΜΟΥΣΕΙΟΝ ΤΗΣ ΠΟΛΕΩΣ ΤΩΝ ΑΘΗΝ
ΙΔΡΥΜΑ ΒΟΥΡΟΥ

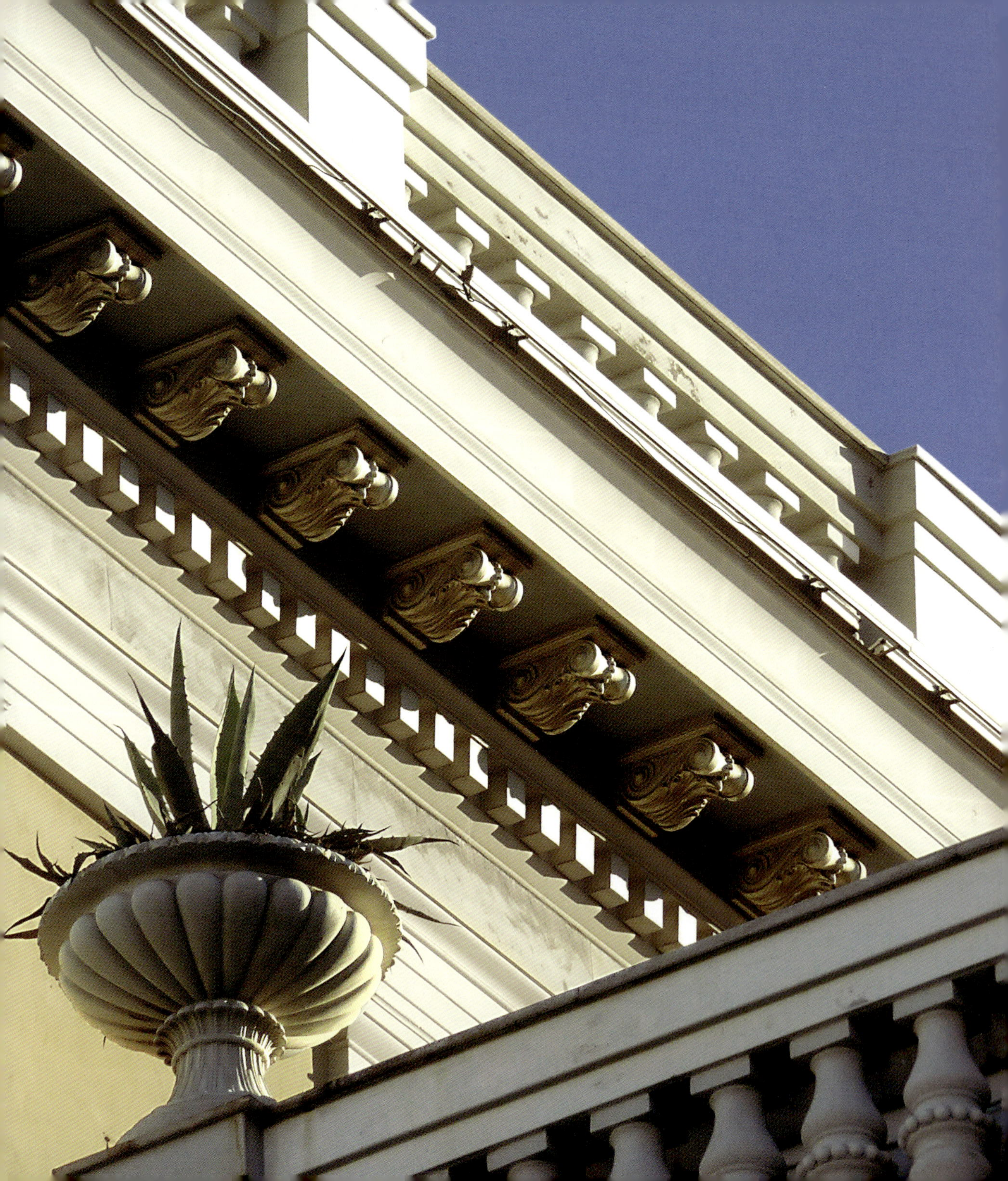

KOTZIA SQUARE

Kotzia Square, built in 1874, formerly known as Loudovikou Square and later renamed Kotzia Square for the first mayor of Athens, Konstantinos Kotzias. The excavation of an ancient road, tombs, and parts of the city's ancient fortification, add another layer of historical significance.

Three imposing buildings, the National Bank of Greece, the Old City Hall, and the Melas Mansion, surround the square, creating a triptych of neoclassical brilliance.

The National Bank was founded in 1841 by Georgios Stavros, a banker, and benefactor. It's closely associated with the civic conflict known as Iouniana that took place on its grounds. The factions were the "Pedinoi," from the valley, and the "Orinoi," from the mountains. The "Pedinoi" were supporters of the English party, while the "Orinoi" supported the French and Russian parties. In July of 1836, the antipathy between the two parties culminated in one of the bloodiest civil war battles in Athens, resulting in the deaths of two hundred people.

Kotzia Square, *located in front of Athens City Hall, Athinas 63*

KOTZIA SQUARE

The Old City Hall, designed by Panagiotis Kalkos between 1871 and 1874, is the second building worth exploring. Inside, one can admire the work of known Greek painters, including murals by Fotis Kontoglou, one of the most influential Post-Byzantine artists in Greece. A large oil painting depicting St. Paul the Apostle teaching the Athenians the Christian religion, 1877, completes the visit.

Of course, no important work could be complete without the presence of Ernst Ziller. The third building, known as the "Melas Mansion," crowns the square, adding another architectural masterpiece to his long list of achievements. Commissioned in 1874 by the wealthy wheat merchant, Vasilios Melas, it was originally planned to be used as a high-end hotel named "Grand Hotel d'Athenes," though the plan never materialized. Heavily influenced by Viennese architecture, the building showcases turrets, arches, and wide verandas at the top. Considered the largest Athenian private building of its time, its construction cost about 1,000,000 drachmas, an exorbitant amount for the period.

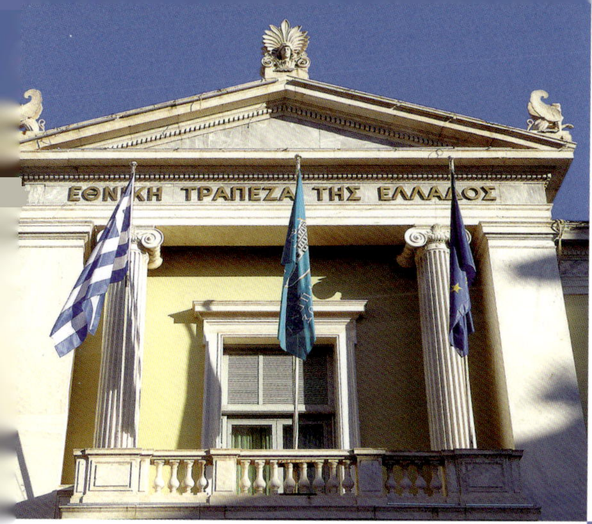

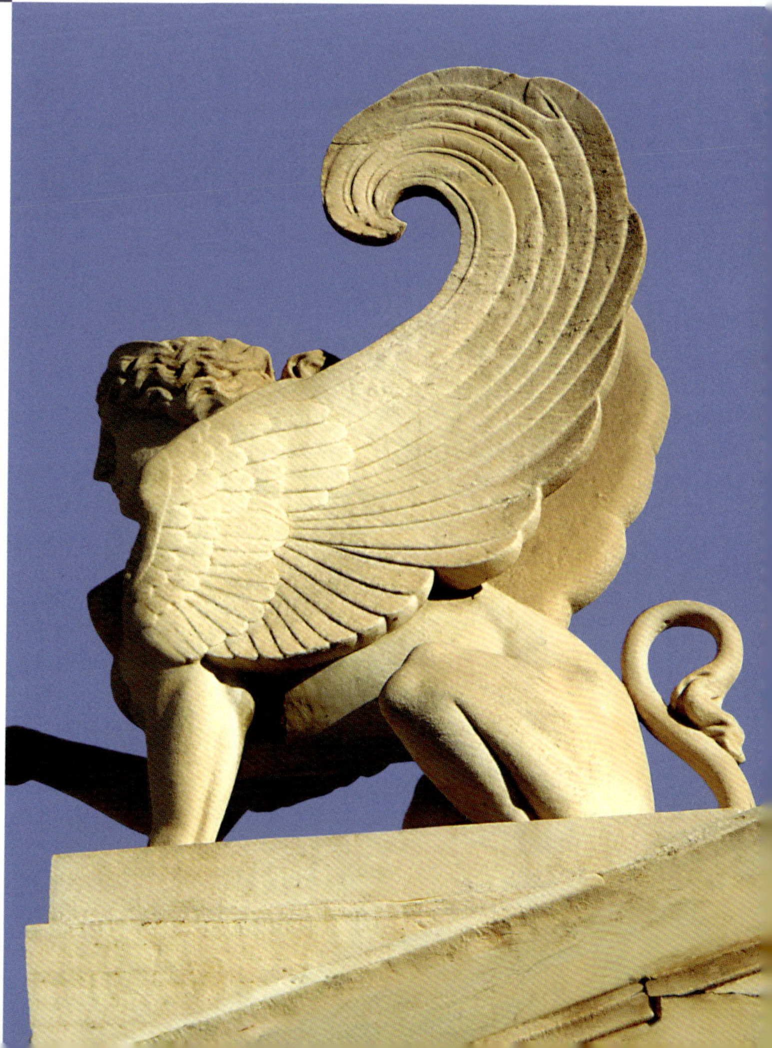

Previous Page: *Melas Mansion, architectural design by Ernst Ziller*

Top: *First National Bank of Greece located on the corner of Aiolou and Stavrou Streets, funded by Georgios Stavros*

Right: *Stone carving of winged sphinx on the National Bank's facade; the combination of the lion's body and the human head is interpreted as a symbol of strength and intelligence*

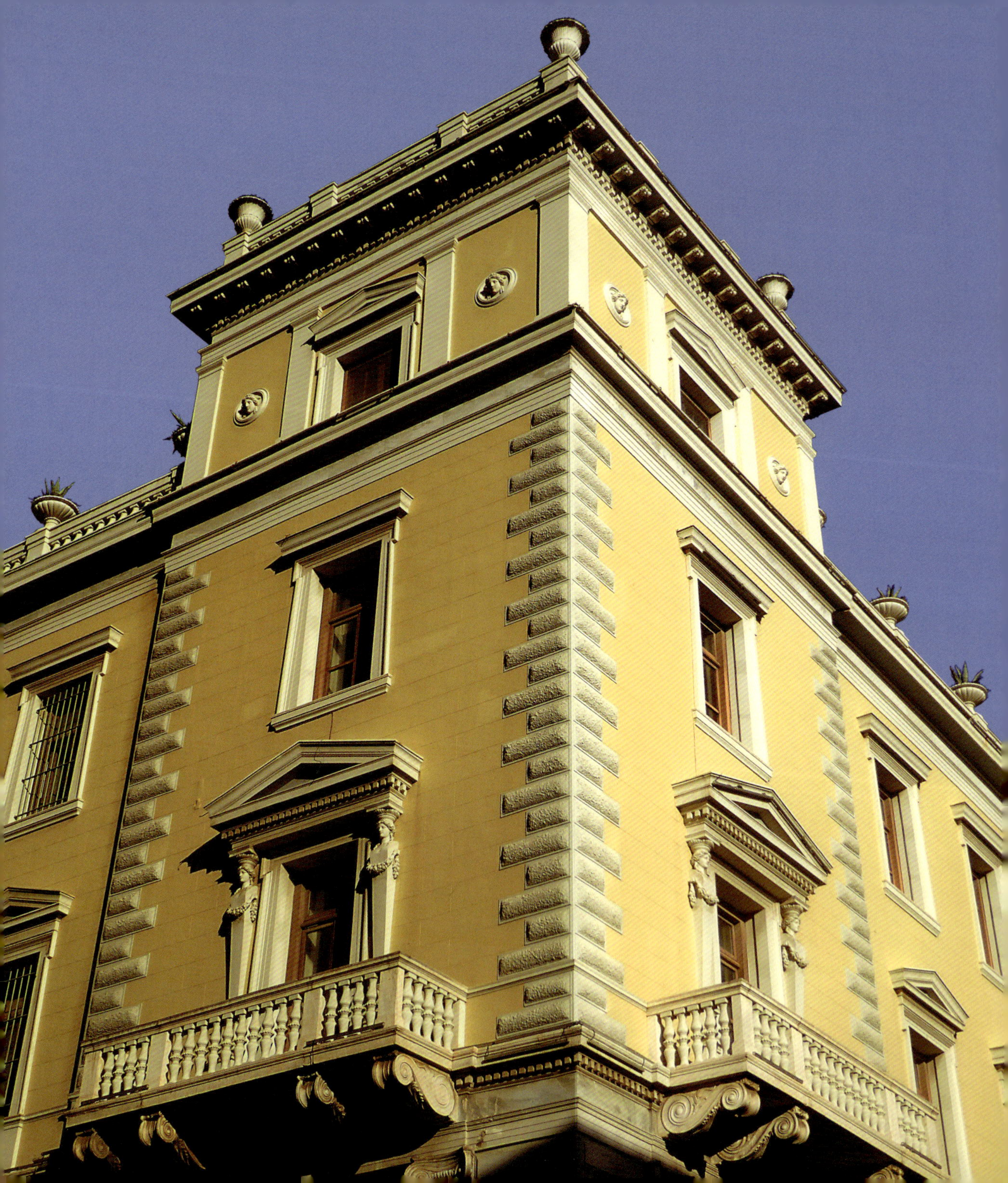

KOTZIA SQUARE

In 1881 the Athens Stock Exchange and later the Athenian Club, 1888-1894, were housed here, and by 1900, the Athens post office set up its headquarters. The letters, arriving at Piraeus Port, were brought to the square on mules. The postman, standing on a wooden box, called the recipients' names. Letters not claimed were burned on the spot.

Today, walking in Plateia Kotzia is like tip-toeing between two worlds. A breath away from the Athens fish and meat market, the fountain offers a respite to many Athenians from the hot summer months. As the sun sets, the dynamic changes, and groups of immigrants and refugees emerge. Most live in the nearby areas of Metaxourgeio or behind Omonoia Square, two deeply displaced neighborhoods in Athens.

The buildings may be visually impressive, but a sadness permeates the square. The people's lowered heads speak of conflicts, just like the one that took place historically in the square, and of losing loved ones and homes.

Opposite: *Melas Mansion, example of mature neoclassical architecture*

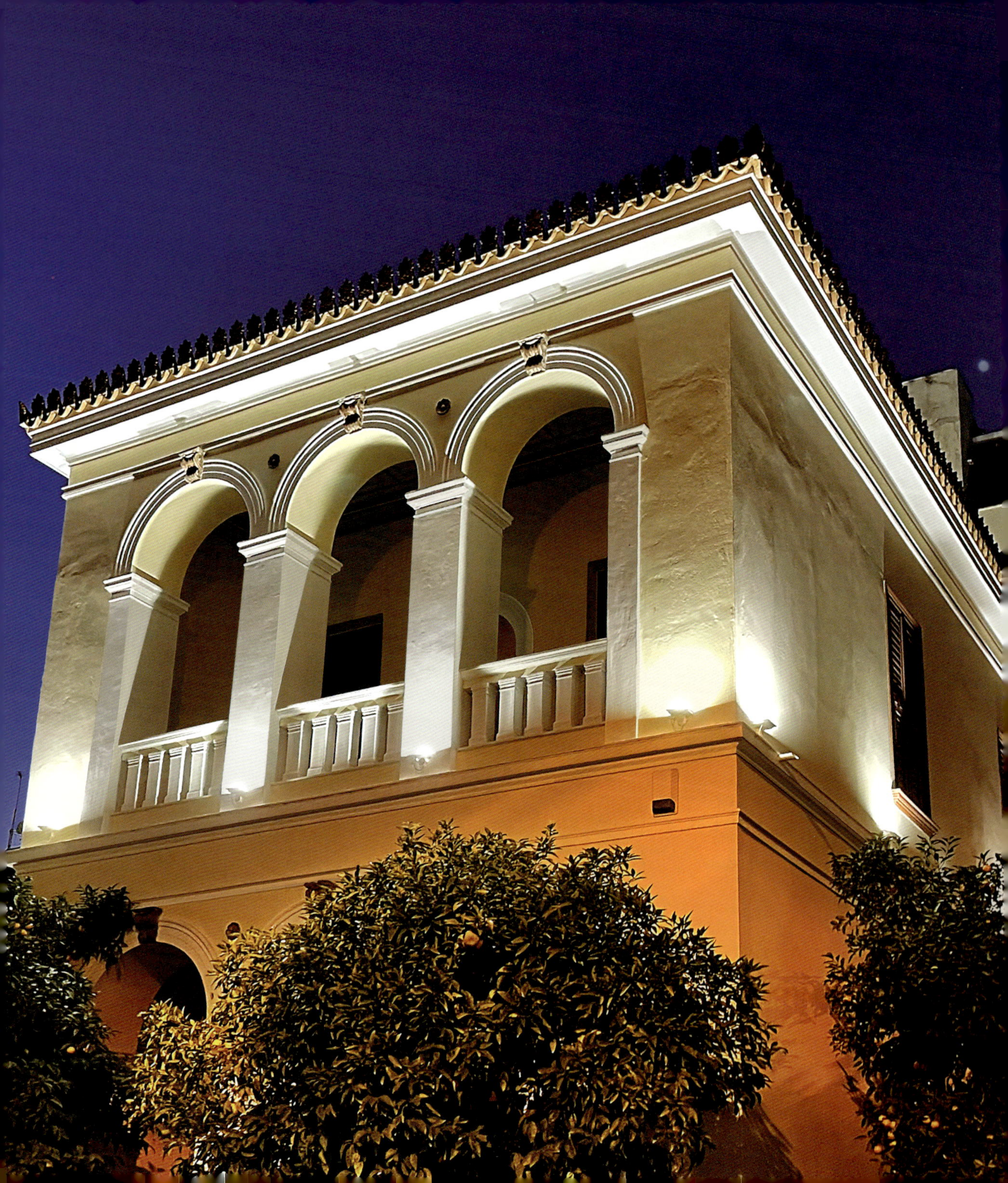

MUNICIPAL GALLERY OF KALLITHEA SOFIA LASKARIDOU

A woman standing on a balcony looks down upon her garden. Her eyes, once bright, have lost their luster, and her hand, once holding a paintbrush, now rests on a cane. Death is nearing, but she's not afraid. Life has been generous to her. At ninety-five, she can still think clearly. Her eyesight is blurry, but it's better this way. Sometimes she thinks that her entire career was spent reaching this point of awareness, to paint with inverted eyes so as not to miss what's important.

The woman caresses the onyx brooch on her lapel. She's aristocratic, well-educated, and privileged. She's traveled far and wide. She's met important people, artists and writers and intellectuals. She took classes at famous art schools and exhibited her work in famous salons, when other women of her age could only hope for marriage.

She also knows that this house, with its curved arches, painted ceilings and thick walls, will be her resting place. She smiles at the thought. This house only brought her happiness. It's here that she held her first canvas, here that she mixed her first paints, and here that she learned that all was possible.

Municipal Gallery of Kallithea Sofia Laskaridou, *120 Laskaridou Street, Kallithea; Hours: Daily: 10:00 a.m. – 2:00 p.m. and 6:00 p.m. – 9:00 p.m.*

MUNICIPAL GALLERY OF KALLITHEA SOFIA LASKARIDOU

Walking on Laskaridou Street in the Kallithea district, one can't help but notice a magnificent two-story building designed in pure neoclassical form by Paul Ziller, Ernst Ziller's younger brother. The house belongs to Sofia Laskaridou, the first woman to be accepted at the Athens School of Fine Arts.

Laskaridou was born in Athens in 1876 in an affluent and highly educated home. Her father was a wealthy merchant and her mother a pioneer in women's education and proponent of physical education for young girls. Sofia's sister, Irini Laskaridou, was the founder of Kallithea's first kindergarten, as well as the "School for the Blind." It was also Irini who translated the Braille system of tactile writing into Greek.

Encouraged by her mother, Sofia Laskaridou headed a group of female art students, who petitioned the king to allow women to take the same courses with the same renowned teachers as men did, and to have equal access to grants, prizes, and scholarships. Their petition was granted.

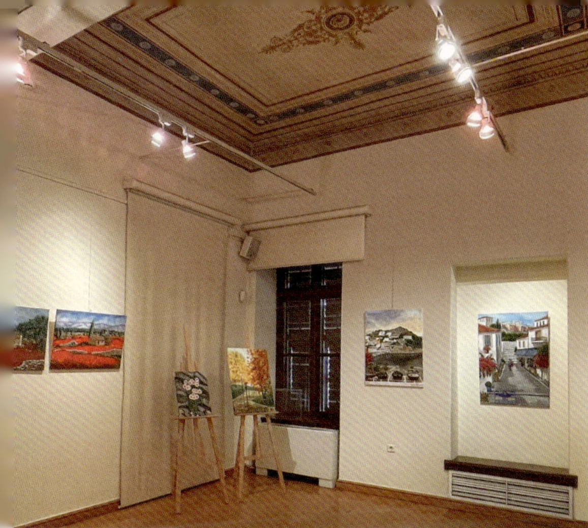

Top: *Exhibition room; the house hosts many cultural events for the municipality of Kallithea*

Right: *Self-portrait of Sofia Laskaridou, National Gallery – Alexandros Soutsos Museum*

Following Pages: *Laskaridou House on a bright spring day*

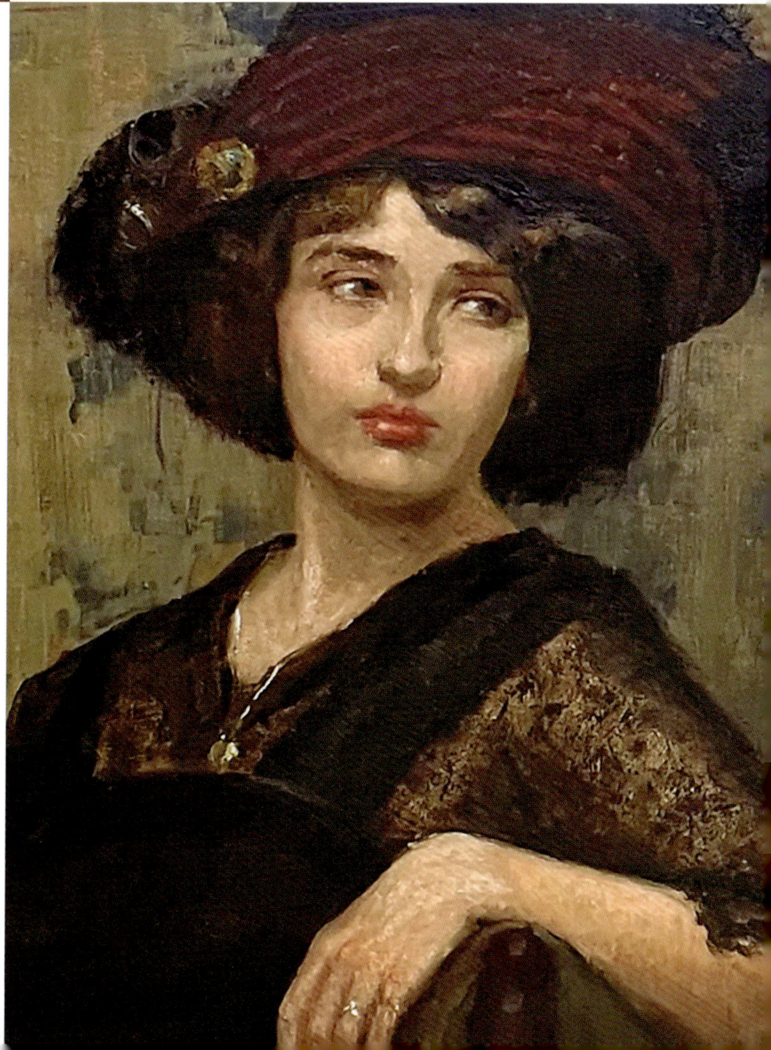

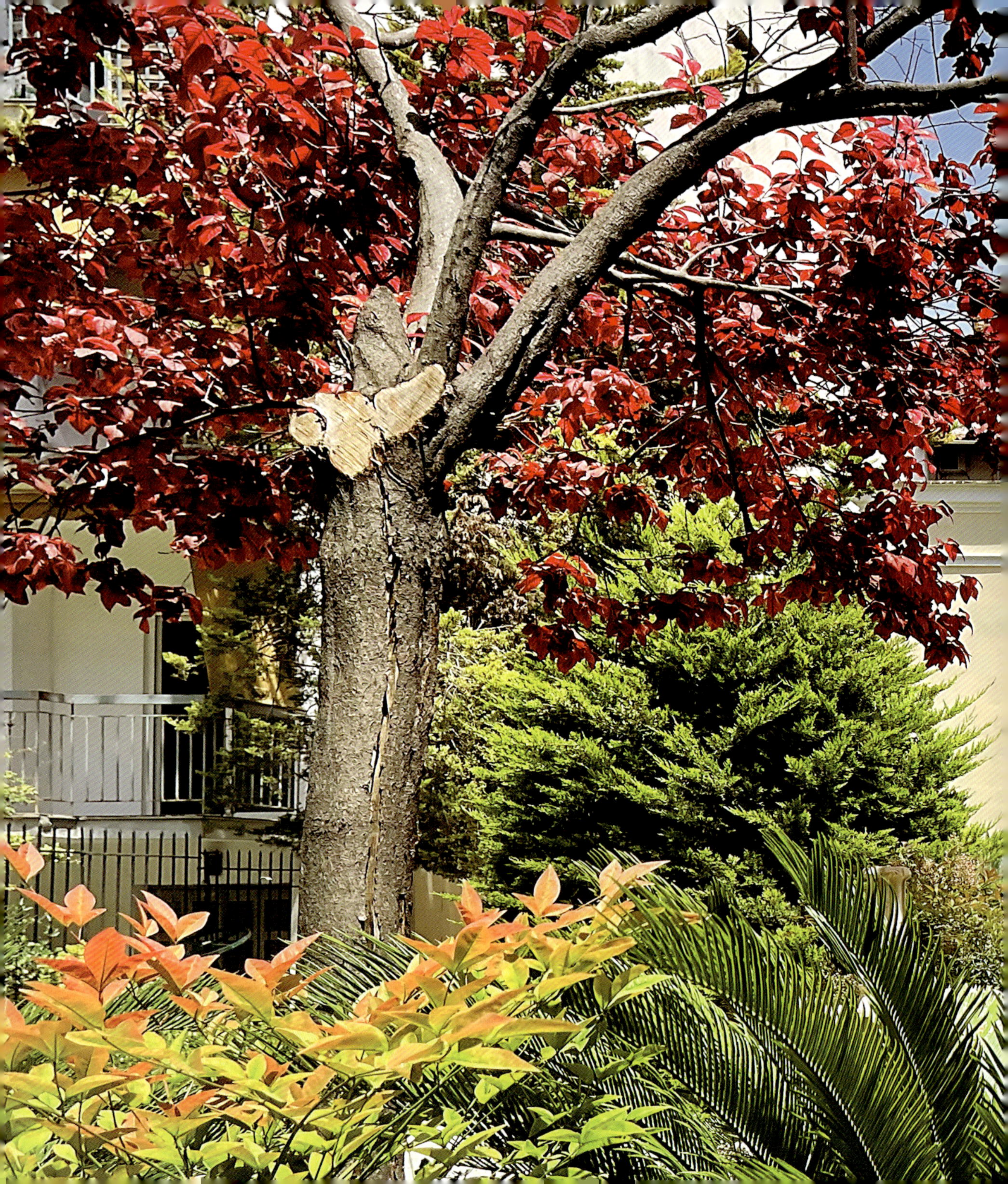

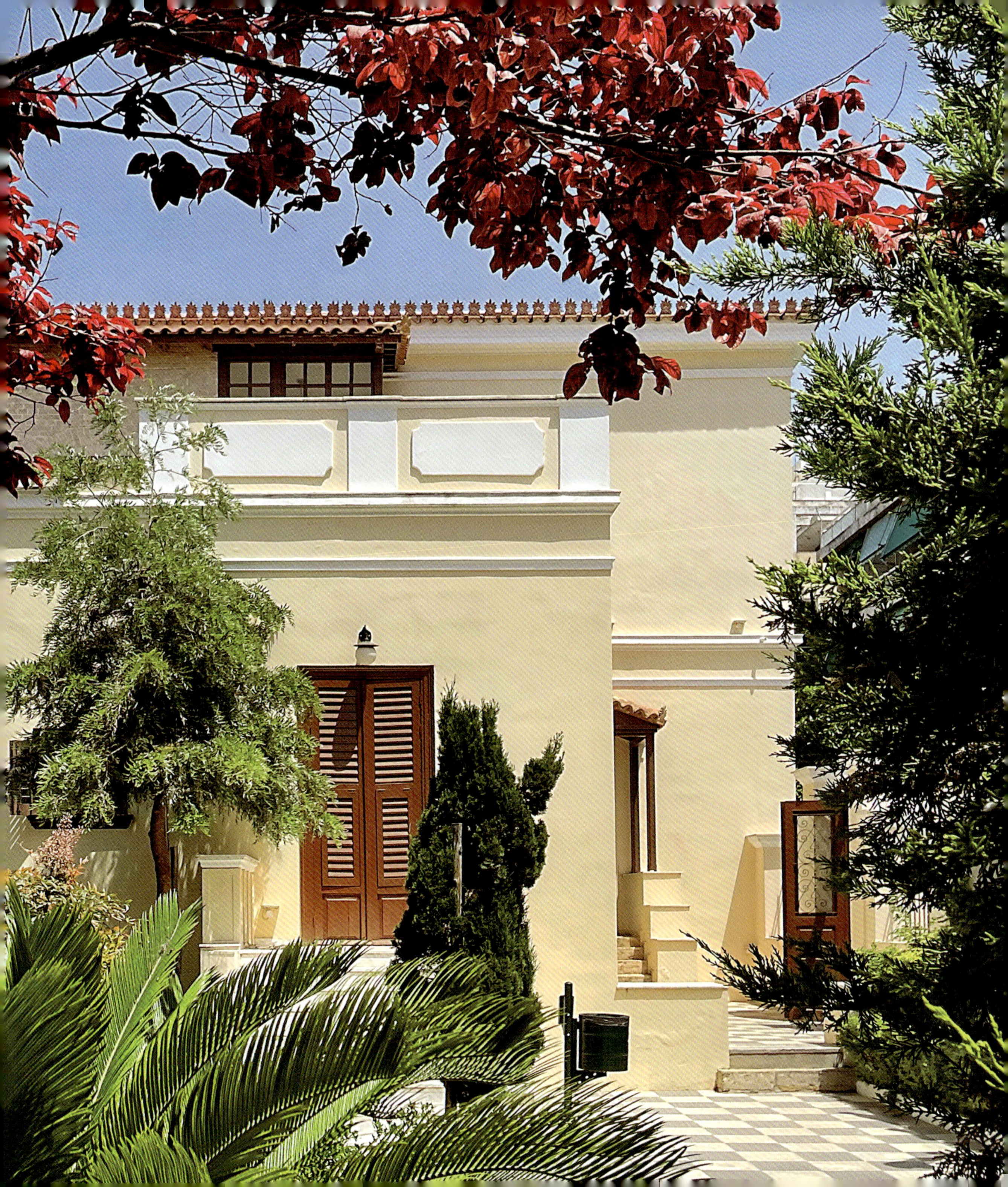

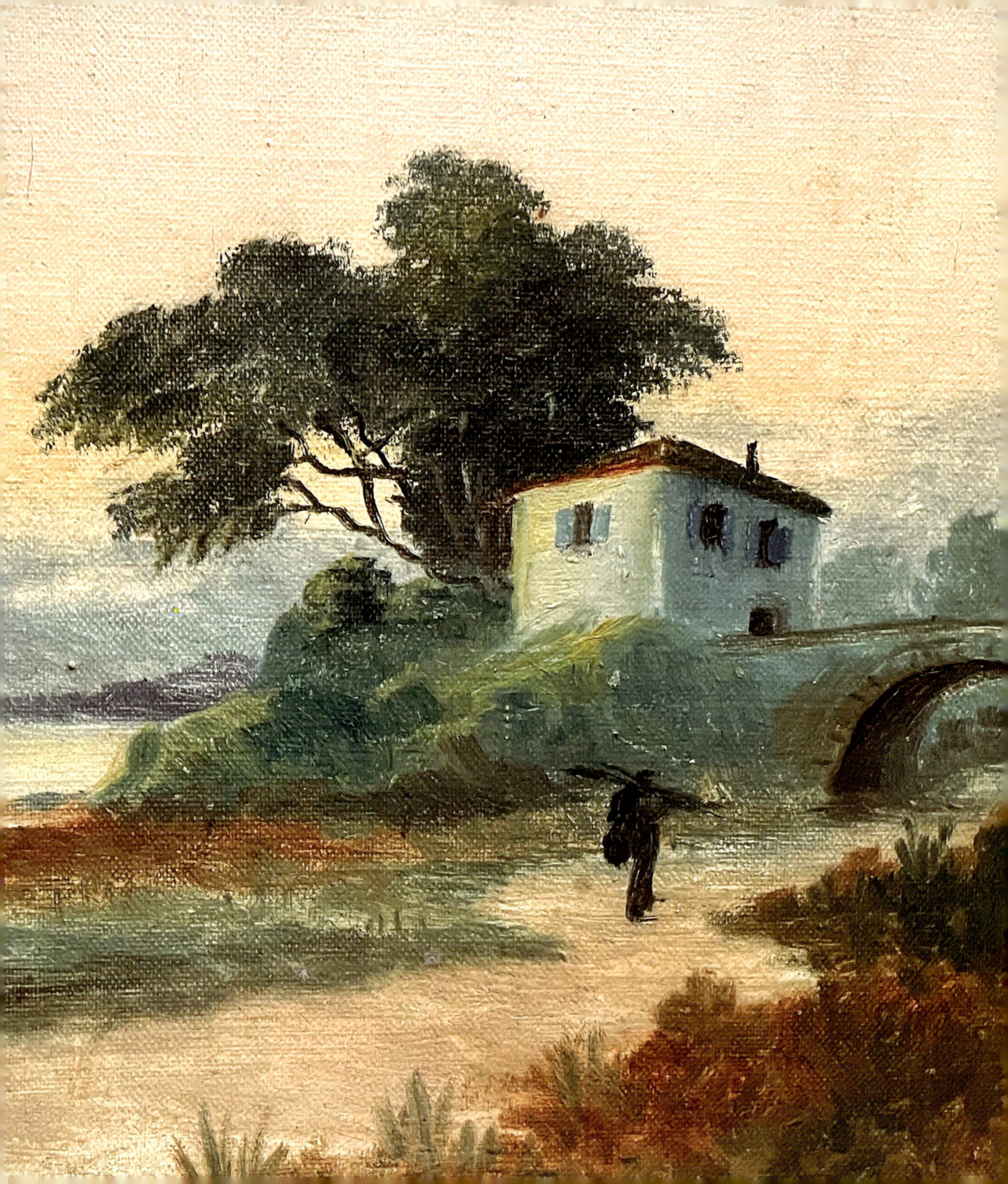

MUNICIPAL GALLERY OF KALLITHEA SOFIA LASKARIDOU

In true fairy tale style, during one of her walks, Laskaridou met Pericles Yannopoulos, an ardent Philhellene with extreme nationalistic ideals. Their affair was passionate, but when he proposed to her, Laskaridou chose to pursue her career and left for Munich. In 1910, Yannopoulos, disillusioned by his limited success and the disregard for his ideas, committed suicide.

Although devastated by his death, Laskaridou never stopped painting, and her career flourished. She permanently returned to Greece in 1916, and slowly retreated into her home, where she died at the age of ninety-five.

Largely unknown to the public, Laskaridou's work has left an important mark on Greek modern art. Some of her paintings can be viewed at the National Art Gallery of Athens, but also at her home in Kallithea, which now houses the Municipal Gallery of Kallithea.

A few trains stops away from the city center, it's here that one can experience her true essence, imagining her walking the grounds with color always in her eyes.

Opposite: *Detail from a painting by Sofia Laskaridou*

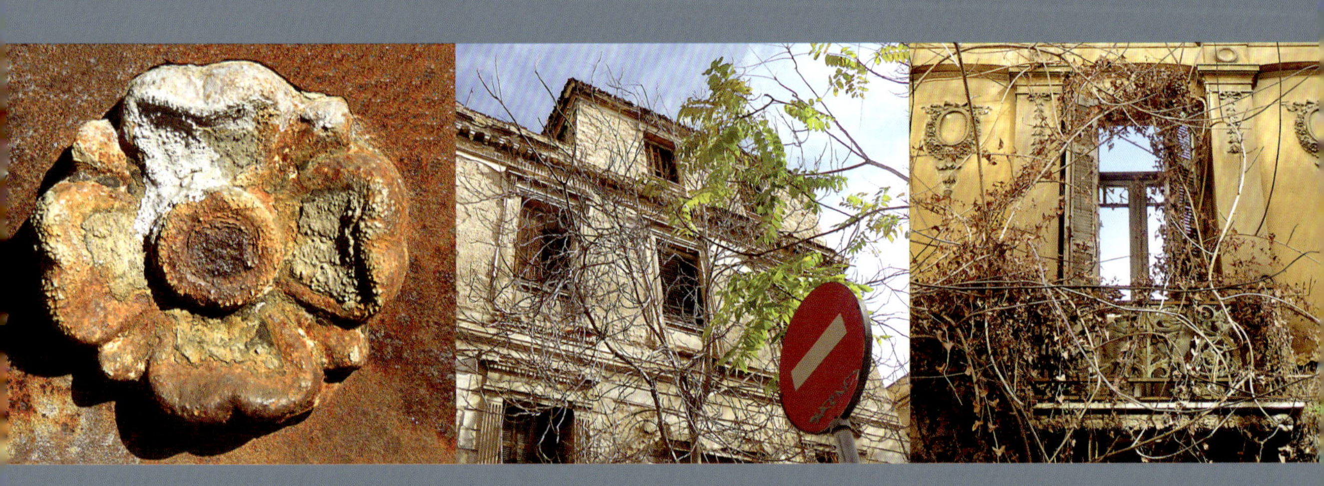

FORGOTTEN GLORY

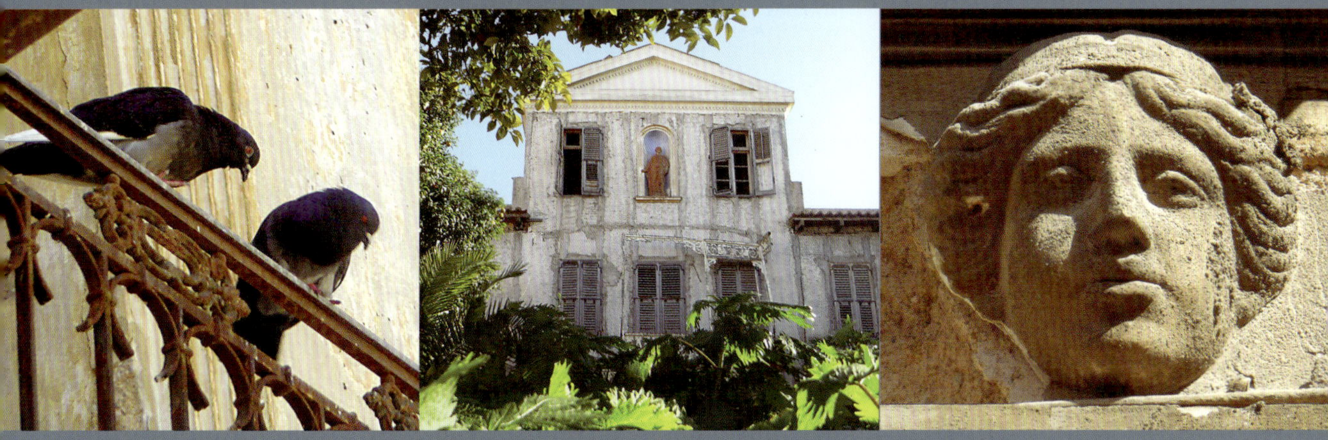

Walking around Athens, it's hard not to notice the great number of buildings left to decay. Some are stunning neoclassical mansions with marble statues, ornate freezes, cast iron balconies, and colonnades. Others are humbler, with tiled roofs and clay figureheads on the cornices. These houses are the silent witnesses of an Athens that no longer exists but is imprinted in the city's soul.

Broken windows, falling mortar, trees thrusting out of rooftops, winding stairs leading to hollow floors, and attics occupied by squatters and pigeons, fuel the imagination. There's something powerful and poignant about these houses that raises questions. Who were the original occupants, and what happened to them? Where did they come from, and what kind of lives did they live? Records exist for some of the historical buildings, but for the rest of them, there's very little to go by.

At the onset of the twentieth century, the character of Athens drastically changed. More and more people moved away from the city center to escape pollution and be closer to nature.

INTRODUCTION

Neighborhoods that were once desirable to live in were slowly abandoned. The inheritors of these homes, faced with heavy property taxes and maintenance expenses, were unable to maintain them, and the buildings were left to decay.

There are about seventeen hundred abandoned houses in Athens. Another two hundred are under protective status to be restored, but the lack of funds, and the excruciating bureaucratic process have left the plans unrealized. So these beautiful buildings continue to stand on their own, relying only on nature to spare them. Some have become so dangerous they could crumble at any moment; others have been taken over by squatters with little concern for their property or history.

These old houses are such an important part of Athens that it's hard to imagine the city without them. One hopes that the government, as well as private citizens, will invest in these treasures, restoring them. In the meantime, all that one can do is walk around with an open mind, and perhaps they wind may whisper their stories.

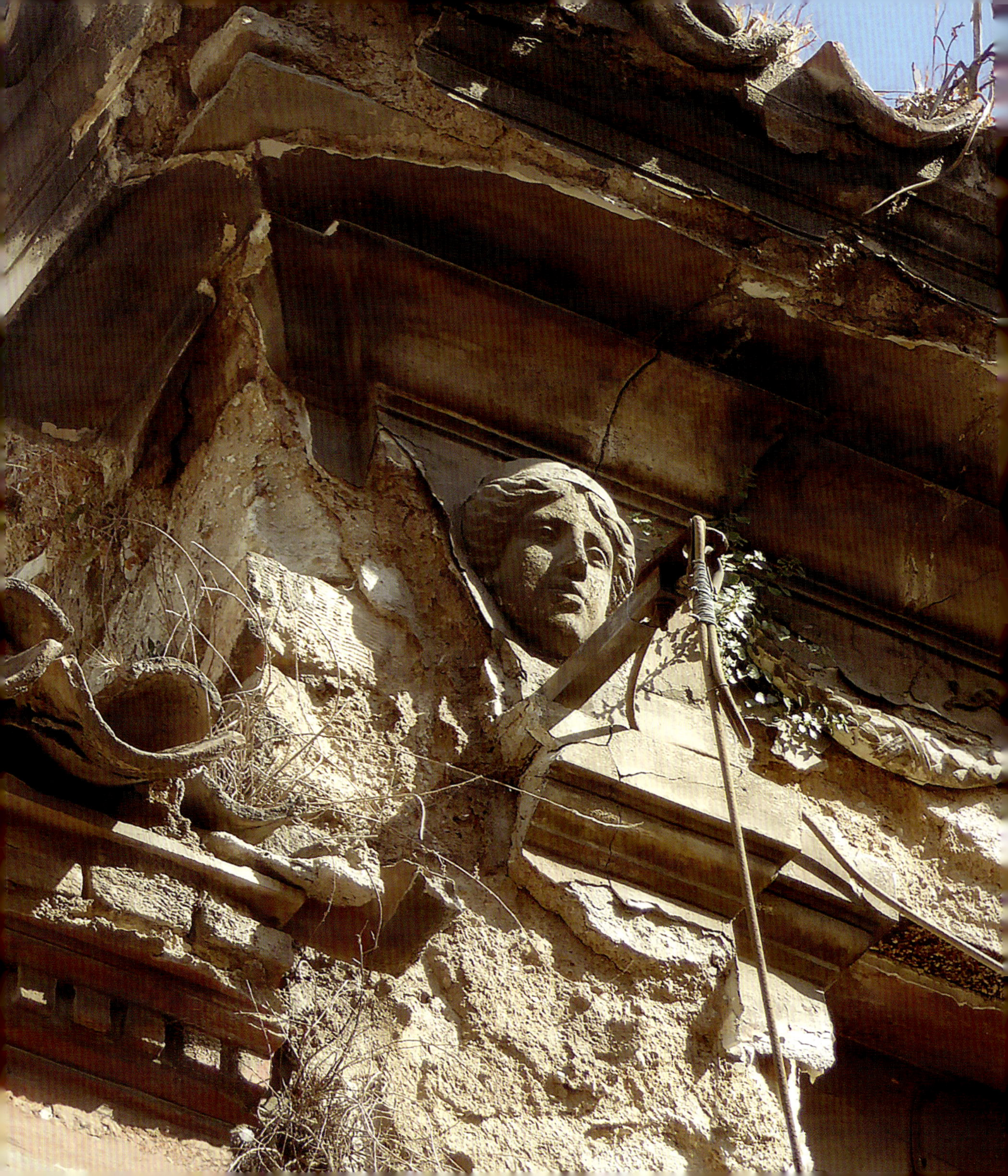

THE KORAI HOUSE

Sunrise. The alleys in the Psyrri neighborhood are still asleep, exhausted by another sleepless night, but someone is awake, observing me. I turn around, startled. A cigarette wrapper dances in the breeze and then flutters away. There's no one here but the wind. I walk a few more steps, but the feeling that I'm being watched grows stronger. Whatever it is, its presence gains strength like the rising sun.

I raise my head, and then I see them. Two female terracotta heads, twin sisters, perched on the façade of an abandoned building. Their faces are serene, almost impervious. They've seen and heard it all; people holding hands, couples kissing, arguments, confessions, and tears.

If you let them, they'll tell you that they've always been here watching over this street. They'll tell you that this home was once filled with beauty, with wide open shutters letting in the light, about children hanging May wreaths on the balconies to welcome spring or throwing confetti and garlands as the Mardi Gras procession passed by.

The Korai House, *name inspired by the author, Hebe's Street, Psyrri; terracotta women representing ideal neoclassical beauty*

THE KORAI HOUSE

I take some photographs and walk away, their serene faces still imprinted on my mind. Months pass by. I decide to go back and find out more about the building, but where to? The alleys are so close to identical, it's impossible to retrace my steps. In a way, I feel that I've failed them. Like so many others before me, I admired their beauty, but now I bypass them, abandoning them once again in the quiet space. Perhaps that's what they wanted all along.

A few years go by. It's late afternoon, and the streets are flooded in a brilliant light. I take it all in, grateful to partake in this moment of beauty. That's when I see them, their delicate terracotta heads peeking through a patch of shrubbery. Weeds have cracked through their heads, almost splitting them in half. I wonder when nature will take its final toll, receding their features deeper and deeper until they're completely erased.

The building with the Korai is located at Hebe Street, but be patient. It might take time to discover them; or you may think that you've bypassed them. Stay alert, and when you least expect it, they'll reveal their beauty, letting you see them in their full glory.

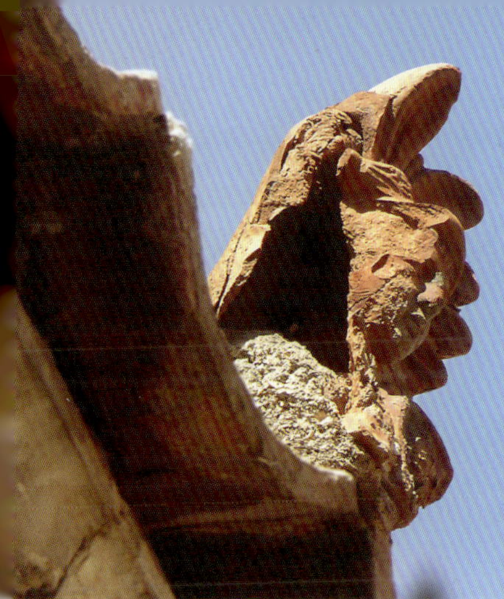

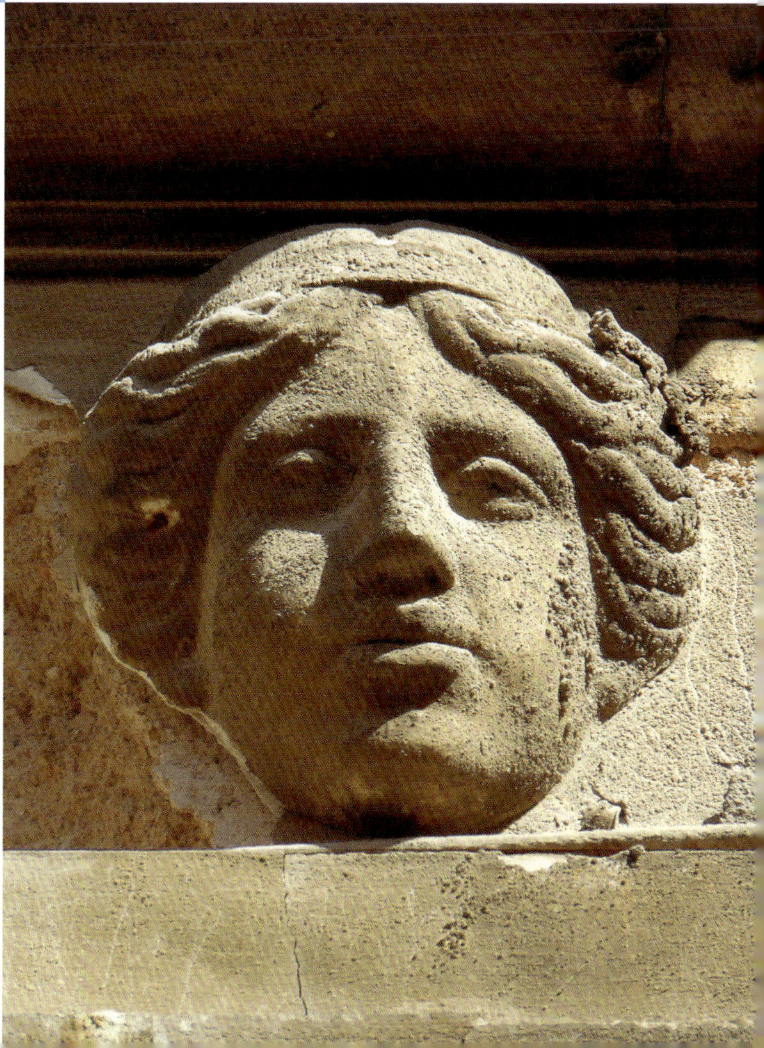

Top: *Detail of Acrokeramon, a clay decoration on the edges of a tiled roof; a design element in popular neoclassical architecture*

The Acrokerama can appear singularly at the corners of a house, or in a row running around the parameter of the roof; subjects include: flowers and deities, with Hera and Hermes as the most popular choices

Right: *Clay figurehead of woman, probably a nymph or a deity*

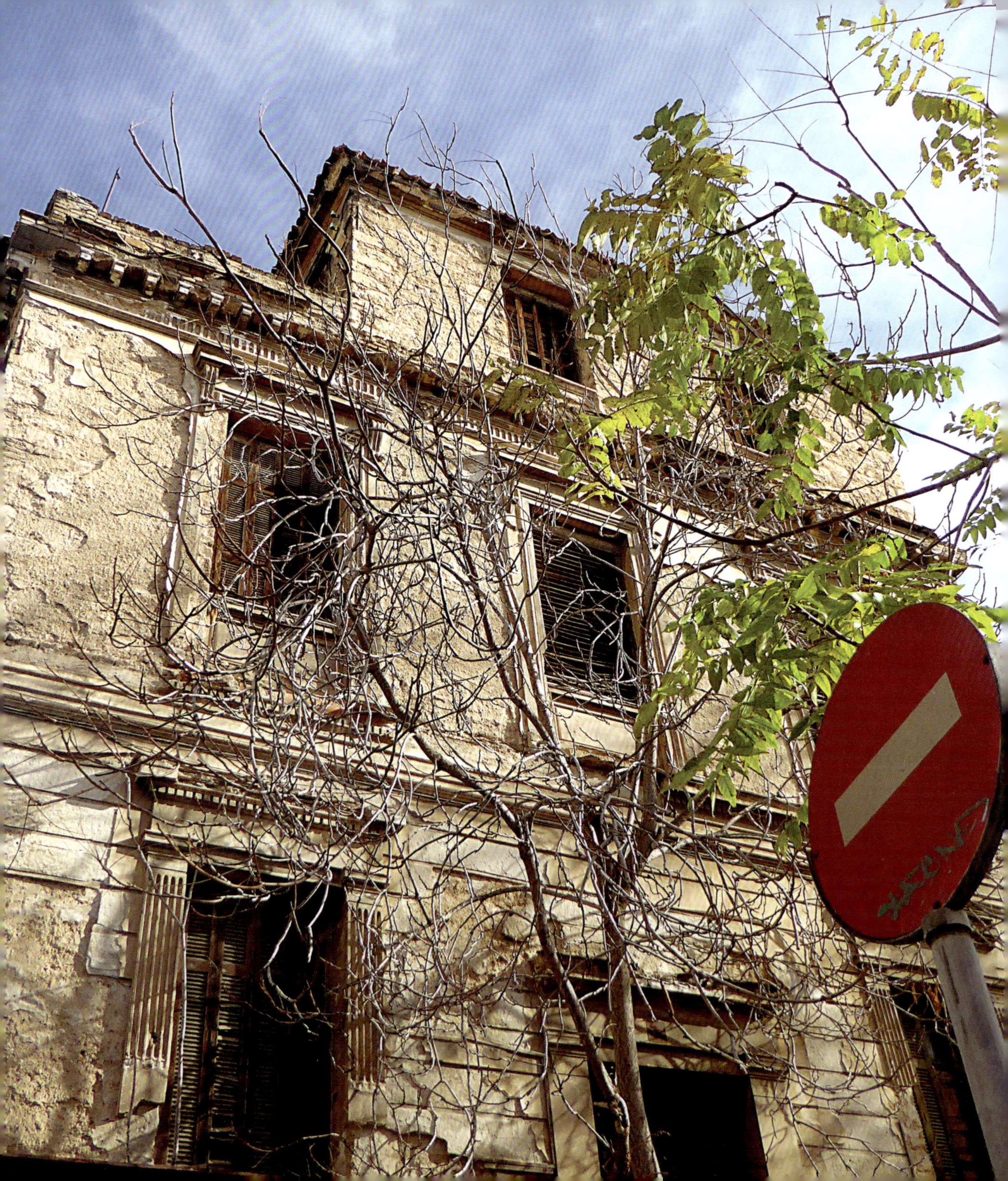

KALOGIROU HOUSE

Walking on Piraeus Street, cars, trucks, and motorcycles zooming by, raising clouds of soot and exhaust fumes. At first glance, there's very little to draw one's attention to. The area is mostly industrial, devoid of character with hot summers and cold winters, but if you let your eyes adjust, some stunning structures emerge, all of them abandoned now.

According to the original city layouts by Stamatis Kleanthis and Eduard Schaubert, Piraeus Street was to lead directly to Omonoia Square, where the new palace was to be built. The plan never materialized, and those who rushed to buy property, soon realized that their value was lost and moved out, letting the buildings decay.

However, it's exactly this decay, and the mystery that surrounds the previous occupants, that brings me back again and again. Hidden between the cement and the apartment buildings constructed in the early sixties, one can find a treasure trove of information about the life and spirit of nineteenth-century Athens.

Kalogirou House, *Kalogirou and Psaromiligkou Street, Psyrri; the street was named after Greek Independence revolutionary monk, Samuel Kalogirou*

KALOGIROU HOUSE

A cluster of motorcycles parked on the pavement blocks my way, so I cross the street to avoid them. A side street catches my attention, and I head towards it. I look up, astonished to find myself in front of a massive building occupying almost half the block. A group of smaller houses stands adjacent, like children hovering next to their mother for shelter.

The street is a haven for the displaced and the homeless. Men crouched at the steps of the buildings shoot heroin in broad daylight, as others drag cardboard boxes preparing their beds for the night. Their eyes are furtive, full of suspicion, so it's better not to linger.

The street is named after Samuel Kalogirou, a patriot monk in the Greek Independence War. Kalogirou lived in Kougki of Souli, a town in the Ioannina district. When the people of Souli agreed to surrender their arms to the Ottomans, Kalogirou refused to leave and stayed behind with the elderly and wounded. When Ali Pasha's men arrived, Kalogirou set the nearby warehouse on fire, blowing up himself and the weaponry.

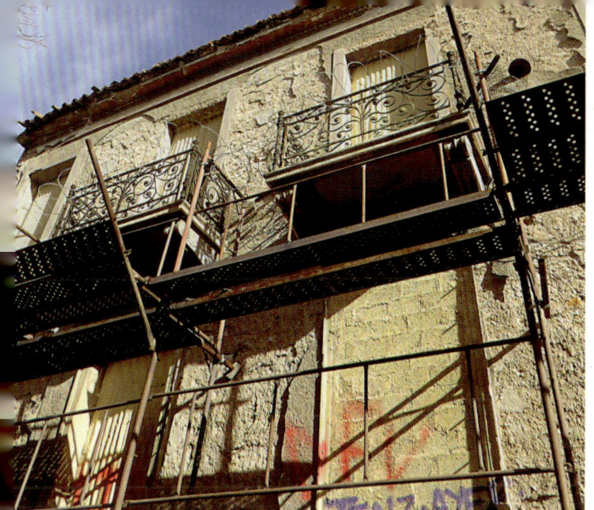

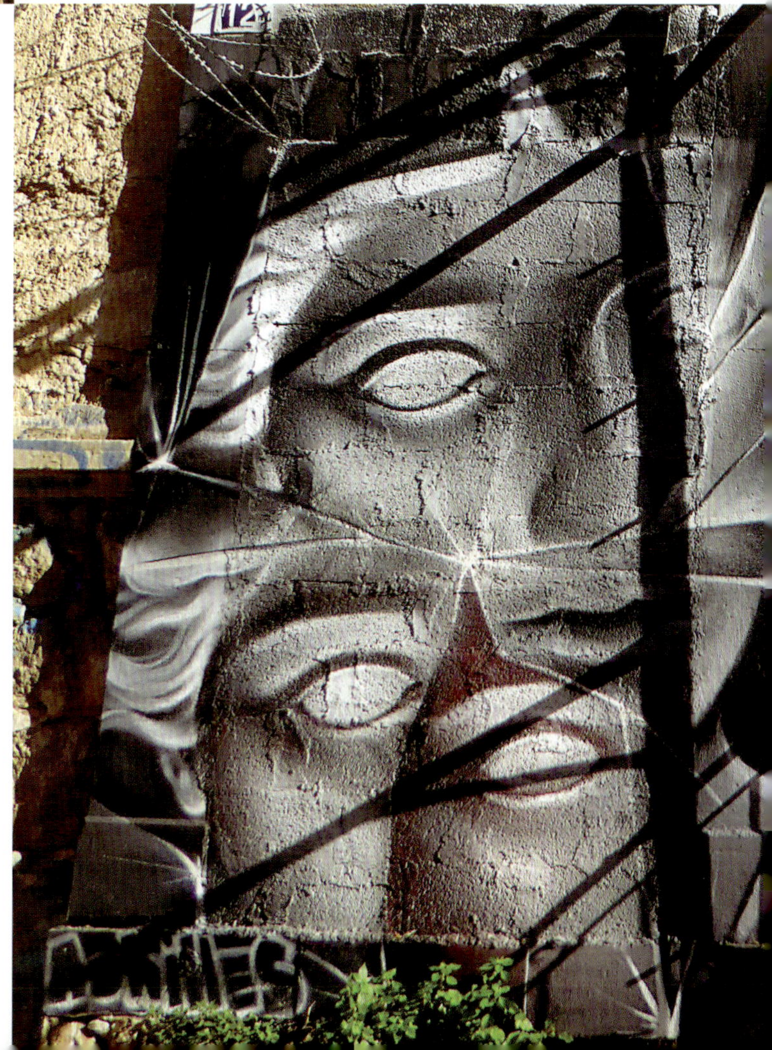

Top: *Protective scaffolding and windows blocked with cement to deter drug users and squatters; some of these mansions remain privately owned and others have been transfered to the Greek government*

Right: *Mural by Achilles; a popular and thought provoking street artist*

Following pages: *Commanding view of the building on Kalogirou Street; owners unknown*

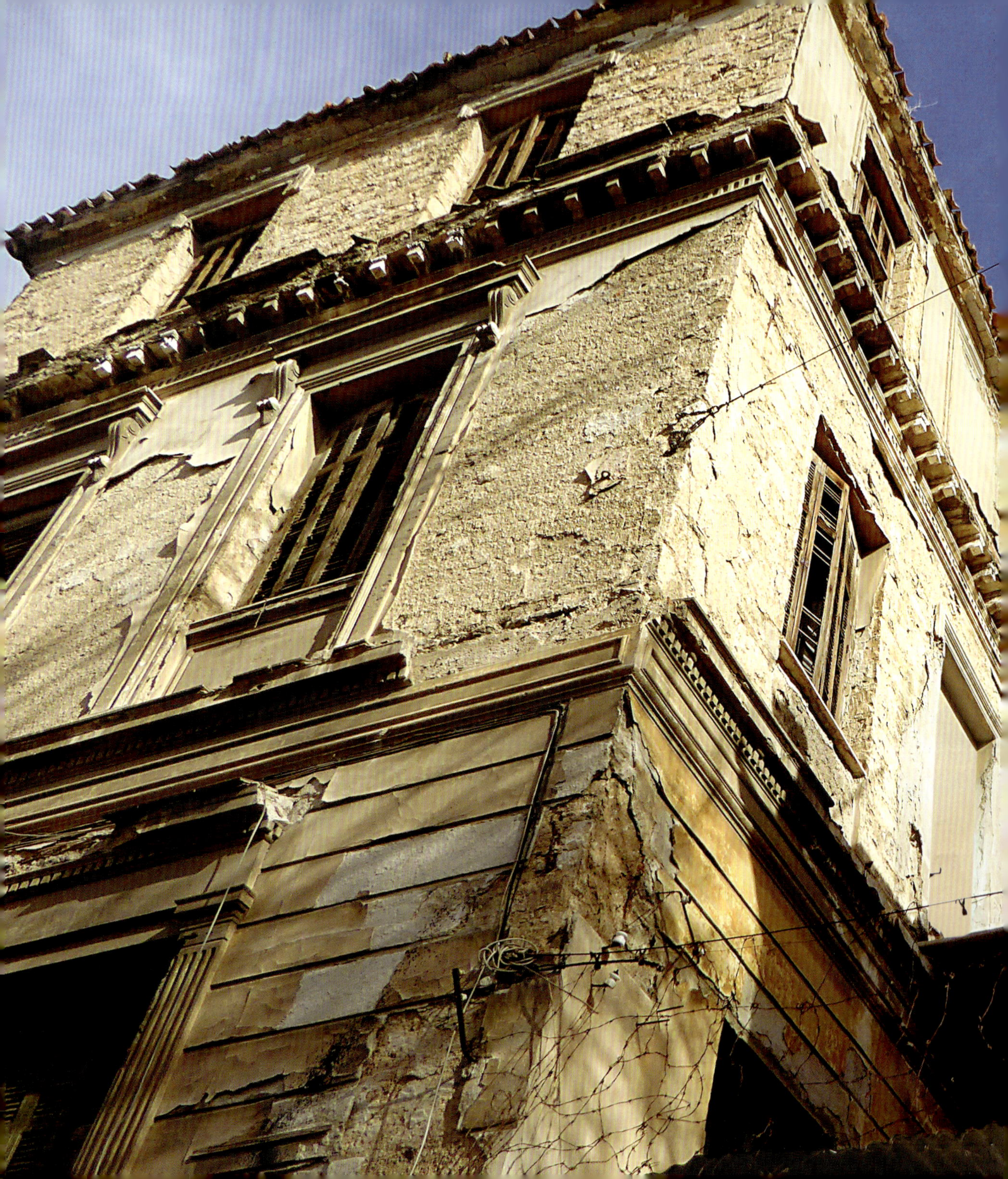

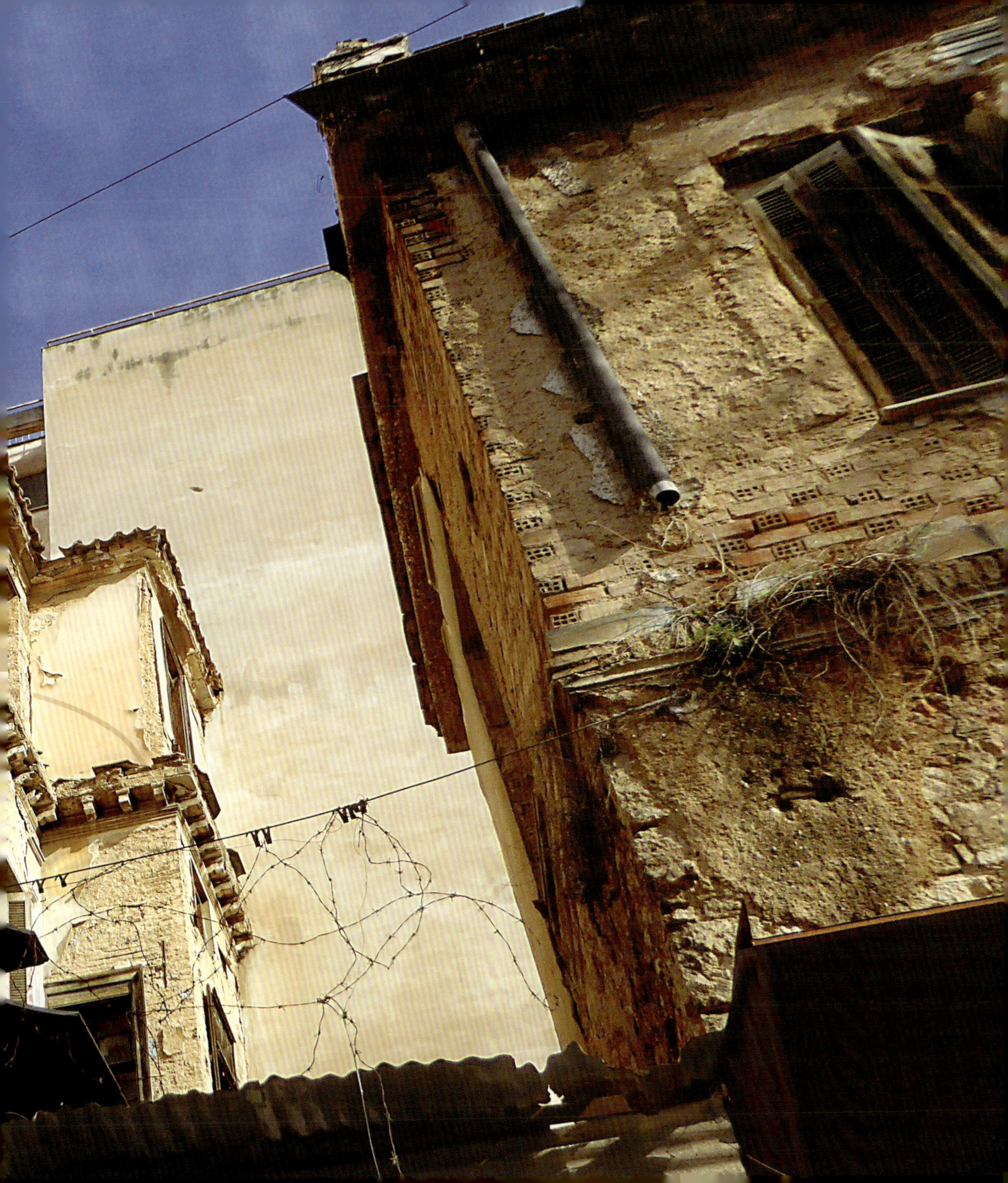

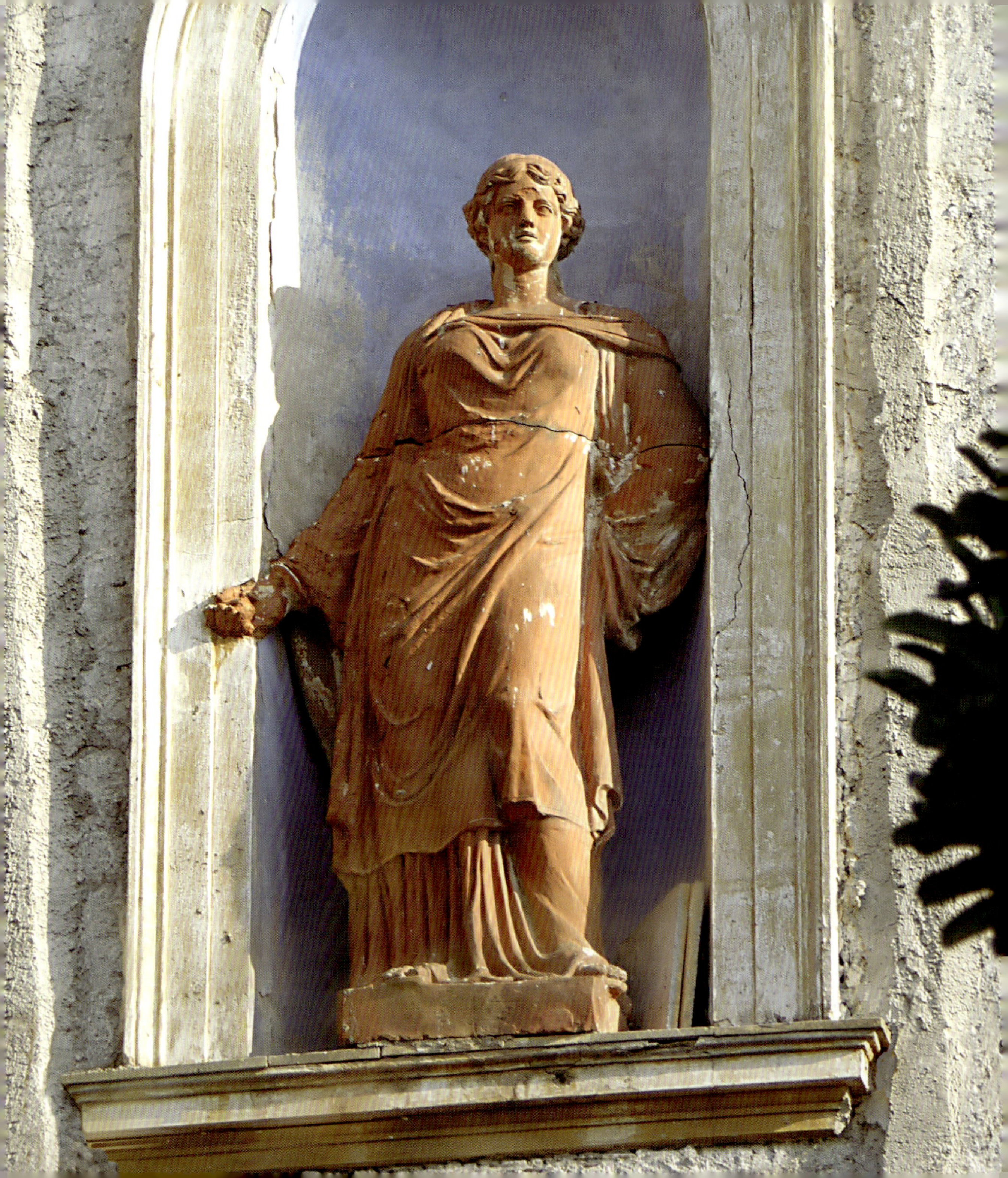

KOLETTIS MANSION

Summer afternoon in Plaka. Most of the visitors have retreated to their hotels to avoid the heat, and the few remaining seek shade under the trees. We are at the Brysaki area, one of the most visited and most enchanting parts of Plaka, which rests at the foothill of the Acropolis and a breath away from the Ancient and Roman Markets.

Meticulously restored homes, painted in the most luscious colors, with geraniums cascading from the windowsills, dot the streets, stealing one's heart away. Amidst all the beauty, the observant traveler will notice a neglected mansion receding into the background surrounded by tangerine, palm, and cypress trees.

The mansion, with an enigmatic terracotta figure perched in a niche, speaks of wealth and privilege. The woman draws you closer, beckoning. Standing amidst the tattered shutters, she has stories to share about dances lasting until dawn and political deals negotiated or broken.

Kolettis Mansion, *Polygnotou 13, Plaka; residence of Greek politician Ioannis Kolettis with free standing terracotta figure in niche*

KOLETTIS MANSION

This is the house of the first prime minister of Greece, Ioannis Kolettis, a deeply controversial figure. Kolettis navigated his political career by shifting sides until he ended it in support of the French party. His house was notorious for shady transactions, known as "rousfetia." It was not uncommon to see people gathered at the gates, begging for favors that he granted or rejected based on personal profit.

There's a story that goes hand in hand with Kolettis' personality. A friend of his brought him a small monkey as a gift. Kolettis became very attached to the animal, and he was always seen walking with it on his shoulder. The monkey, like its owner, proved to be extremely nasty, annoying guests by stealing their hats and gloves. That's how the popular expression "Kolettis monkey" was born, which refers to someone being a pest.

Despite promises to restore the mansion and house the poet Konstantinos Cavafy's archive, the mansion remains abandoned, with the enigmatic statue as its sole inhabitant. Stop by and greet her, and if you're fortunate enough, you might even notice the faint smile on her lips.

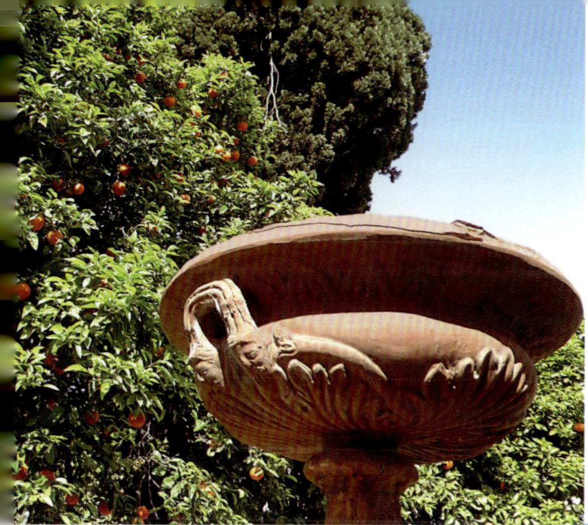

Top: *Terracotta flowerpot inspired by nineteenth-century neoclassical designs*

Right: *Adjacent building housing the Ephorate of Antiquities and Private Archaeological Collections*

Following pages: *Kolettis Mansion surrounded by cypresses, palm trees, and weeds; the building, owned by the Greek government, was to house Konstantinos Cavafys' poetry collection, a plan that has yet to materialize*

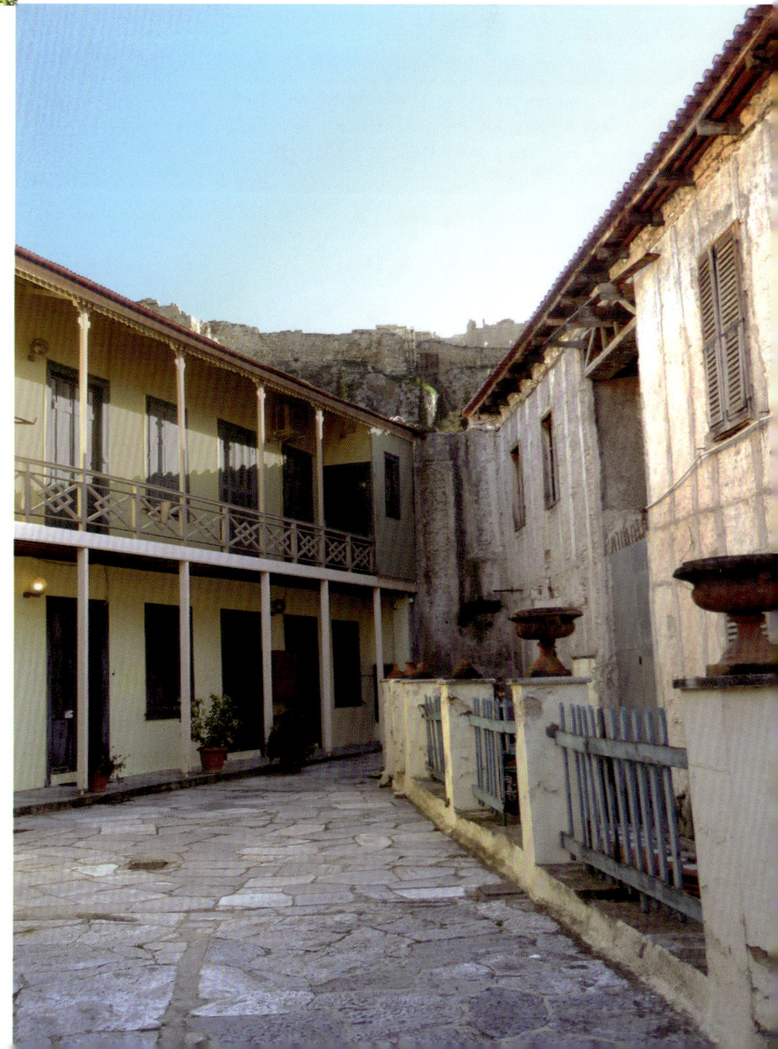

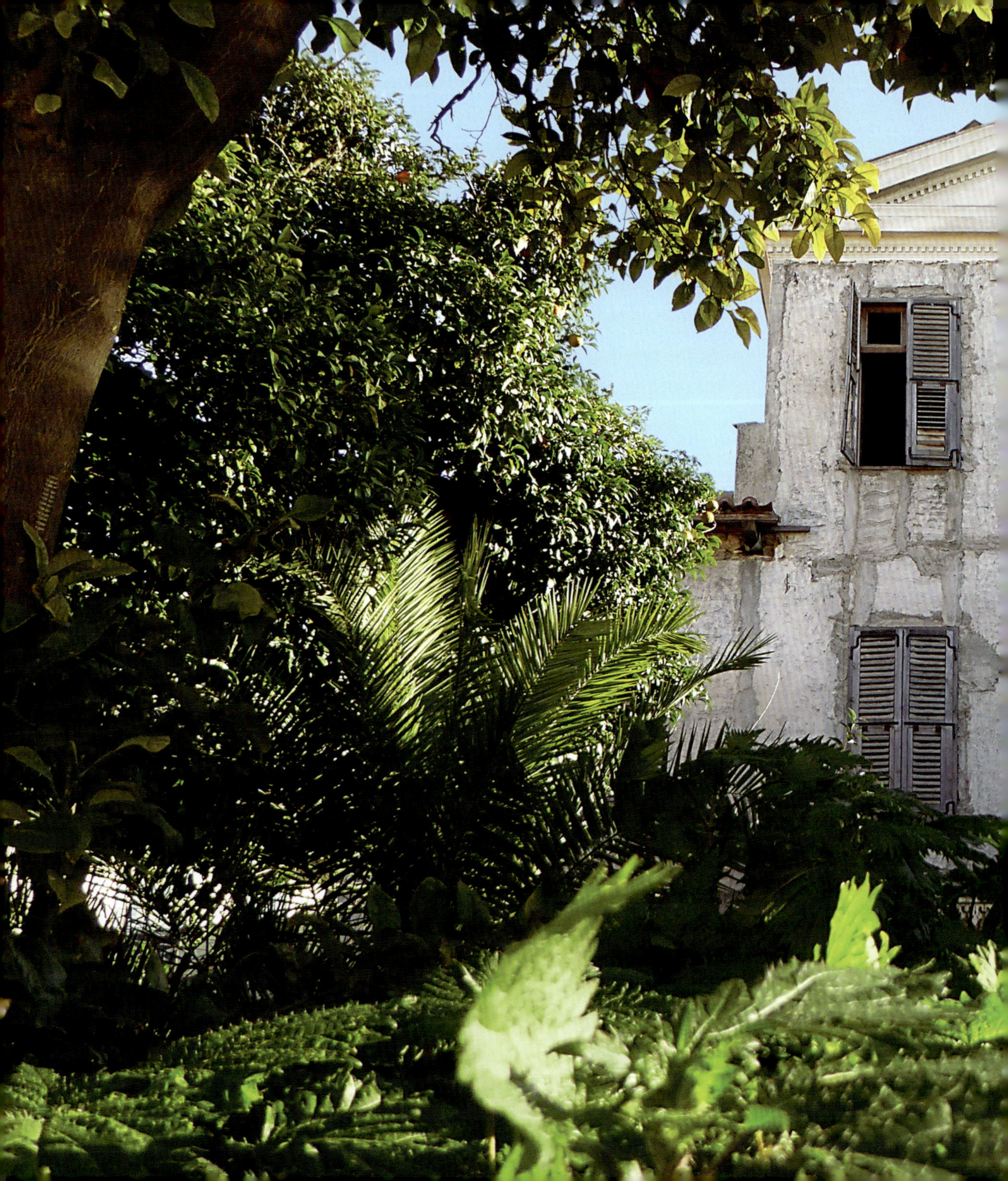

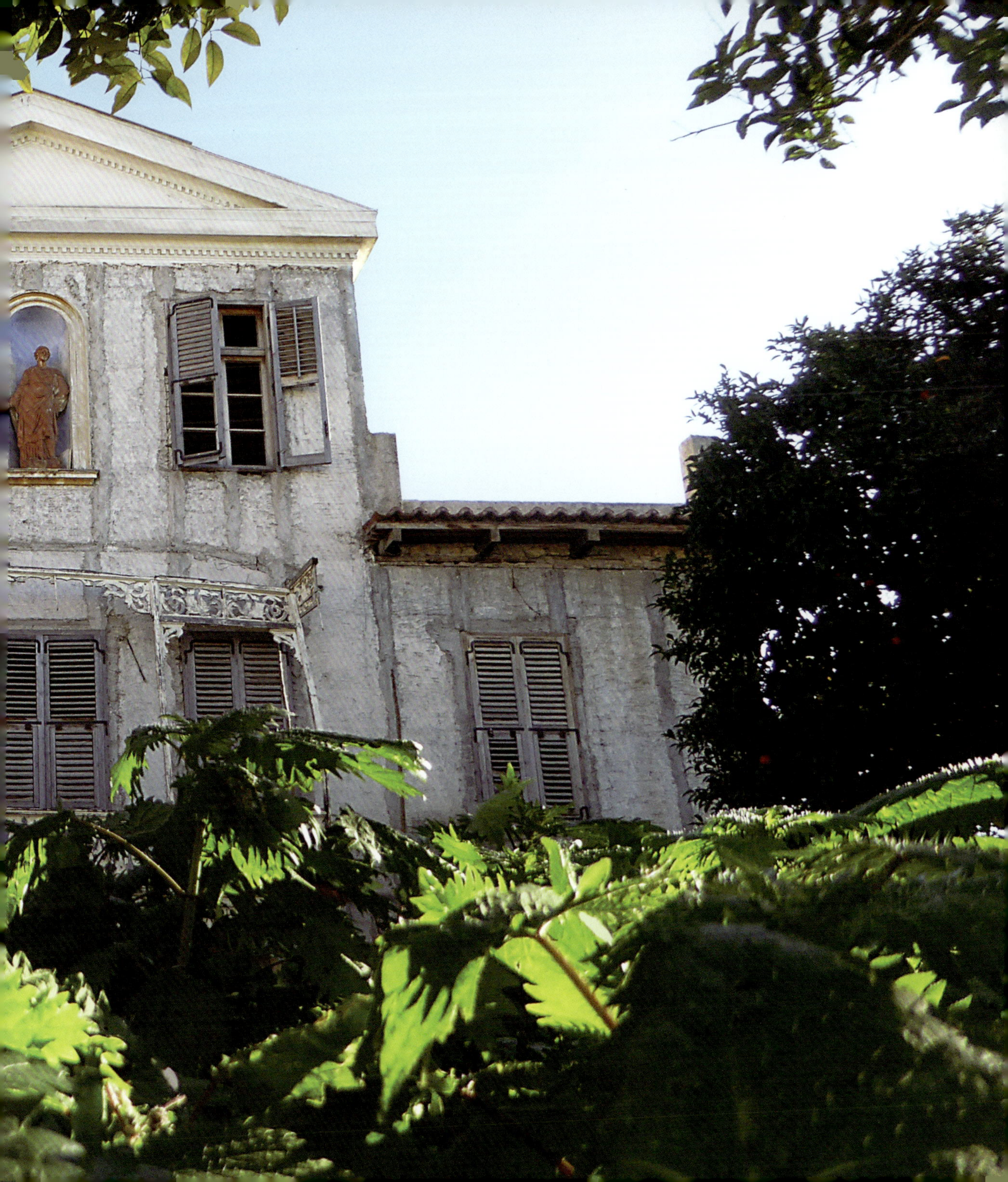

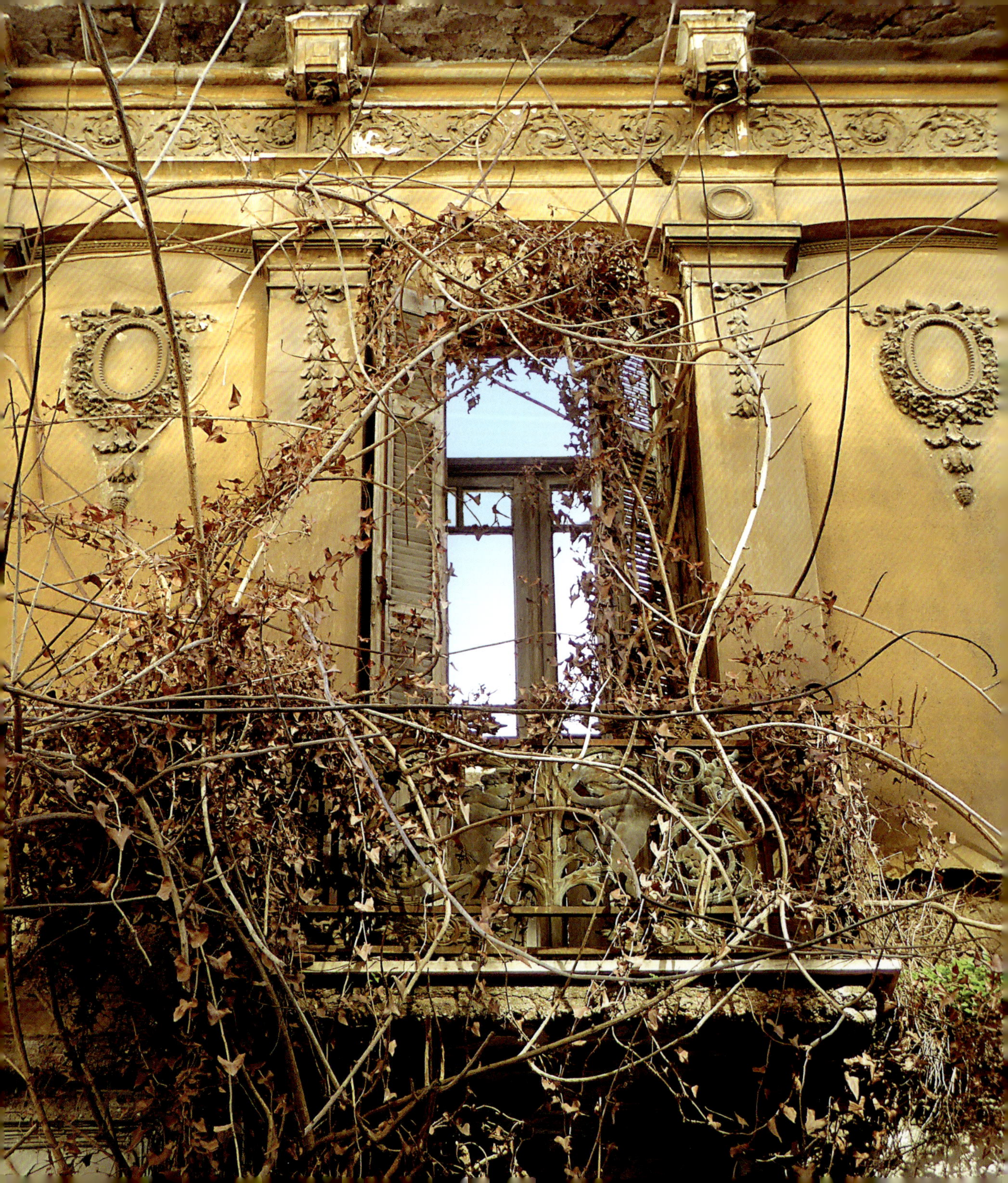

EVMORFOPOULOS MANSION

Tucked neatly into a small alley, steps away from the bustling streets of the Psyrri neighborhood, a magnificent mansion stands alone, gazing at the sky. Painted in a deep ochre color, with flowery cartouches on its walls and playful cherubs made from cast iron, one can't help but wonder how it's possible for such beauty to be left decaying.

Withered branches sprout out of the broken shutters, the hands of the furies in an ancient play, as clouds float in and out from the structure's empty shell. The building, nearly occupying the entire block, speaks of times of past grandeur and wealth.

There's something profoundly regal about this mansion that asks you to stop and take notice. There's an immediacy about it of something lost and now found, a part of a dream stored deep in the subconscious and you're back to reclaim it. Yet the memory will not last long and the day will come that the excavators will roll in knocking down the walls and tearing away the house's heart.

Evmorfopoulos Mansion, *5 Evmorfopoulou Street, Psyrri; neoclassical mansion with elaborate cartouches and cast iron balconies*

EVMORFOPOULOS MANSION

Not much is known about the house and its inhabitants, but once, it must have been a wonder to behold. Maybe it belonged to a wealthy family that moved into the area with the intention of being near to the King's palace in Omonoia Square, a plan that never materialized. Perhaps it was the house of a successful merchant or a foreign ambassador.

Others say that the house belonged to a relative of Manos Eleutheriou, one of the most prolific lyricists, poets, and writers of modern Greece. Either way, it must have been a true wonder for a child to play in these enchanting grounds, skipping rope or sipping cold lemonade under the watchful eyes of the adults.

Standing before the building, an irresistible desire takes over to climb through the boarded doorways and cross into this magical world. One feels envious of the pigeons and the cats, free to roam the grounds or the squatters, who at some time or another, have found shelter in these grounds, and for the moment being the only rightful owners.

Opposite: *Pigeons, the most popular inhabitants of abandoned homes, observing the passersby*

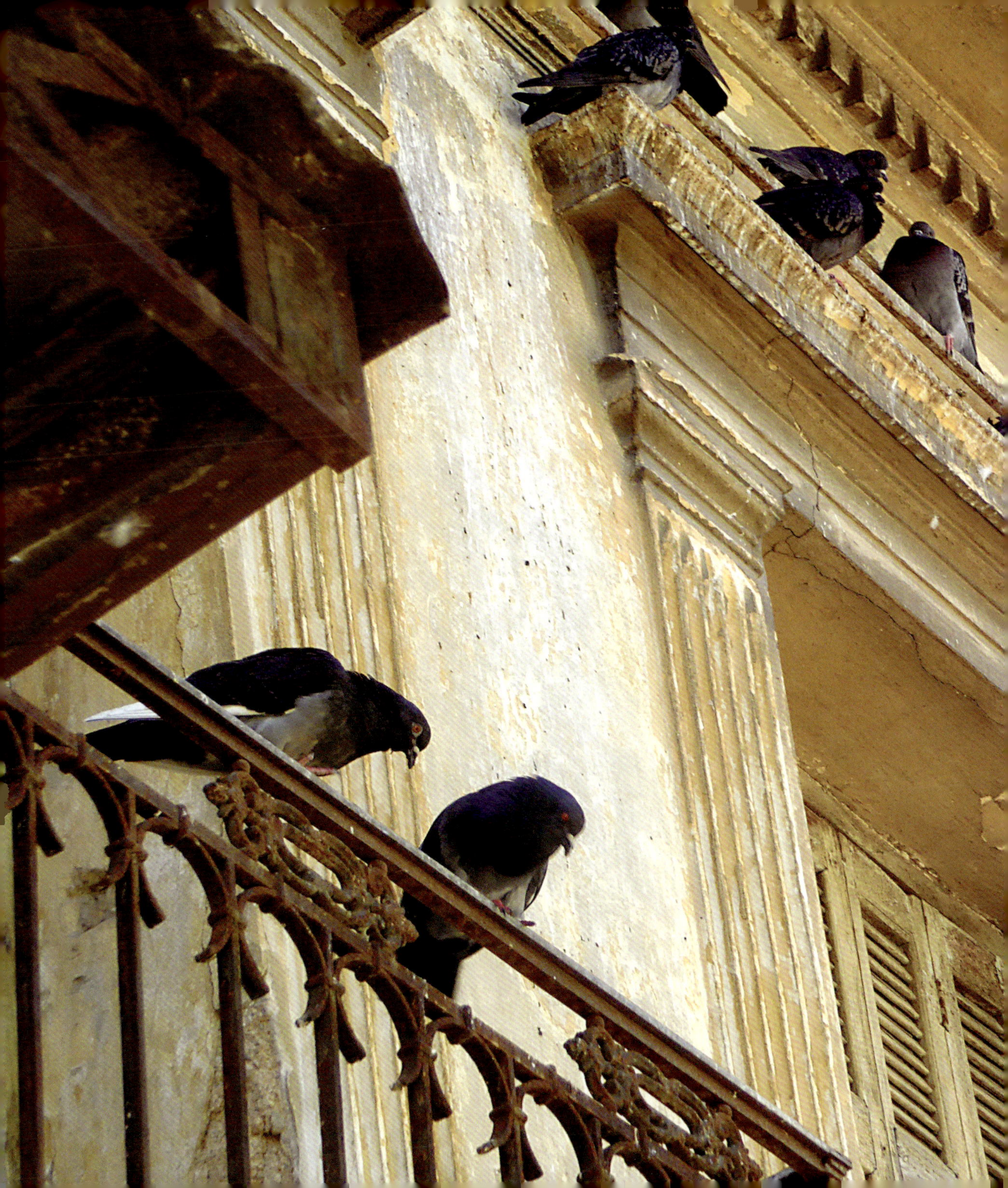

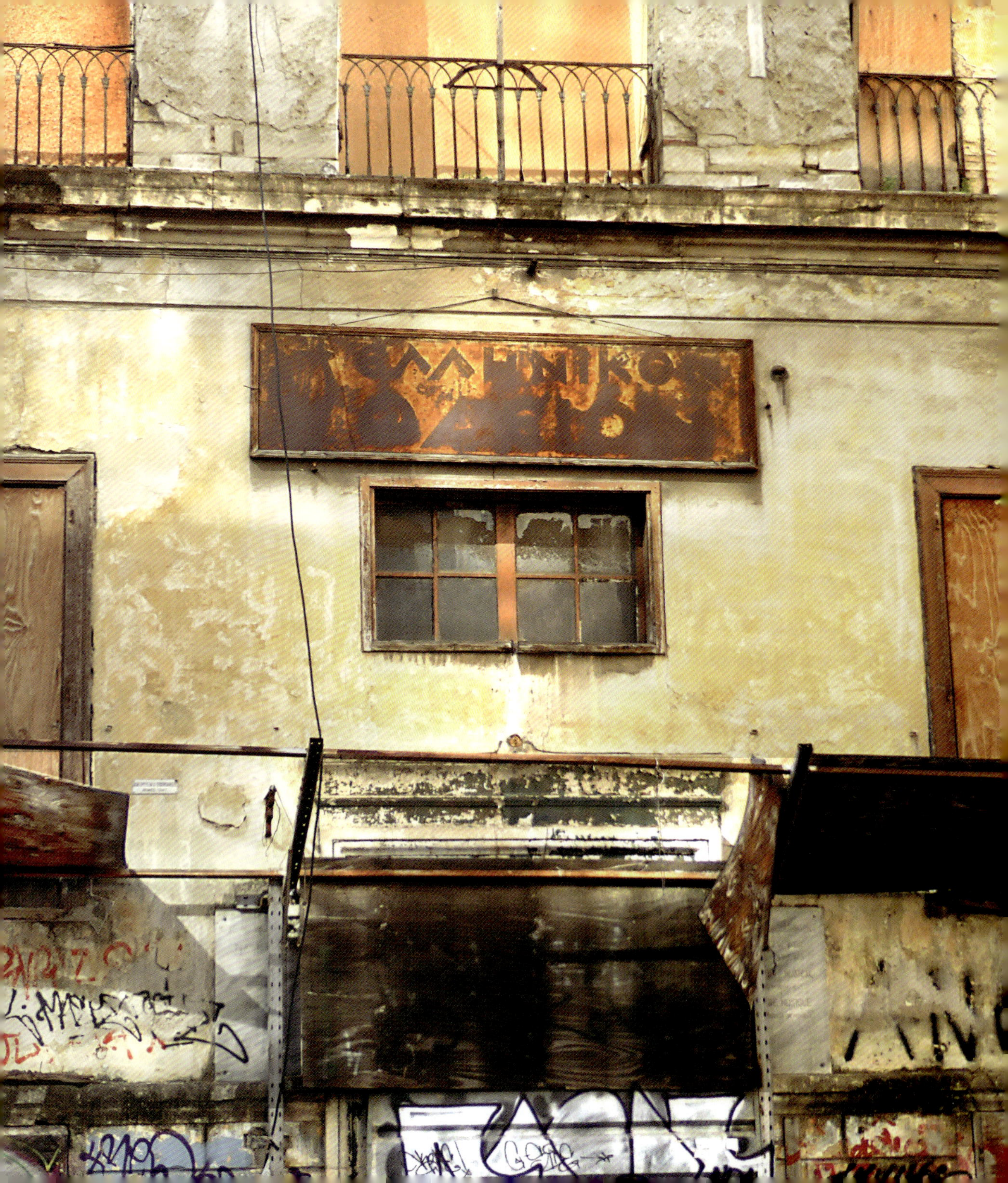

ANTON PROKESCH VON OSTEN MANSION

One of the first mansions built in Athens, Anton von Osten's house stands on a hardly known street, unless you fall upon it by happenstance. Its high walls, reminiscent of a fortress with tall windows, now barricaded by cheap plywood, and surrounded by high gates, speak of times gone by. A rusty sign with the words Greek Music Academy, barely readable, adds an extra layer of nostalgia.

Anton von Prokesch Osten was an Austrian diplomat, general, and intellectual with a sincere love for Greece. He was nominated with the title "von" for his bravery in the Middle East, and was the first ambassador of Austria to be dispatched to Athens.

Osten wanted a house that not only afforded him the luxuries that he was accustomed to, but also a place where all the intellectual, artistic, and political elite of Athens could gather. The design of the mansion is attributed to Adolf Lueders on plans by Karl Roesner. The austere and almost forbidding lines of the exterior were softened by a spacious garden that extended into the back.

Anton Prokesch von Osten Mansion, *3 Feidiou Street; faded sign of the old Music Academy of Athens*

ANTON PROKESCH VON OSTEN MANSION

Hans Christian Andersen described the residence as having winding stairways, floor to ceiling mirrors, and elaborate frescoes, a true jewel in the still unadorned Athens. Osten's wife, Irene Kiesewetter von Wiesenbrunn, an accomplished musician, was known for her extravagant ballroom dances and literary salons.

In 1854 the house was bought by Eleni Tositsa, a major benefactor to many cultural and educational establishments in Greece. After her death, the house was bought by Heinrich Schliemann, who lived there until the completion of his family residence at "Iliou Melathron."

From 1899 until 1919, the house became the Music Academy of Athens under the guidance of the Austrian pianist, Lina von Lottner. Some of the most outstanding Greek musicians and composers performed and taught there, helping others to find their calling.

With little left of the old times but the rusty sign, it's a wonder to imagine that music once rose out from the garden, caressing the nearby homes.

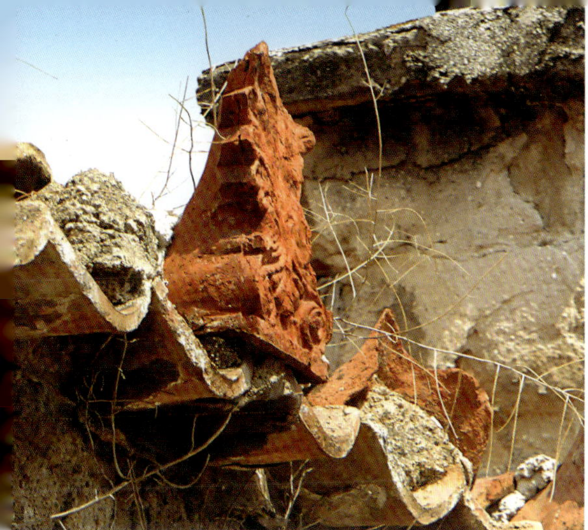

***Top:** Side view of "Acroceramon;" the mansion was known for its extensive garden grounds and variety of trees and flowers; building design by Adolf Lueders on plans by Karl Rosner*

***Right:** Bookstore "Fos," meaning "Light," specializing in religious themed books*

***Following pages:** Art Deco lamp posts in front of the mansion*

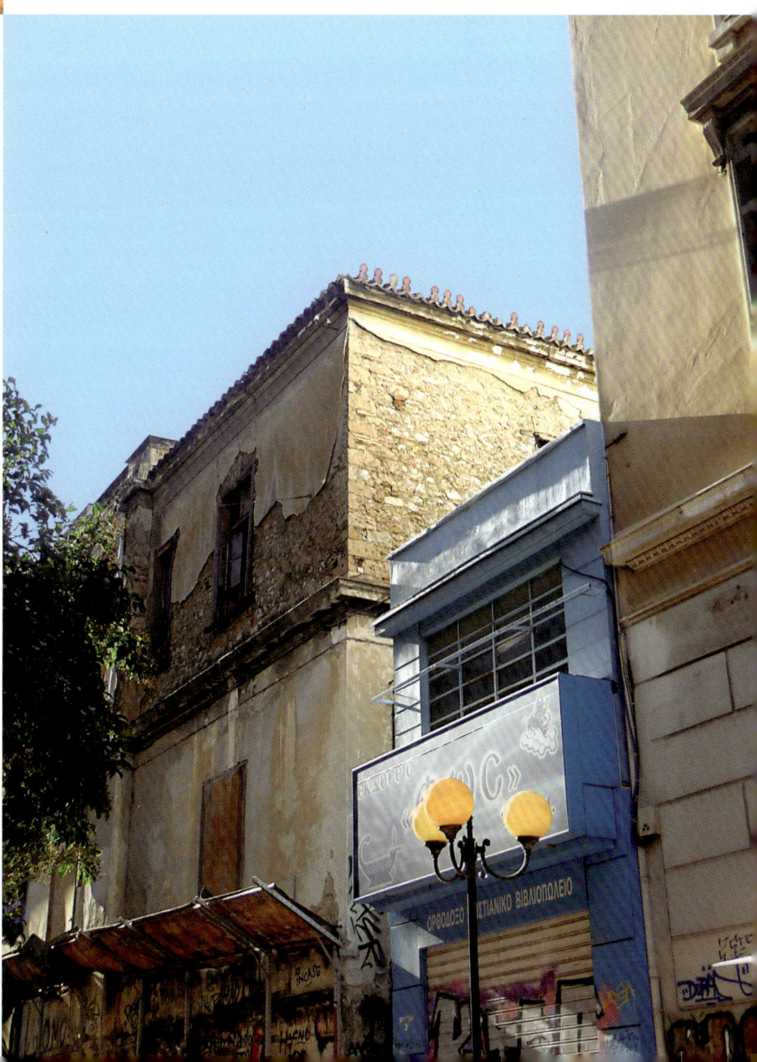

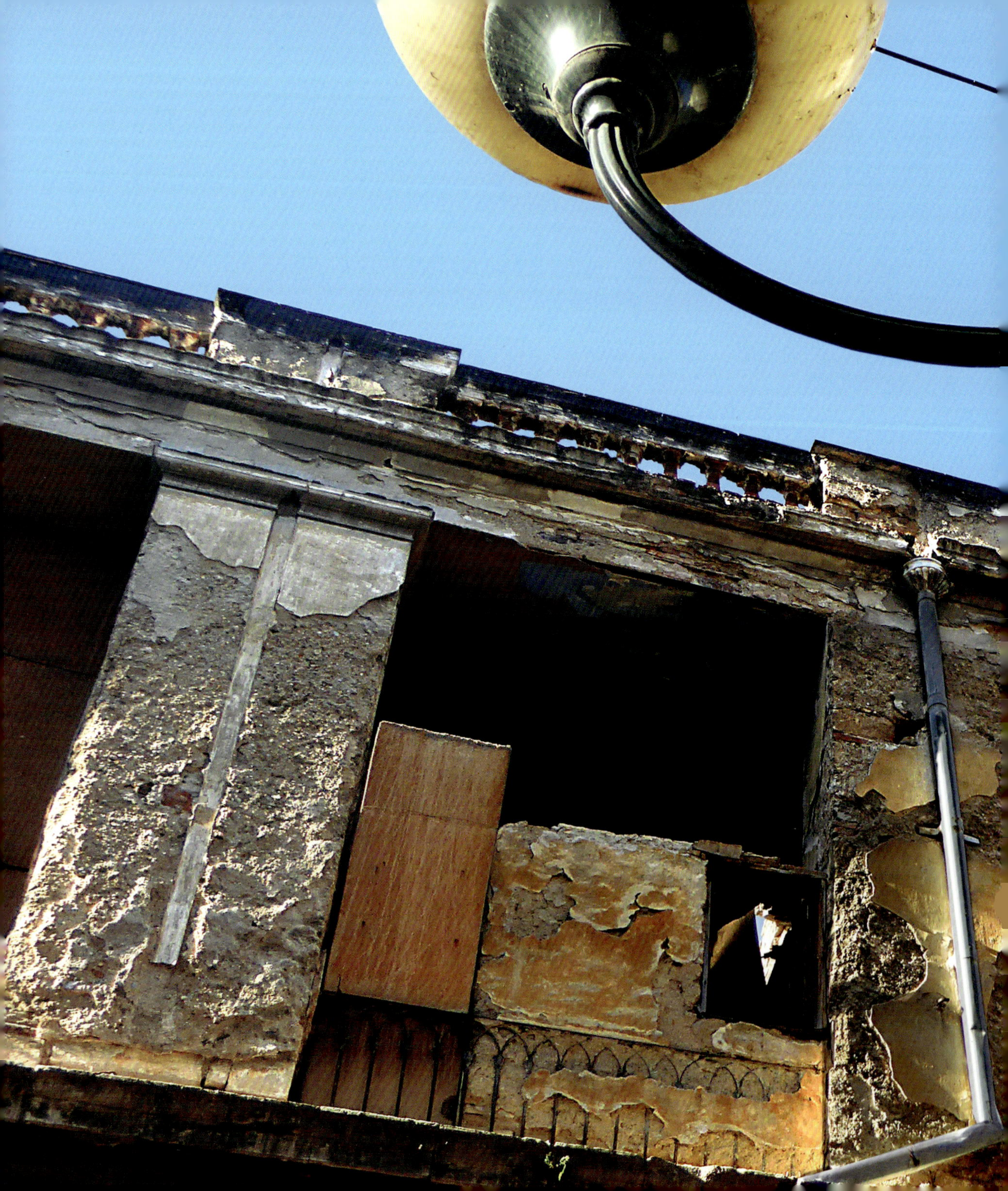

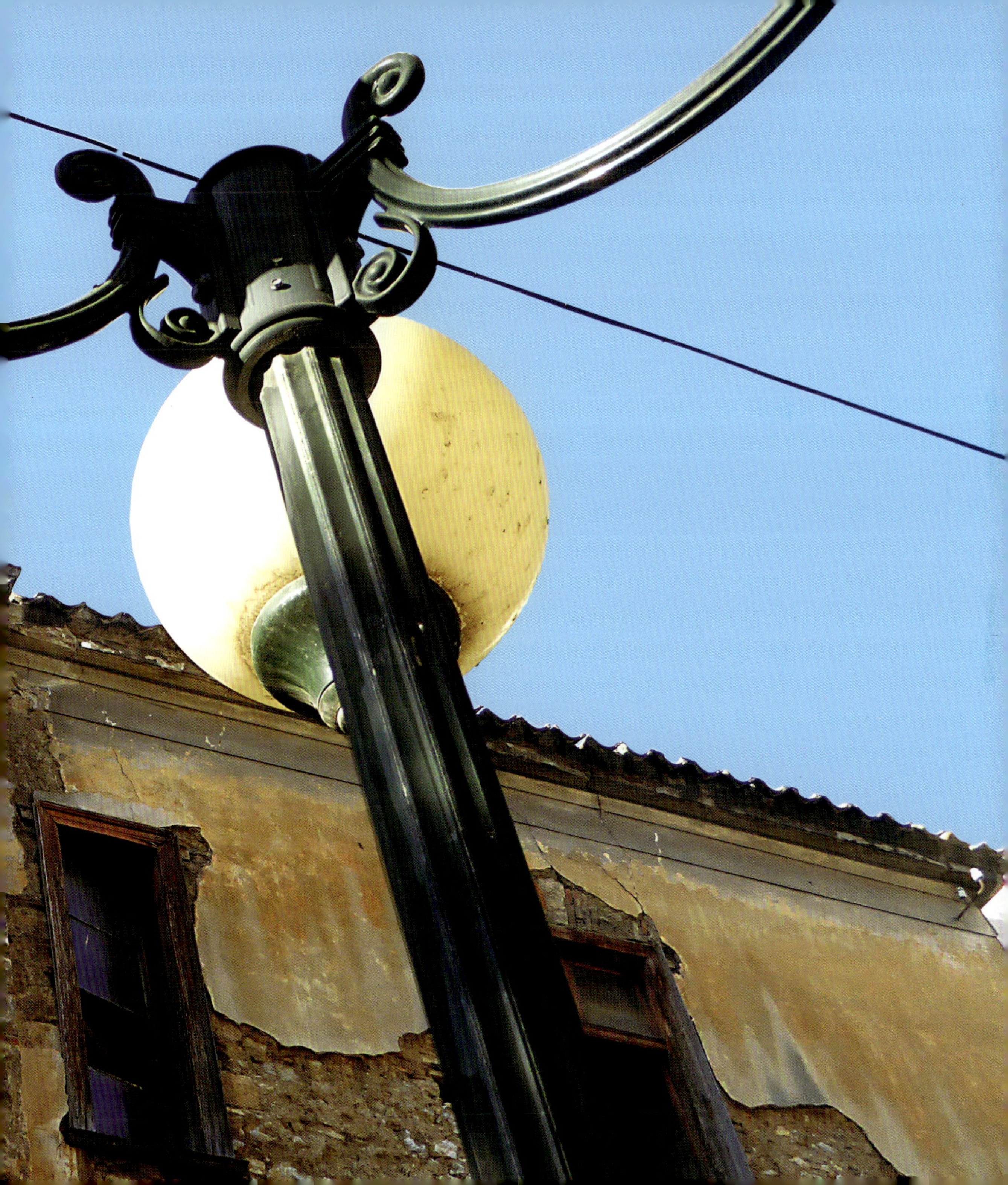

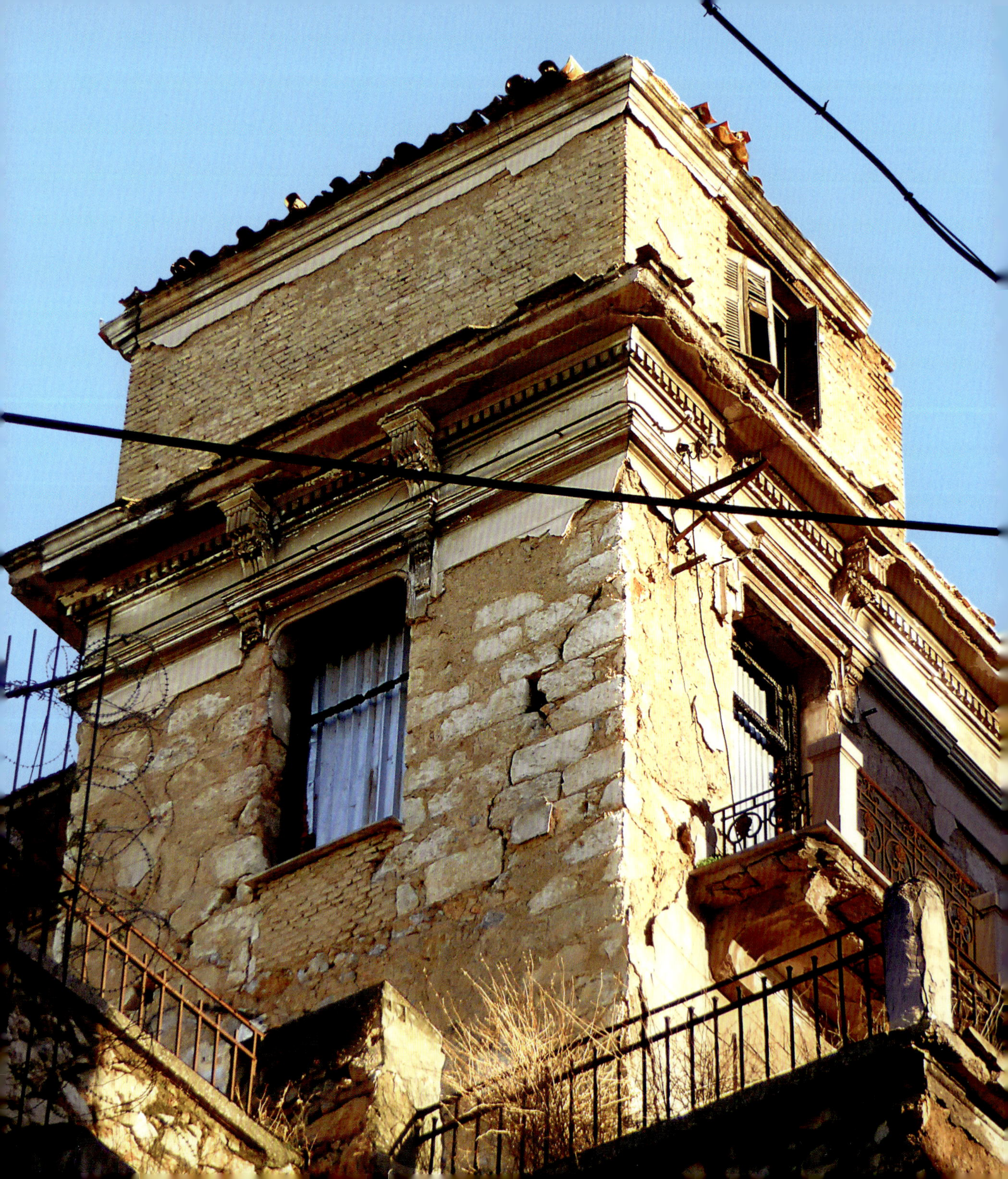

AIOLOS TOWER

Built out of stone in the early twentieth century, the Aiolos house is striking in its appearance. Perched below the Strefis Hill in the Exarcheia neighborhood, its massive structure resembles a watch tower or a fortress ready to defend the neighborhood from invisible enemies.

The mansion, very appropriately, is named after the god of the winds, Aiolos, because of the gusty winds that always seem to surround it. Stone masonry, reinforced concrete balconies, rails made of wrought and cast iron, give the house an air of luxury and ingenuity for its time.

Yet, the first time I encountered it, I couldn't help but think that there was something foreboding, almost ominous, about it. The stone steps that lead to the first floor displayed no sense of welcome, and the house's name, "Aiolos," carved on a marble slate above the entrance resembled a funerary stela. The shuttered windows and padlocked doors did little to ease this sense of uneasiness. This was not a place to linger but it lured me in like a trap never to come out.

Aiolos Tower, *Kallidromiou 78 and Themistokleous Streets, Exarcheia*

AIOLOS TOWER

I returned to the house on different days and seasons trying to understand my emotion, but the feeling never changed. When sunny, the light accentuated the cracks and crevices that so desperately needed repair and on winter days, the hovering clouds and the howling wind weighed down upon the structure with an unerring bleakness.

The mansion belonged to the twin brothers Iliopoulos who inherited the house from their father with the promise that they never sell or alter it. The brothers stayed in the mansion until their deaths in 2000, although nobody really remembers them.

The house, like so many other buildings, was left to its fate and soon it was occupied by squatters. A great fire in 2018 almost destroyed its interior, but the structure still stands as impassable as ever.

The father's wish has been fulfilled; the only way this house will ever be altered is to tear it down.

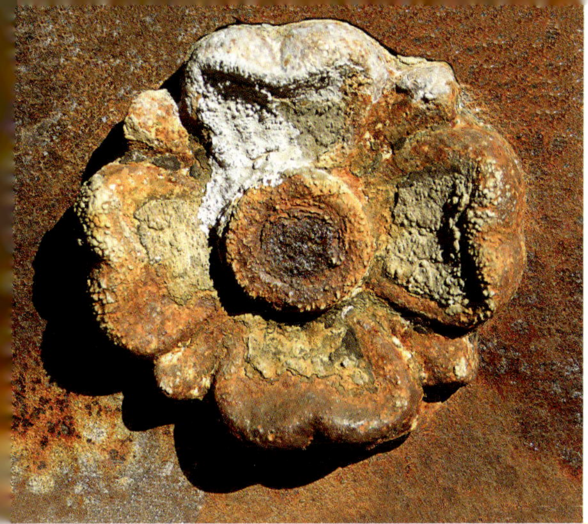

Top: *Rosette detail in cast iron*

Right: *Stone masonry, reinforced concrete balconies and rails made from wrought and cast iron*

Following pages: *Aiolos Tower, owned by the Iliopoulos brothers residing there until their deaths in 2000*

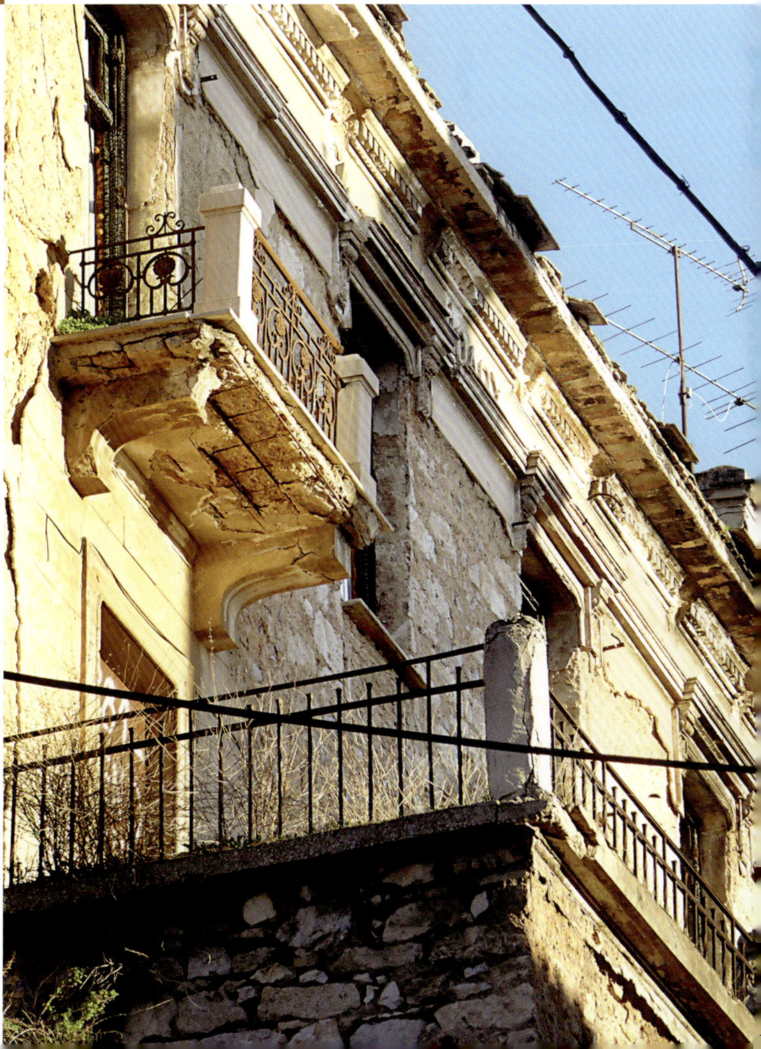

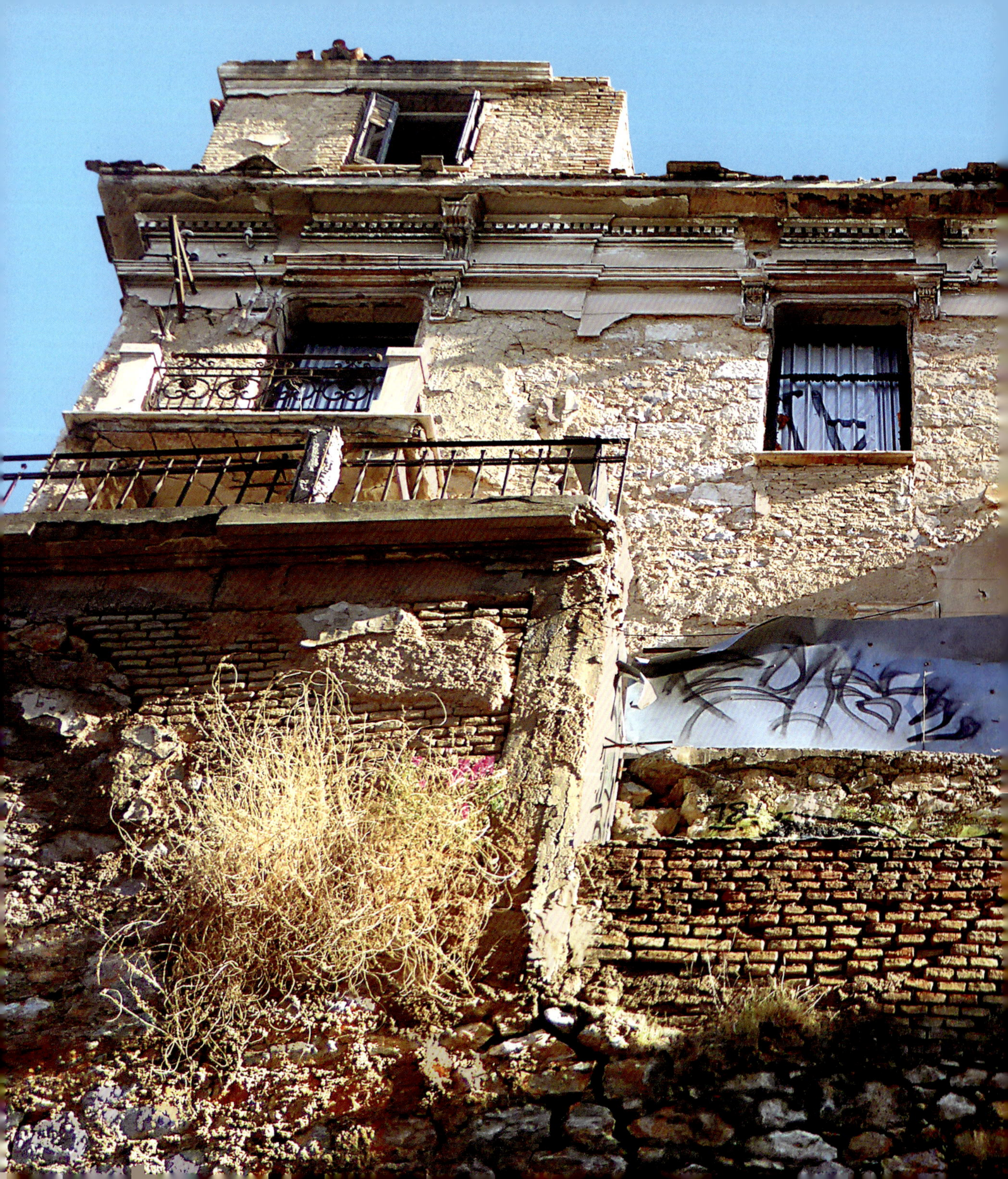

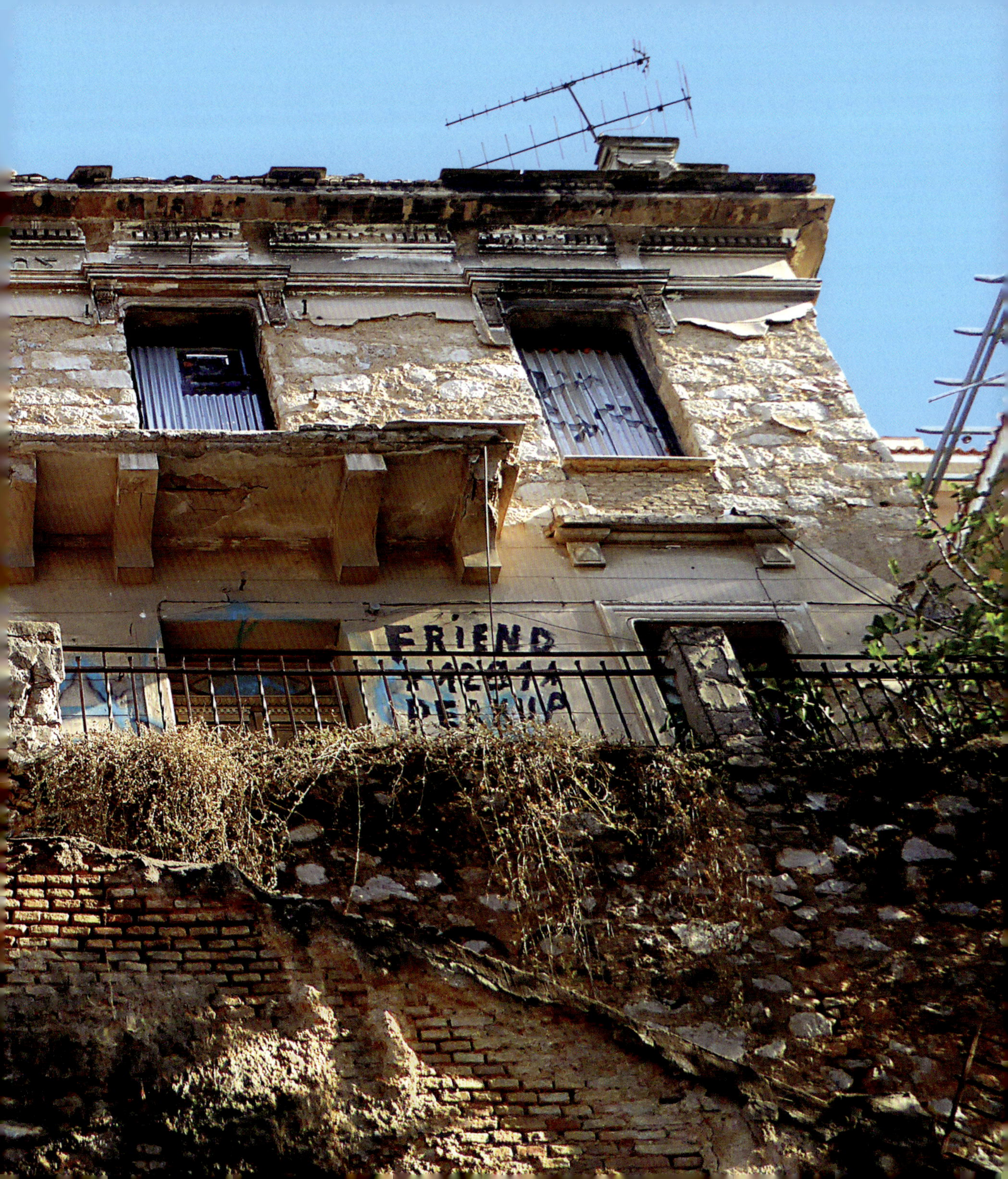
FRIEND

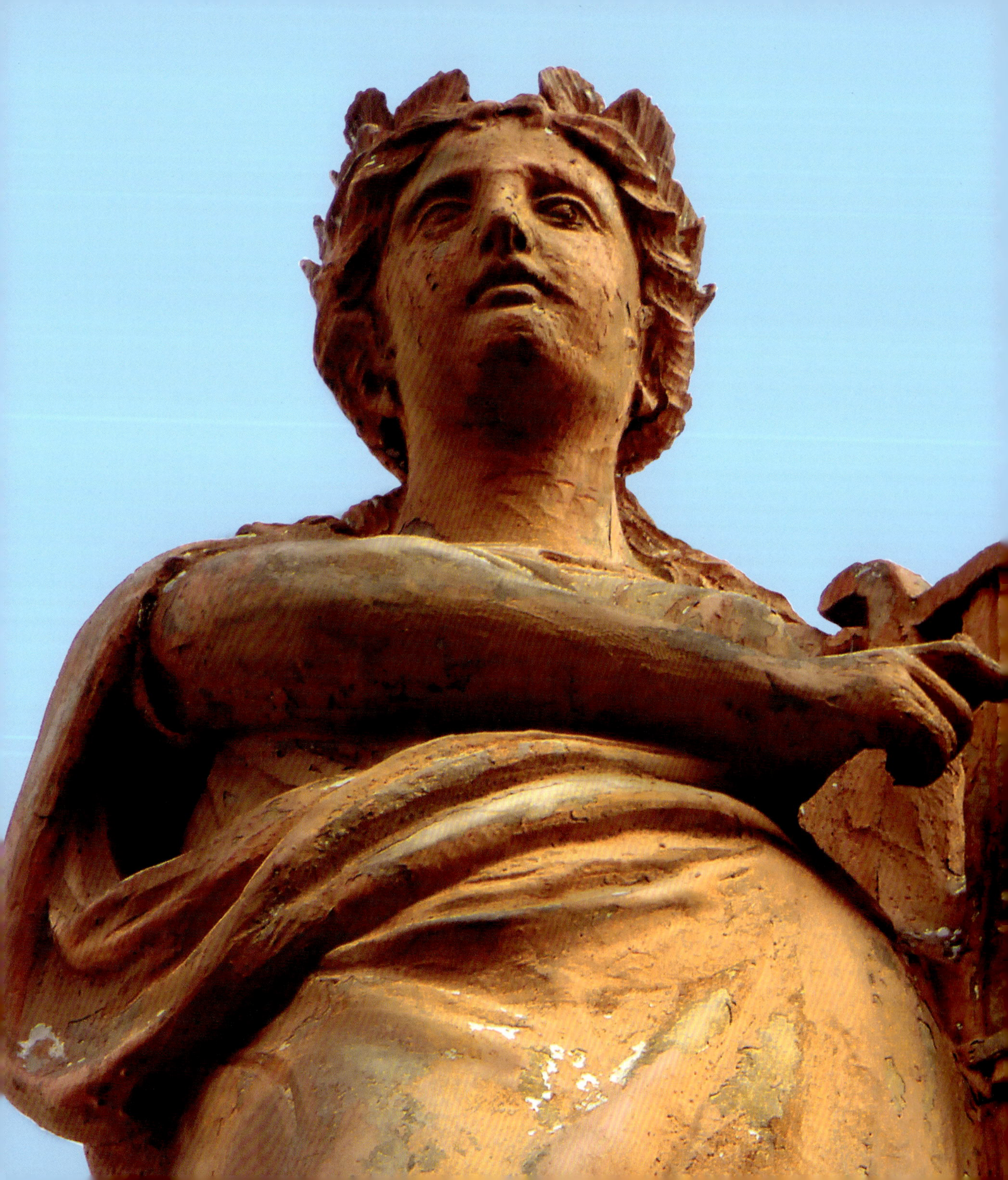

THE MUSE'S HOUSE

A cloudy November morning. There's a chill in the air, a reminder that winter is not far away. I'm walking around Omonoia Square with no plan or direction. The forecast has predicted rain. The absence of sunlight makes the streets look moody and withdrawn.

This is the Athens that is hurting, and nobody seems to be doing anything about it. An Athens where the poor and unwanted live isolated and which outsiders rarely visit. Tired and decaying, it's the Athens that expects nothing, because hope seems lost. Immigrants and refugees hover in their darkly lit homes, and when night falls, drug dealers, pimps, and gangs take over the streets, adding nothing but insecurity and fear.

It's pouring now, and thunder roars. I find shelter below the door of a small antique store. The windows are covered in grime. I squint to see inside. A world of magic unfolds before me; old toys, statues, mirrors, oil lamps, and rusty clocks. Lightning tears the sky, and the street is immersed in a silver glow.

The Muse's House, *name inspired by the author, Satovriandou Street, Vathis Square; pondering figure possibly depicting Art; house occupants unknown*

THE MUSE'S HOUSE

I look upwards, my eyes meeting with two terracotta figures standing on the roof of yet another abandoned building. Their presence catches me by surprise. Rain pours down their gracious features. There's something playful, almost mischievous about them. Perhaps there have been others before me caught by surprise, a constant source of amusement for them.

The first figure, a hand over her mouth, as if pondering something, and clutching a scroll in her other hand, seems practical, a woman of science, perhaps. The second one, with eyes focused on the horizon and a wreath crowning her hair, seems more ethereal, a woman of the arts maybe. The rain is now unrelenting, and I'm drenched to the skin.

I return on another day. A man in a faded t-shirt appears on the balcony adjacent to the building and looks at me with suspicion. "What are you doing here?" he bellows. "I'm trying to find some information about this house," I answer, but the man has already slammed the door in a huff. The terracotta women, seem to be enjoying this. If they had voices, I'm sure they would have forewarned me about their grumpy neighbor.

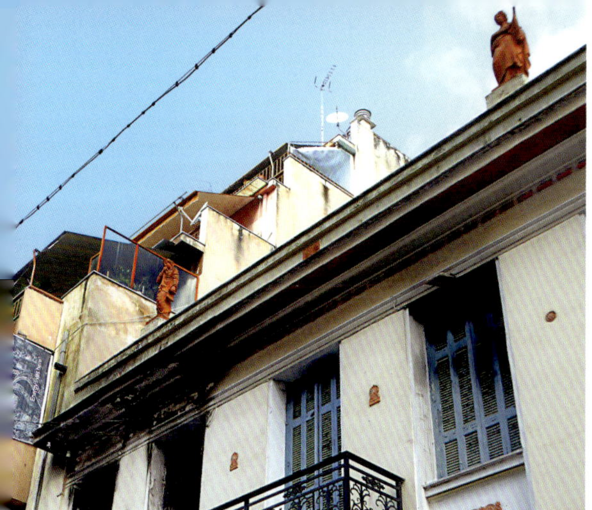

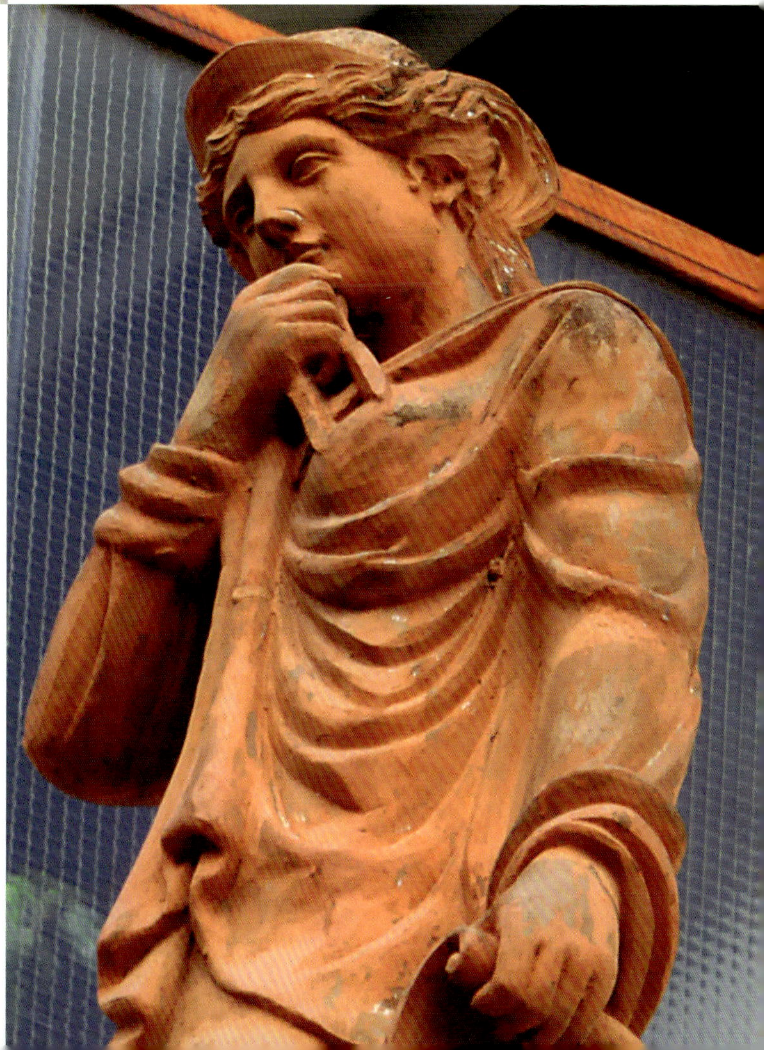

Top: *Standing terracotta figures facing Satovriandou Street; house interior destroyed by fire*

Right: *Close up of terracotta figure probably depicting Science*

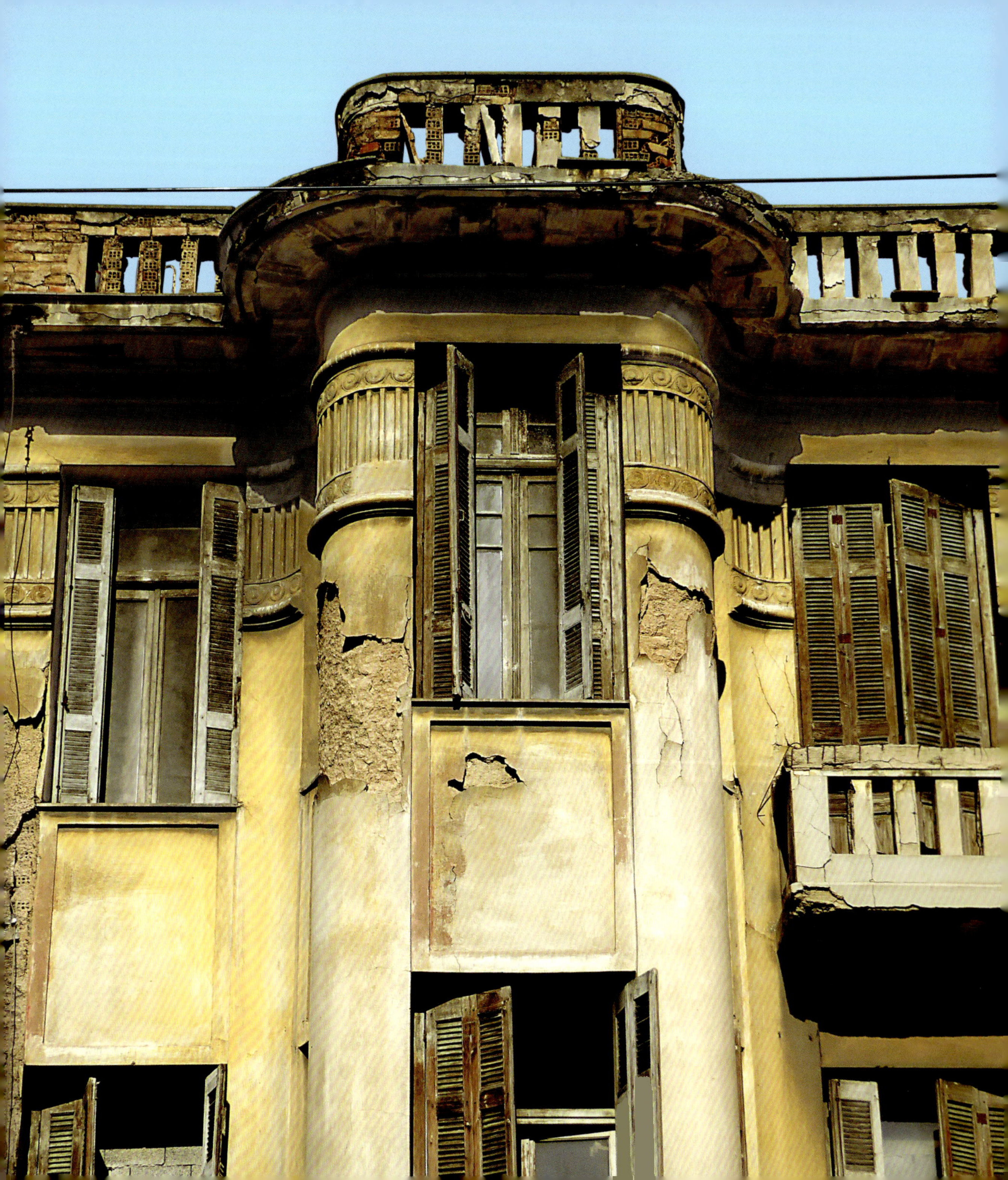

AGIOU KONSTANTINOU MANSION

Opening night, and the Greek National Theater sparkles under the stars. Beams of light cascade down the walls, illuminating the perched statues. The line grows longer. Men and women dressed in elegant clothes patiently wait to enter.

Across the street, the homeless and the addicts withdraw deeper into Agiou Konstantinou Park, readying to partake in their own drama. These are the forgotten ones, hailing straight out of an ancient tragedy, and when the curtain falls and the applause fades, there's nothing but darkness and a sense of hopelessness.

Agiou Konstantinou Street must have been a wonder to see, with horse-drawn carriages trotting up and down the street, carrying the aristocracy. Even the King frequented the theater, entering through a side door that led up to the first balcony, where he and his entourage watched the plays.

Today, the contrast cannot be more extreme, but Athens is a city that thrives on dichotomy. Surprises await everywhere.

Mansion at Agiou Konstantinou Street, *46 Agiou Konstantinou Street, near Omonoia Square and the Greek National Theatre*

AGIOU KONSTANTINOU MANSION

A little further away from the theater, a building with circular colonnades rises into the night like a ship's funnel. The building is engulfed in darkness, almost menacing. Nobody walks here but transients, and the unknown.

There are ghosts living here. I can sense them hovering in the dark, men, women and children of the past. A feeling of sadness overtakes me. Again and again, it's difficult to accept that so many glorious buildings are left to their undignified fate until they collapse.

I return early the next morning, filled with the anticipation of what I may encounter. A group of men furtively look around and disappear into a small street. The sun rises higher, casting shadows on the building's walls.

I notice that the windows on both floors are obstructed by cement blocks, except for the middle one with the half-open shutters. Did I really see someone? The thoughts of ghosts have been dispelled; it's the humans that write and erase history.

Opposite: *Fluted column with popular late nineteenth-century designs*

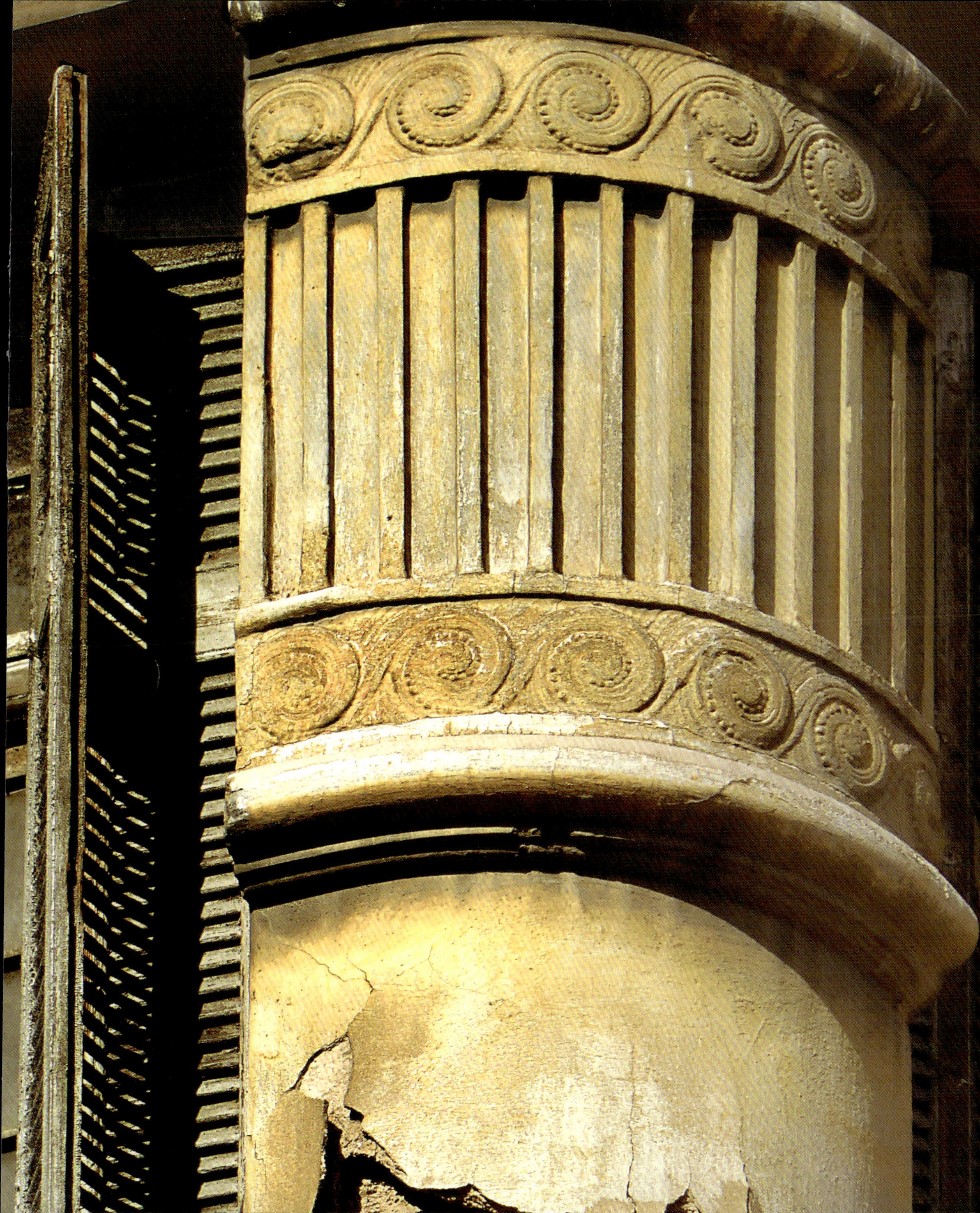

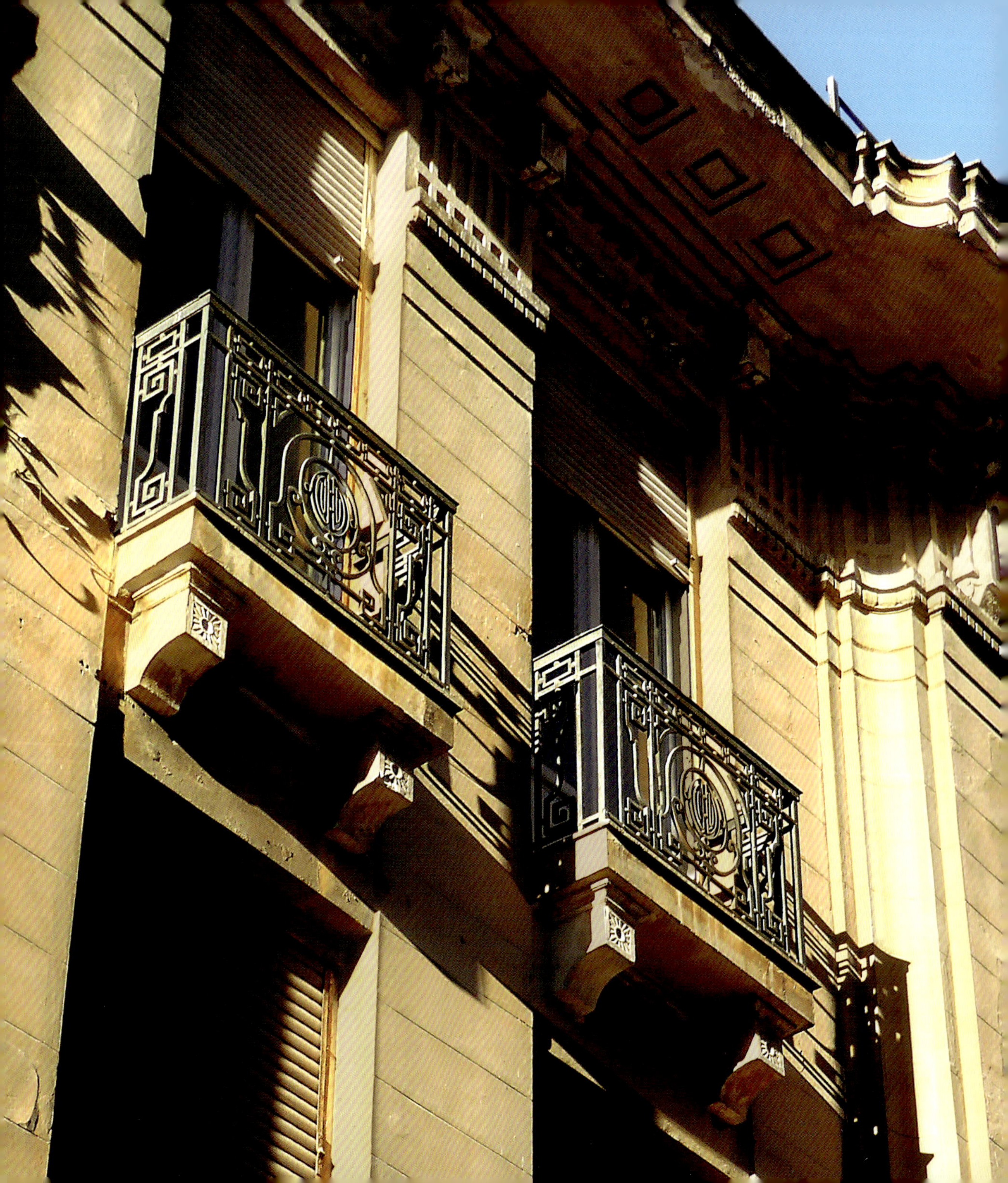

MAVROMICHALIS STREET MANSION

Late afternoon on Mavromichalis Street. Sunlight floods the narrow paths, setting the buildings ablaze. I'm here by happenstance, after a long walk in Exarcheia. My mind is alert. This light makes me giddy; it pours through me like a balm. Moments like this I'm grateful to be alive, to be a part of this inexplicable world that catches me by surprise. I know the moment is fleeting, so I want to run around and shout, "Look! Look up!"

That's when I see it, immersed in light. A building so exquisite it resembles a palace or an ancient temple. The side of the building has collapsed, adding more drama. I try to take it all in. Everything about this mansion speaks of artistry and care. The top floor shutters are half open and appear to be more modern, but the details on the building's facade denote mature, nineteenth-century architecture.

I walk around trying to discern something that will allow me to understand the building's history, or the lives of the people who lived here, but the front door is hermetically closed. I walk away, hoping that one day this splendid building will find its rightful owner once again.

Mavromichalis Street Mansion, *Mavromichalis Street 47; early twentieth-century building, currently under renovation*

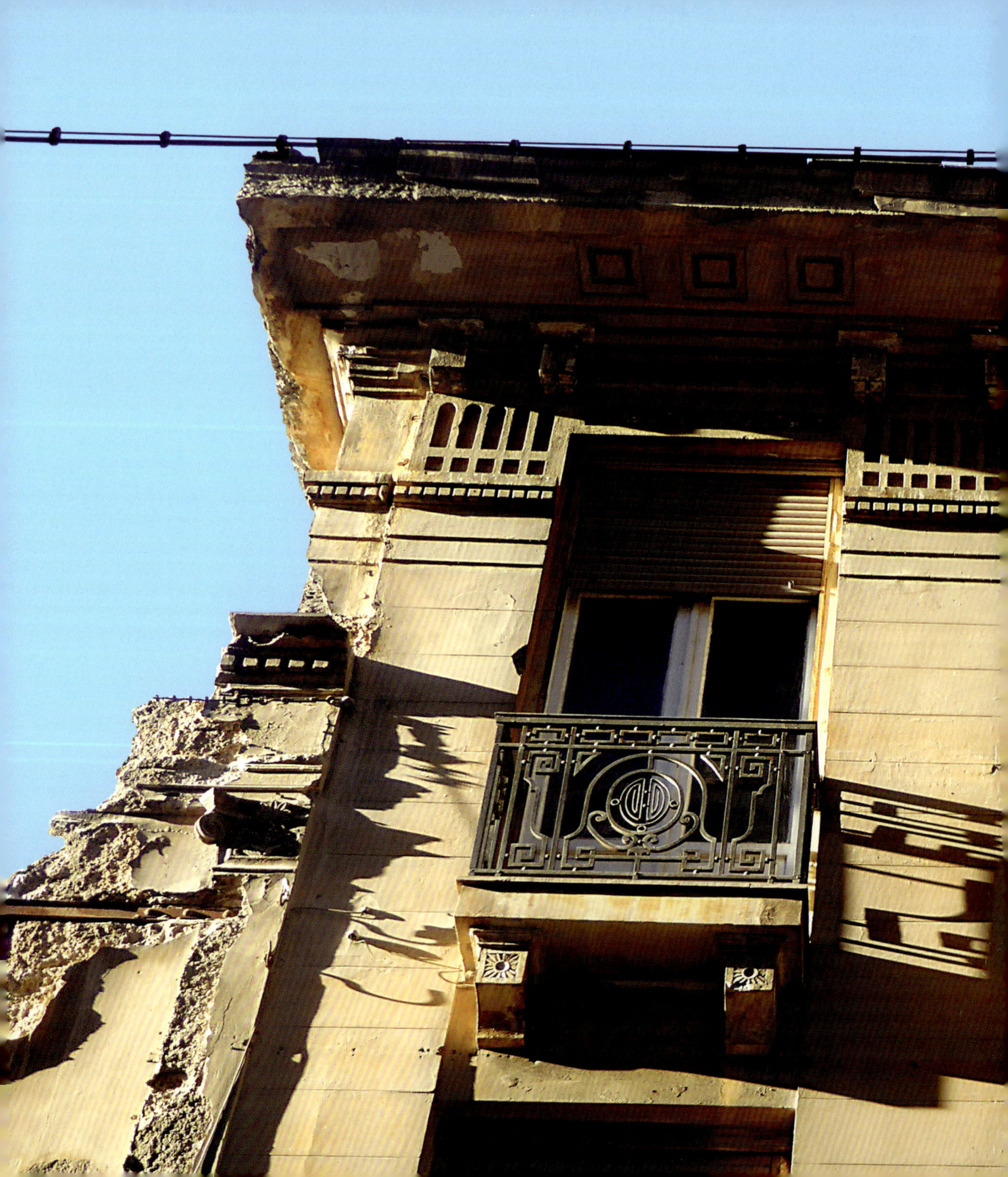

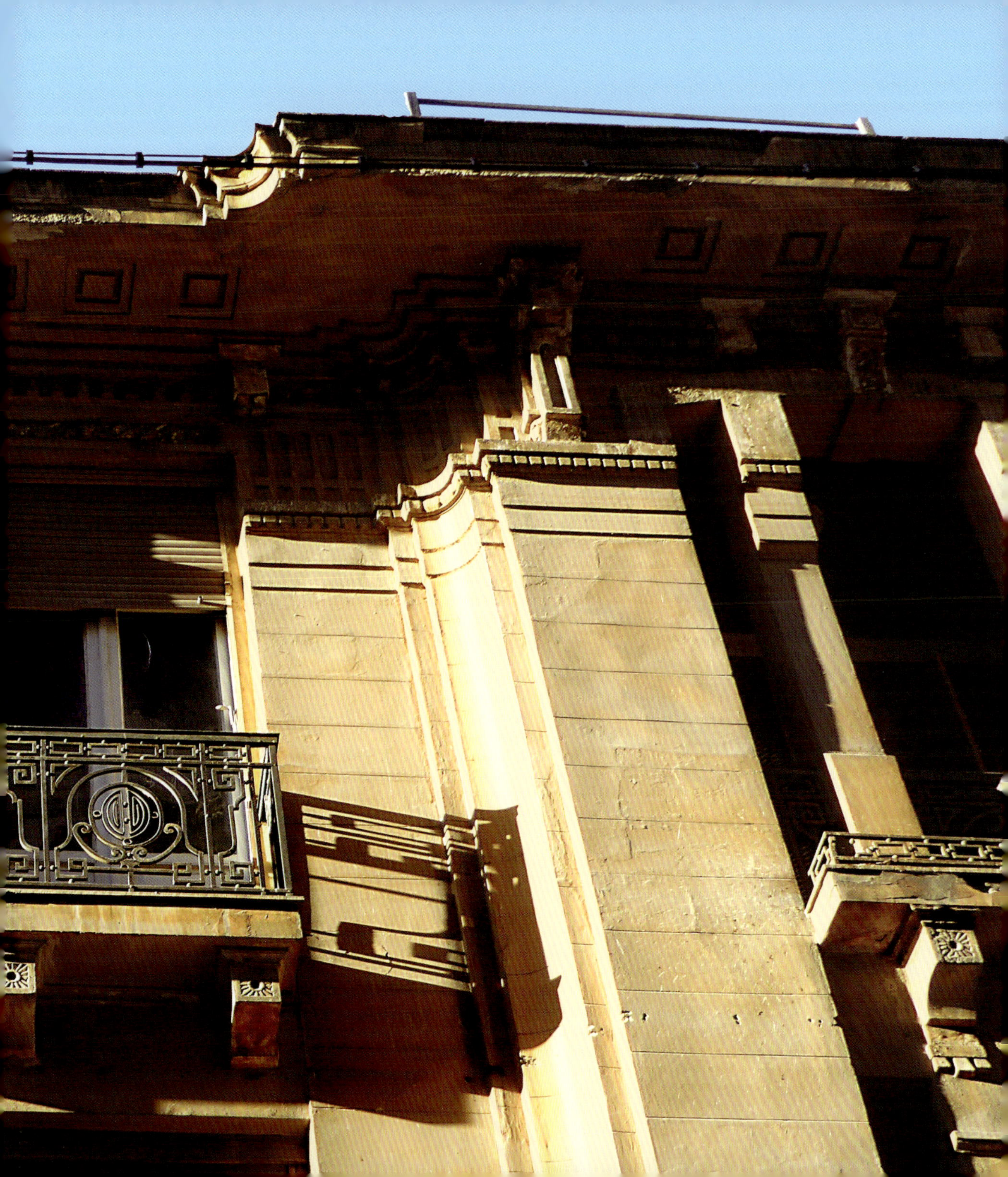

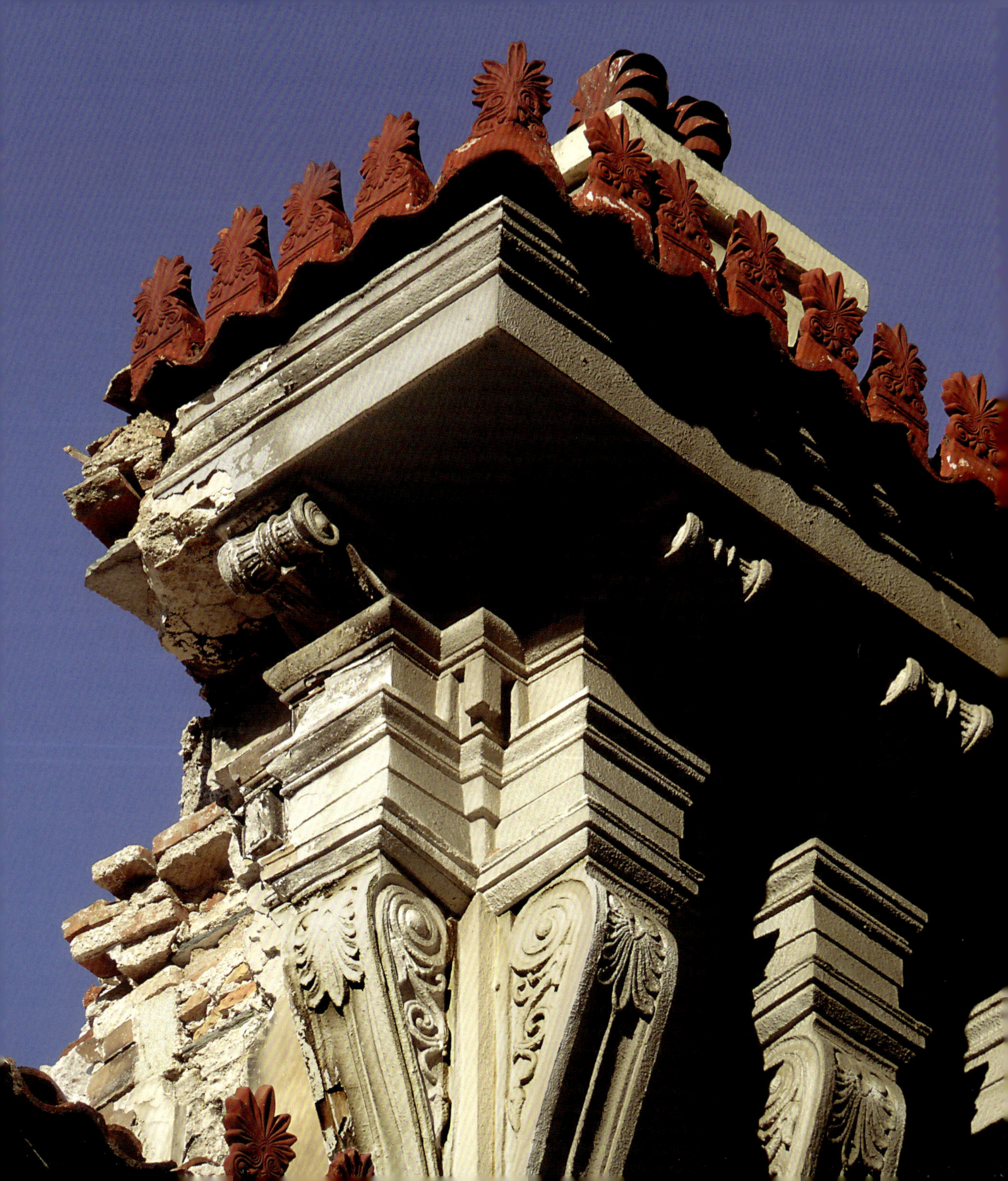

ATTIKON – APOLLON CINEMA COMPLEX

February 2012; the height of the protests against Greece's austere economic measures. The neoclassical building on the corner of Christos Ladas and Stadiou Streets is burning. Sirens tear at the night as an epic battle ensues against the wind. Twelve more fires erupt in different parts of Athens set by thugs and neofascists. When daylight arrives, there's nothing left but smoldering ashes.

The building, designed by Ernst Ziller between 1870-1881, on behalf of Chian banker Stamatios Dekozis Vouros, is destroyed, its shell the only reminder of its past. Valtis' pharmacy, Mousios' barber shop, the new Ministry of National Economy and later the Costa Boda store, were a few of its famed tenants.

But it was the construction of the "Attikon" cinema that put the building on the map and turned it into a renowned entertainment center. Built between 1914 and 1920, in Neo-Baroque style and based on drawings by the architect Alexandros Nikoloudis, "Attikon" marked the beginning of the construction of the great viewing halls.

Atticon – Apollon Cinema Complex, *Stadiou Street, Athens*

ATTIKON—APOLLON CINEMA COMPLEX

Opulent, with spacious seating and ornate designs, it opened its doors to the public in 1916. Four years later, in the same building, the "Apollon" cinema was added, turning Stadiou into one of the liveliest streets in Athens.

From 1929 onwards, "Attikon" cinema operated under the direction of "Skoura Film," the film dynasty of the Skoura brothers. During the German occupation of the The Second World War, "Attikon" cinema was renamed SoldatenKino Victoria, and Apollon into Kino Apollo. Skouras was ordered to show films only for German troops with subtitles in German and Italian.

It's ironic that the two theaters survived both the German occupation and the ensuing civil war, only to find their doors closed in such an undignified way. For many Athenians going to Attikon was a night long event, followed by a walk on the brightly lit Stadiou Street and a stop for dessert or ice-cream in one of the many pastry shops that dotted the street.

Plans for the restoration of the building abandon. Conflicts of interest between the private and public sectors remain in limbo, leaving yet another historical part of Athens to its fate.

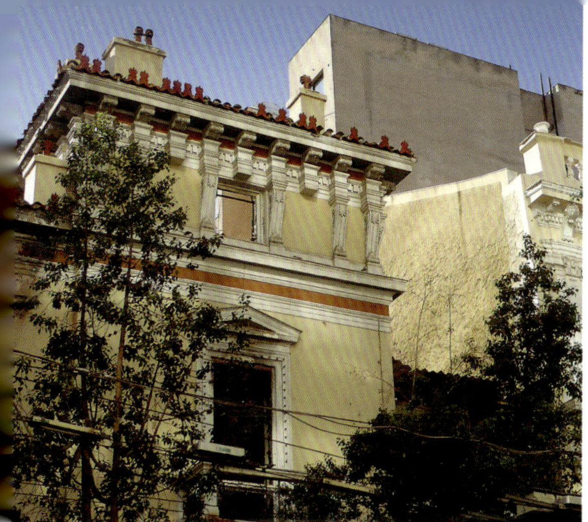

Top: *View of the burned building from Stadiou Street, once housing the high end "Costa Boda" store and the Ministry of National Economy*

Right: *Detail of acanthus flowers and sea shells*

Following pages: *The building showing the extent of fire still waits to be restored*

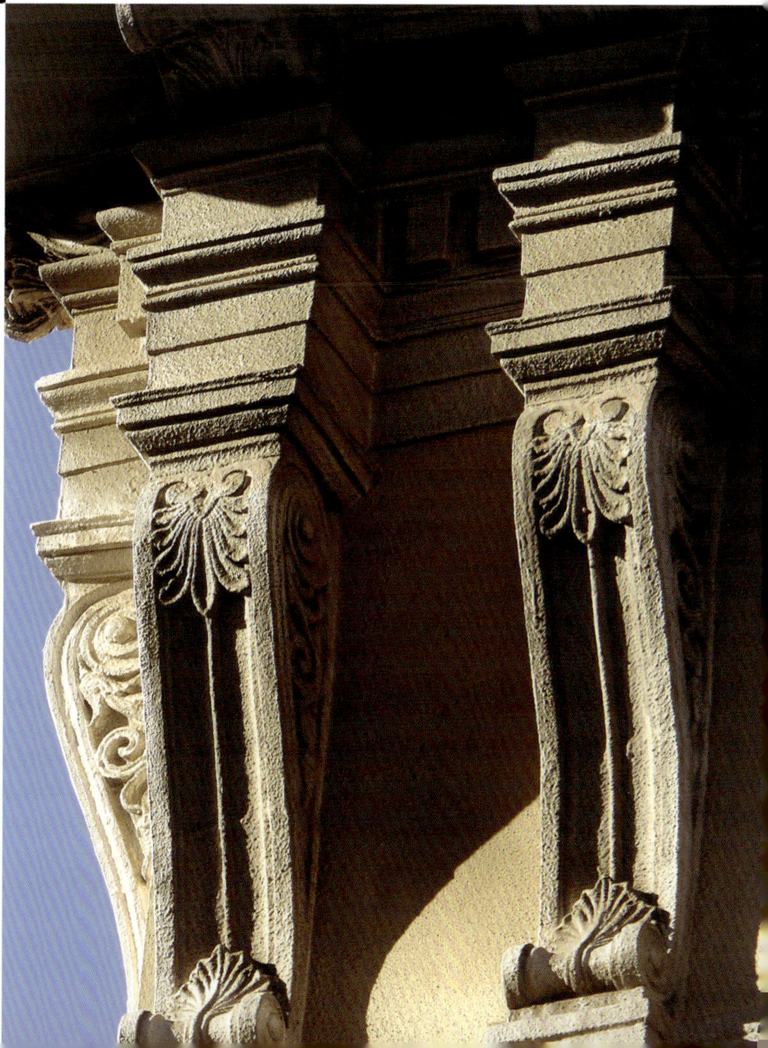

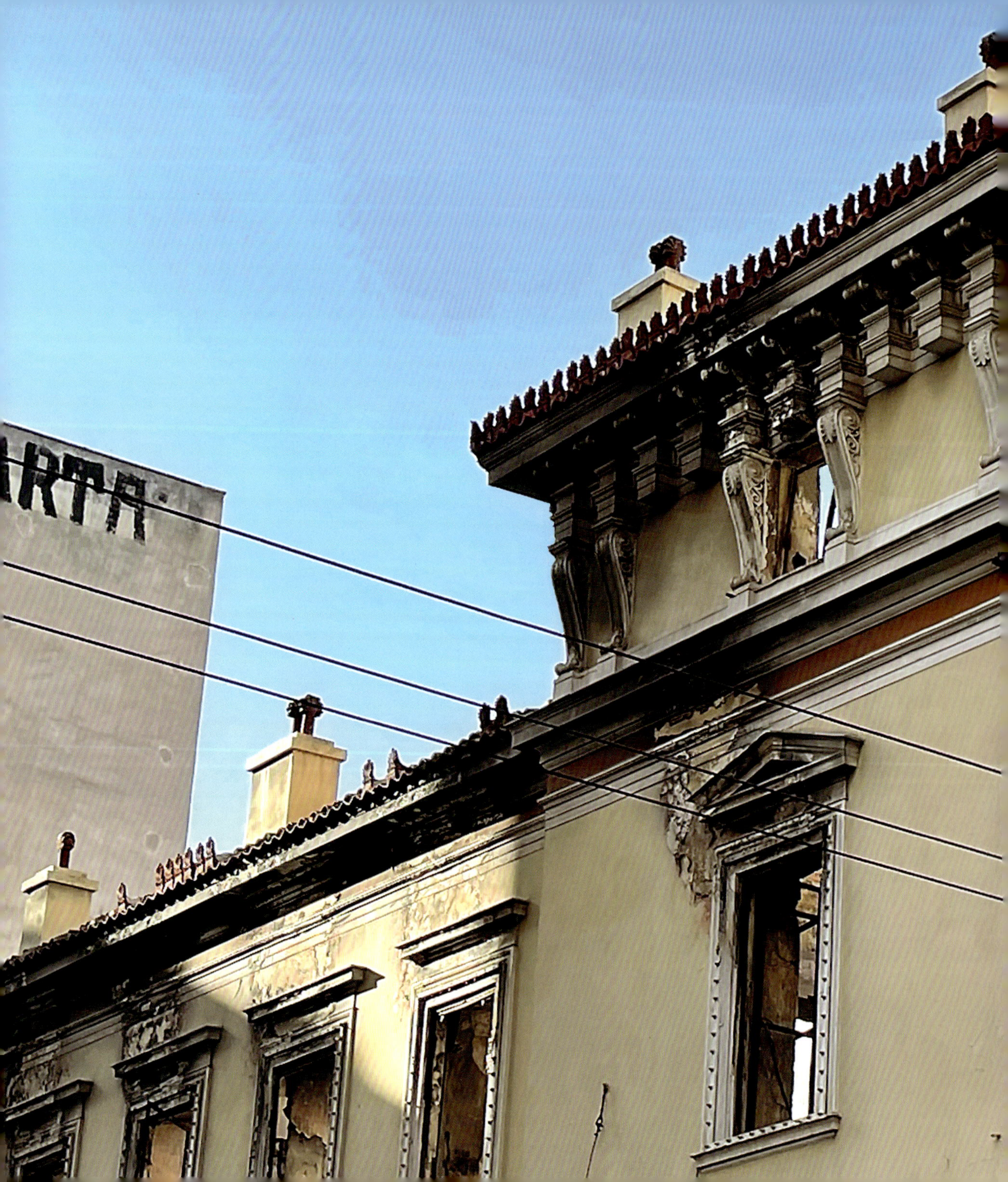

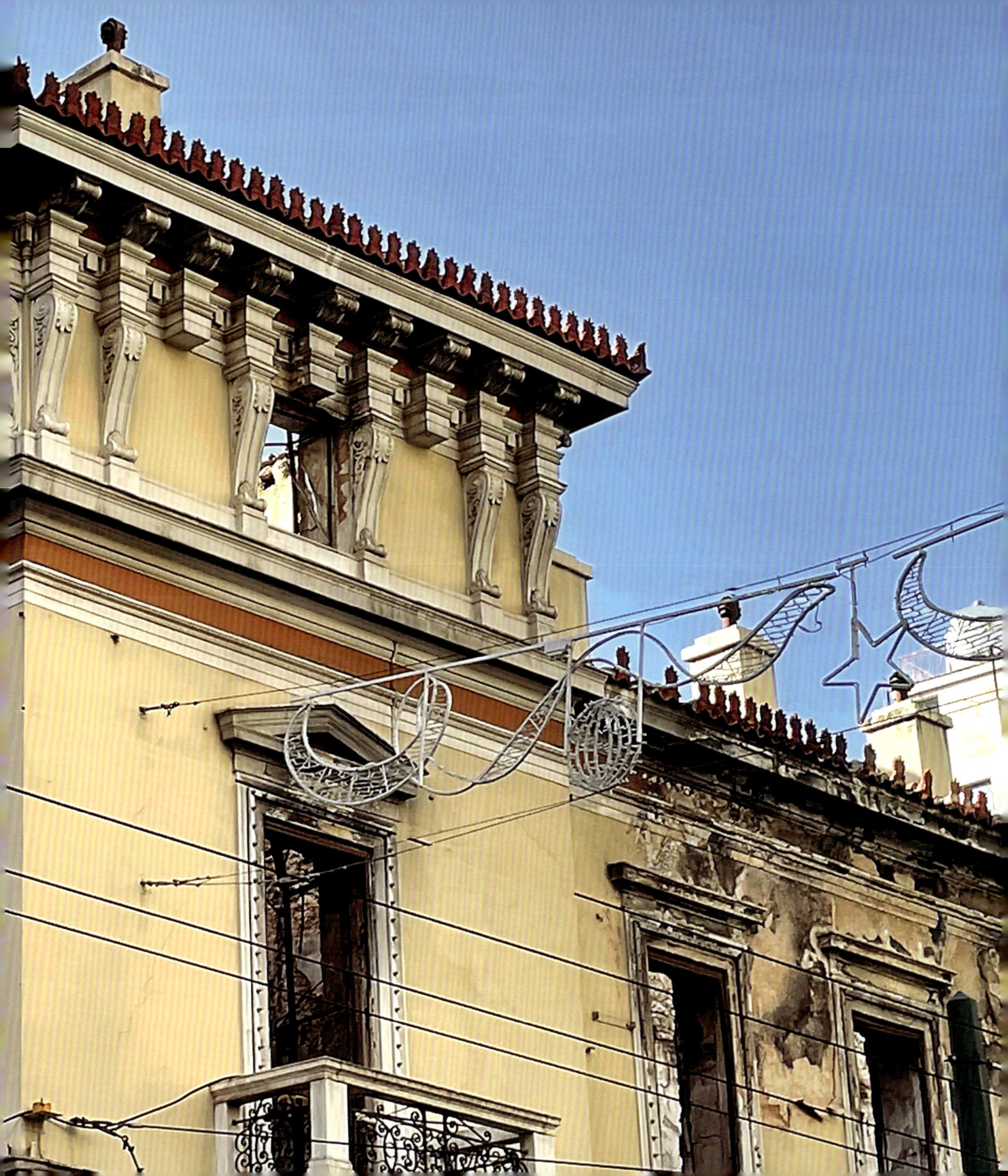

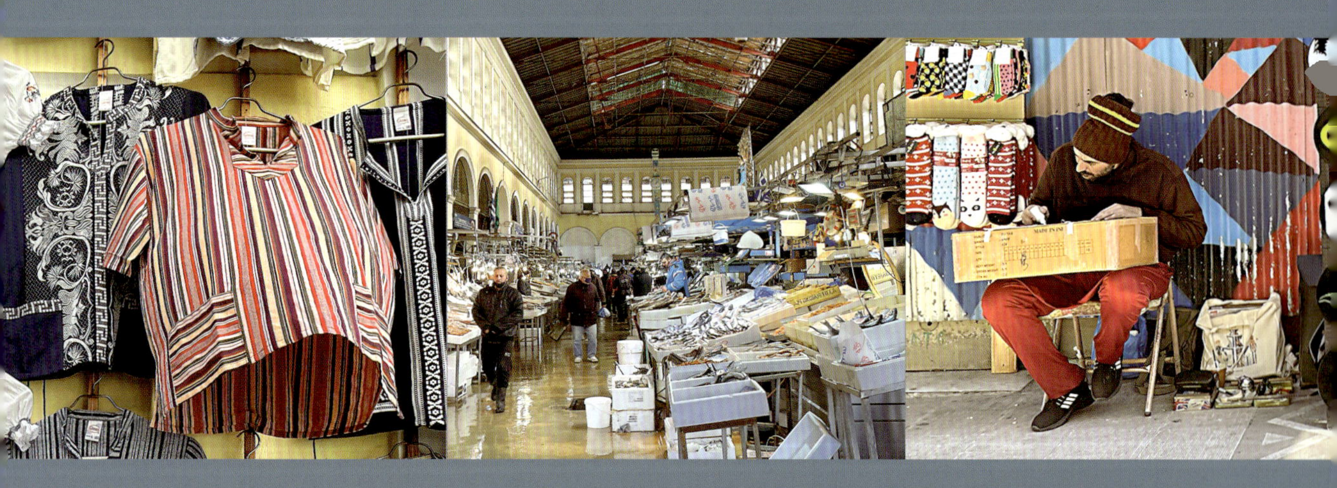

THE HEART OF COMMERCE

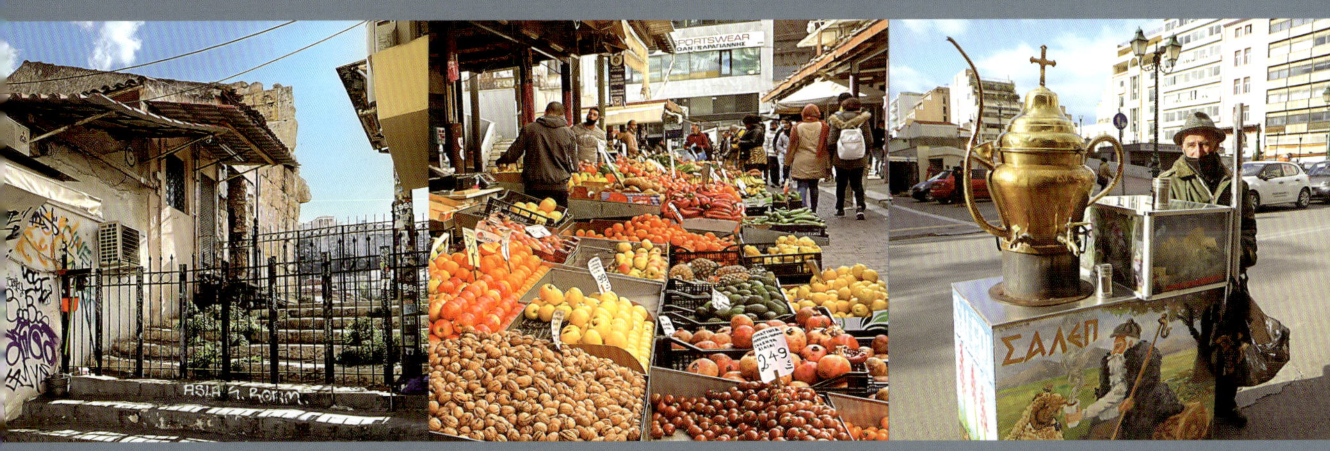

F

Following the Greek Revolution of 1821, Athens was nothing but a poor village. Streets were nonexistent, and the small paths were filled with dirt and garbage. The burgeoning growth of *flomos*, a plant with highly poisonous fumes, was equally dangerous for people and animals.

Fallen columns, scattered stones, and overflowing springs made it difficult to move around, and during the winter months, entire sections of the city were cut off. The lack of a sewerage system and garbage collection led to the spread of diseases, such as cholera, malaria, and typhoid, affecting entire neighborhoods.

Kleanthis and Schaubert, the original architects of the city's planning, named the first paved streets after the names of classical gods, a tradition that other architects followed, adding the names of philosophers and dramatists. Streets such as Athinas, Ermou, Aiolou, Sophocleous, among others, were born.

INTRODUCTION

Official road construction began in 1834, with Piraeus Street connecting Athens to the port. It was around the same time that the triptych of the commercial streets of Athinas, Ermou, and Aiolou were built, which became known as the city's axis.

By 1850, the first squares, bridges, and parks were constructed, followed by the creation of a sewerage system. By 1896, the lamps were replaced with gas lamps, bringing Athens closer to other European capitals, although Athens never completely assimilated Western and Eastern traditions.

Commerce, as in ancient times, flourished, attracting many merchants, investors, and benefactors who were eager to help the country find its footing. Hotels and coffee shops were built, and travelers and intellectuals followed, making Athens a place of inspiration and residence. The streets buzzed with activity, as merchants, visitors, artisans, and miracle workers moved about impressing people with their exotic goods, and once again creating history.

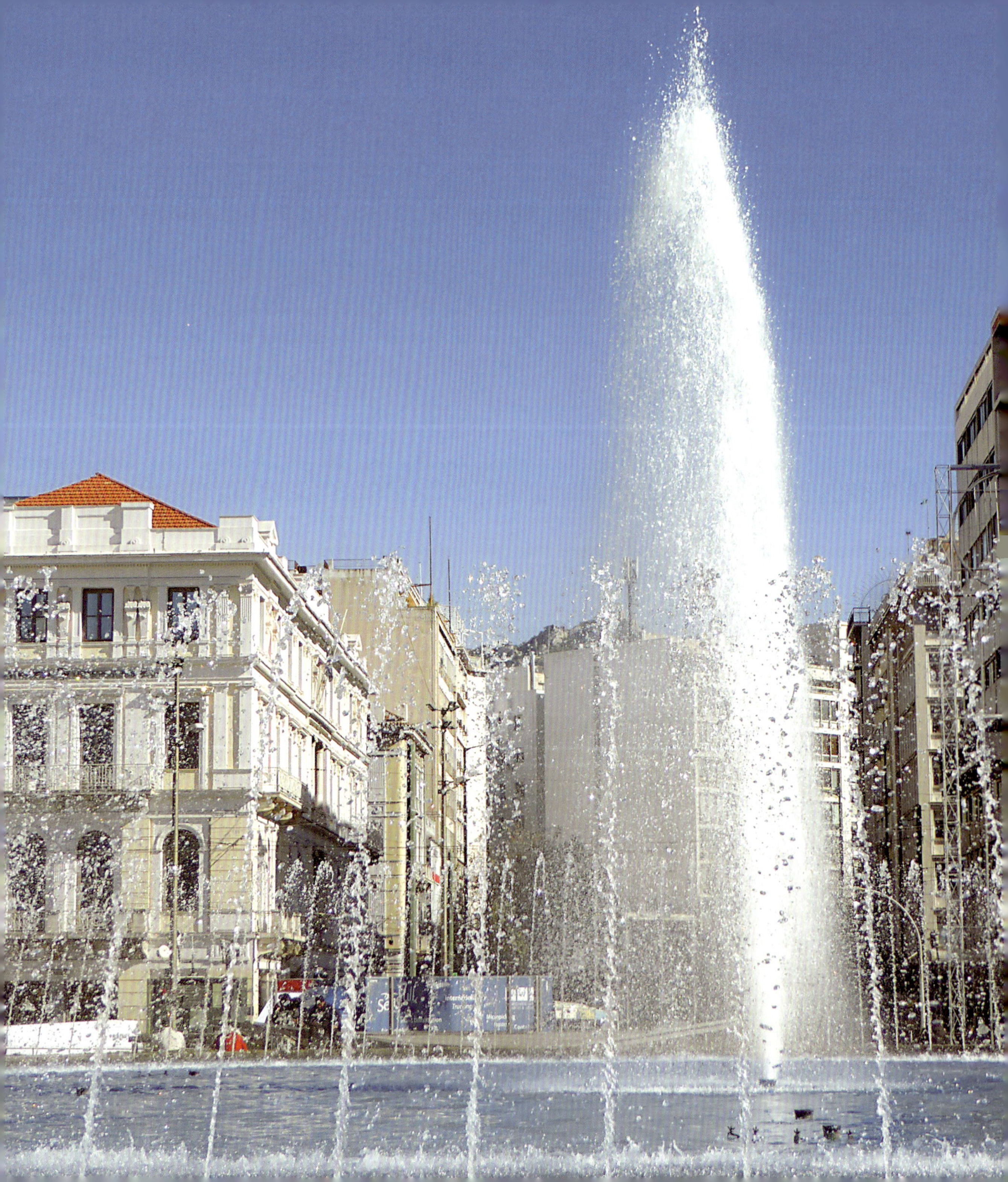

OMONOIA SQUARE

No matter where you are, at one point or another, you'll find yourself in Omonoia Square, the major hub of the city. Cars, taxis, motorcycles, and buses perpetually go around and around like in Dante's inferno. Some of the oldest hotels, most of them abandoned or in decay, surround the square, adding an extra layer of despair and grandeur.

At the turn of the nineteenth century, the area was a large ditch filled with rubble and garbage. Grapevines, stables, and small hovels were the most one could find. As the city grew, the need for a connecting point between the smaller streets became evident, so around 1850, the vineyards were uprooted, and the square was built and named after King Otto.

During his reign, it became a vital gathering place for political speeches and demonstrations between pro- and anti-King supporters. After the King's ousting in 1862, the square was renamed Omonoia, meaning Unity Square, the name that still holds to this day.

Omonoia Square, *major hub of commerce and gathering place of refugees and immigrants*

OMONOIA SQUARE

By 1895, a major subway line was constructed from Piraeus to Athens. The square was transformed into a beautiful garden with iron rails and a variety of palm trees, as seen in many postcards of the time period.

Around 1930, the square got its circular shape and was decorated with the statues of the nine muses placed upon columns, a design that never agreed with the people's taste, and they were eventually removed. By this time, the character of the square was already changing. The wealthy moved closer to Syntagma Square or to Kolonaki, with Omonoia becoming a meeting place for refugees and those looking for work. The major hotels came to disrepair, closed or were relegated to cheap accommodations for sleep and prostitution. The glory of Omonoia Square had officially come to an end.

Walking around today, a bittersweet feeling prevails. The senses are assaulted. Stunning neoclassical buildings stand next to cheap stores, run down tavernas, and souvlaki stands. Refugees and immigrants gather at the square, sitting on the grass around the fountain, waiting for an opportunity that never arrives.

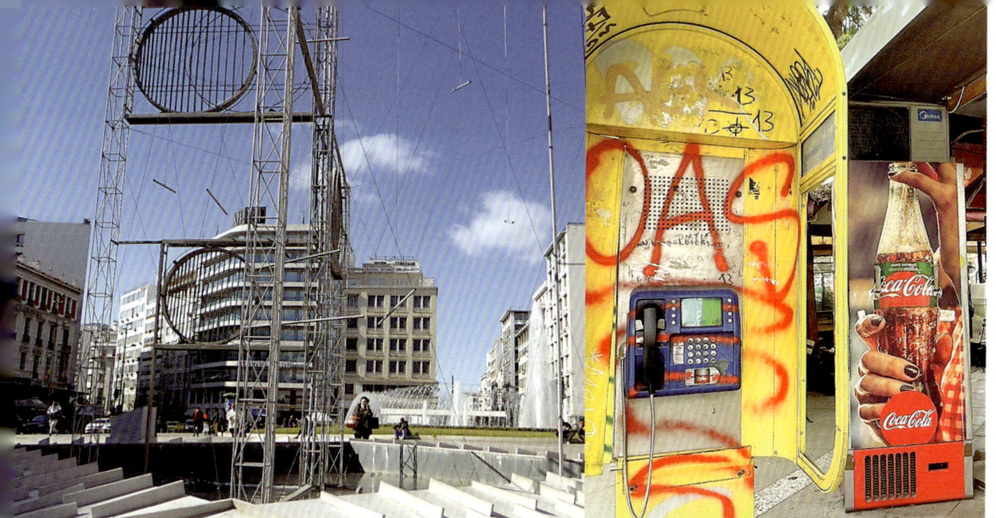

Top: *Sculpture by George Zongolopoulos, donated to the City of Athens by the Onassis Foundation*

Top Right: *Old style phone booth*

Right: *Christmas tree at sunset*

Following pages: *Omonoia Square with Acropolis seen through the newly minted fountain*

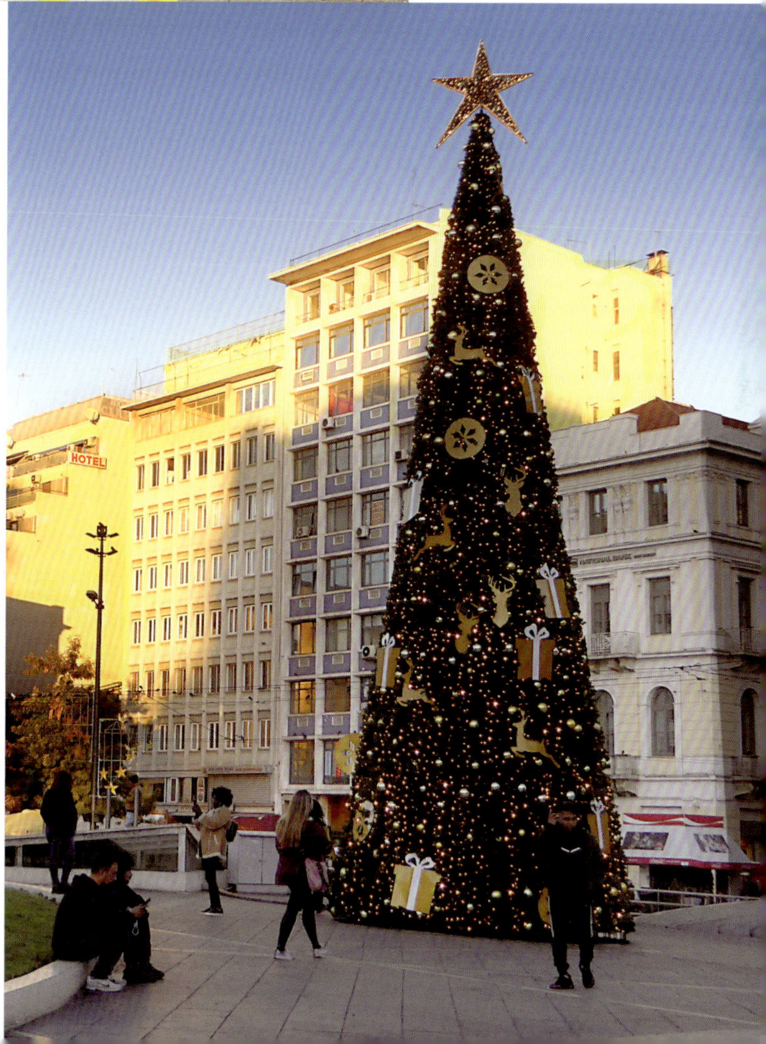

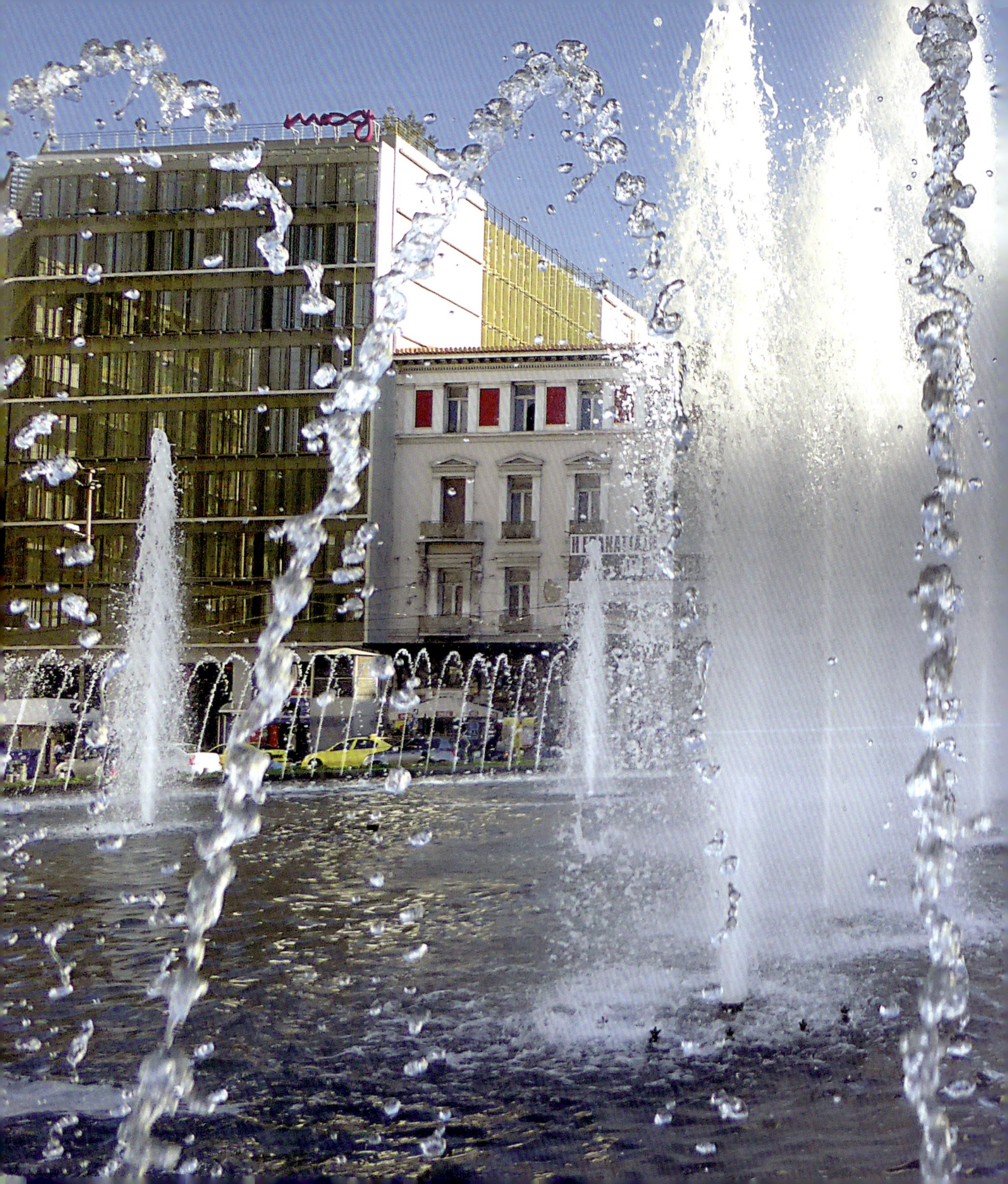
moxy

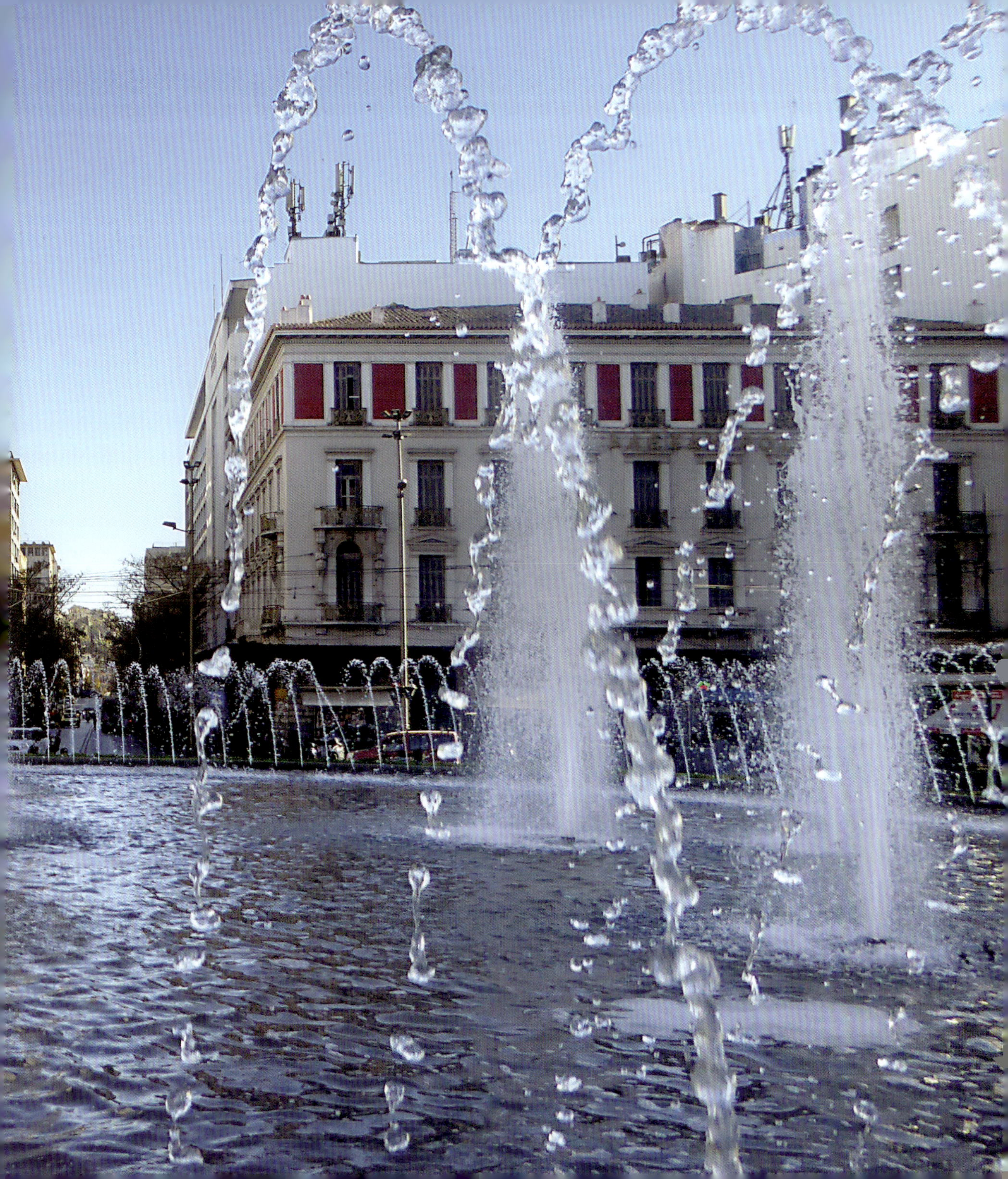

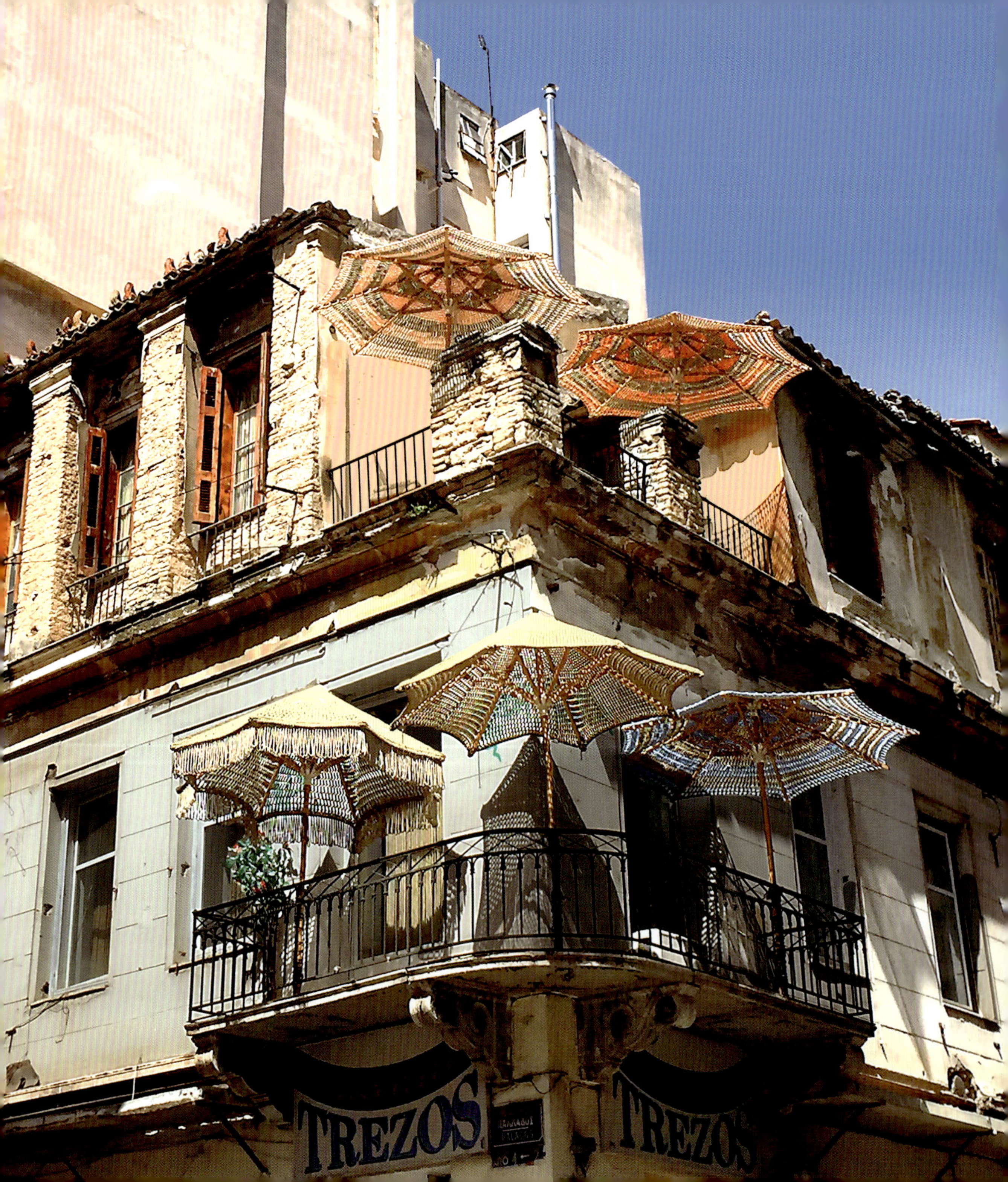
TREZOS
TREZOS

ATHINAS STREET

A man wearing a red vest and a tall hat shakes a copper bell, bellowing, "Come! Last chance to see the bearded woman and the camel with two heads all the way from Egypt!" Across the street, two men, their bodies rubbed in oil, slide and roll on the dirty street as the crowd cheers them. Further away, a barber in a filthy white apron prepares to extract a man's tooth. Charlatans and quacks march around beating drums and blowing trumpets, promising miracle cures.

This is Athinas Street, named after the goddess Athena, also known as the "Street of Miracles" or "Monster Street" because of all the curiosities presented there. Along with Aiolou and Ermou Streets, it connected the "old section" of the town, starting at Monastiraki and ending at Omonoia Square.

Home of merchants, the street buzzed with activity. Small, two-story buildings were erected along the street, the lower floors functioning as shops and the upper ones as residences. Small hotels were also built to accommodate the many travelers and salesmen who frequented the area.

Athinas and Pallados Streets; *popular corner specializing in furnishings and crafts*

ATHINAS STREET

Coffee shops, confectionery stores, and bakeries soon appeared, among them the famous "Brown Bakery," the only English-speaking store that sold bread and other English products. Towards 1850, the first horse-drawn carriage station was introduced, transporting passengers to various parts outside Athens.

After The Second World War, Athinas Street, like so many other nearby streets, fell into disarray becoming a haven for criminals, pimps, and prostitutes. Most of the hotels closed, and those that survived were converted to brothels. Once a thriving place of commerce, Athinas became a shadow of its former self with people leaving in fear and poverty.

Still, the street never lost its charm, and to this day, it continues to surprise. Chaotic, with small stores selling baskets, sandals, rugs, curtains, and army clothes, it seamlessly combines the old with the new.

If you're lucky enough to visit the street during late spring, you'll be enchanted by the rows of purple blooming trees known as jacarandas. A street of miracles, indeed.

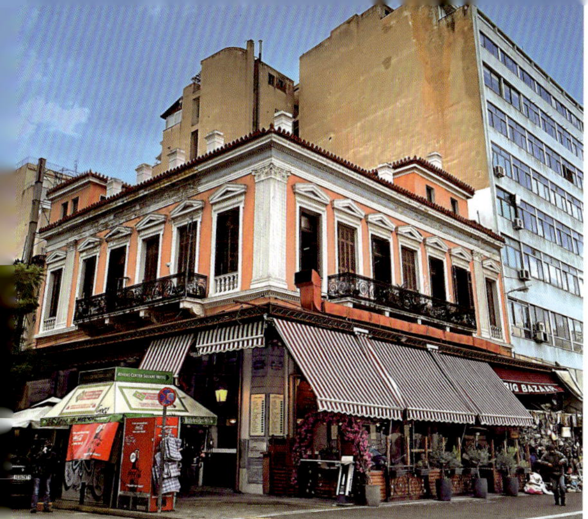

Top: *"Neon Xenon," nineteenth-century hotel for modest income travelers, renamed "Hotel New York," in 1912; today the building houses an antique store*

Right: *Share Fund of Civil Servants building designed by Vasilios Kouremenos, notable for its mosaic representations of Greek mythology*

Following pages: *Blooming jacarandas trees in front of a neoclassical building*

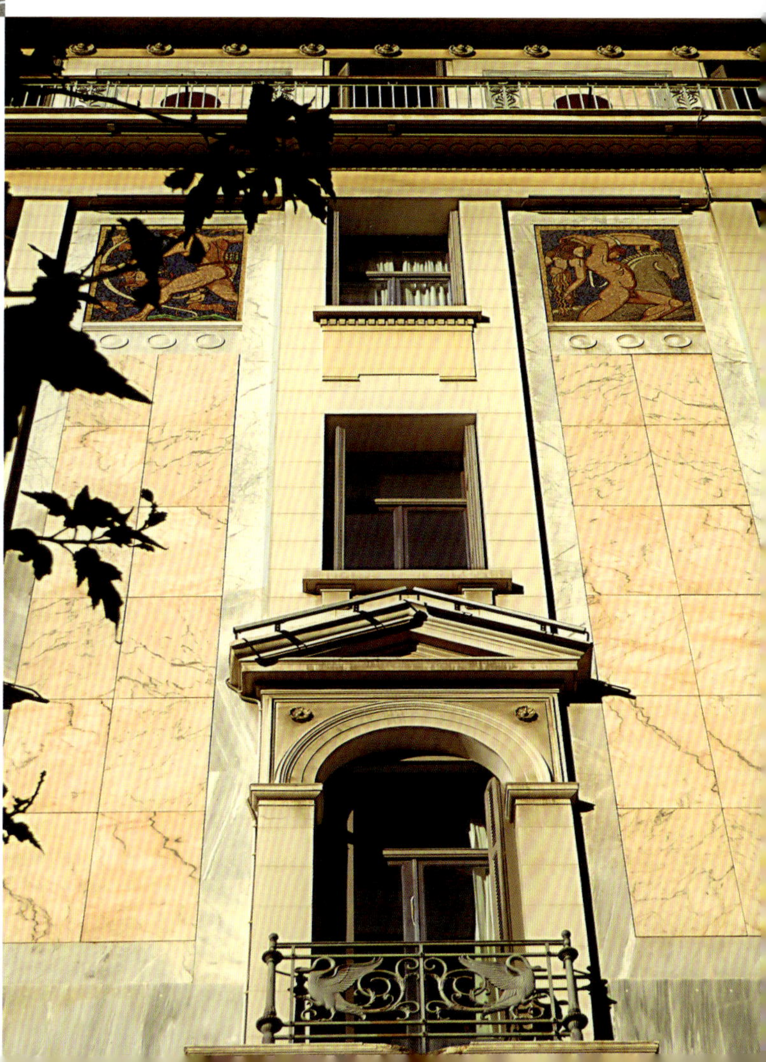

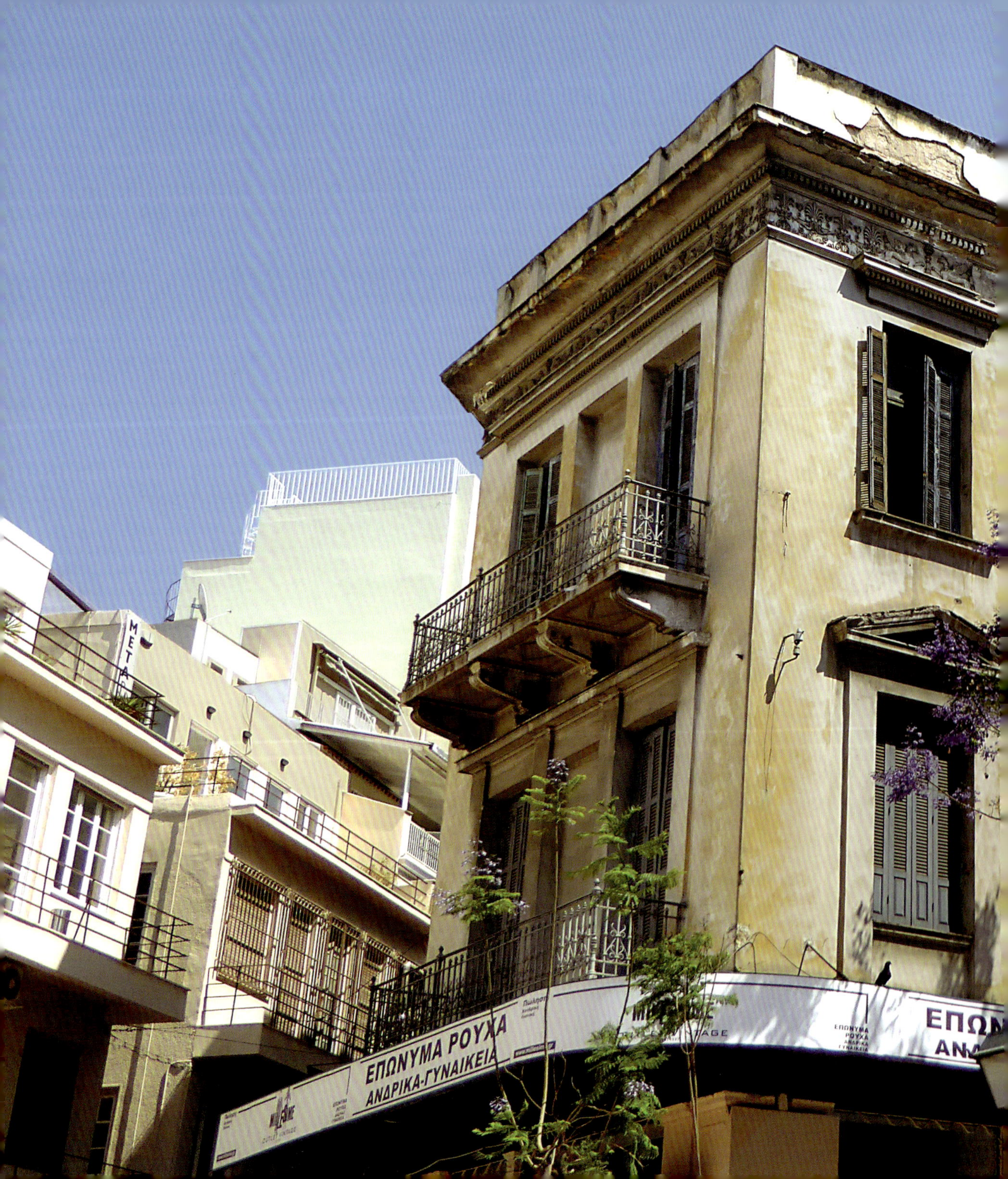
ΕΠΩΝΥΜΑ ΡΟΥΧΑ
ΑΝΔΡΙΚΑ-ΓΥΝΑΙΚΕΙΑ

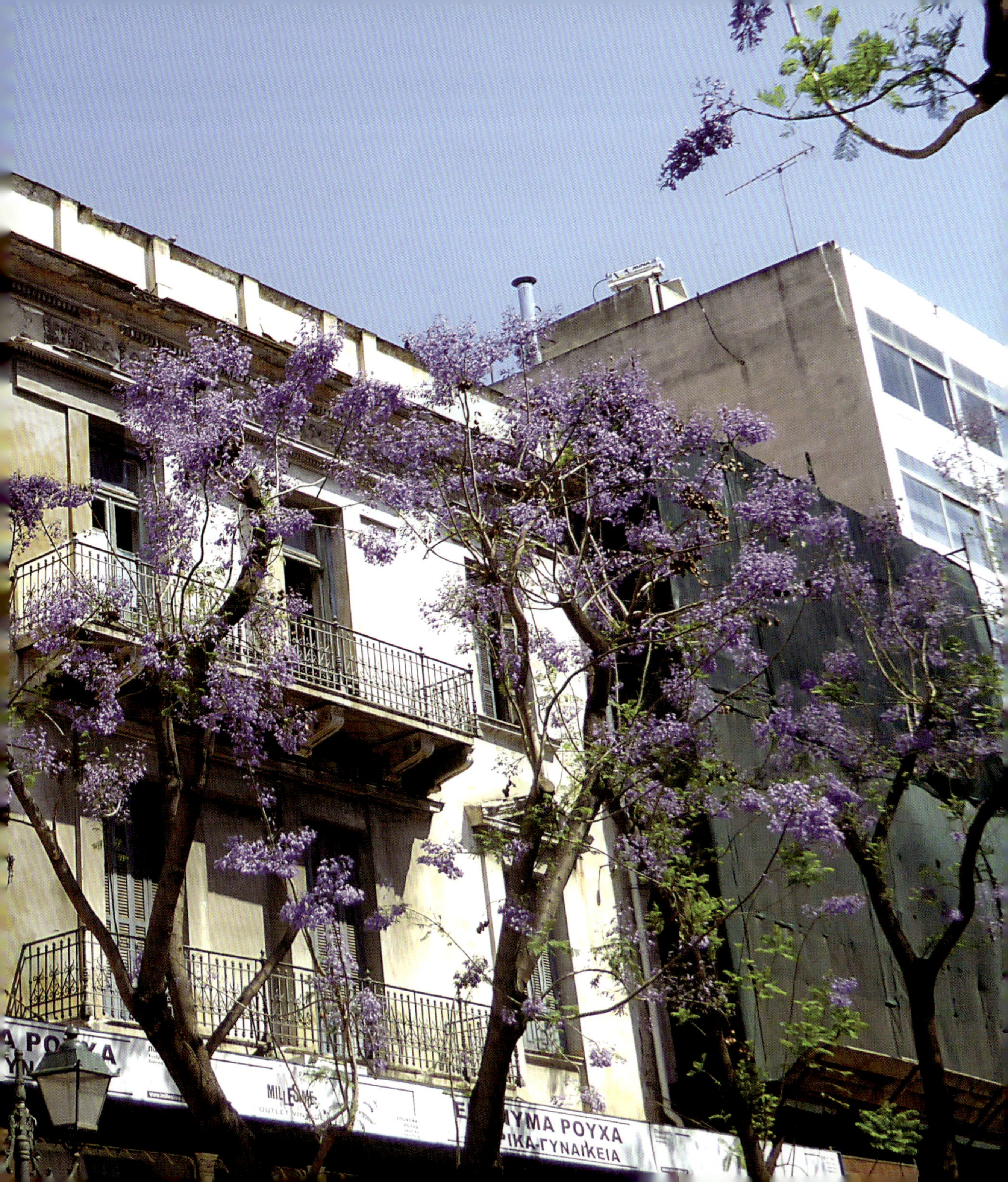
MILLESIME
OUTLET
ΡΟΥΧΑ
ΓΥΝΑΙΚΕΙΑ

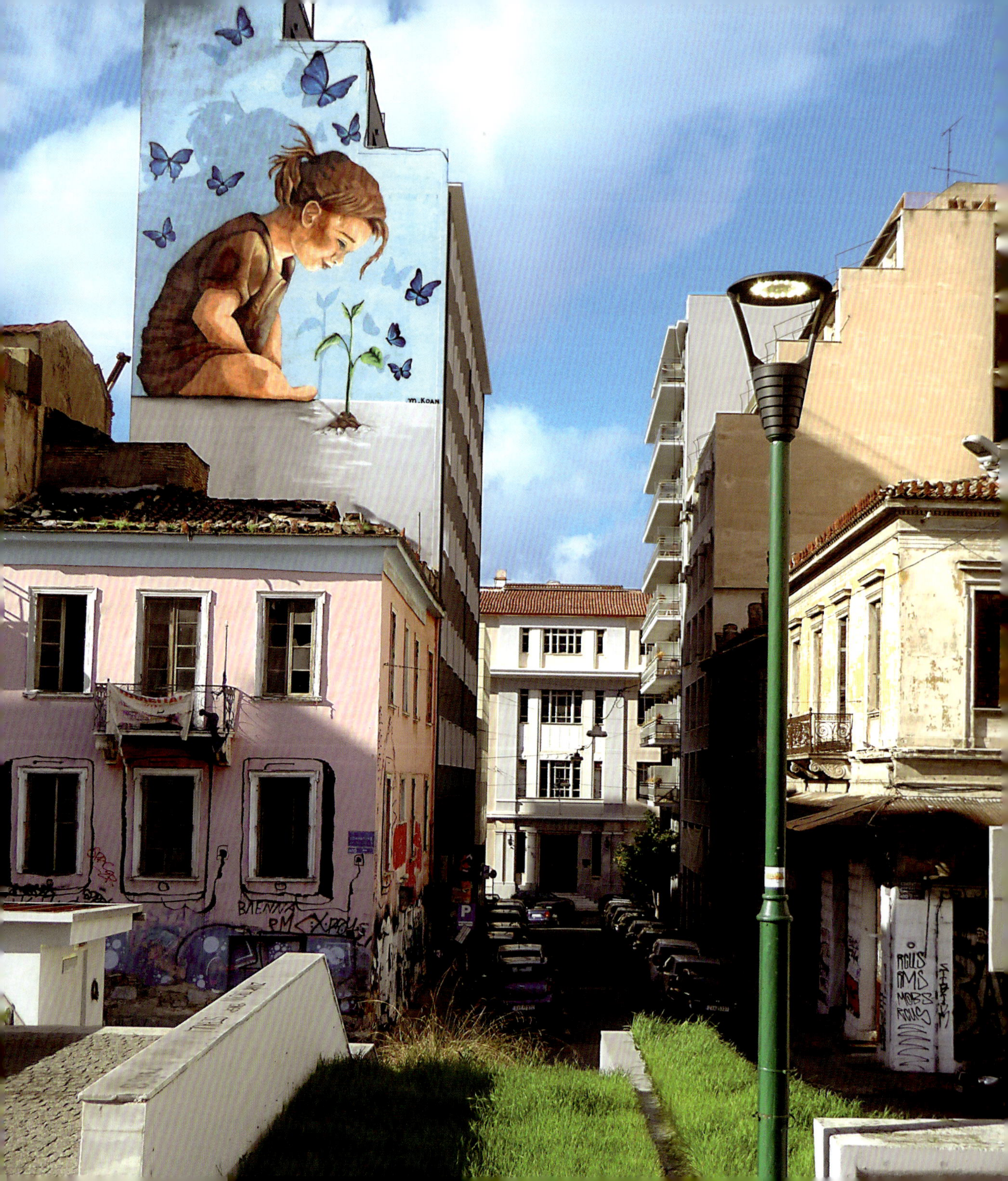
m.KOAN

VARVAKEIOS MARKET

Christmas is nearing. The market is bustling with activity, as merchants and customers argue over prices. Some come from high end restaurants looking for the latest delicacies; others come simply because the place has the most affordable prices, and the freshest produce.

I walk around taking it all in, when a man in a blue apron almost shoves a snapper into my face. "Fresh out of the water!" he shouts. A little further away, a tiny Greek flag sticks out of a grouper's mouth. Its left eye has been speared and hangs on the ice. A butcher raises his cleaver and chops off the head of a lamb, as a boy with sleepy eyes turns on a hose and washes the blood away. Kiosks selling nuts, dried fruit, spices, and herbs entice the senses, making it impossible to decide what to get.

The market is named after Varvakis, a Greek benefactor and ex-pirate with a bounty placed on his head by the Ottomans. Varvakis was responsible for the construction of many important buildings around Athens.

Varvakeios Market, *Sokratous 6, Theater Square, "Plateia Theatrou;" mural by artist Melina Koan*

VARVAKEIOS MARKET

Never educated, he left a great part of his fortune to the Greek State for the construction of schools, among them the first Lyceum in Athens, known as "Varvakeios Sxoli," now destroyed. The market once adjacent to the school is also named after him.

Built at the intersections of Aiolou, Athinas, and Sophokleous streets, the Varvakeios Market is a late nineteenth-century building based on the plans of the architect Ioannis Koumelis, who got his inspiration from other European marketplaces. The characteristic part of the market is its metallic roof and large glass ceiling windows that allow light to pour in.

After two major fires in 1884 and in 1928, the market was rebuilt to its present design. Many famed late-night restaurants existed in the side streets, including "Ipeiros," which still stands in the same spot after 150 years. On Sunday afternoons, when the market is closed for the weekend, "Rebetika" music flows from the old taverna named "Stoa ton Athanaton," meaning the "Gallery of the Immortals."

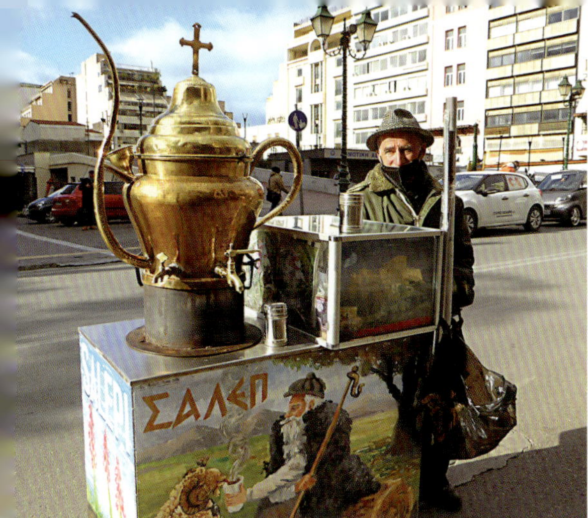

Top: *Street vendor selling "Salepi," a winter beverage made from flour extracted from the tubers of Orchis mascula and flavored with cinnamon or ginger*

Right: *Varvakeios Market with characteristic metallic roof and large glass ceiling windows*

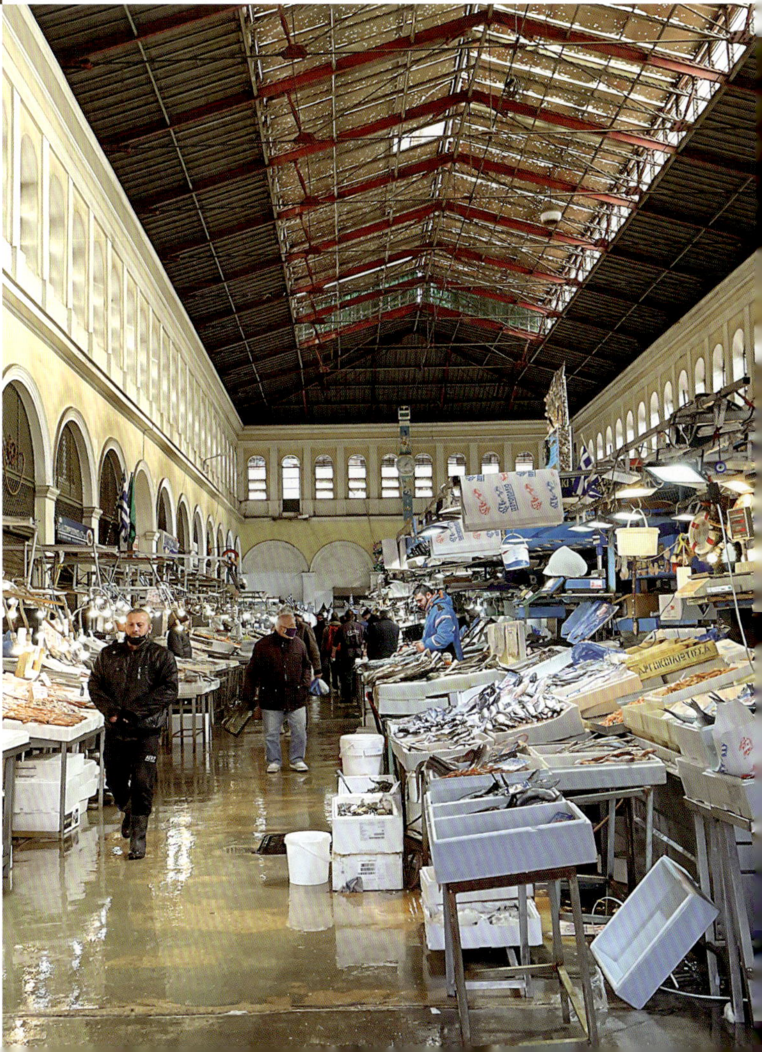

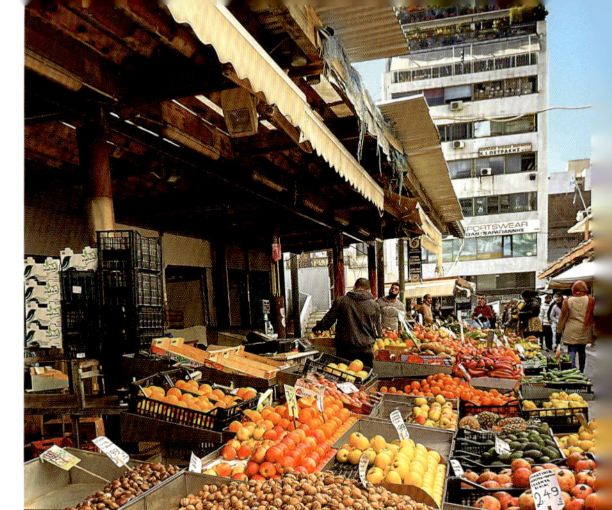

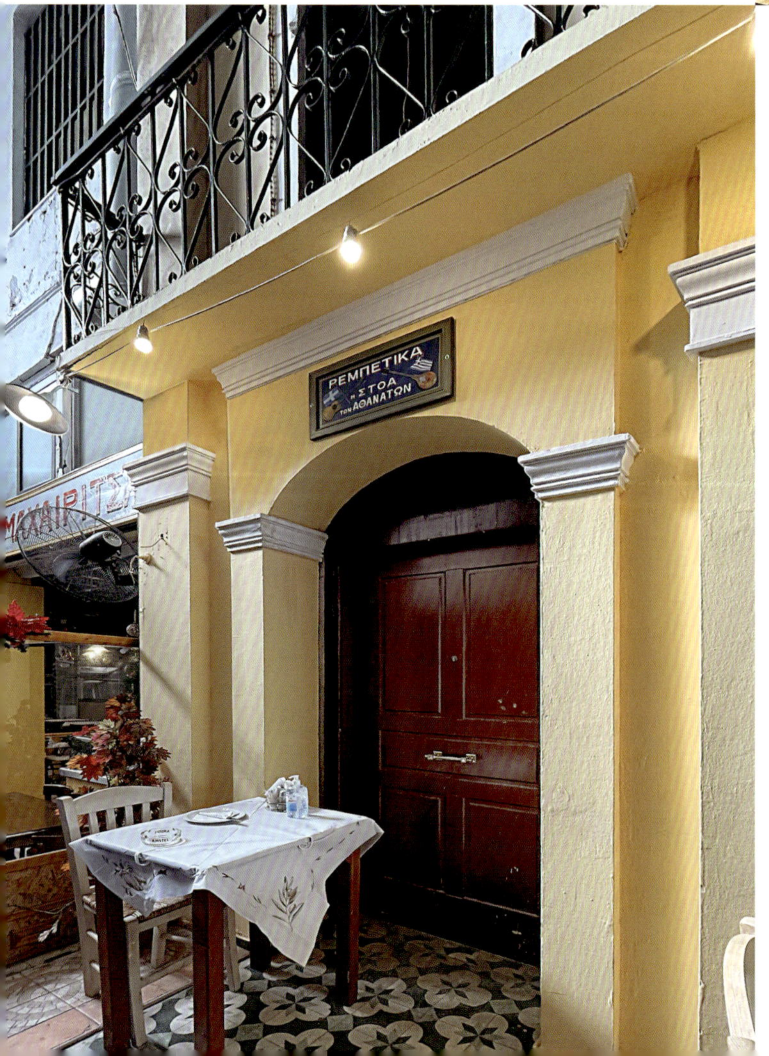

Top: *Outdoor fruit and vegetable market completes the day's shopping*

Left: *Taverna named "Stoa ton Athanaton," meaning "The Gallery of the Immortals," specializing in Rebetica music*

Following pages: *Cast iron awning representative of nineteenth-century markets*

VARVAKEIOS MARKET

As night descends, the market takes a shadowy turn. The area, home to many refugees and immigrants, unveils another side, much harsher. Groups of young men spill onto the streets looking for drugs or to rob an unsuspecting person. Cell phone and ATM thefts are common and so are racial attacks and street skirmishes. Drug addicts and the homeless roll out their cardboard boxes, finding shelter in front of a doorway or under a bench.

The street is transformed into a place of darkness and very few reminders of the morning activities. The sight raises questions. How can one justify this abrupt change? In nearby Monastiraki Square people weave their way amidst the street vendors and artists, buying souvenirs or strolling through the narrow alleys, yet as soon as one reaches the market, an invisible wall is raised, a kind of a signal that you have crossed into unexplored waters. A shame really, because the market and the square hold an unsurpassed beauty and an historical interest waiting to be recognized.

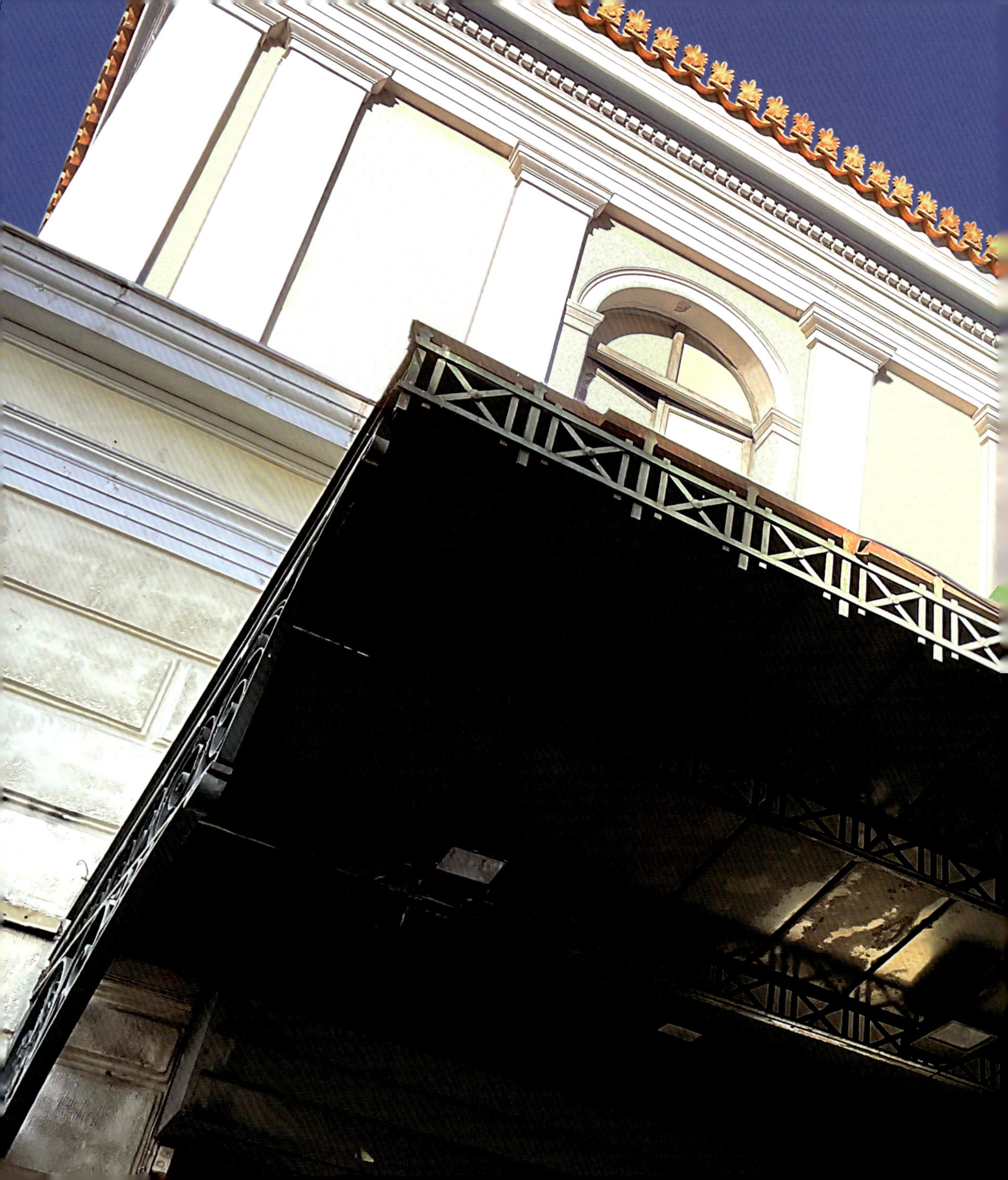

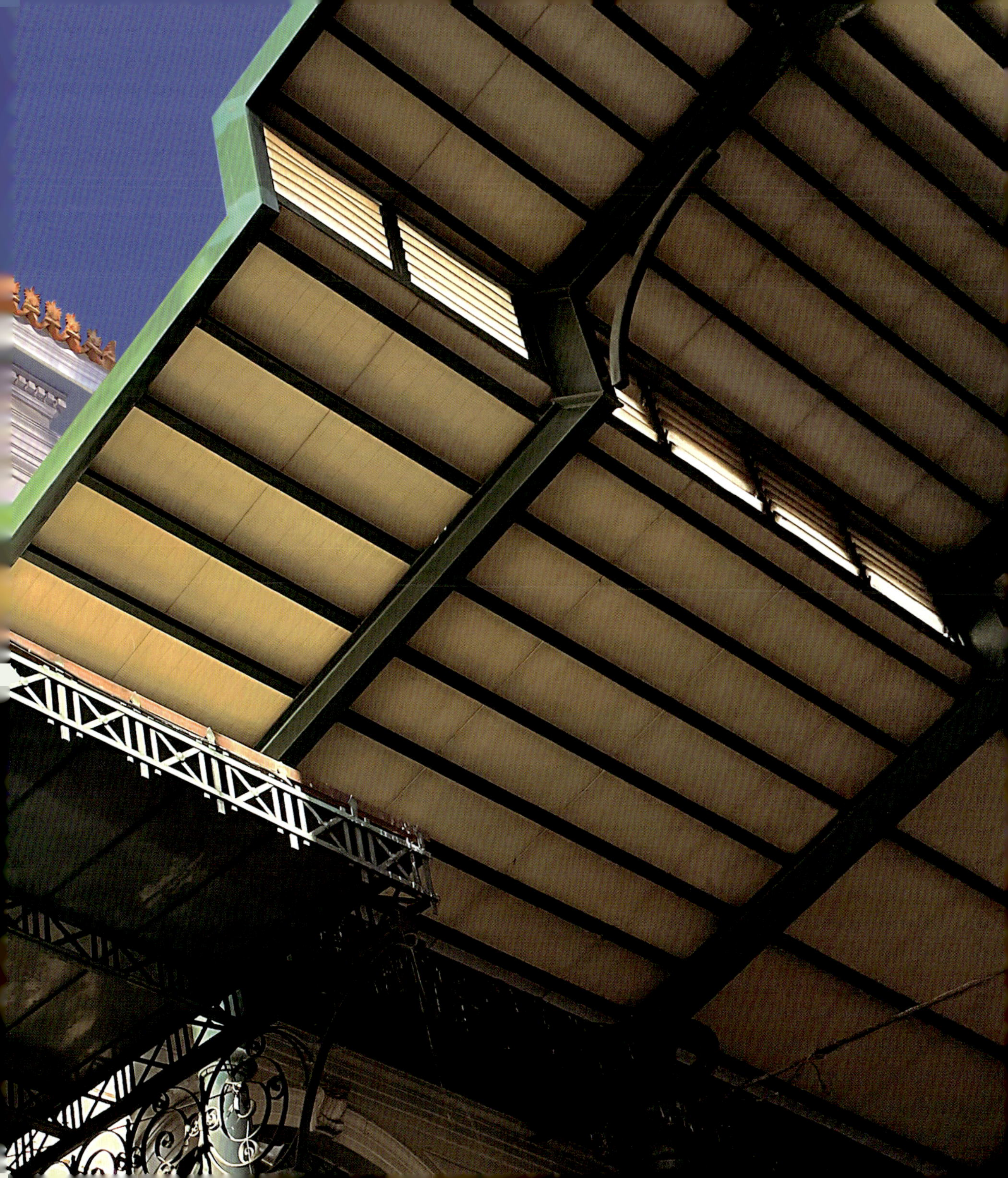

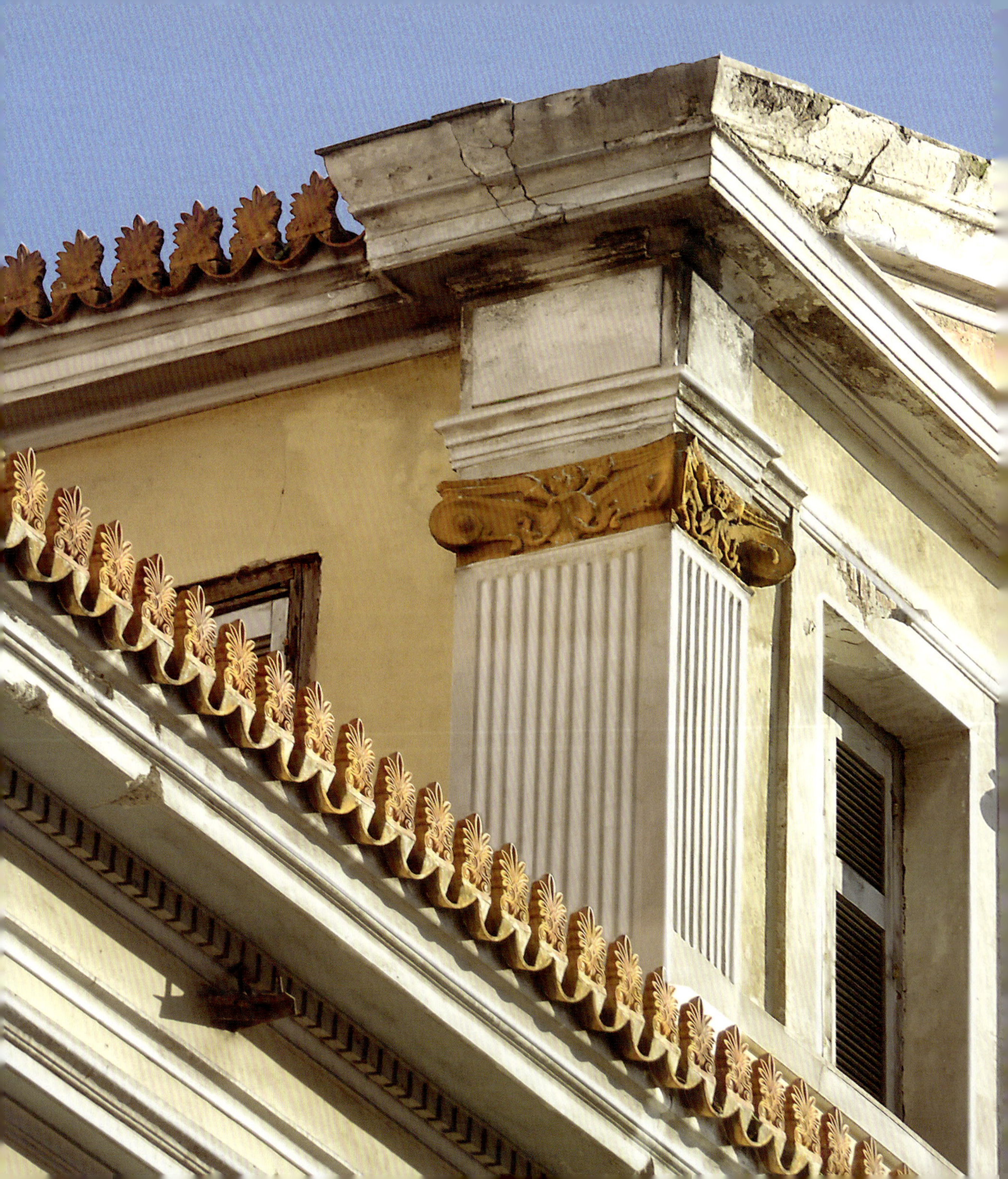

AIOLOU STREET

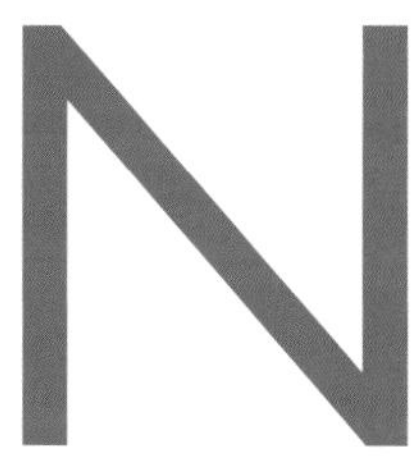

amed after Aiolos, god of the wind, Aiolou Street is one of the oldest streets of Athens. Built in 1835, the street was nothing but a narrow strip that led from the center of the old market to the hills of the Acropolis, known as "The Castle."

As the capital emerged, Aiolou Street quickly became one of the most important commercial streets in the city. Based on plans of architects Kleanthis and Schaubert, it was the starting point for all other commercial roads to follow. Surrounded by cafés, patisseries, and all other kinds of commercial and non-commercial stores, it was known as the political, commercial, and economic decision making center of the city. The many kafeneia often functioned as gathering places to discuss politics, often against King Otto's autocratic reign.

By the mid-nineteenth century, the street had become one of the most important areas of hospitality in the city. About fifty-five hotels were built, all for the use of visitors and merchants. The hotels were painted yellow,

Aiolou Street, *detail of Efstathiou Simou's residence, secretary in the Ministry of Finance and advisor of the Secretary of Finance*

red, and blue, rarely white, and consisted of a top floor functioning as sleeping quarters and the ground floor functioning as the dining area. "America," "Bosporus," and "Byzantium" are among the most famous ones on the street, and so was "Francois Tavern," a place where many foreign travelers frequented.

It was on Aiolou Street that the first bookstores opened. Hat, umbrella, glass, and houseware factories followed, as well as many pharmacies, such as the "Royal Pharmacy" and the famous "Krinos." These pharmacies were equally involved in the political life of the city, and it was here that the more educated gathered, not only to have a tooth removed, but also to discuss the latest in politics. These pharmacies were known as "mini parliaments," and it was here that one could gage the direction in which the nation was heading.

Today, Aiolou Street remains one of the busiest commercial streets of Athens, attracting low-income people, immigrants, students, and those looking for a good bargain.

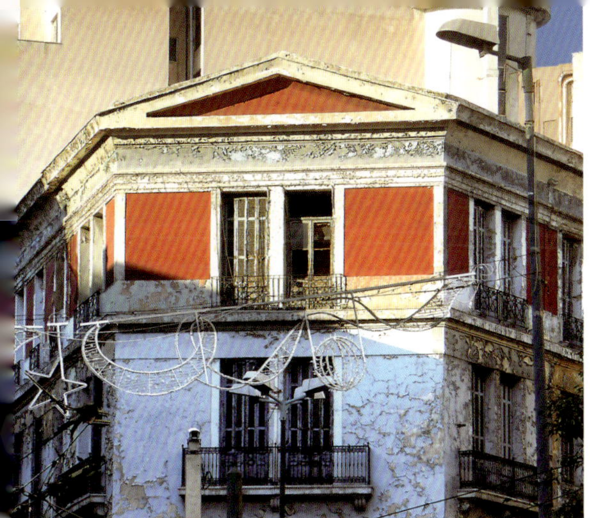

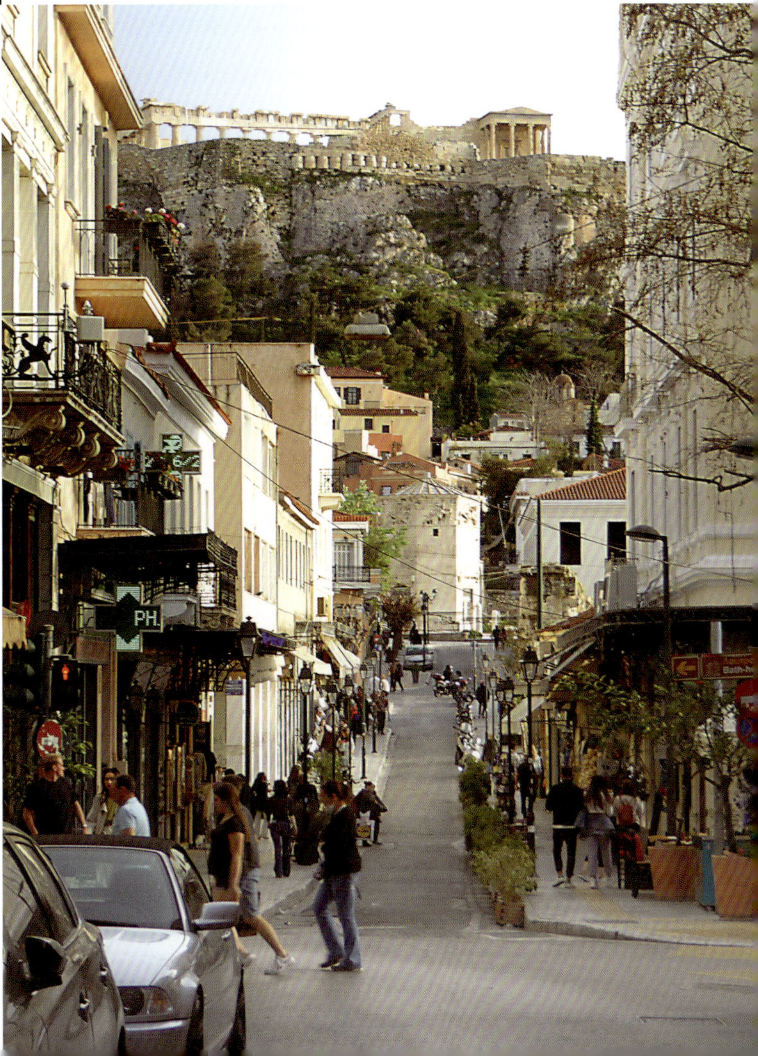

***Top:** Neoclassical building at Aiolou and Stadiou Streets painted in terracotta red and sky blue, characteristic color combinations of nineteenth-century buildings*

***Right:** Aiolou Street, named after the god of wind, Aiolos, with view of the Akropolis and the "Tower of the Winds" monument*

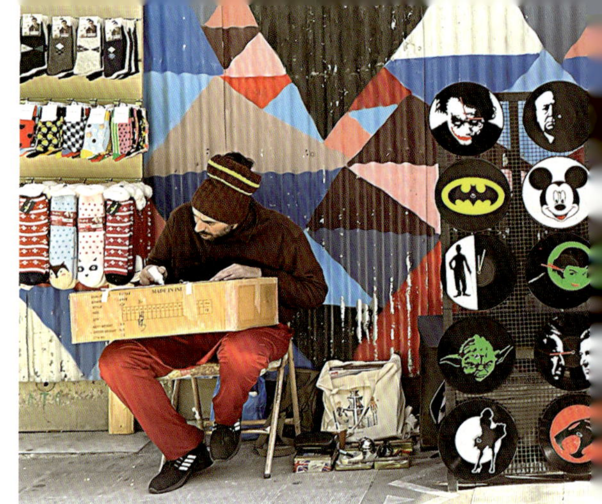

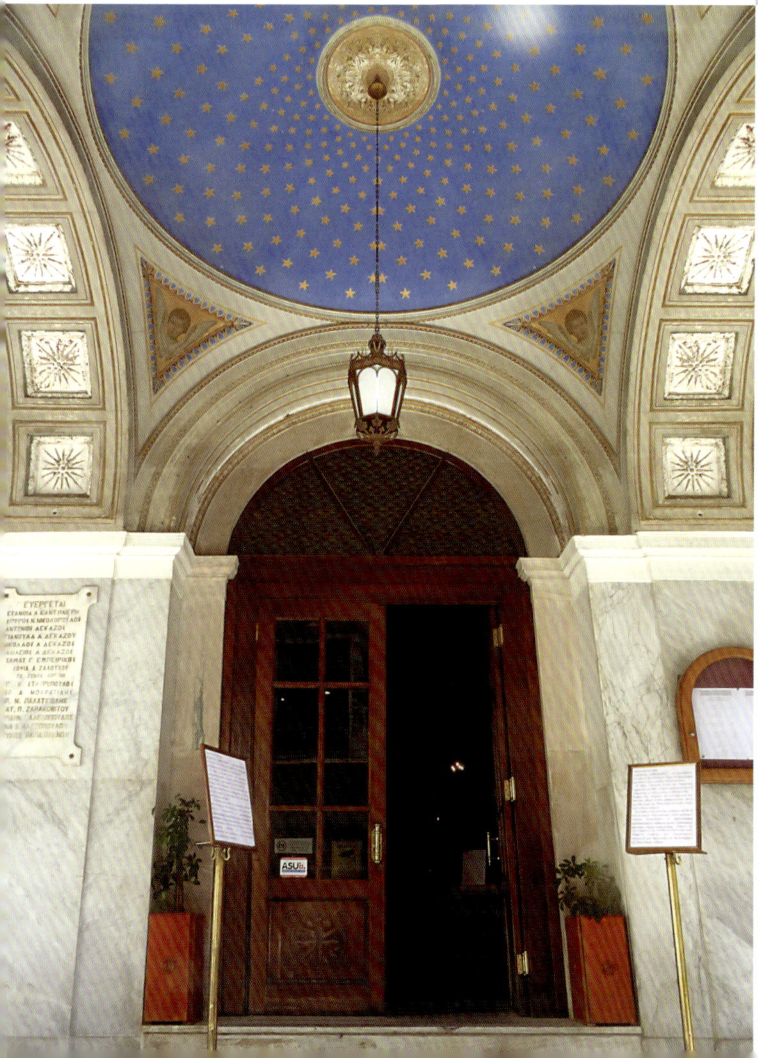

Top: *Street artist on Aiolou Street on a busy Saturday morning; background mural by Achilles*

Left: *Agia Irini Church, the first Cathedral of Athens, where King Otto was coronated, located on Agia Irini's Square, a popular gathering place*

AIOLOU STREET

Tucked off Aiolou Street stands a highly historical square known as Agias Irinis' Square. Once the flower district of Athens, one could buy plants, seeds, and particularly lavender.

Agia Irini's Church, a masterpiece of Byzantine architecture, was the first Cathedral of Athens. Some of the most important political and social events took place here, including King Otto's coronation. It is said that during the ceremony, the young prince was not wearing his crown nor holding his regalia, because the shipment was delayed, a harbinger of his often delayed responses to all pressing matters.

Agia Irini's Square, with its tightly set tables and jubilant crowds, is the best place to hobnob and watch people pass by. Small restaurants and cafés serve mouthwatering treats, as street musicians wander about. Grab a chair, if you can find one. Who knows? Maybe you'll catch a glimpse of King Otto and Queen Amalia, dressed in Greek attire, walking down the marble steps surrounded by people waving flags.

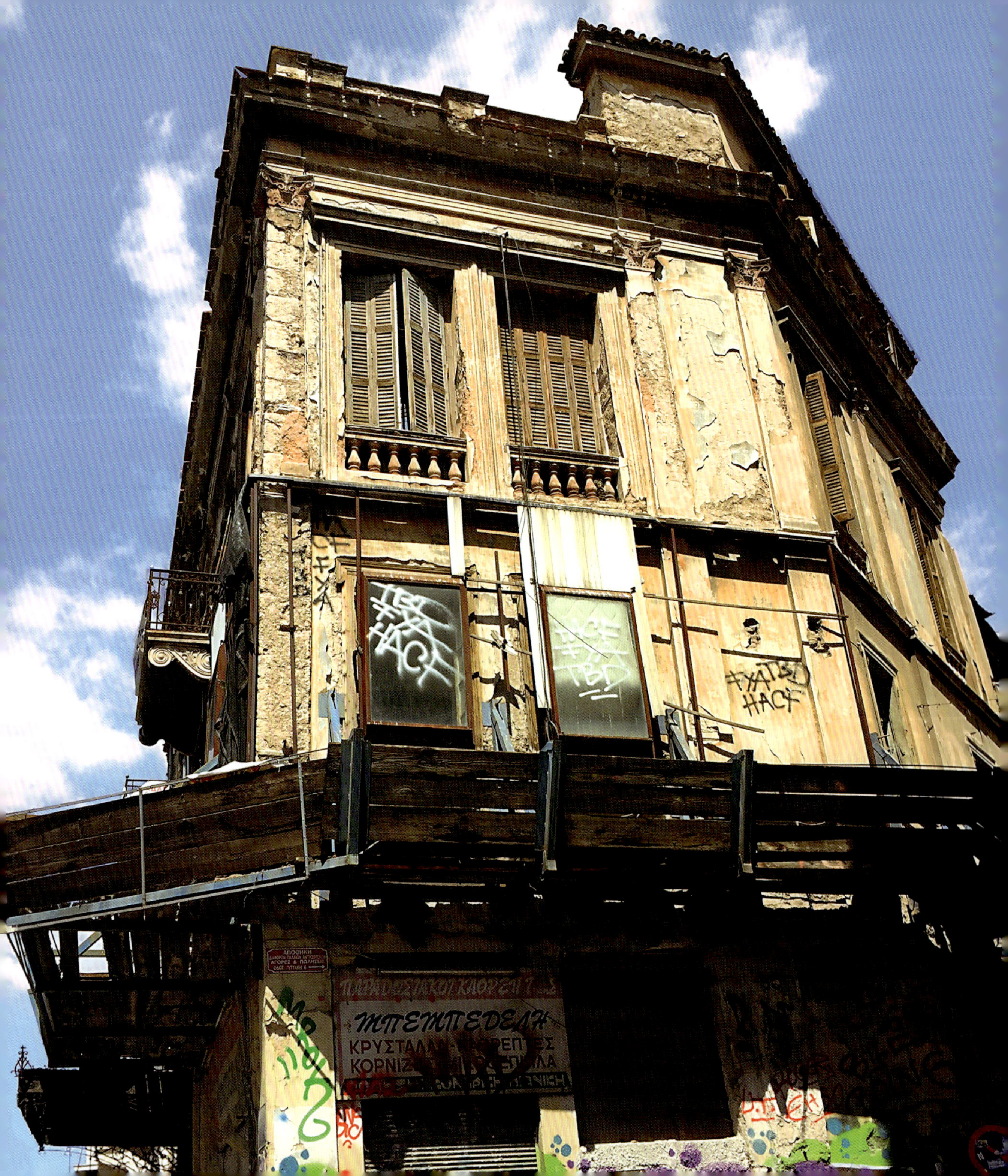
ΑΠΟΘΗΚΗ
ΑΓΟΡΕΣ & ΠΩΛΗΣΕΙΣ
ΜΠΕΜΠΕΔΕΛΗ

ERMOU STREET

The weekend has arrived and Ermou Street is packed with crowds, carrying shopping bags. Long lines form in front of well-known department stores, where one can find the latest fashions. Street vendors and musicians snake their way amongst the crowd, adding an extra note of entertainment to the already busy street.

Ermou Street, also known as "Ermaiki Odos" and named after Hermes, the god of commerce and travelers, is the third significant commercial street of Athens. It begins at Thission Station and the Kerameikos Cemetery and ends at Syntagma Square, where the Greek Parliament stands.

In Ottoman times, Ermou was a narrow path with small houses connected to each other through arches. The southern part of the street, closer to the ancient cemetery, was occupied by small shops selling handmade shoes and sandals, inns, and taverns that were mostly frequented by people of the night and the underworld.

Ermou Street, *representative nineteenth-commercial building standing in decay*

ERMOU STREET

The northern part of the street was associated with high society and became an important shopping center for the wealthy. Even the King himself had his favorite store, named "Pomonis Jewelry," which carried an exquisite collection of gold jewelry. Another important store was Rudolph Mayfair's gift shop, which specialized in European antiques and artifacts. Queen Amalia was often seen on its premises buying German artifacts.

In Ermou Street, one could find two types of tailors for men: the "Ellinoraftes," who specialized in traditional Greek attire, and the "Frangoraftes," for those who preferred European clothes. For the ladies, the choices were easier. They all went to France Lizier, a well-known seamstress who founded the first European atelier for women in Athens.

The economic divide between the two sections of the city started at Kapnikarea Church, an eleventh-century church, which is still standing and open to liturgy. The church was dedicated to the Virgin Mary and took her name from the word "kapnikon," a smoke tax administered to the city in Byzantine times.

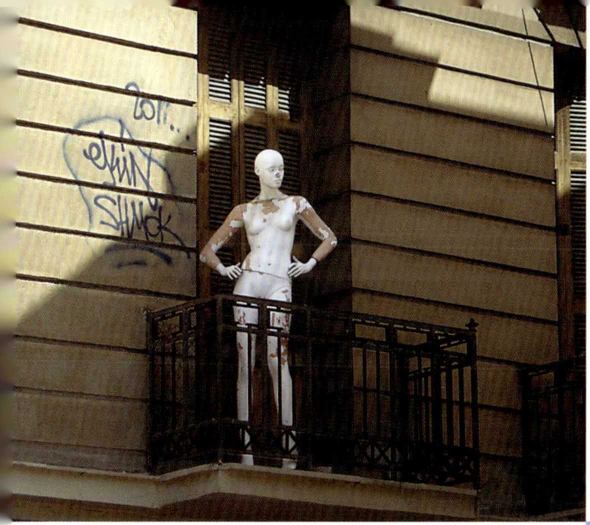

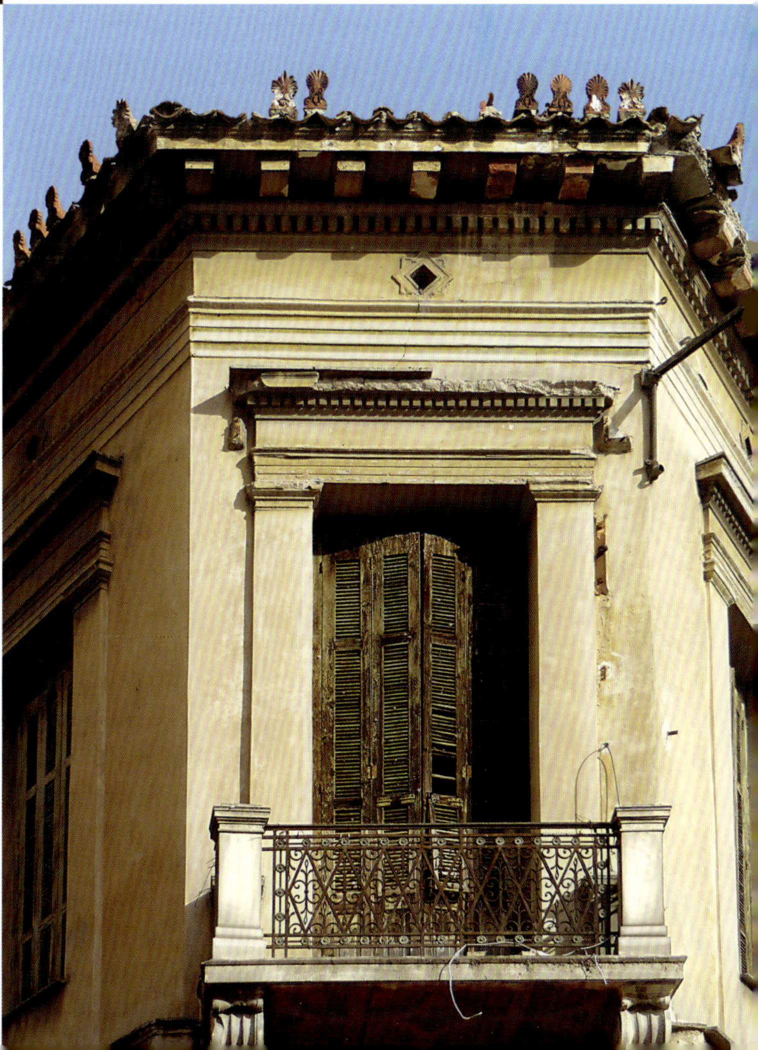

Top: *Beloved mannequin on balcony, a quintessential symbol on Ermou and Artemidos Streets*

Right: *Neoclassical house with Star of David, belonging to Noah Yusurum, a well-known merchant of the area*

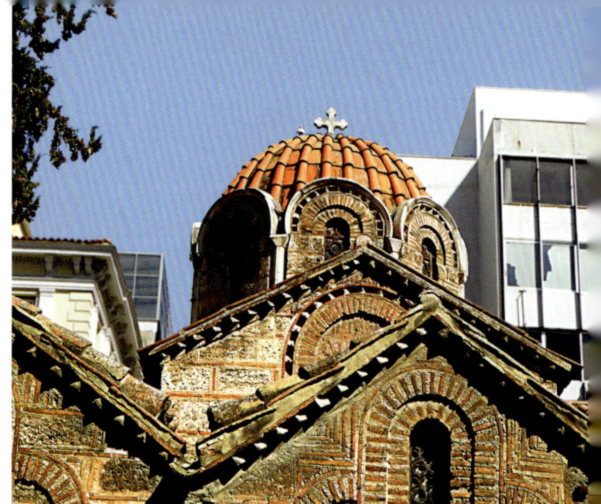

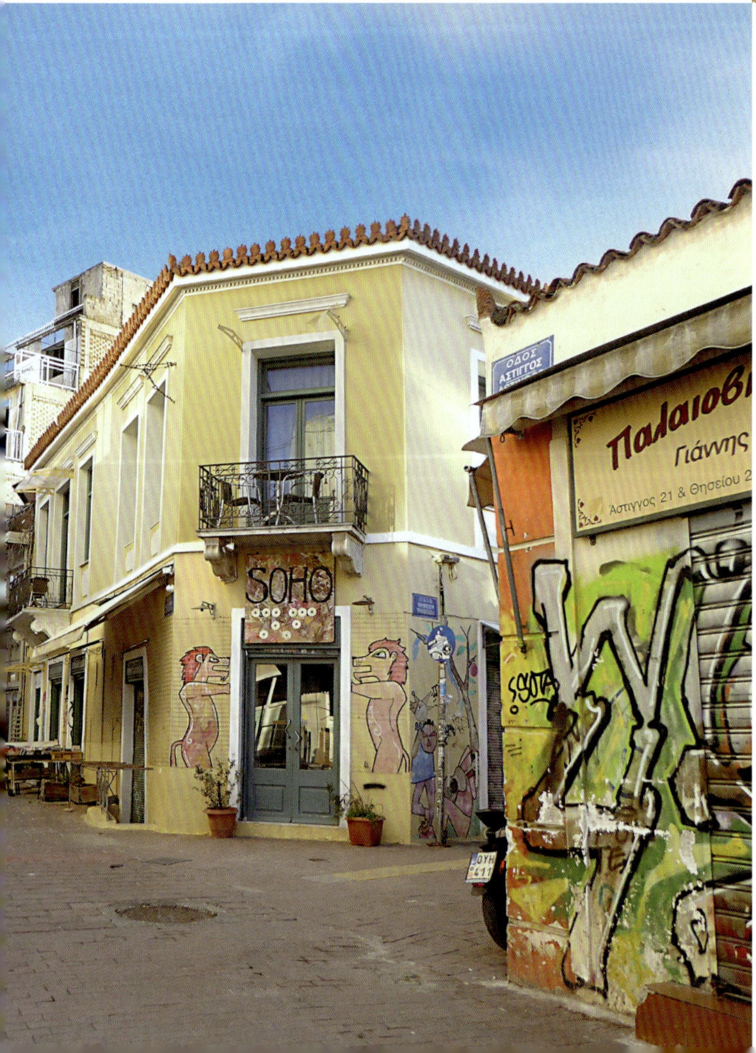

Top: *Eleventh-century Kapnikarea Church, once dividing the lower part of Ermou Street where the poor vendors stood and the upper part where the aristocracy shopped*

Left: *Corner of Astiggos and Thisseos Streets, a popular crossroad for finding old books and magazines*

ERMOU STREET

Count Botsari's and Lazarou Giourdi's mansions, among others, built in pure neoclassical style, added a cosmopolitan air to the street. Galleries and photography shops, such as Elli Sougioultzoglou-Seraidari's, also known as "Nelly," and famous for her photographs of naked dancers on the Acropolis, bookstores, and stationary stores, such as the one of Athanasios Pallis, made Ermou Street one of the most desired places to be and be seen.

Wealthy and poor gathered in the nearby cafés to admire or mock, depending on the mood, the exotic outfits, and to court the beautiful shoppers. At one point, a group of women got so irritated by the attention they were receiving, held a demonstration, demanding equal rights to dress as they pleased, and without any comments, or disturbances.

Towards the end of the nineteenth century, Ermou and Stadiou Streets became the two most important commercial streets of Athens, eclipsing Aiolou's and Athinas' fame, which were eventually reduced to secondary commercial streets.

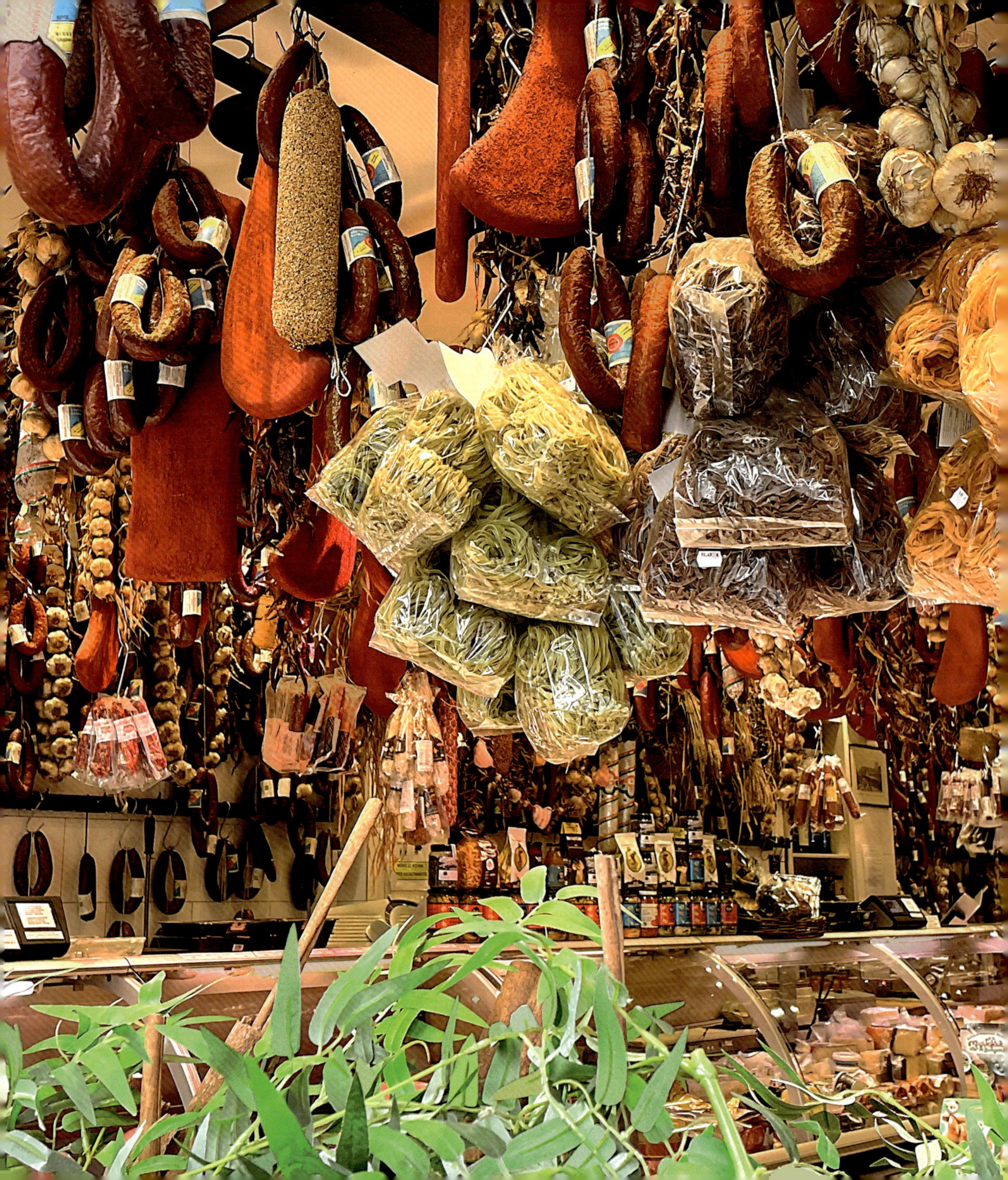

EURIPIDOU STREET

Imagine you're standing on a street with your eyes blindfolded. You've lost your way and there's nobody to help you. You are left with only your hearing, touch, and smell to guide you. The sounds around you are intimidating; there's traffic coming from every direction. The pavement is uneven, so you can lose your balance at any moment. People swirl around you, speaking in all languages: Pakistani, Chinese, Afghani, Greek, Turkish, and Armenian.

You touch a wall to regain your composure. Some plaster falls. A sweet scent catches you unaware, and you walk towards it like a bee to honey. The closer you step, the more intoxicating the scents. Someone takes your hand and draws you in. He offers you sweet tea with apple and cinnamon and removes the blindfold from your eyes. Your world is suddenly transformed.

You've reached one of the most enticing part of Athens, Euripidou Street, where colors, food and spices tease the senses. A world where various nationalities meet to sell their products and where customers patiently wait in long lines to be serviced.

Euripidou Street, *small commercial alley famous for its exotic foods, pastrami, cheeses, and spices*

EURIPIDOU STREET

Euripidou Street is another small commercial road adjacent to Monastiraki Square, filled with vendors and family businesses. As the Varvakeios Market grew, many shops spread out to nearby Euripidou Street. At first the road was known for its variety of cheeses, among them the famous cheese store, "Strouga tou Moria," belonging to the Mpitsika family and still operating to this day.

Soon other stores were introduced, selling pastrami, sausages, herbs, and spices. The street was also known for its night life, and the gathering of "older" prostitutes, women above forty, and men who gambled in small hotel rooms, something that hasn't changed much since the old days.

In 1922, with the arrival of the first refugees from Asia Minor, Euripidou Street was named "the gut and stomach of Athens" because of the variety of produce one can find there. Today, Greek, Middle Eastern, and Asians work side by side, making the street a true melting pot.

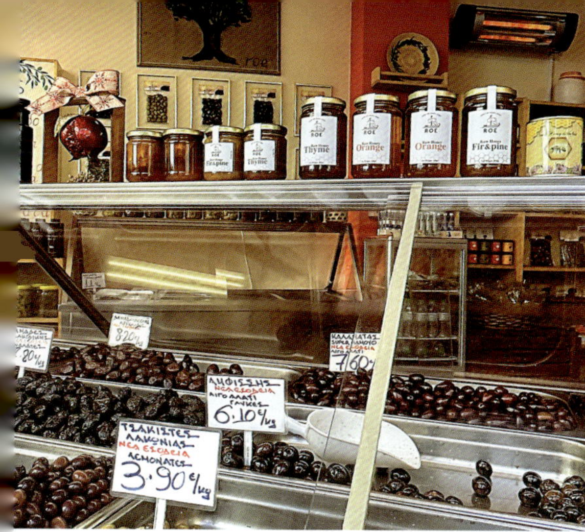

Top: *Small store selling a variety of olives and honey*

Right: *Old sign advertising Kotsopoulos factory specializing in restaurant equipment and furnishings*

Following pages: *Colorful spice store specializing in South Eastern products*

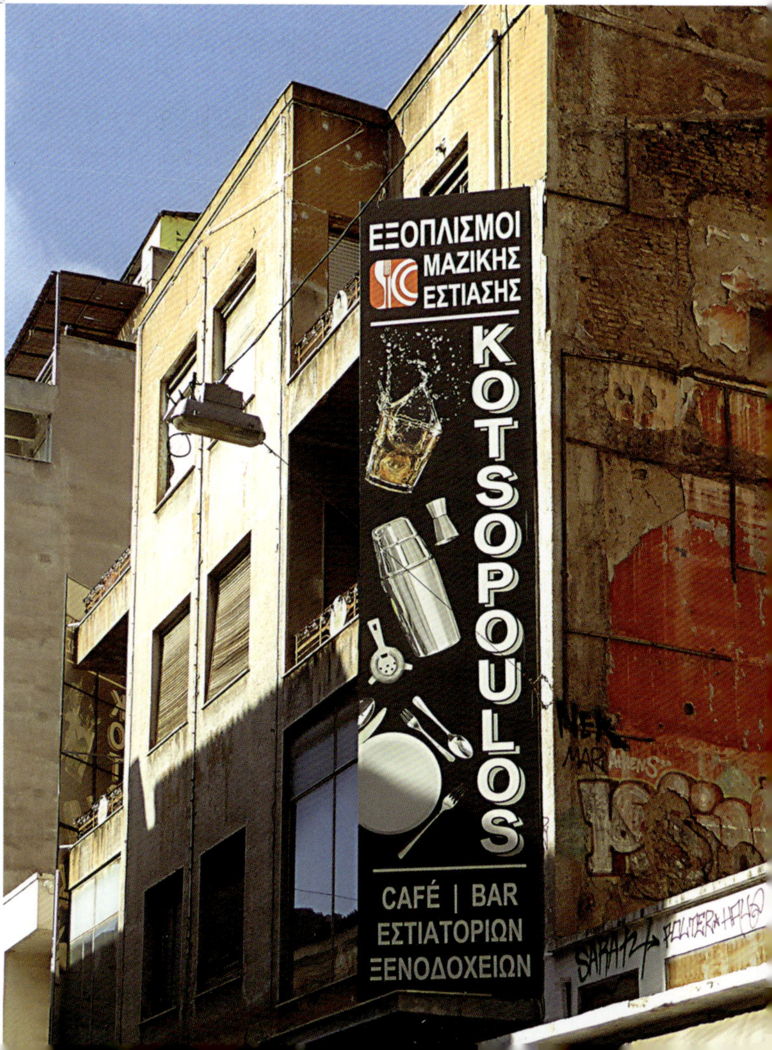

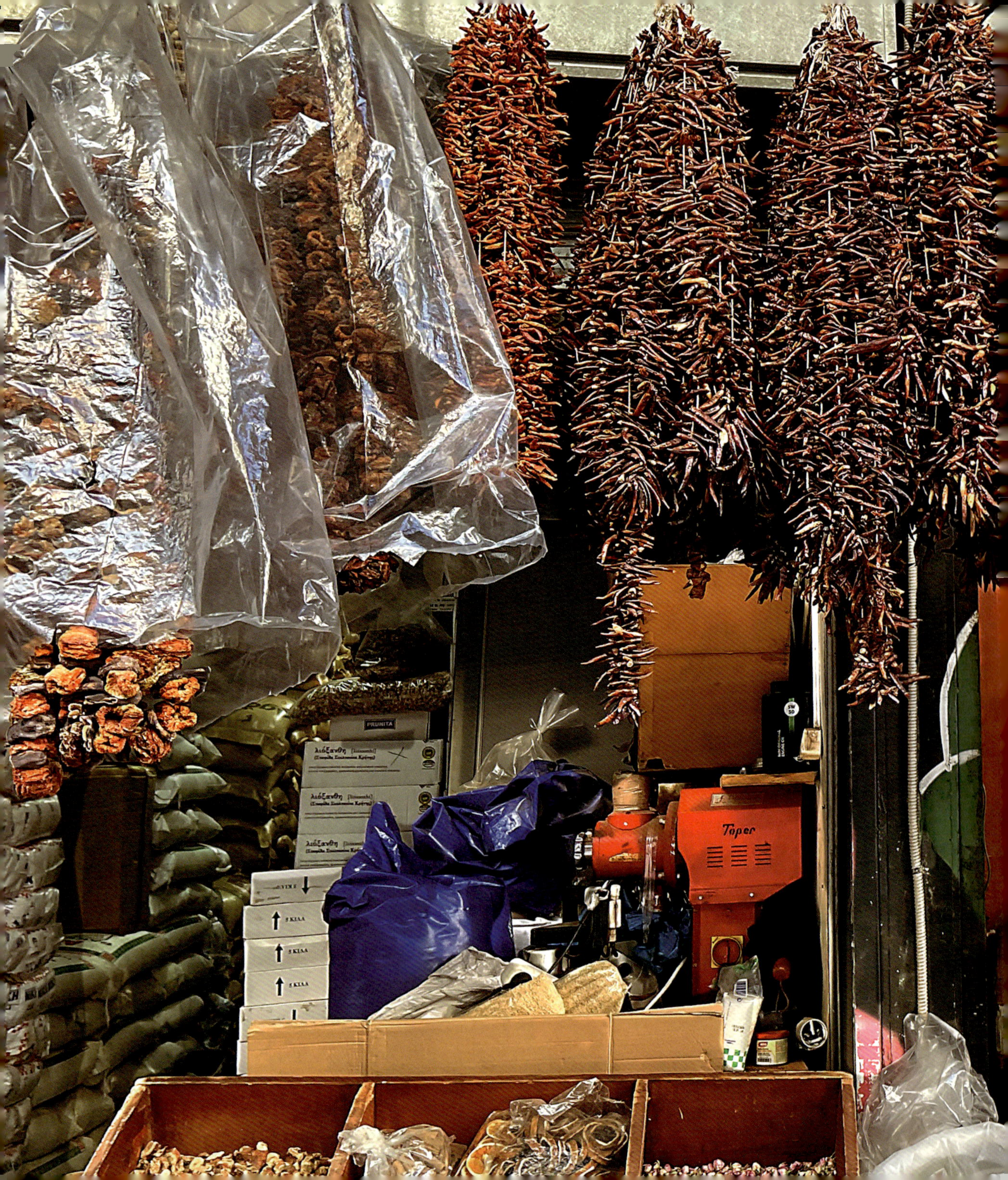
PRUNITA
Toper

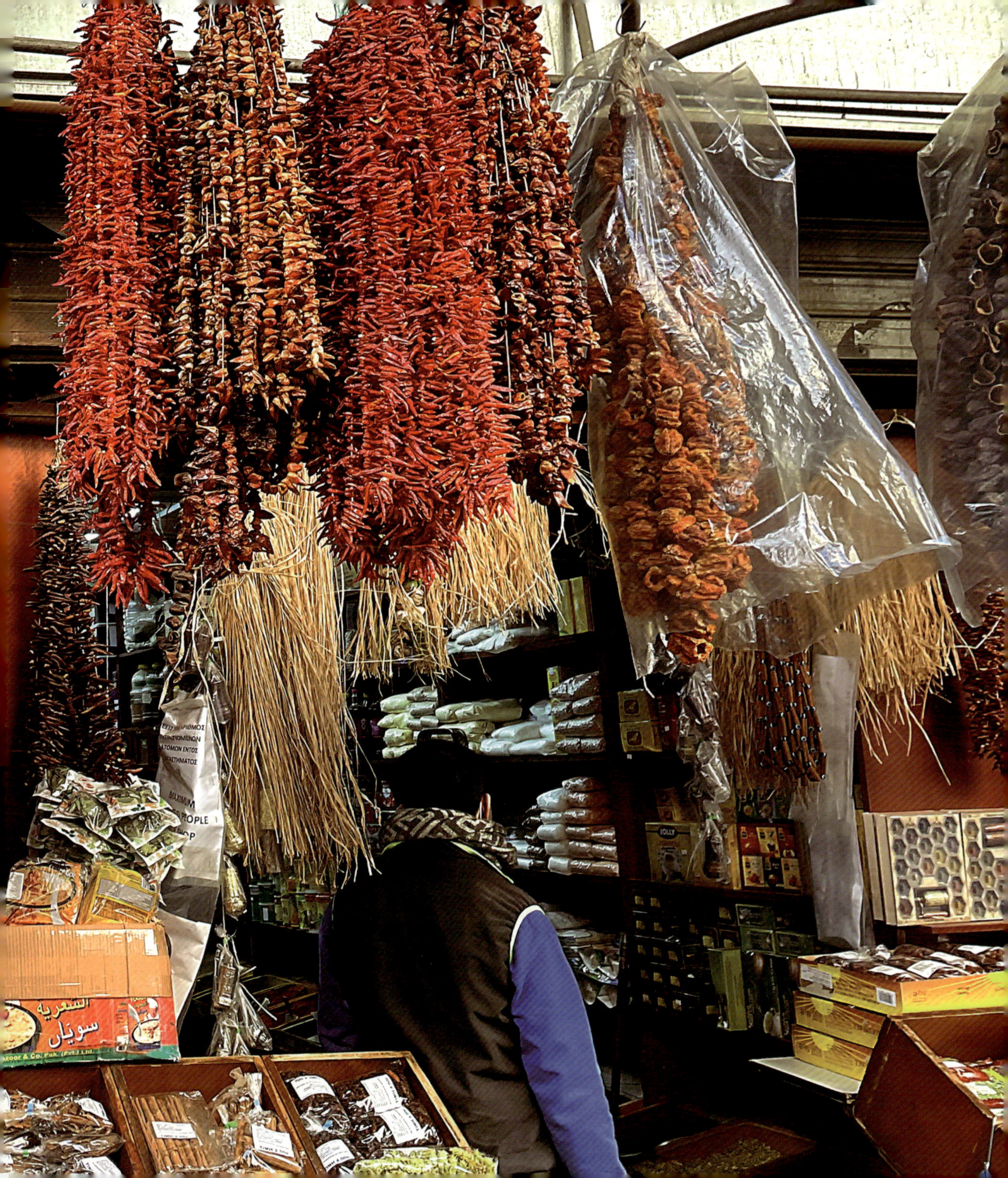

السعريه
سويان
& Co. Pak. (Pvt.) Ltd.
JOLLY

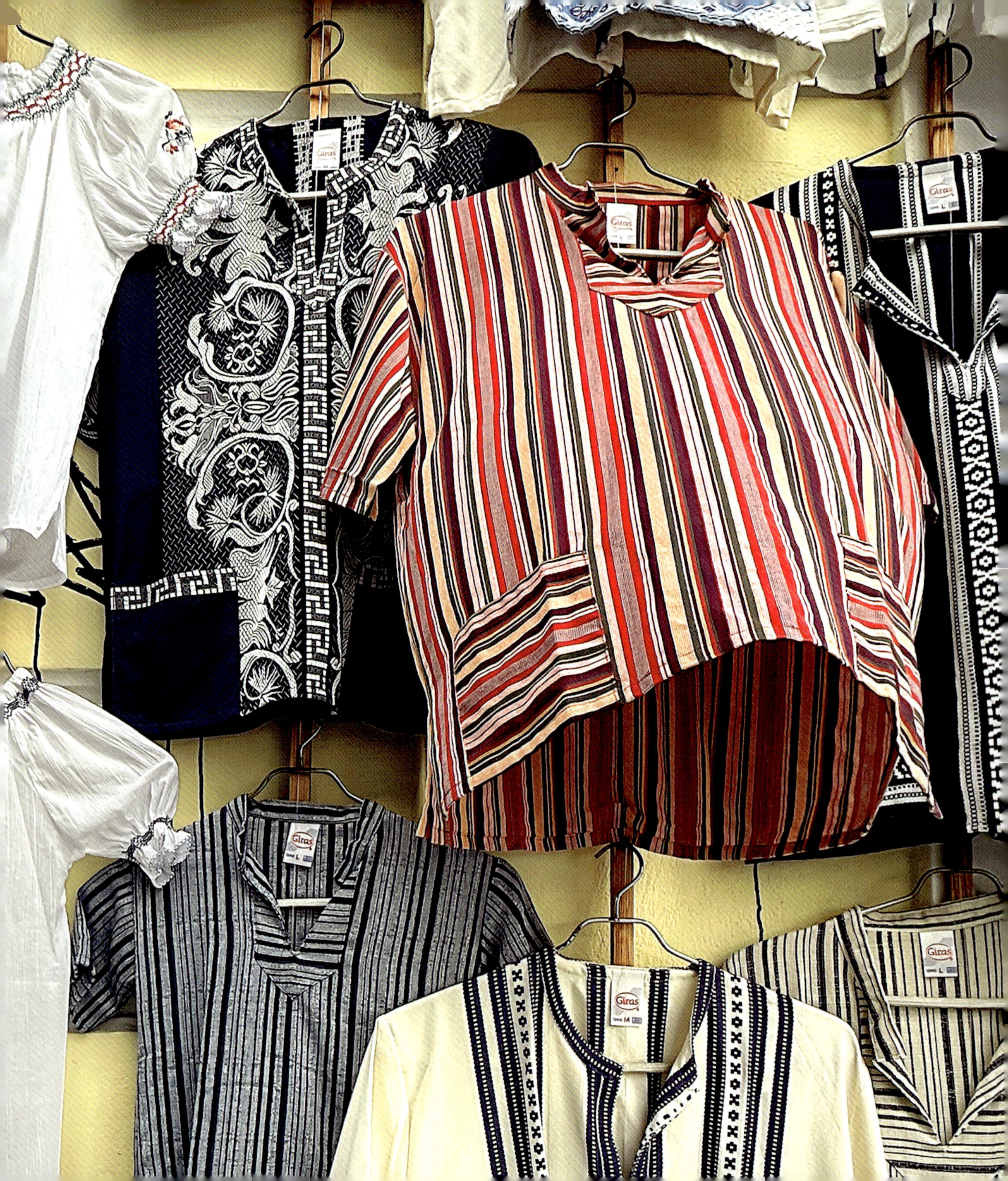
Giras
Giras
Giras
Giras

MONASTIRAKI

I'm eight years old, walking up Pandrosou Street with my father, heading to my elementary school, "Hill Memorial," that still stands in one of the oldest parts of Plaka. The store owners roll up their shutters preparing for another busy day. They hose down the street and dust off their windows. A world of color emerges.

I stop before my favorite sandal store and wave at Mr. Melissinos, the sandal maker and poet. I'm very shy of him, almost a little afraid, but I admire his thick mustache and large smile. Further down, the Metropolis Cathedral towers above us like a benevolent giant. We stop before an ecclesiastical store selling church paraphernalia and priests' outfits. The sparkling stones on the miters intrigue me.

Later, as a teenager, I walked down Hephaestus Street with my friends, bargaining for worn out Levi jeans, a luxury item back then. The outfit was completed with military boots and a messenger bag with peace signs and handwritten messages. We drank coffee overlooking the Acropolis and the Ancient Market. Our youth made us giddy. We were invincible.

Pandrosou Street, *one of the most visited streets of Athens; shirts in traditional Greek designs*

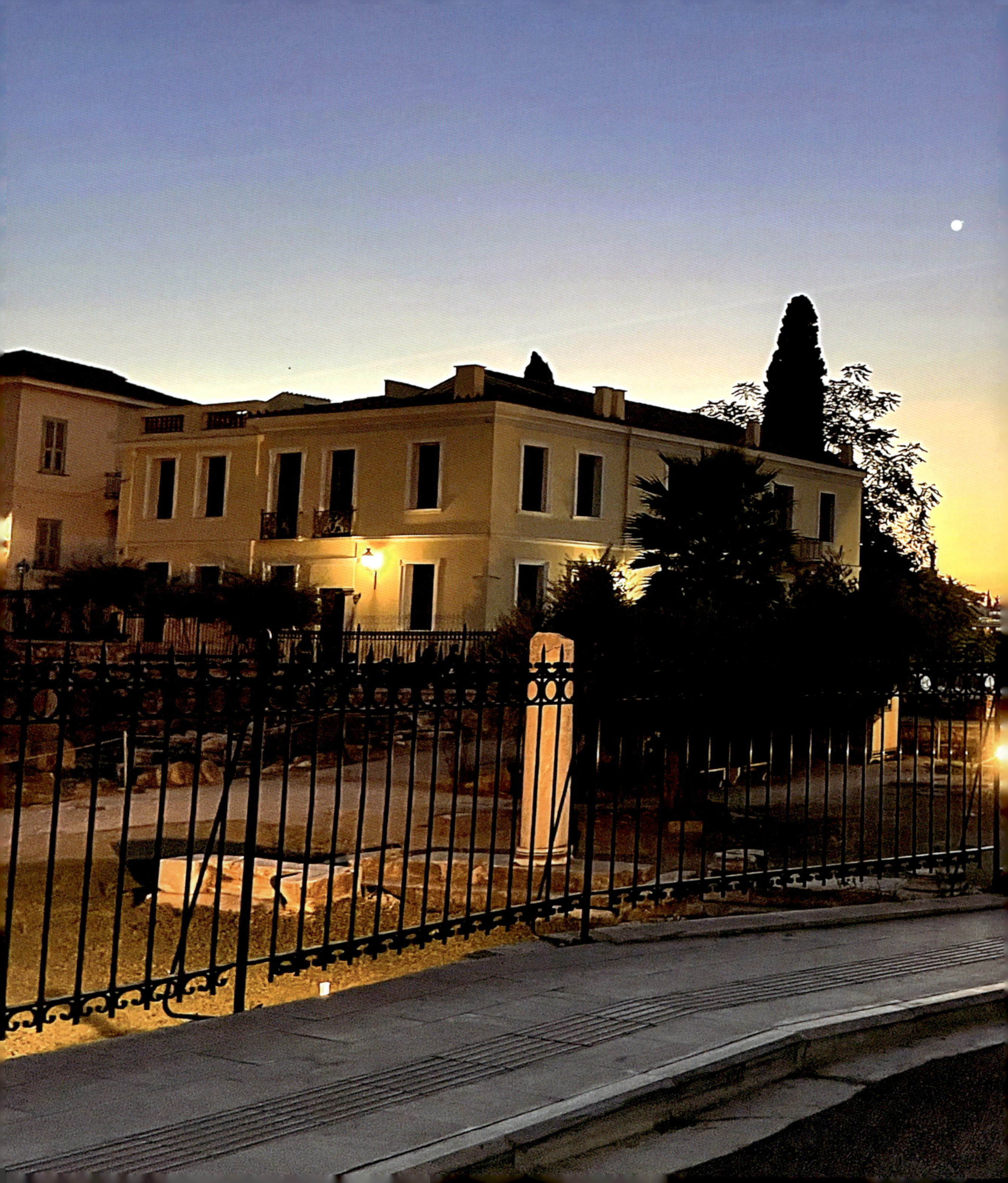

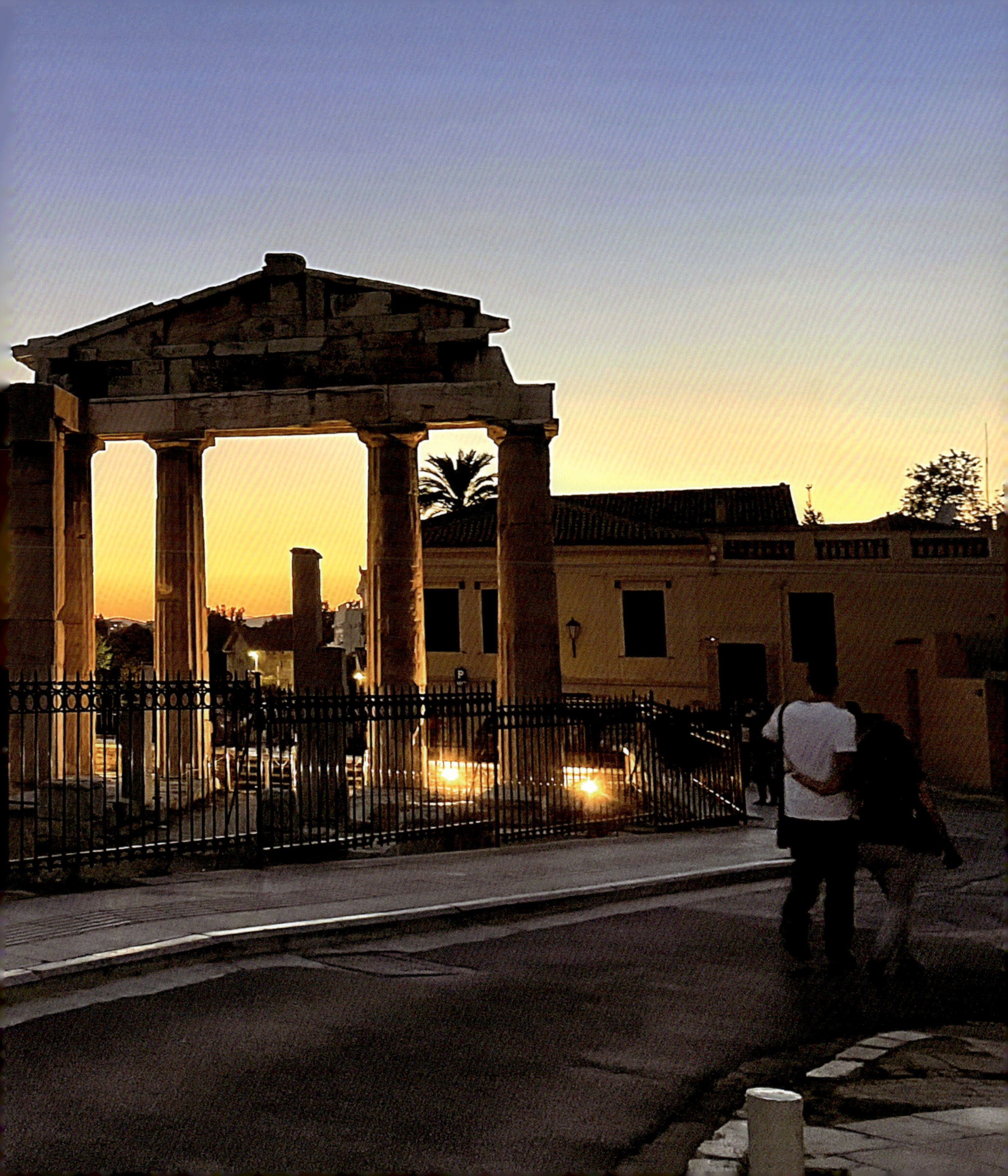

MONASTIRAKI

Monastiraki is one of the oldest and most popular neighborhoods in Athens. Its name derives from the eleventh-century monastery dedicated to the Virgin Mary that once stood in the same location where a smaller church now stands. After the construction of the subway station, a large part of the monastery was demolished, and the square was renamed "Monastiraki," meaning "small monastery."

By the mid-nineteenth century, at the intersection of Ermou and Athinas Streets, the first horse drawn carriage station was created, transporting visitors from Piraeus port to Athens. This added extra clout and excitement to the area, which also attracted many of the acrobats, wrestlers, and miracle workers that used to perform in Athinas Street.

Another famous site in the square is the Tzistaraki's Mosque, built in 1759 by Mustafa Aga. The saying goes that in order to find cement, Mustafa destroyed a column of Zeus, causing a plague epidemic. The mosque has had many uses and has functioned as a jail, an armory, and a storage area. Today the building hosts the Museum of Traditional Ceramic Arts.

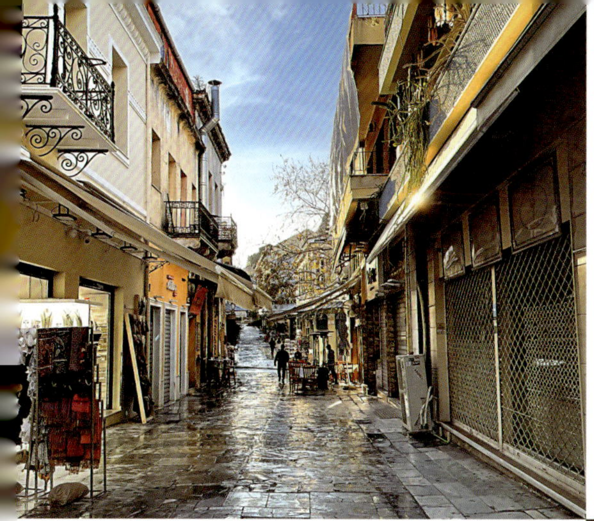

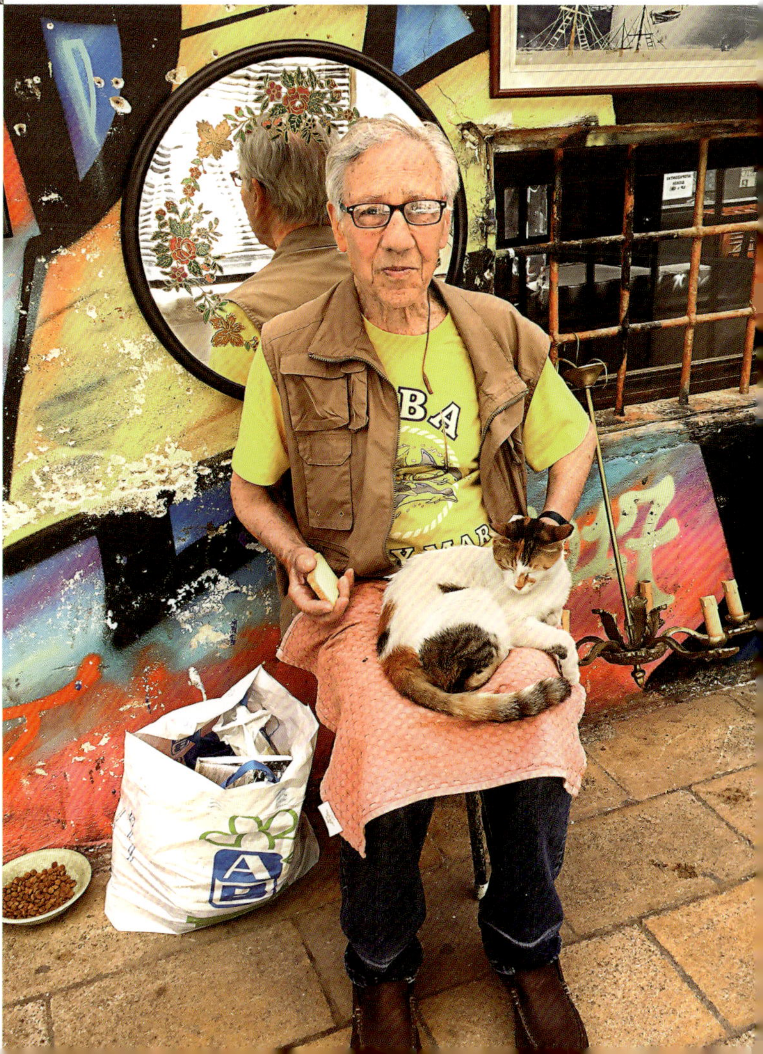

Previous pages: *Sun setting above the Roman Market in Plaka*

Top: *A rainy October day with clouds parting as small stores lift their shutters*

Right: *Antique store owner with his beloved cat*

Following pages: *Tzistaraki's Mosque, once used as a jail, armory, and storage area. Today the building hosts the Museum of Traditional Ceramic Arts*

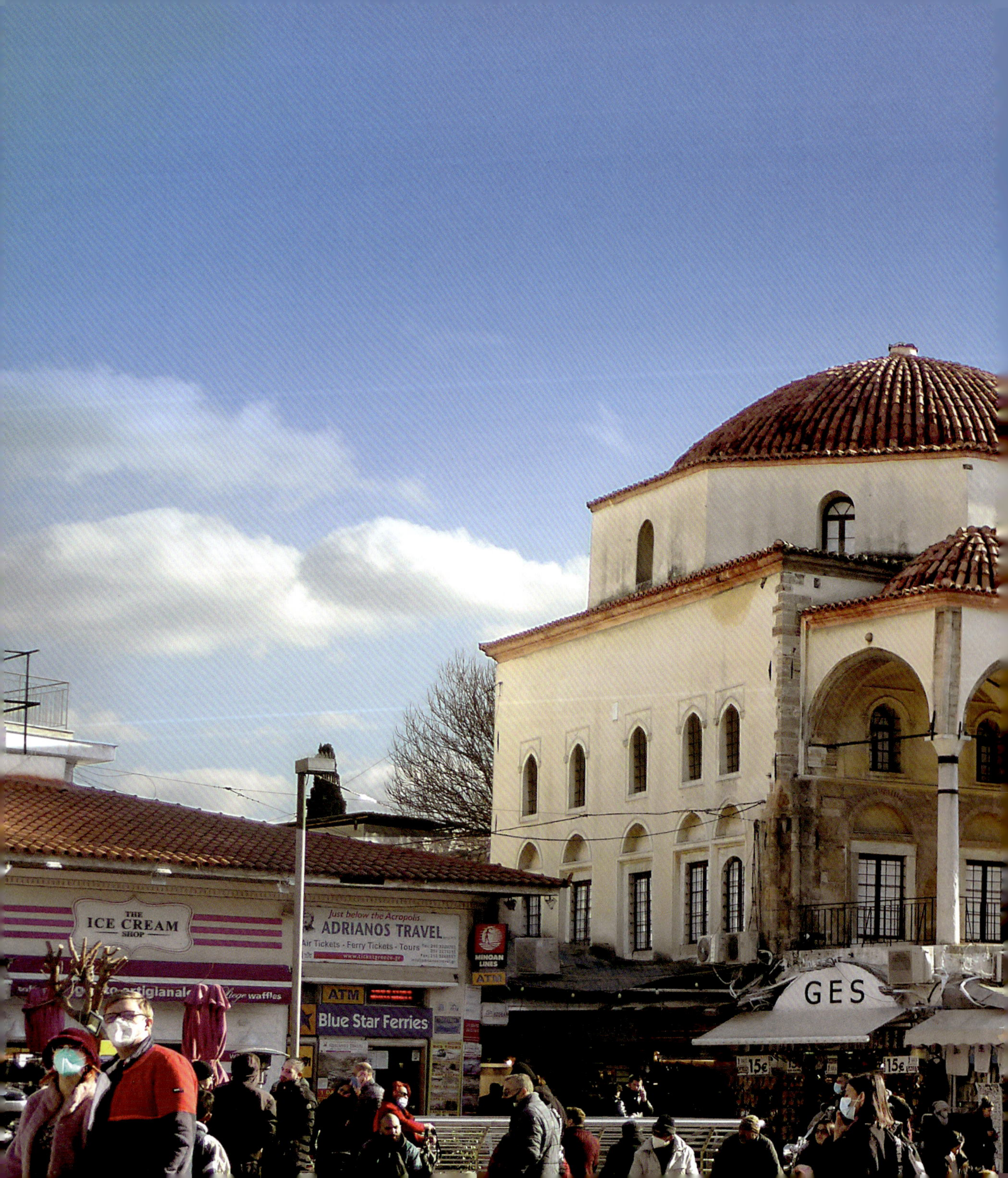
THE ICE CREAM SHOP
Just below the Acropolis...
ADRIANOS TRAVEL
Air Tickets - Ferry Tickets - Tours
MINOAN LINES
ATM
ATM
Blue Star Ferries
GES
15€
15€

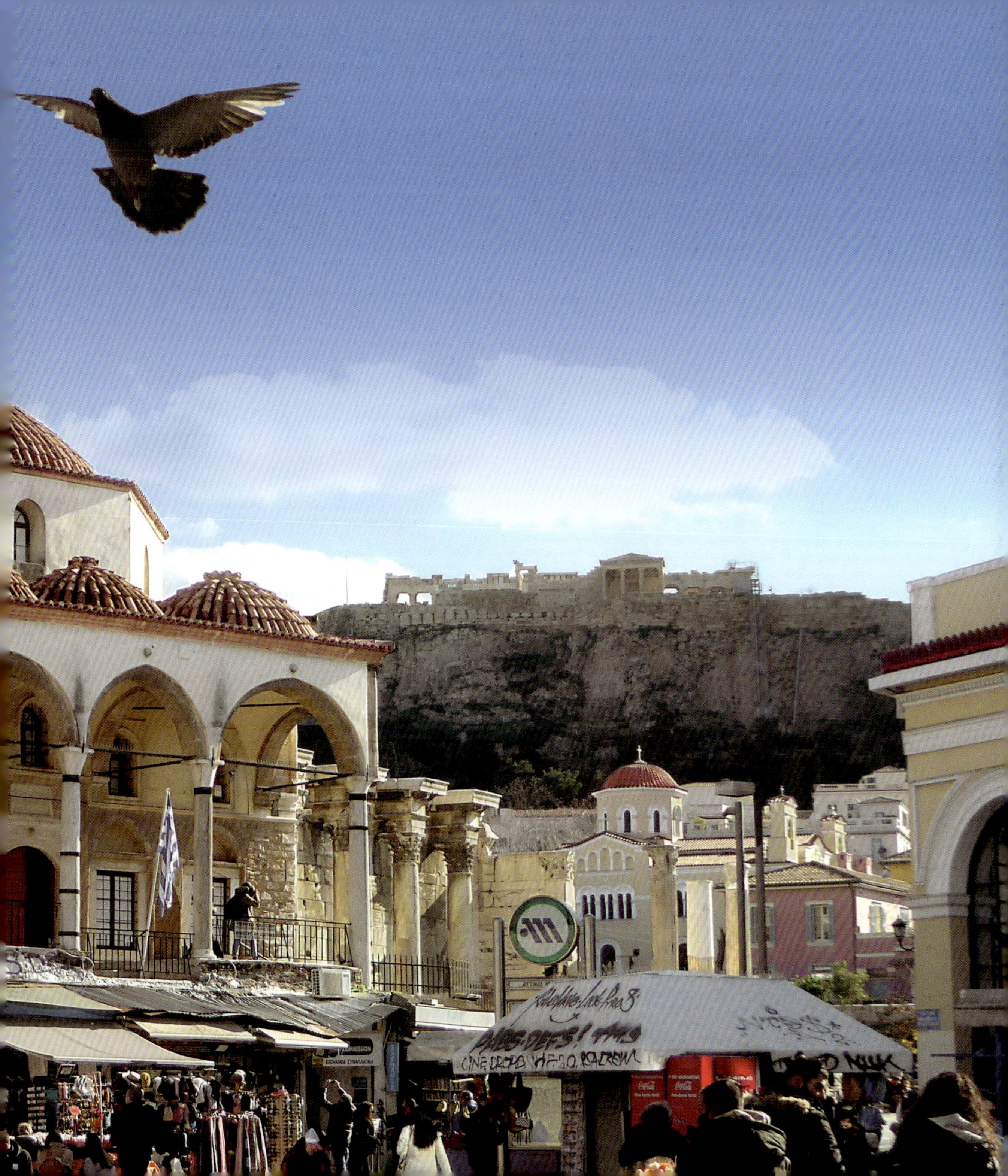

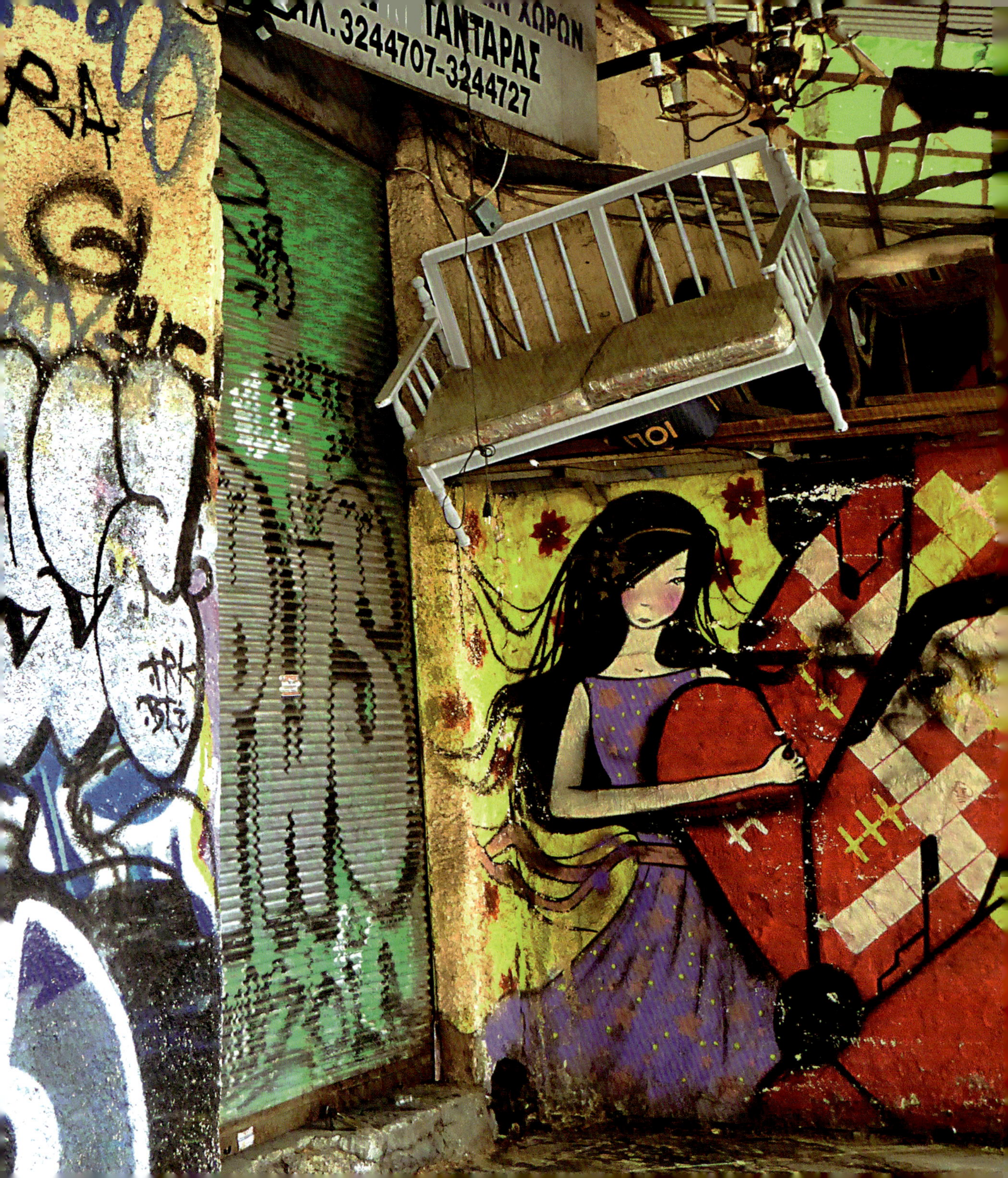
ΧΩΡΩΝ
ΤΑΝΤΑΡΑΣ
3244707-3244727

ABYSSINIAS SQUARE

Saturday morning on Abyssinias Square. Color everywhere dazzling under the light. Furniture, mirrors, art works, cast statues, coinage, jewelry, light fixtures, anything and everything one can imagine can be found here. There's something for every taste and purse. The prices range from a few euro to thousands. Look carefully, you never know what treasure awaits you.

Be forewarned. The store owners have already sized you up and they've already decided if they should cut you a deal or overcharge you. Hundreds of customers, rich and poor, have passed through the square, so don't intend to fool them. The ironic nickname, "loukoumades," or "sweet donuts," was given to them indicating their rough ways and grumpy dispositions.

The name of the square derives from the old Abyssinian population that originally settled in the area. By 1860 the small square was formed where used objects and clothes were sold. The square was known as Yusurum named after the Jewish merchants Elias and Noah Yusurum who established the first antique store on the square.

Abyssinias Square, *famous flea market and gathering place for antique enthusiasts and those looking for a bargain*

ABYSSINIAS SQUARE

As the story goes, after a downpour, he stopped at the square to rest and dry his clothes. While waiting, several passers-by became interested in buying the clothes. Yusurum did not miss the opportunity and that day he sold them all. An experienced tradesman with a winning personality, he decided to set up a permanent bench in the square. Other traders gathered following his example and the bazaar was established. At first only secondhand clothes were sold, so the modern expression, "Did you get your clothes at Yusurum?" implies their used quality.

In 1918 the Antique Dealers Association was formed, with the president elect a descendant of Noah Yusurum. To this day, if you search, you'll find a Yusurum family member maintaining an antique store.

Once the stores close for the night and the alleys grow quiet, let yourself be immersed in good food and music at "Abyssinian Café," or the near by "Cyclaminon" restaurant, two of the oldest establishments in the square.

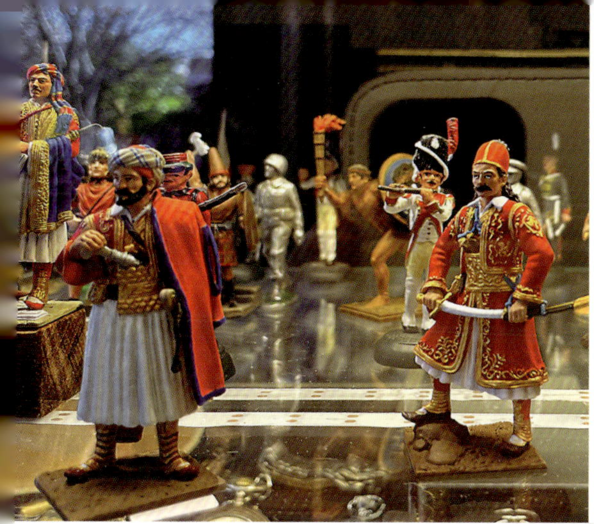

Top: *Rare miniature figures of Greek Independence Revolutionary Heroes*

Right: *Used books and ephemera store*

Following pages: *Antique window front with statue of goddess Artemis and other artifacts*

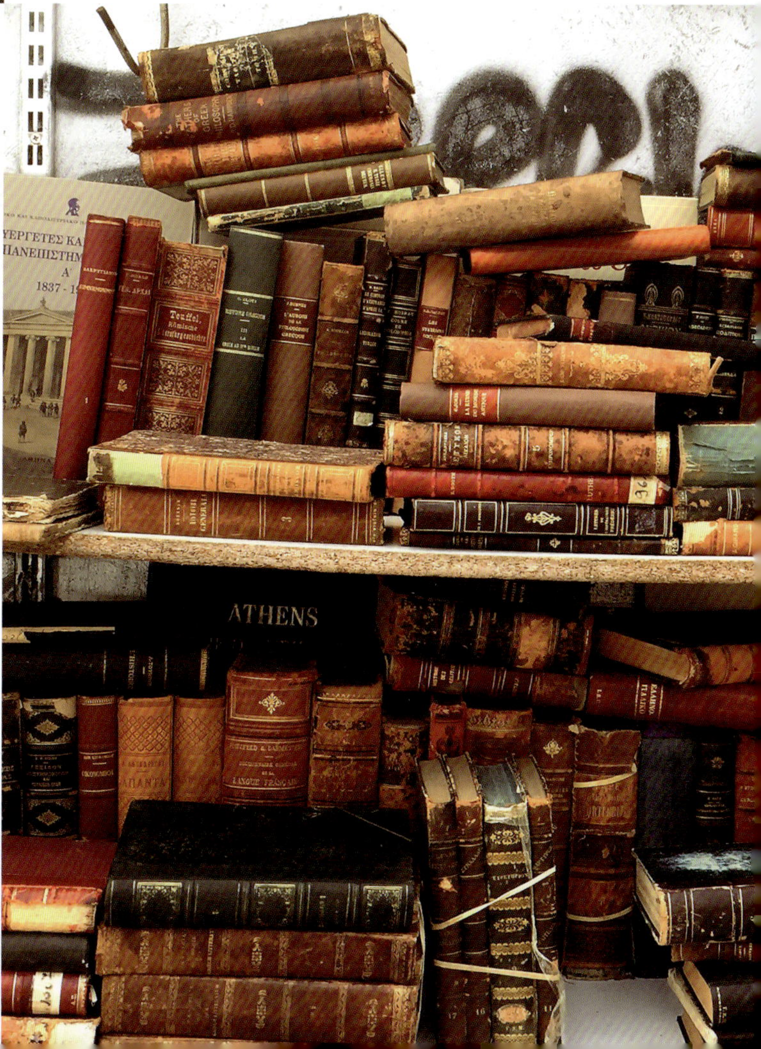

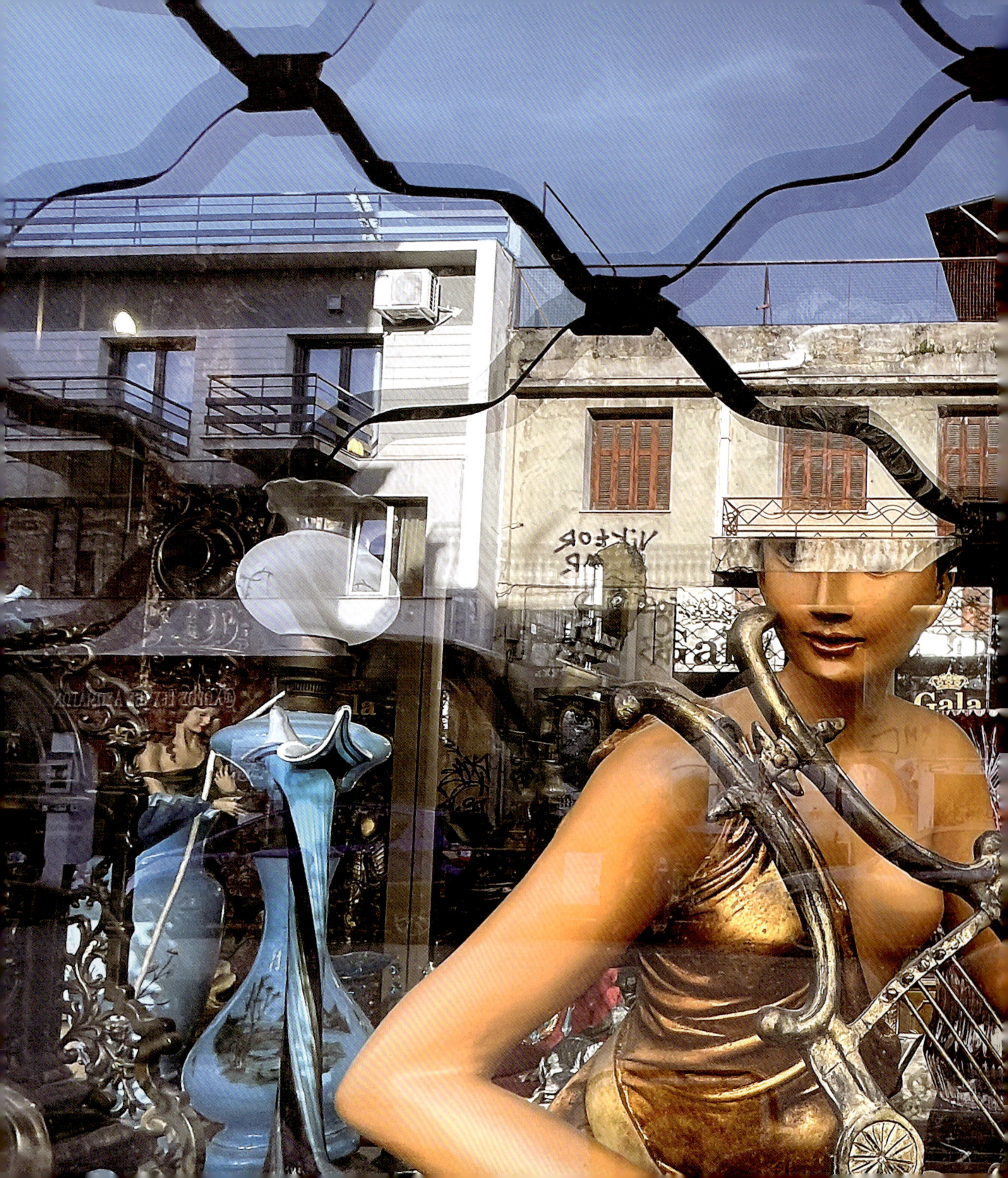
Gala

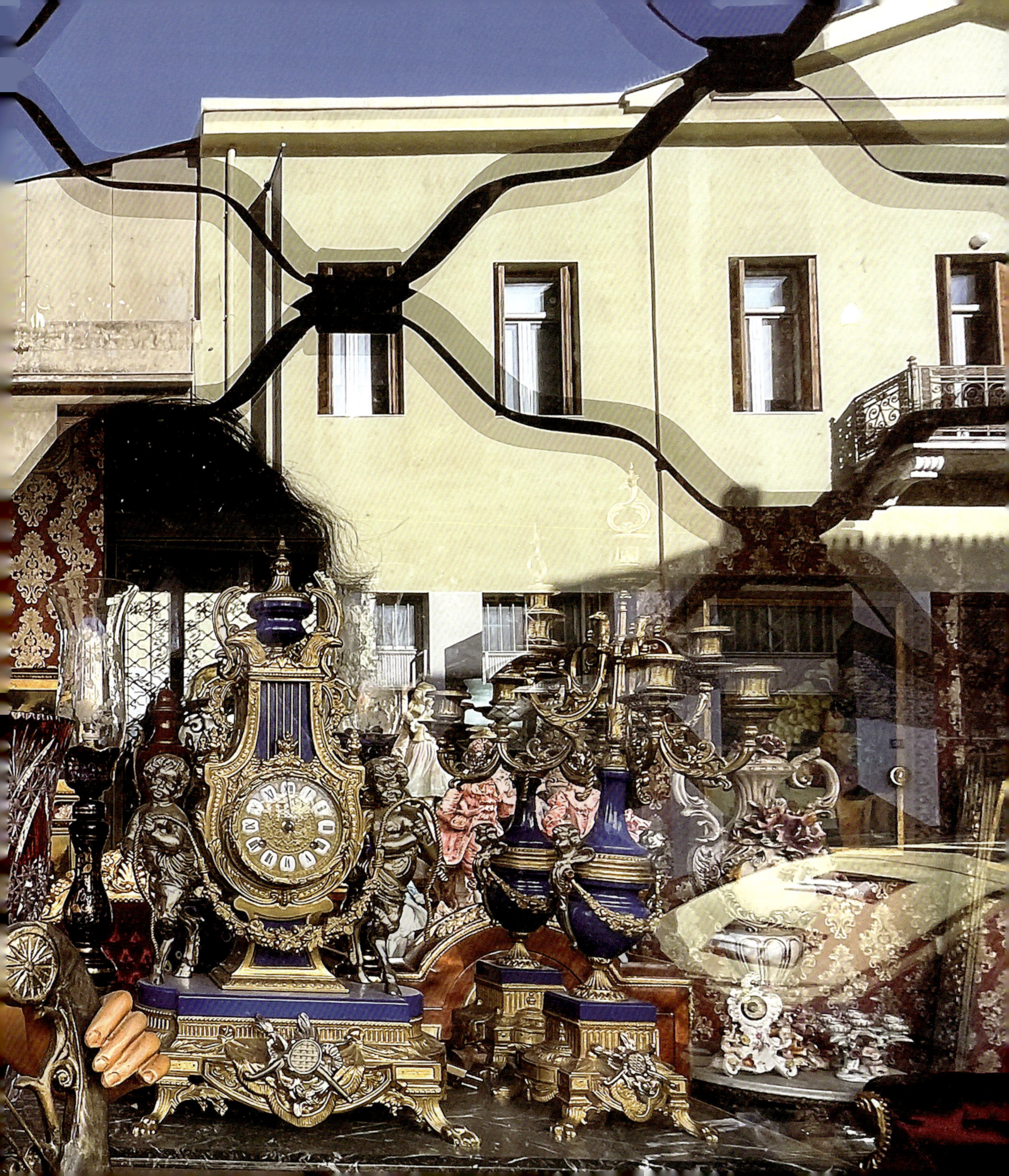

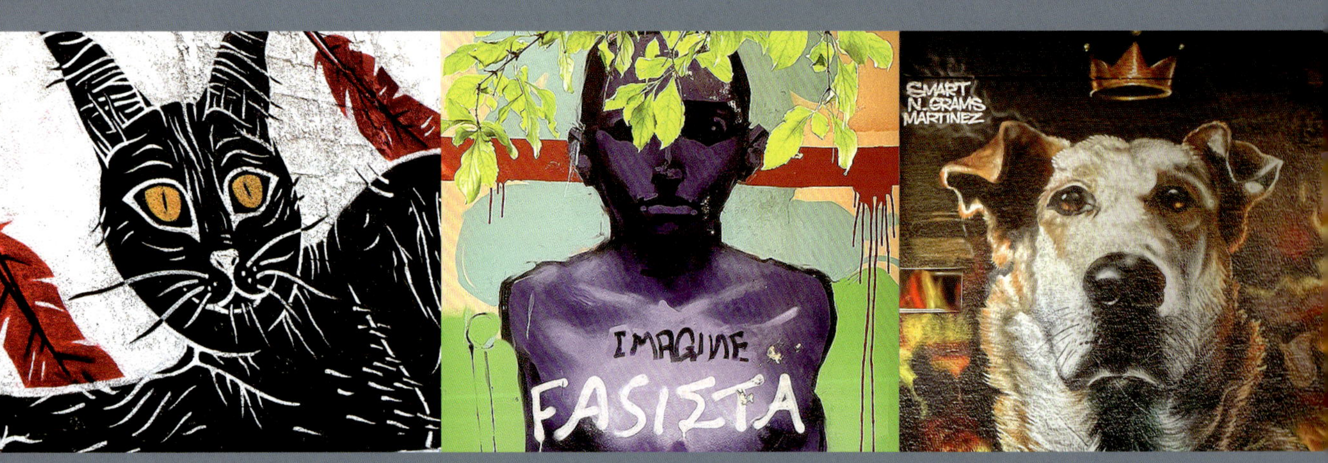
IMAGINE
FASISTA
SMART
N_GRAMS
MARTINEZ

NEIGHBORHOODS OF ILL REPUTE

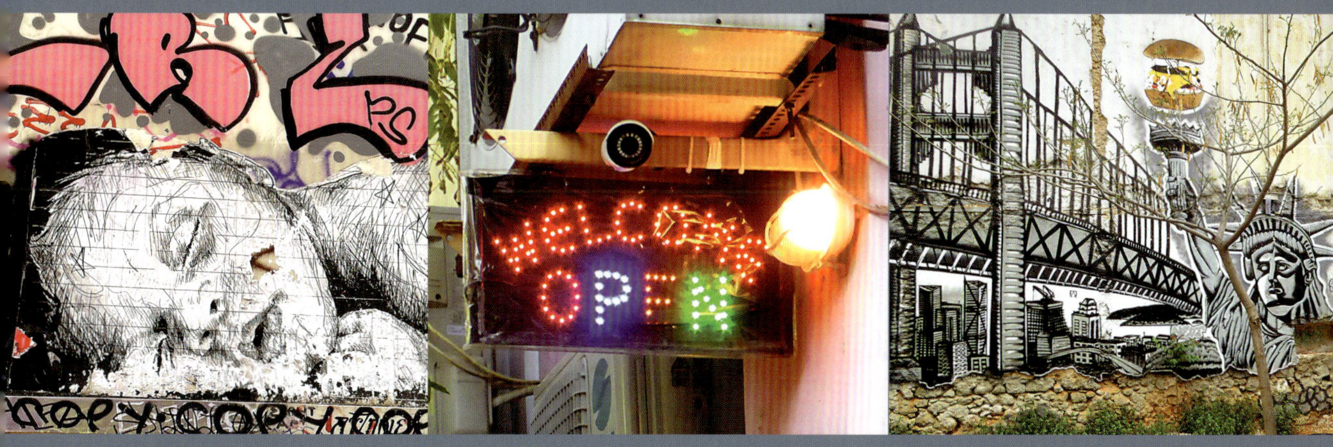

While the title of this section, Neighborhoods of "Ill Repute," implies run down and even dangerous areas, the intention is not to pass judgment, but to introduce some neighborhoods with equal historical and sociological importance that are often misunderstood or ignored.

I was fortunate enough to have grown up in Athens at a time when everything was in flux and the city was going through a transformative political period. The military junta had just collapsed, and an air of optimism was felt everywhere. People, tired of living in fear and oppression, spread their wings with the hope of bringing changes that mattered to all.

The "I" became "we." To ignore those in need was frowned upon. Students joined political parties, ranging from socialist to the far left, and marched for better education, healthcare, and wages. Musical festivals were attended in fully packed stadiums, where the music of Theodorakis, Markopoulos, Xatzidakis, and Xarxakos soared into the night sky.

Areas such as the Exarcheia and Psyrri were places of inspiration and so were the many bookstores and small tavernas, known as "koutoukia," where people gathered to listen to music, talk politics, and everything else in between. Conflicts with the police were common, and so were smashed windows and store fronts. The young were argumentative but also innocent, living the greatest times of a generation.

While the city celebrated its newly found freedom, at the other side of town the conditions of life remained abhorrent. People in the areas around the Metaxourgeio, Gazi, and Kolonos lived under the constant fear of gangs and criminals. Brothels, gambling joints, and opium dens pushed out those who could afford to leave, while an influx of refugees and the extremely poor moved in. Thefts, stabbings, and rape were common occurrences, while the police often turned a blind eye.

Today, these areas are changing. Young people have moved in, bringing with them an air of acceptance and the promise that different groups can coexist. The road is not an easy one; economic hardship and racism, complicate matters. The city needs uplifting. It needs vision, financial commitment and the belief that transformation is possible.

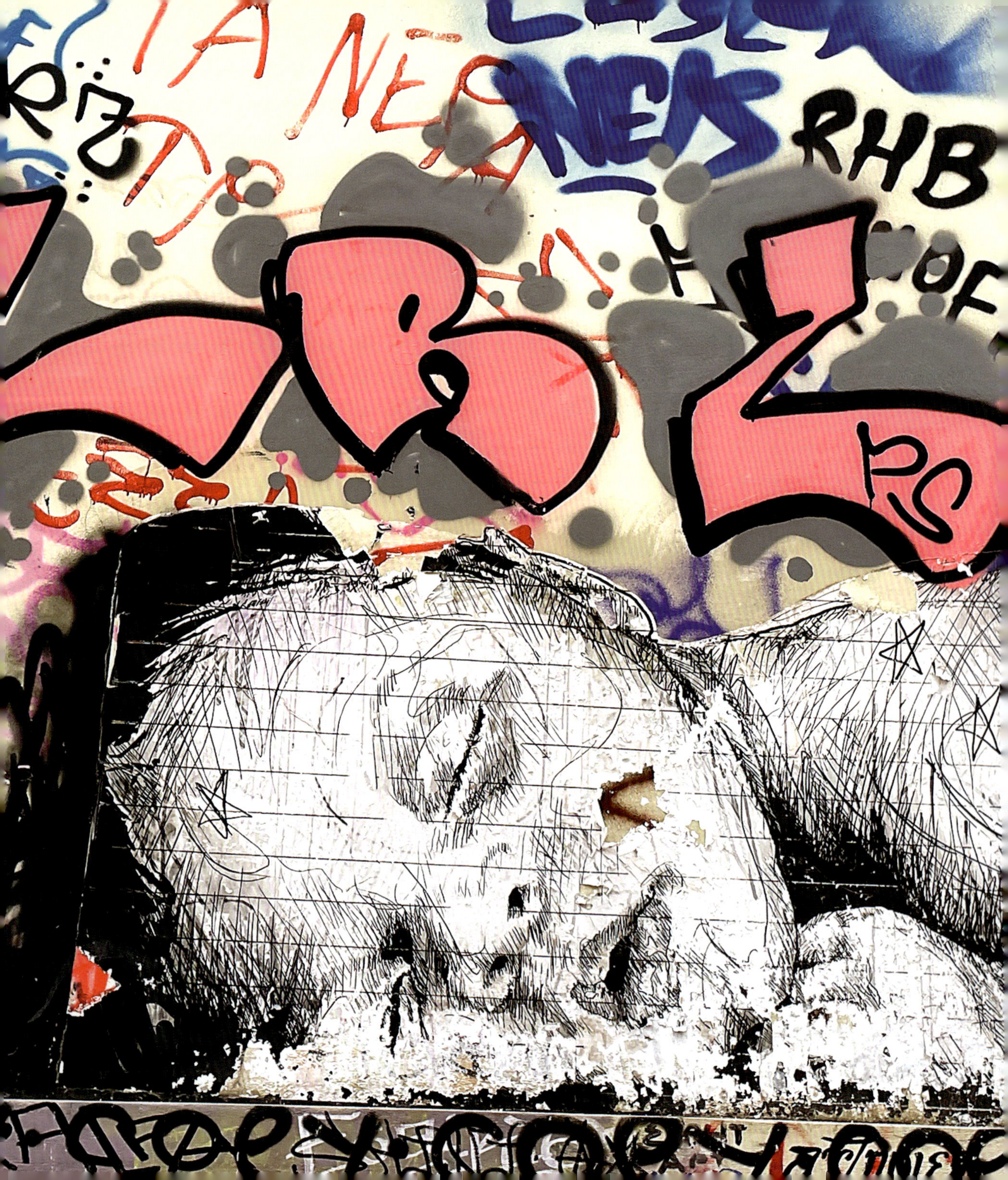
RHB

EXARCHEIA

For many, Exarcheia is synonymous with counterculture, eclectic bookstores, quaint cafes, music venues, and Avant Garde galleries. It's a place where artists, poets, musicians, writers, and students gather to talk about art and politics. For others, it's synonymous with graffiti filled walls, anarchists, transients, and Molotov cocktails. A place where anarchists and cops collide, often with casualties. Exarcheia is everything mentioned above and nothing at all. If you ask the locals, they'll simply tell you that it's only another neighborhood.

Originally, the area was called Neapolis, and it was the first suburb to appear outside the neighborhoods of Plaka, Thission, and Psyrri. The area was first inhabited by workers from the islands who came to Athens to help with the construction of the many neoclassical monuments. Each island had its own specialists: woodcarvers and loggers from Andros; quarry cutters from Tinos; well makers from Naxos; and builders from Karpathos.

At first, the neighborhood functioned independently from the city, since most of the necessary things could be found in the neighborhood. The houses of Neapolis were representative of the populist neoclassical

---

Exarcheia, *mural by artist Stms., Exarcheia*

architecture decorated with clay roofs and flanked at the four corners with terracotta heads, known as "akrokerama." They had indoor gardens, and wells for water.

Towards the middle of the nineteenth century, the first students from other parts of Greece arrived to study at the newly founded universities. The rent was cheap, and the locals looked after them, providing them with their basic needs. It was not uncommon to see lines of young men waiting to be fed at the small tavernas. The area very quickly acquired a youthful character, with late night gatherings and music playing, flute being the favorite instrument.

In 1880, the area changed its name to Exarcheia, although the northeastern part is still called Neapolis, named after Basilios Exarchos, a grocer from "Ipeiros." Exarchos was known for the best olive oil in the area, and soon his fame spread to all Athenians who came to Exarcheia to shop.

The flux of students and intellectuals led Exarcheia to be known as the anti-commercial, anti-capitalist neighborhood of Greece, if not Europe.

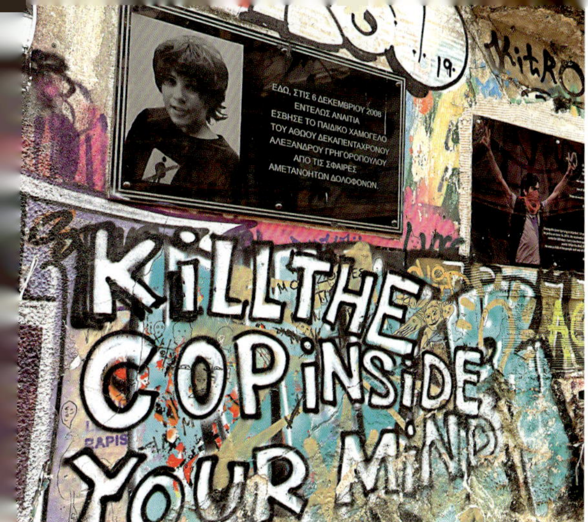

Top: *Memorial plaque commemorating the death of fifteen-year-old student, Alexandros Grigoropoulos, innocent victim of police brutality, Exarcheia Square*

Right: *Mural, Exarcheia Square*

Following pages: *"Dreaming of Matisse," Themistokleous Street and Methonis, Exarcheia*

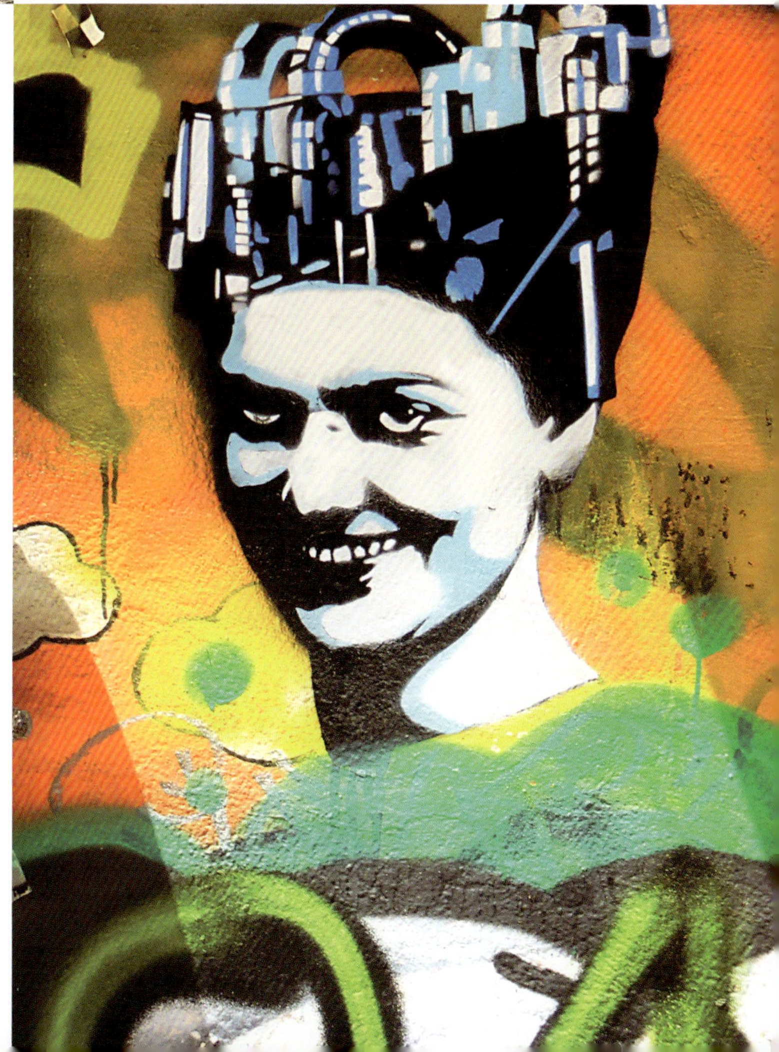

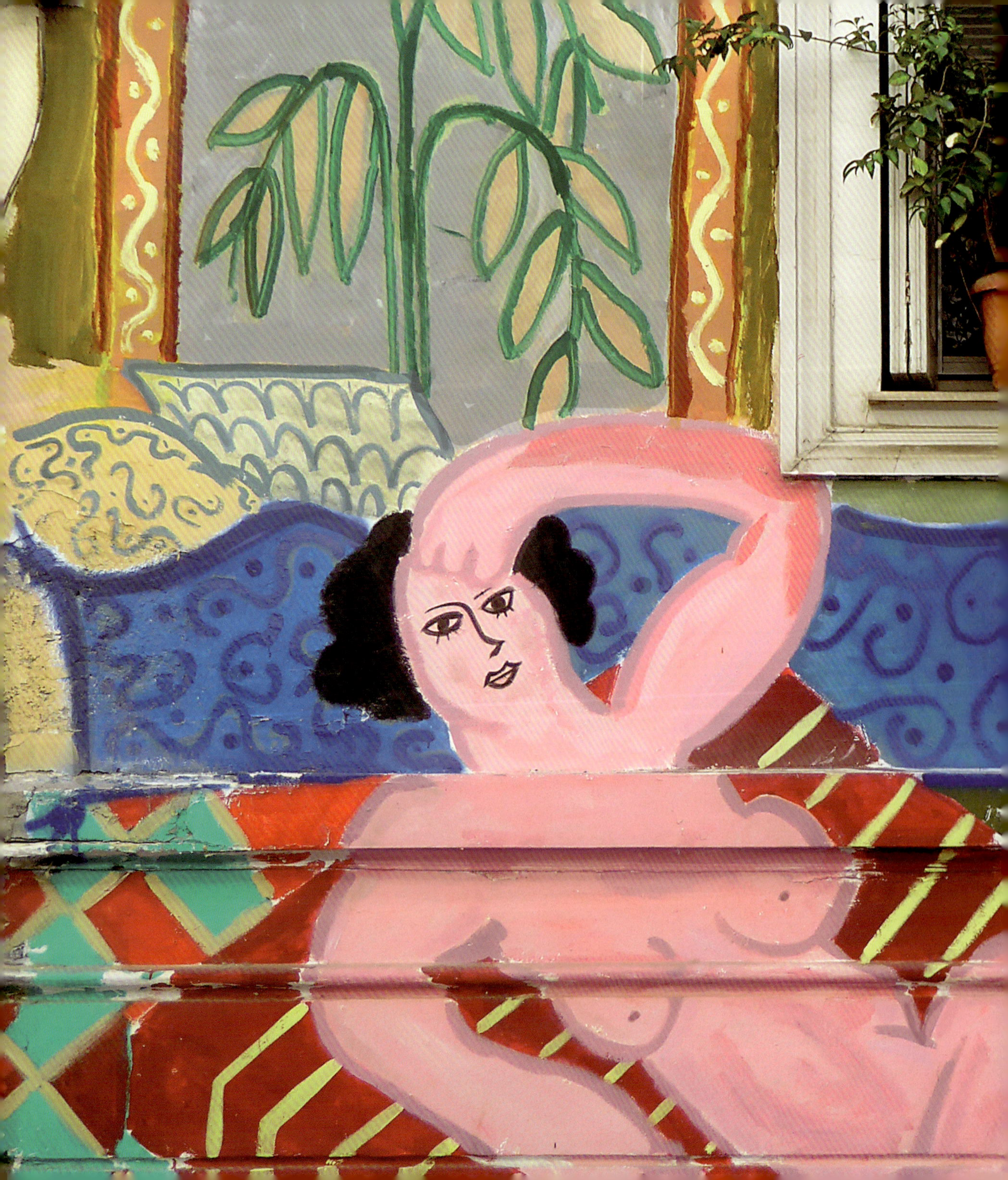

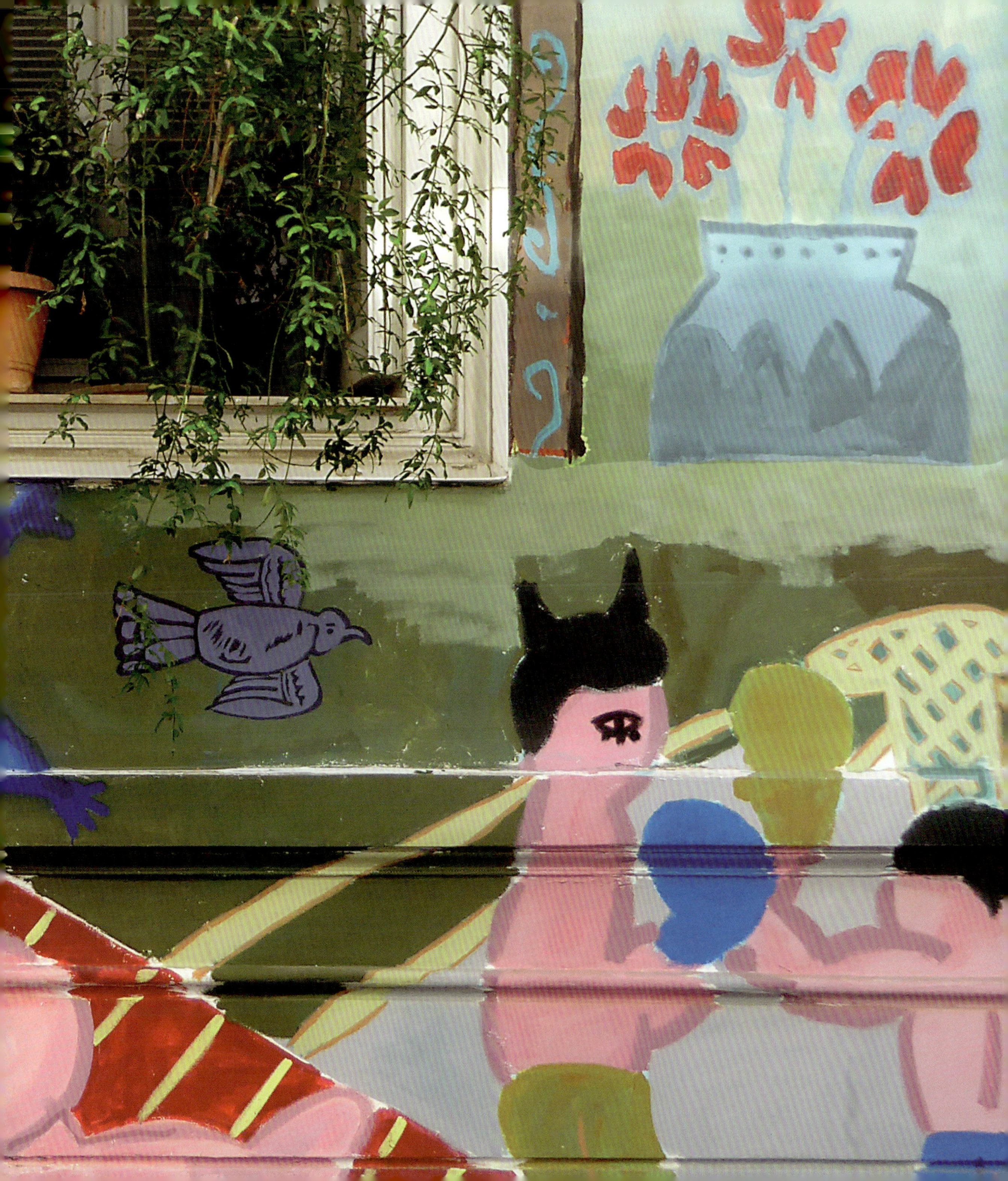

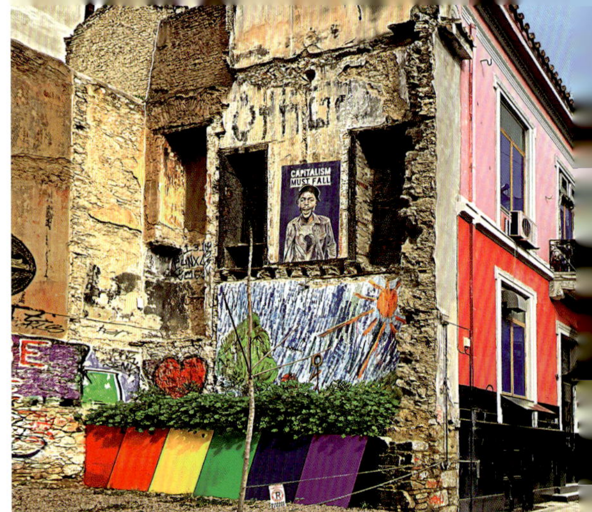

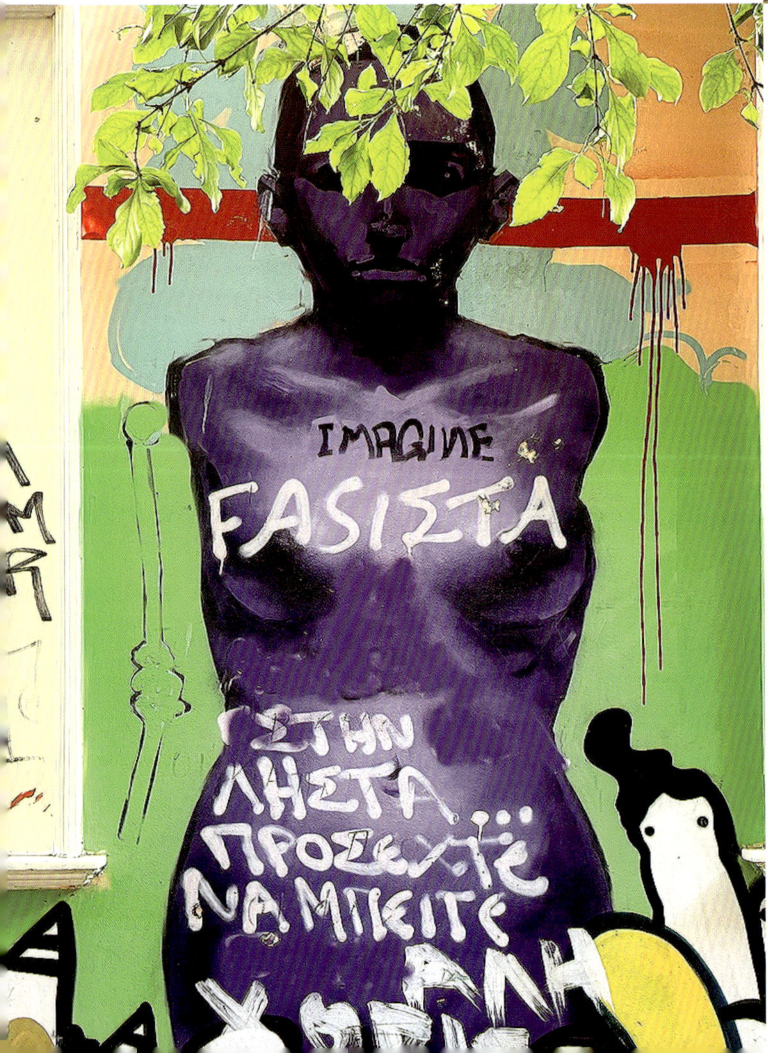

Top: *House painted in LGBTQ Pride colors and Black Lives Matter mural, Exarcheia*

Left: *"Fasista," Methonis Street and "Electric Woman," Exarcheia*

EXARCHEIA

Famous Greek poets and writers lived and worked here, establishing some of the most important publishing houses of Athens.

The first serious clashes in Exarcheia occurred in 1895, when a group of students from the National Technical University of Athens, led by Kleon Raggavis, protested the King's autocracy and the imports of luxury goods, such as gloves, canes, and hats. The students, wearing the traditional peasant hats from the island of Sifnos, clashed with merchants, who wore tattered hats to make fun of the students. The police intervened and many students were arrested. The event is known as "Skiadia," from the brim of the hat that creates shade.

Exarcheia has had a long history of political and intellectual activism. The original anarchists were well educated with ideals, but their messages were slowly diluted. Today, the old anarchists have been replaced by groups of masked men, with no political affiliations, or neo-Nazis often posing as anarchists. However, don't let this stop you; the neighborhood is filled with well-intentioned people, neoclassical buildings converted into quaint restaurants, and outdoor bars. Come visit and let the spirit sway you.

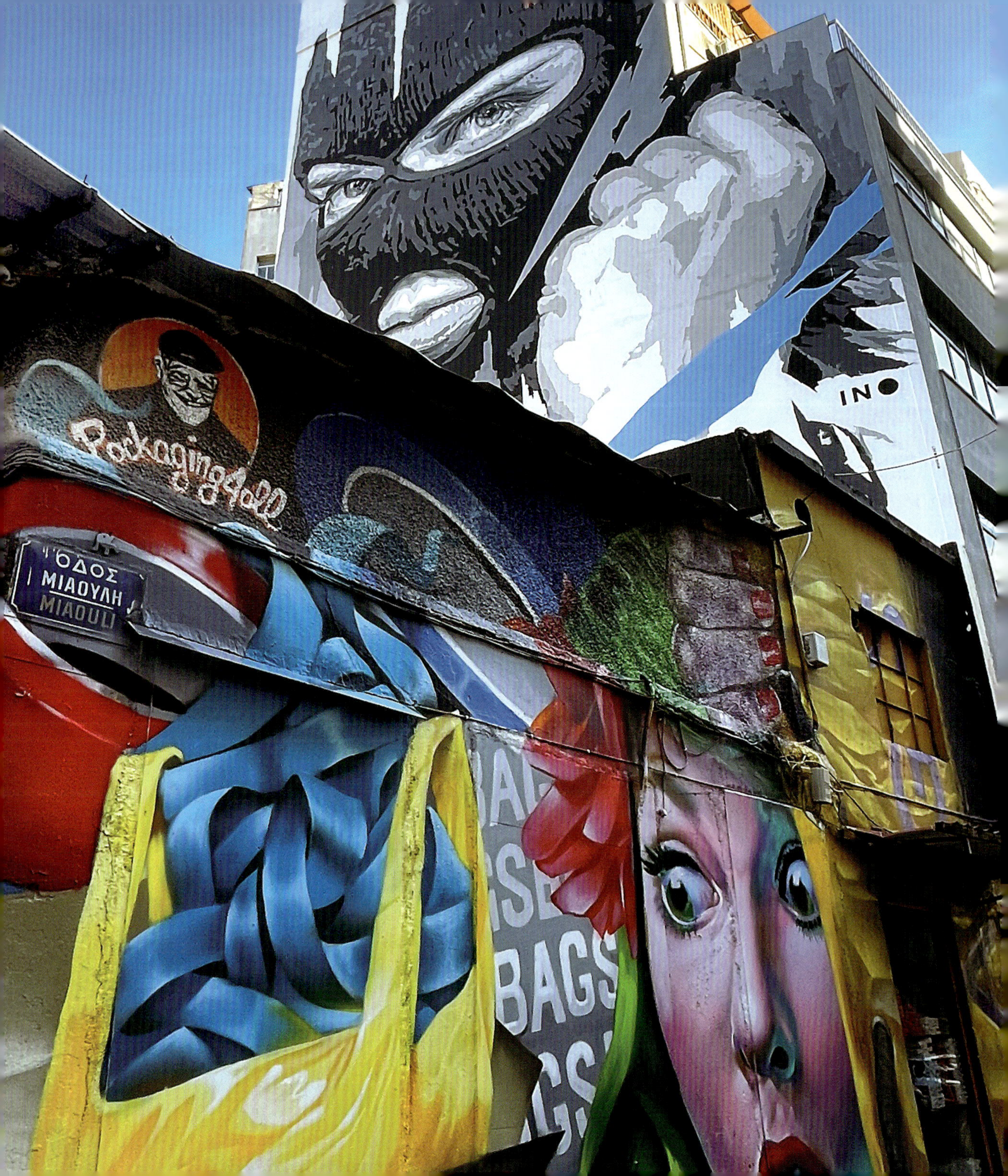
ΟΔΟΣ
ΜΙΑΟΥΛΗ
MIAOULI
Packaging4all
INO
BAGS

PSYRRI

One of the oldest neighborhoods of Athens, named after Psyrris, a wealthy landowner, or from the first workers from the island of Psara who settled there. Psyrri was a tightly built enclave, with small homes, adjacent to each other. The houses followed a simple architecture of two floors, a small balcony, and an inside porch. Small craft shops and vendors dotted the streets, selling the most necessary goods.

Following the revolution of 1821, many prominent merchants moved there, as well as many revolutionary generals, some of them deeply embittered by the political conflicts that followed the revolution. "Plateia Iroon," Heroes Square, a square that still stands today, was known as a gathering place where the old revolutionaries met to discuss politics and express their dissatisfaction.

Psyrri was also the most famed neighborhood where many foreign travelers, visitors, and recorders stayed, Lord Byron among them. Lord Byron rented a room at the house of the widow Makri, wife of the deceased

---

Miaouli Street, *background mural, Apocalypse Now, by muralist INO; foreground mural by Alex Martinez*

British Deputy Consul, Theodore Makris, and her three daughters. Byron fell in love and married the youngest daughter, Teressa, although she was only 13 years old. His famous poem, "Daughter of Athens," was written for her.

Artists and painters also found inspiration there, among them the French painter Louis Dupré, and Yannis Tsarouchis, known for his famous painting titled, "Caryatids House." Another famous inhabitant of Psyrri was the writer Alexandros Papadiamantis. He lived in the district for over 20 years, and for that he was given the nickname the "Hermit of Psyrri."

Between 1862 to 1897, the area became a haven for thieves, murderers, and robbers, and it was considered the most dangerous place in Athens. Various gangs ruled the area, among them the infamous group known as "Koutsabakides." Their trademark look was longish unwashed hair, bangs that covered one eye and a stiff mustache. They dressed in white shirts and black jackets, with one sleeve hanging from the shoulder, and red belts to hold their guns. A black hat, a symbol of mourning for their dead friends, wide-legged pants, and pointed shoes with high heels, were the epitome of the style.

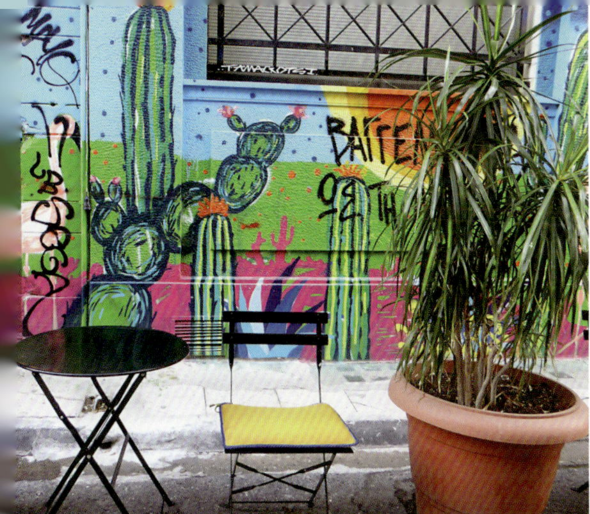

***Top:** "Plateia Iroon," meaning "Heroes Square;" old gathering place for Greek Independence War revolutionaries, today major hub with coffee shops and restaurants*

***Right:** All dogs go to heaven, mural by Smart, N. Grams, and Martinez in tribute of "Loukanikos," or "Sausage," famous Greek riot dog that participated in almost every anti-austerity protest in Athens*

***Following Pages:** 45 Agion Asomaton Street, Caryatids with folded hands, inspiration for French photographer Henri Cartier-Bresson and the Greek painter Yiannis Tsarouchis*

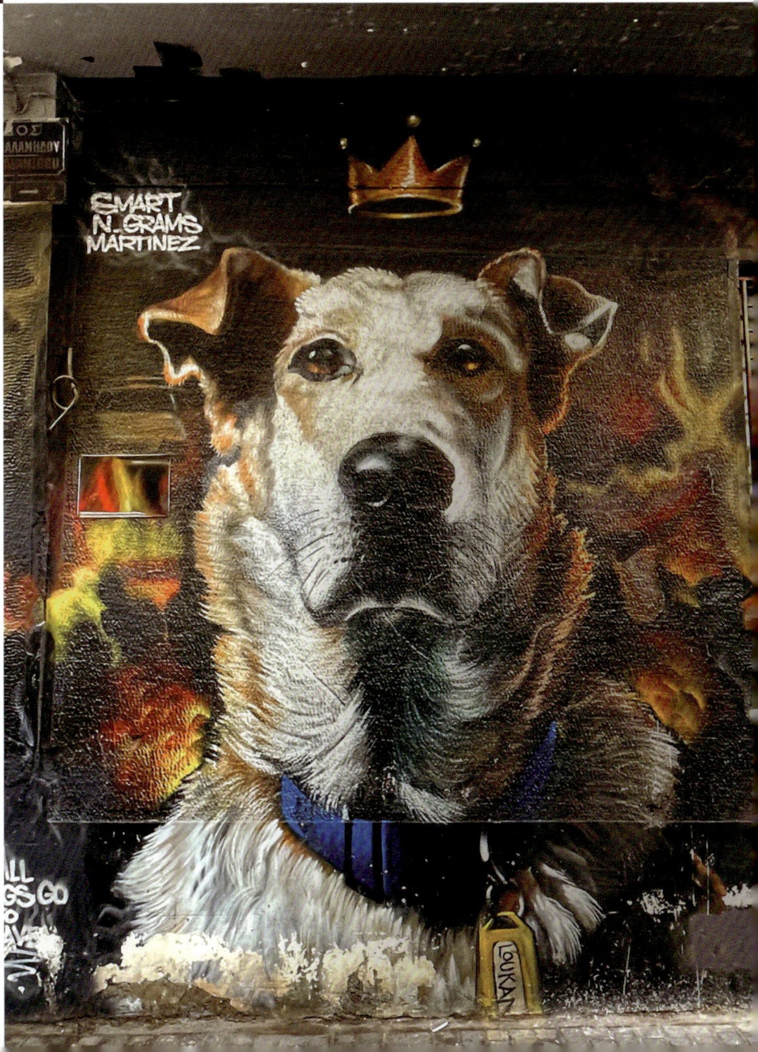

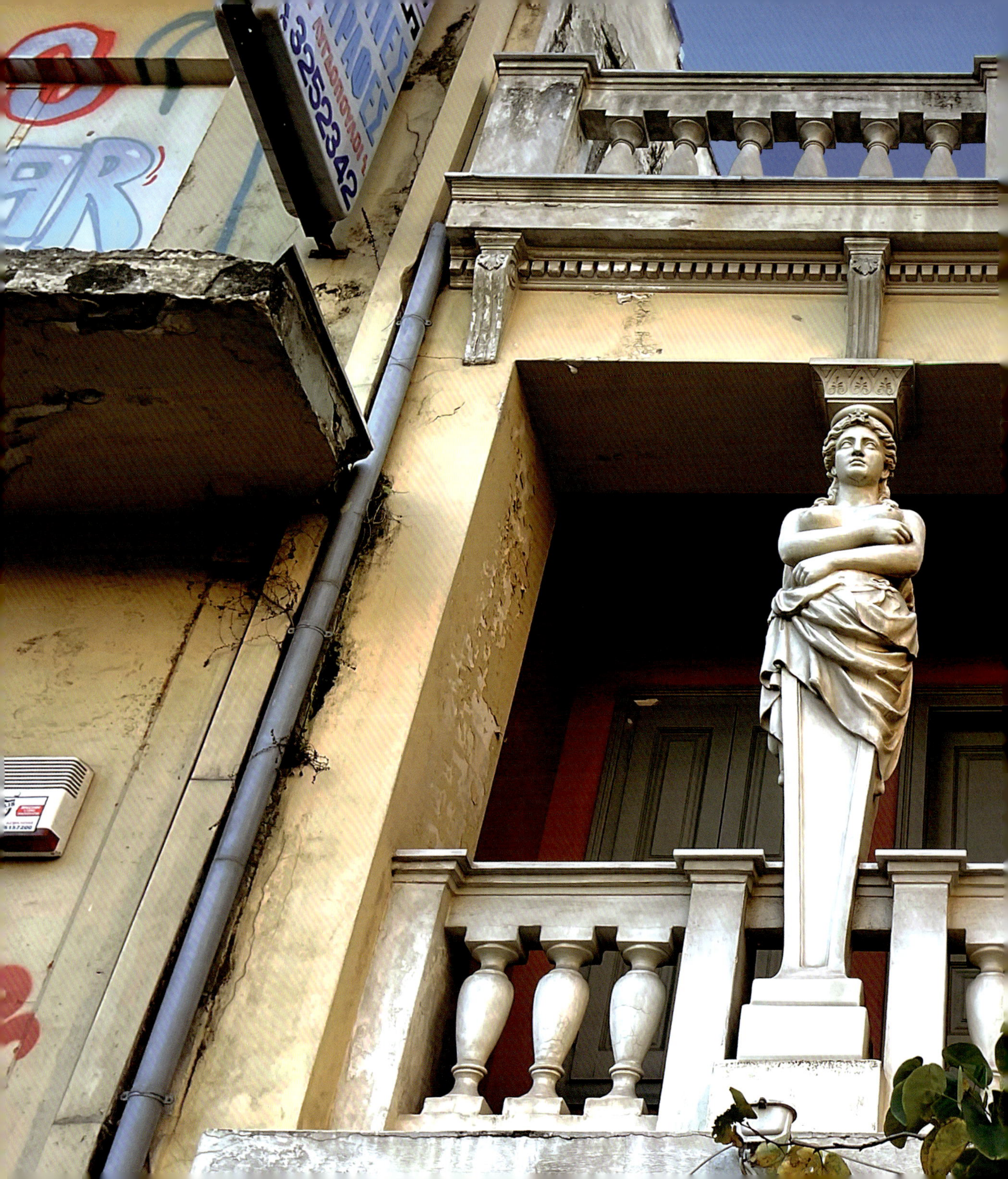
3252342

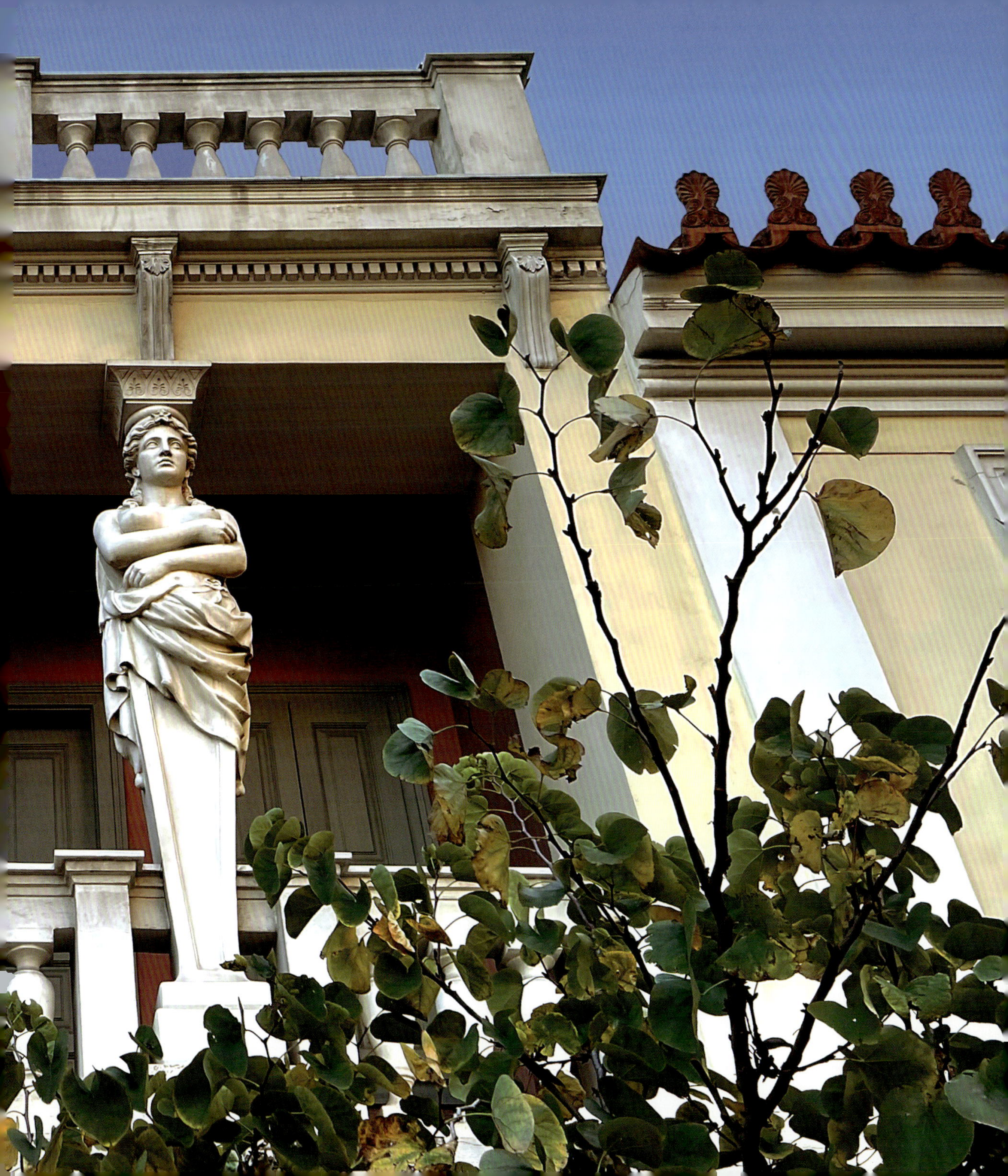

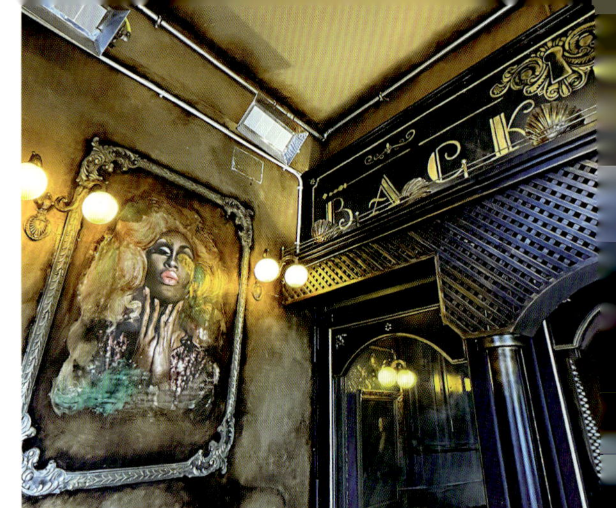

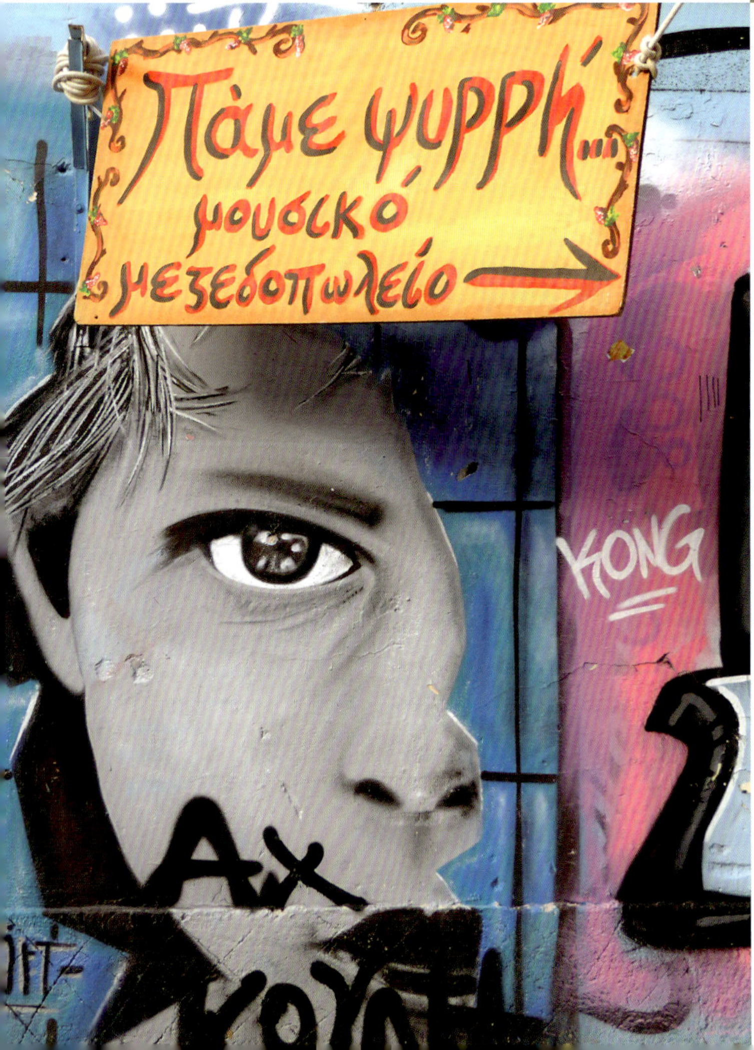

Top: *Popular bar on Sarri Street*

Left: *"Let's go to Psyrri, Mousiko Mezedopoleio," Greek taverna with live music*

Other famous gangs were the "Mortides," a group of men who performed all burials, particularly after the plague of 1854 that hit Athens, and the "Trabucos," named after the famous Cuban cigars they smoked known as "Trabucos." The Trabucos were often brought in by various political parties to create mayhem, threaten, and even murder their opponents.

The reign of the above groups came to an end by 1890, when the police commissioner Mpaikartzis, set upon a campaign for their extinction. At their arrests, the culprits were humiliated by chopping off their hair, tearing their long sleeve and having them destroy their own guns, the ultimate shame for a tough guy.

A very popular musical style, known as "Rebetika," also found a home in Psyrri neighborhood. Most of the songs were written by prisoners and dealt with love, abandonment, drugs, prostitution, and death. Rebetika was inspired by traditional Greek folk music, Byzantine, and Balkan music, along with music from Turkey and Asia Minor. The importance of the songs remains to this day and are considered the most loved and influential songs in Greece.

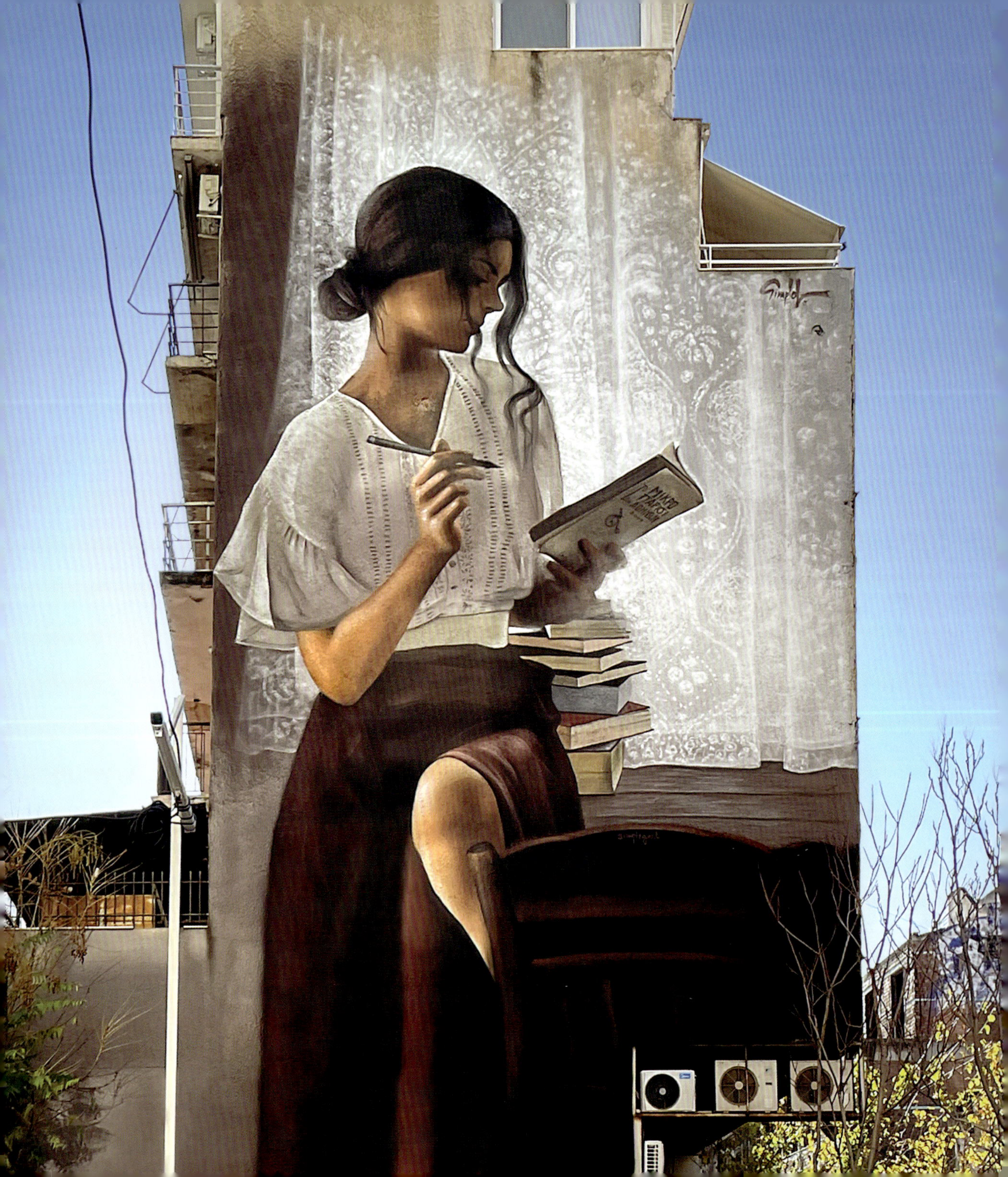

METAXOURGEIO

Early morning on a crisp winter day taking photographs. My sister and I are walking on Iasonos Street, one of the most notorious areas in Metaxourgeio. Bright pink and yellow neoclassical buildings with cypress green shutters stand on both sides of the street, in a sad effort to look inviting. They however do little to erase the sense of decay that clings in the air, as if the street has been soaked in pain.

A group of men hurry inside a building with a "Welcome" sign at the door. Across the street, two more men walk up a basement's steps, still zipping up their pants. It's hardly nine o'clock in the morning, but business seems to be thriving.

Metaxourgeio is one of the poorest, but upcoming, neighborhoods in Athens. It's named after a silk factory that operated during the middle of the nineteenth century under the name, "Serian Company of Greece Athanasios Douroutis & Co," owned by the Douroutis brothers.

Metaxourgeio, *So Many Books, So Little Time, mural by Simple G, 2 Megalou Alexandrou Street*

METAXOURGEIO

The area was also known as the "Minotaur" or the "Waste Dumps" because all the human waste of Athens accumulated there. The stench, depending upon how the wind blew, could reach all the way to the palace.

Illnesses such as typhoid, dysentery, and cholera were prevalent among the many poor families living in the area. They worked primarily in the gas and silk factories, hardly making ends meet. Because of the sewage sludge, fruit trees and vegetables grew in abundance and were sold in the main vegetable markets often causing outbreaks of cholera and typhoid.

The silk factory, originally designed for Prince Georgios Katakouzinos as his private residence, was never occupied because of the stench, and so the house became the silk factory.

A satirical novel by the famous Greek writer Dimitris Psathas titled, "Madame Sousou," best describes the dire conditions of the area and offers an excellent sociopolitical testament of the time period. Madame Sousou is an imaginative woman who wants to move up in society and settle in

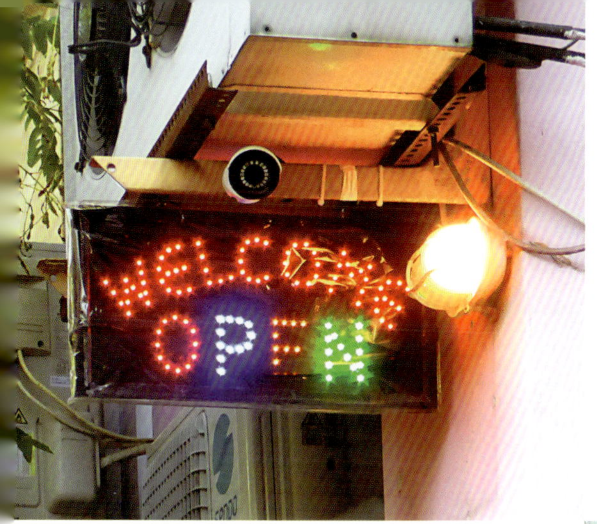

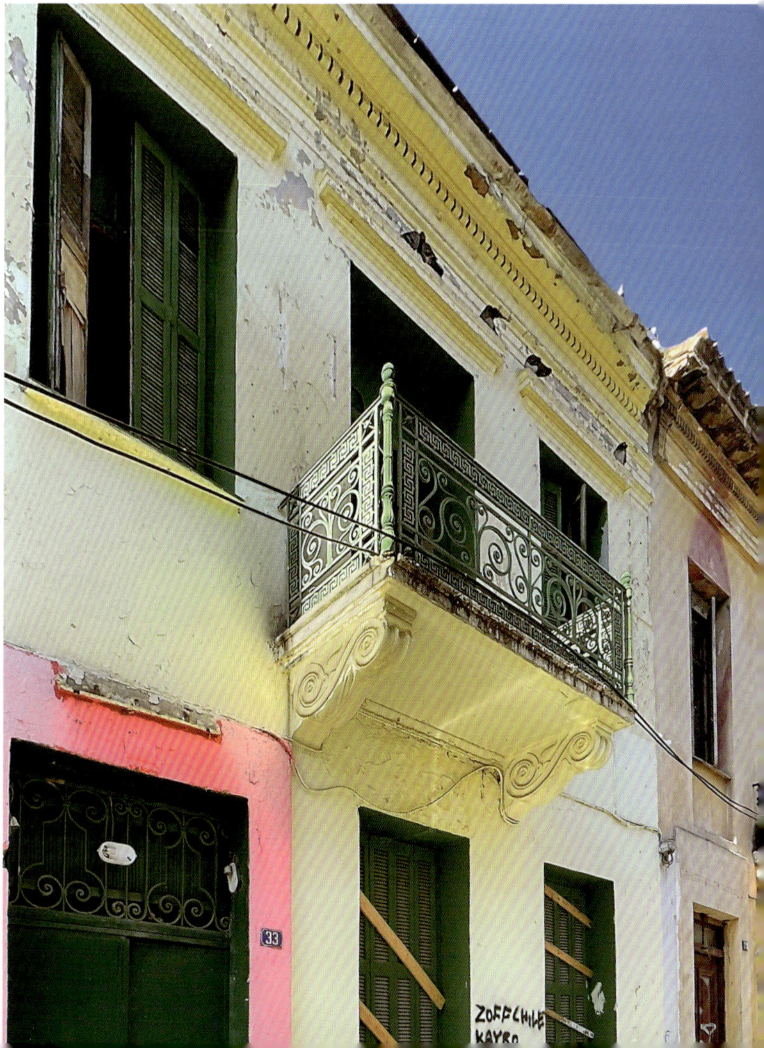

Top: *Sex sign welcoming clients; red light district, Metaxourgeio area*

Right: *Jason Street, famed for its abandoned neoclassical buildings and brothels*

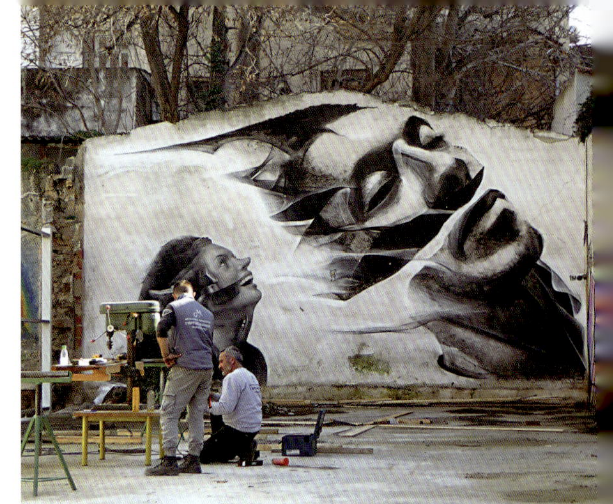

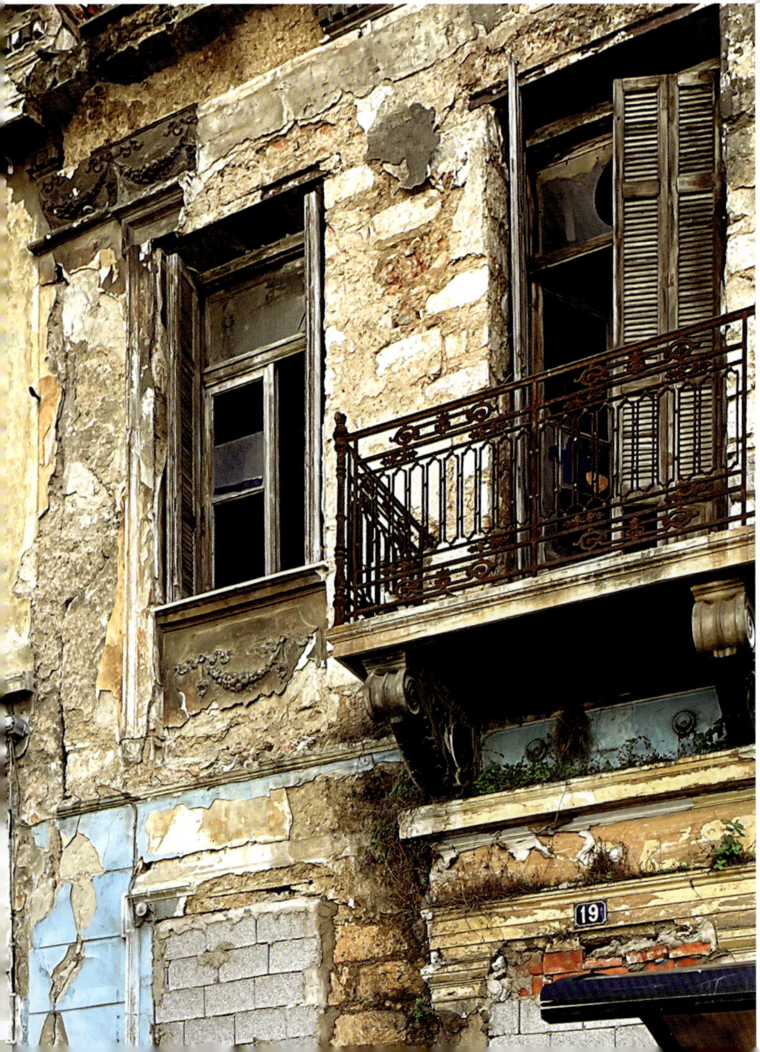

Top: *Alley with hidden mural by artist, INO*

Left: *Abandoned house with old pharmacy sign and gathering place for squatters*

Following pages: *Mural by artists BarbaDee and Onebran on Salaminos Street*

aristocratic Kolonaki, although she never abandons her neighborhood. The novel was adapted as a play and later revised for cinema and television.

Despite the poverty, Metaxourgeio was known for its musical vibrancy, and it was here that the first local choirs were formed under the tutelage of Italian workers, who were hired at the nearby hat factory. "Apokries," or Mardi Gras, was another holiday celebrated with great gaiety. People dressed in costumes and paraded the streets holding the "Gaitanaki," a pole decorated with garlands that children danced around.

Today Metaxourgeio, with its small houses, ground floor buildings, and small abandoned neoclassical buildings, is a place worth exploring. Bars and restaurants, art galleries, lush courtyards, and balconies facing the Acropolis, turn this small neighborhood into a time capsule of nineteenth-century Athens.

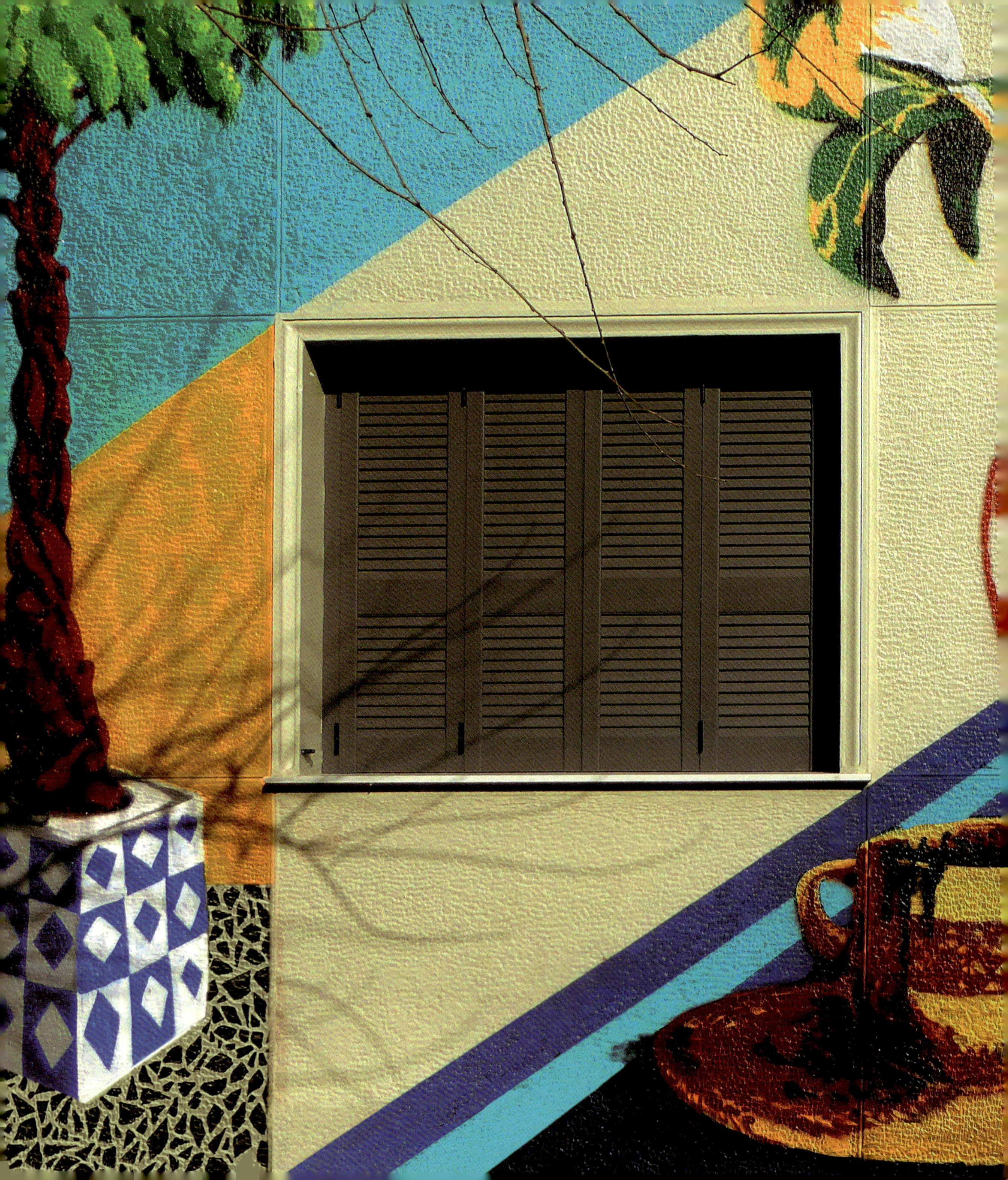

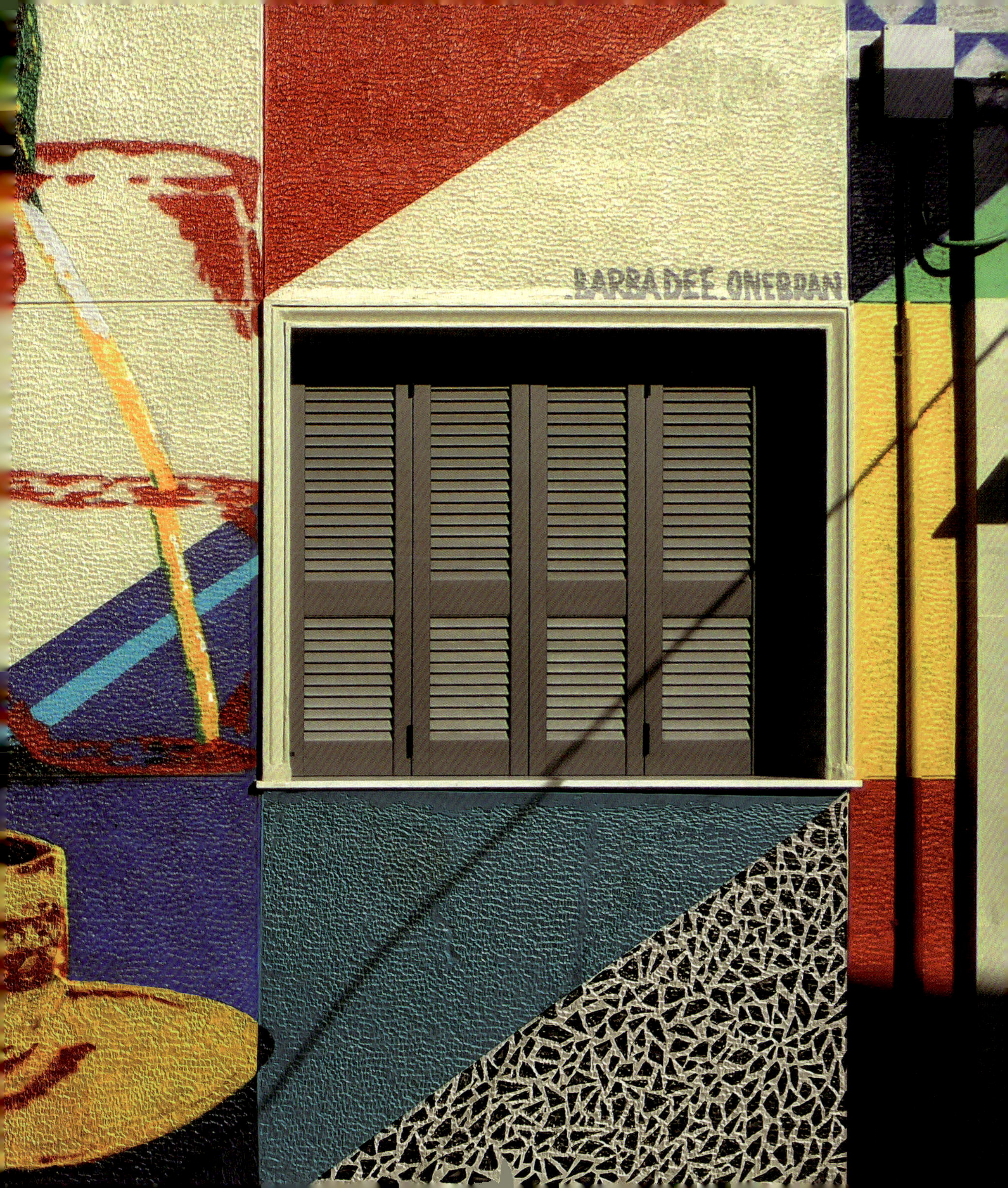

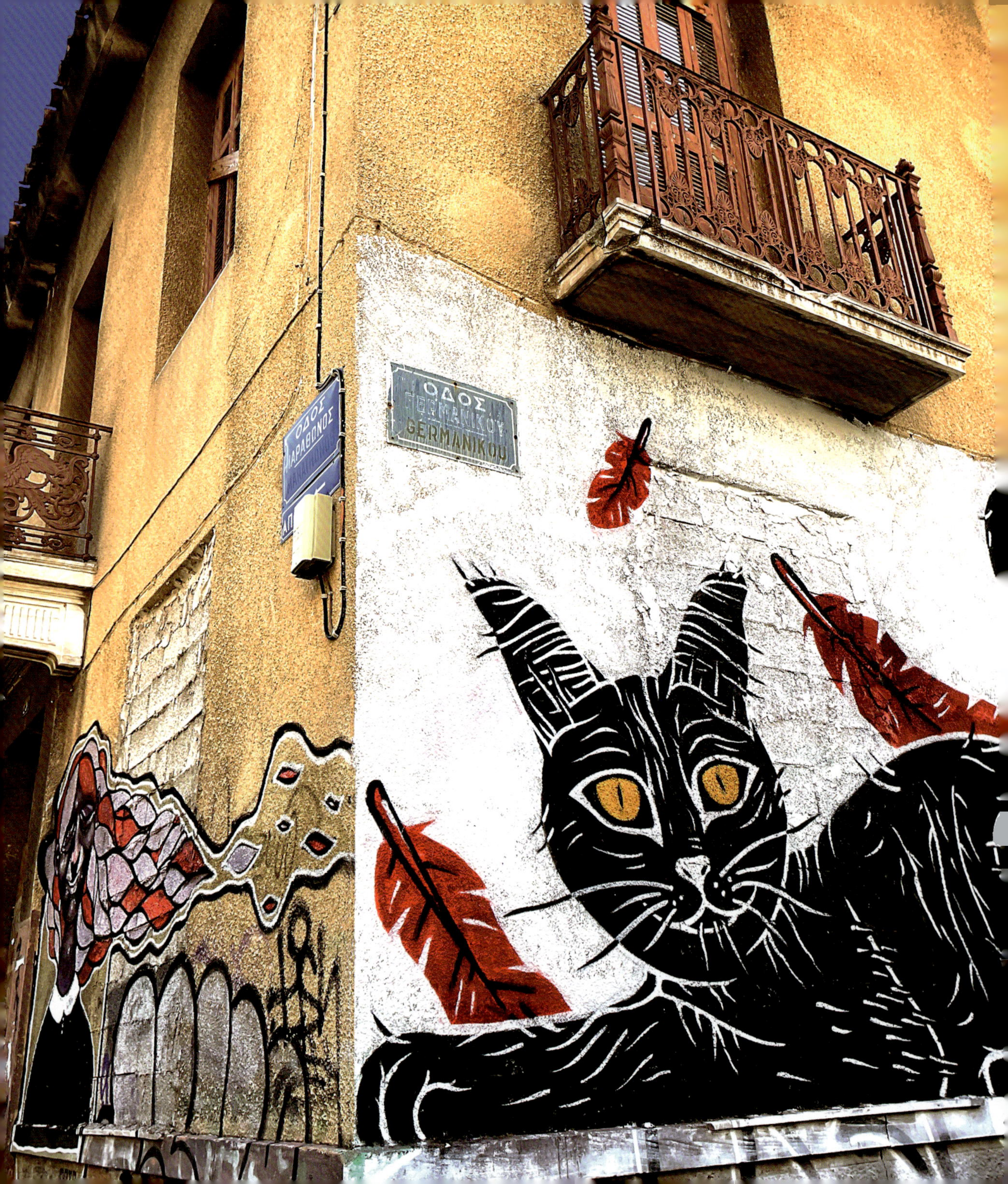
ΟΔΟΣ
ΜΑΡΑΘΩΝΟΣ
ΟΔΟΣ
ΓΕΡΜΑΝΙΚΟΥ
GERMANIKOU

KERAMEIKOS

Early morning in Kerameikos Street. A stray cat jumps over a heap of garbage and scurries away. Above me, the sky stretches bluer than ever. I walk quietly, as if trying not to awaken the ancient spirits of men and women of antiquity whose names and faces have long faded away. Their presence is felt everywhere, coexisting with the modern inhabitants, often visiting them in their dreams.

Kerameikos Street, one of the oldest streets in Athens, was originally known as "Acacia Street," so named after the rows of acacia trees that grew there. Walking on this narrow street is like stepping into the soul of the city and peeling it back, layer after layer. Neoclassical buildings, alleys leading to other alleys, small squares, quaint cafés, art galleries and the ever present brothels, are all a part of this hardly known area that deserves so much more.

The street begins at Omonoia Square and ends in Iera Odos, close to Technopolis and the Kerameikos Cemetery. Kolonou, Kolokynthou, Thermopylae, Salaminos, and Mykalis are a few of the intersecting streets worth losing yourself in.

Germanikou and Marathonos Streets, *cat mural guarding the street*

KERAMEIKOS

Like Alice in Wonderland, every step you take brings you closer to an unexplored world. "Paramythias Street," or Fairytale Street, is one of those enchanting streets. A mysterious tower, once owned by the Jewish family, Sarfati, now functions as the art center, "Communitism." It's here that young people gather at the steps to talk about art or prepare for another exhibit.

The Leontos Avdi Square nearby, named after Leontos Avdi, a member of the communist party, is another quiet spot to relax in with plenty of greenery and trendy restaurants. Opposite the square is the new "Municipal Gallery of Athens" that was once the silk factory.

At the end of The Second World War, Kerameikos, a deeply democratic neighborhood, became the scene of fighting between Greek partisans and British forces. In the walls, one can still see the imprints left by the bullets from the battles fought to determine Greece's political future.

Today, the area is primarily occupied by immigrants and refugees, although a lot of younger Athenians are slowly moving in, tastefully restoring the old homes, and bringing to Kerameikos a new balance and energy.

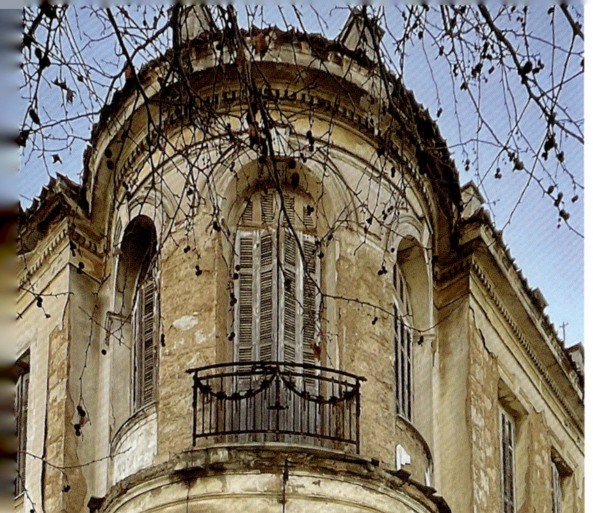

Top: *"Communitism," cultural center promoting arts and the environment; 28 Kerameikou and Paramythias Streets*

Right: *System of a Fraud, by artist INO, Achilleos Street*

Following page: *"Orizontas Gegonoton," or "Event Horizon;" multi space art center; 88 Keramikou Street*

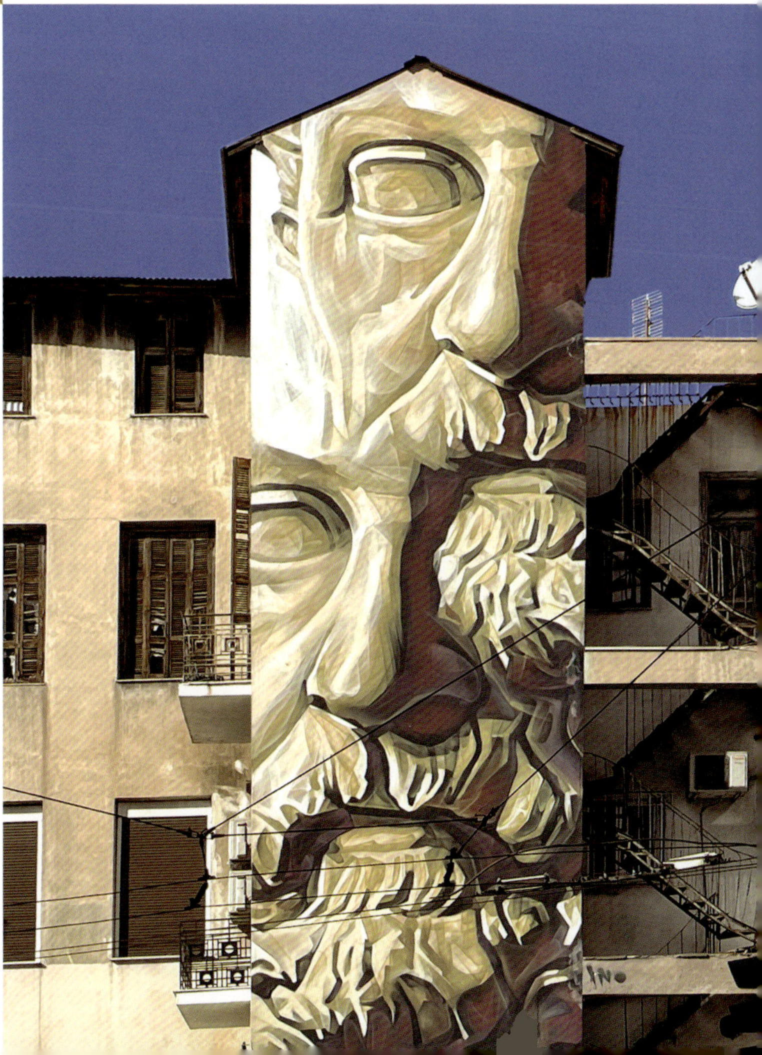

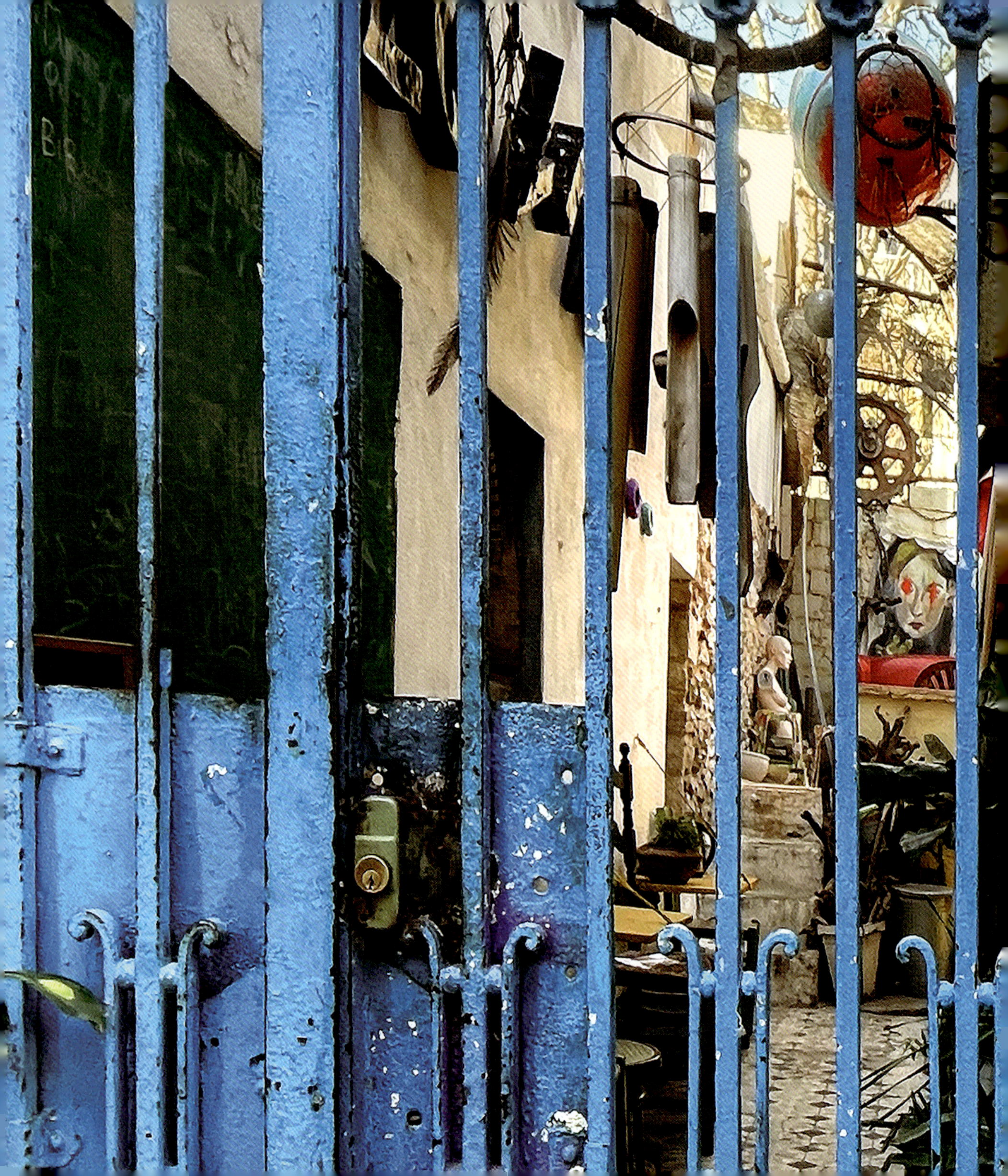

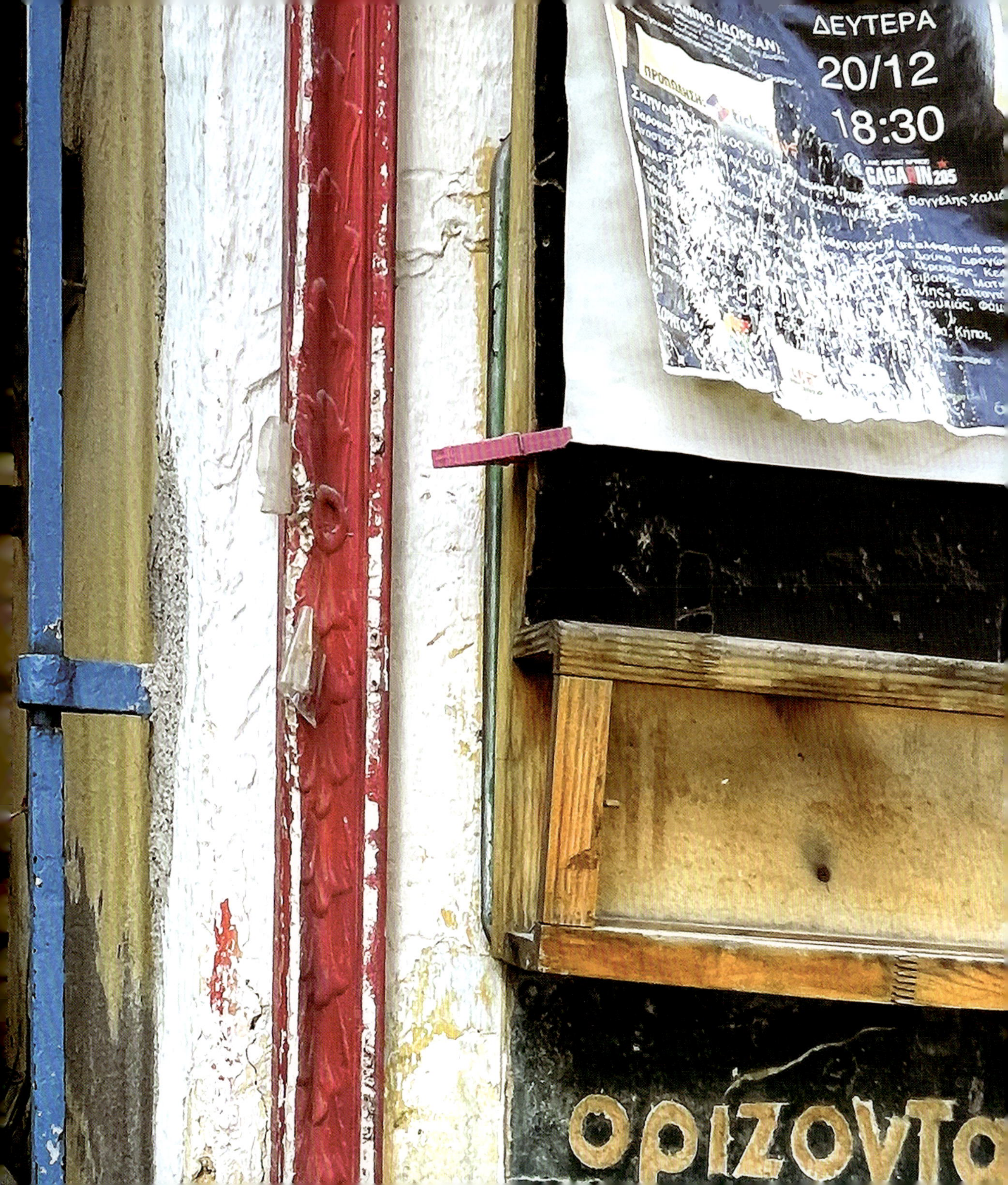
ΔΕΥΤΕΡΑ
20/12
18:30
GAGARIN 205
ΟΡΙΖΟΝΤΑ

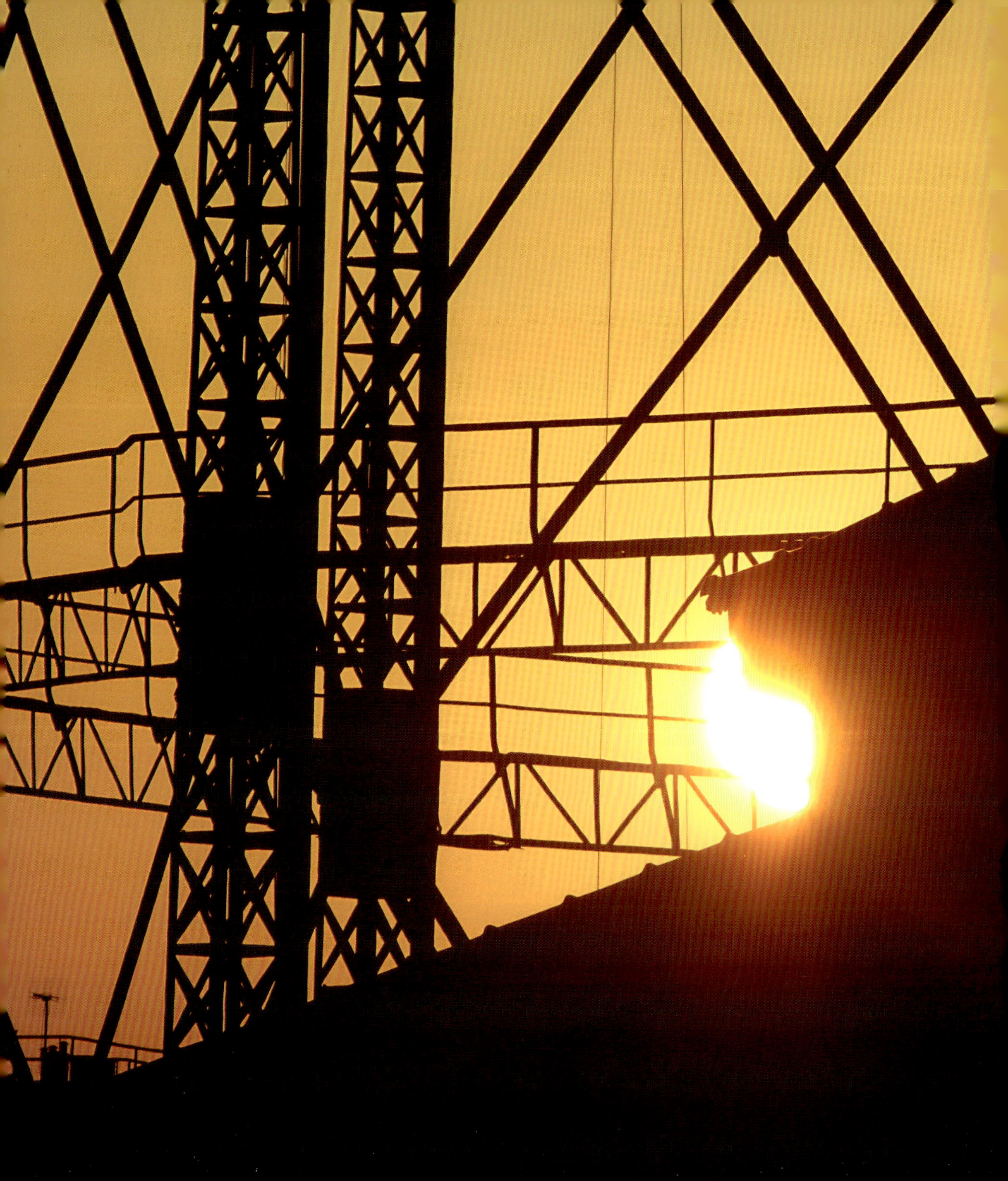

GAZI — TECHNOPOLIS

Towering above Pireos Street, one of the busiest industrial streets of Athens, the Gas Factory marks the skyline with its strength. A gigantic structure of iron and steel, with tall brick chimneys surrounded by barbwire, the factory speaks of darker times.

Its construction started in 1857 under the ownership of Frangisko Feraldi, later to be bought by Fulon den Vol in 1887. Hundreds of workers and their families lived on its grounds and the nearby area, known as "Gazochori," Gas Village, under horrid conditions. The pollution was so bad, the factory was often shrouded in a cloud of smog. Contagious diseases ran rampant, with many people dying unaccounted for. It was not uncommon for the entire area to go on lock down to prevent further contamination of the city. The factory ceased production in 1983.

Gazochori was one of the most undesirable areas to live in, not only because of the pollution, but also because of the many criminals it attracted. Behind the factory on Iaksos Street, the famous "Gaidouropazaro," an outdoor market selling and buying donkeys, took place with all the Athenian underworld present.

Gazi, *100 Pireos Street; sun setting above the Gas Factory, also known as Technopolis, dedicated to Greek composer Manos Xatzidakis*

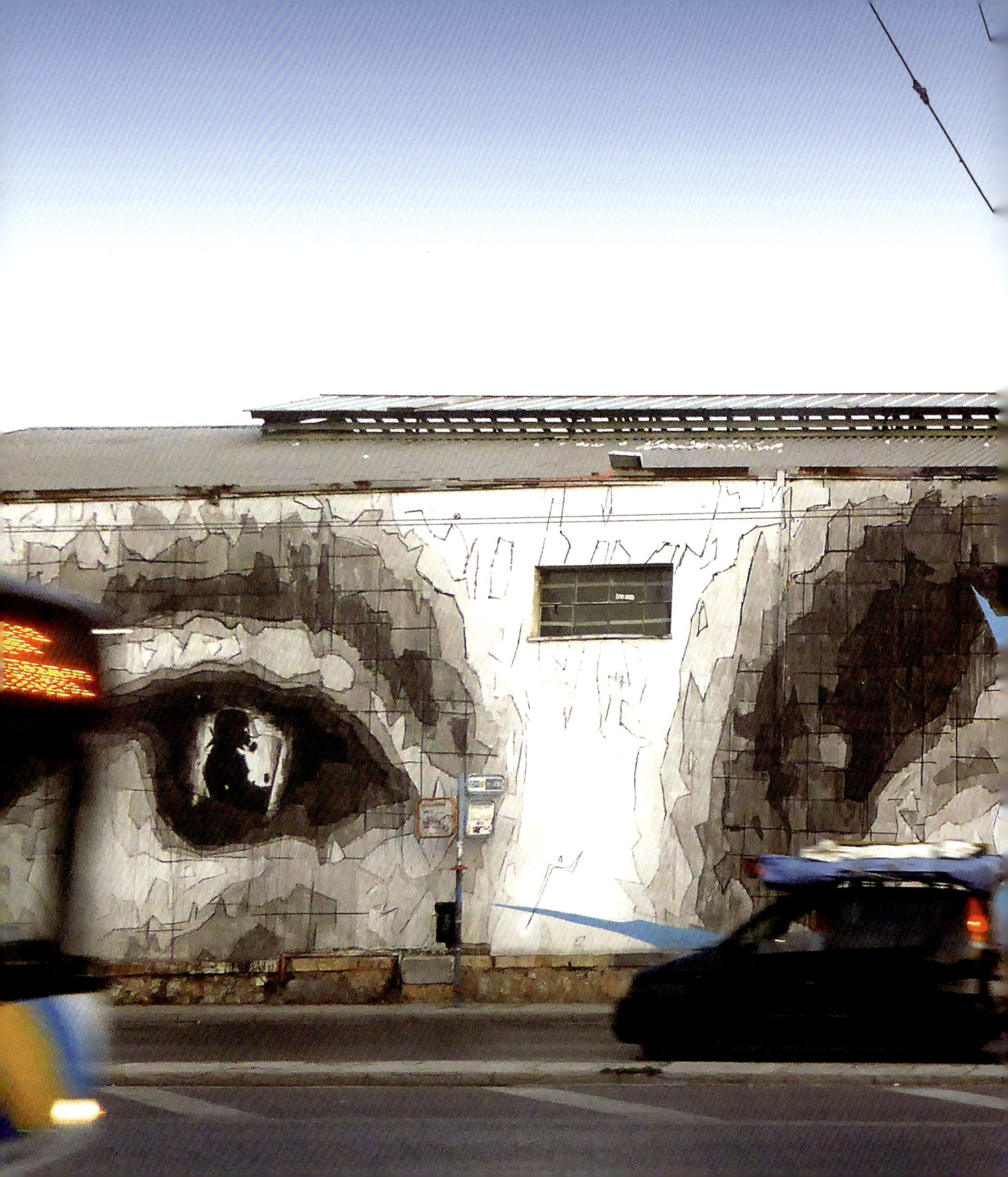

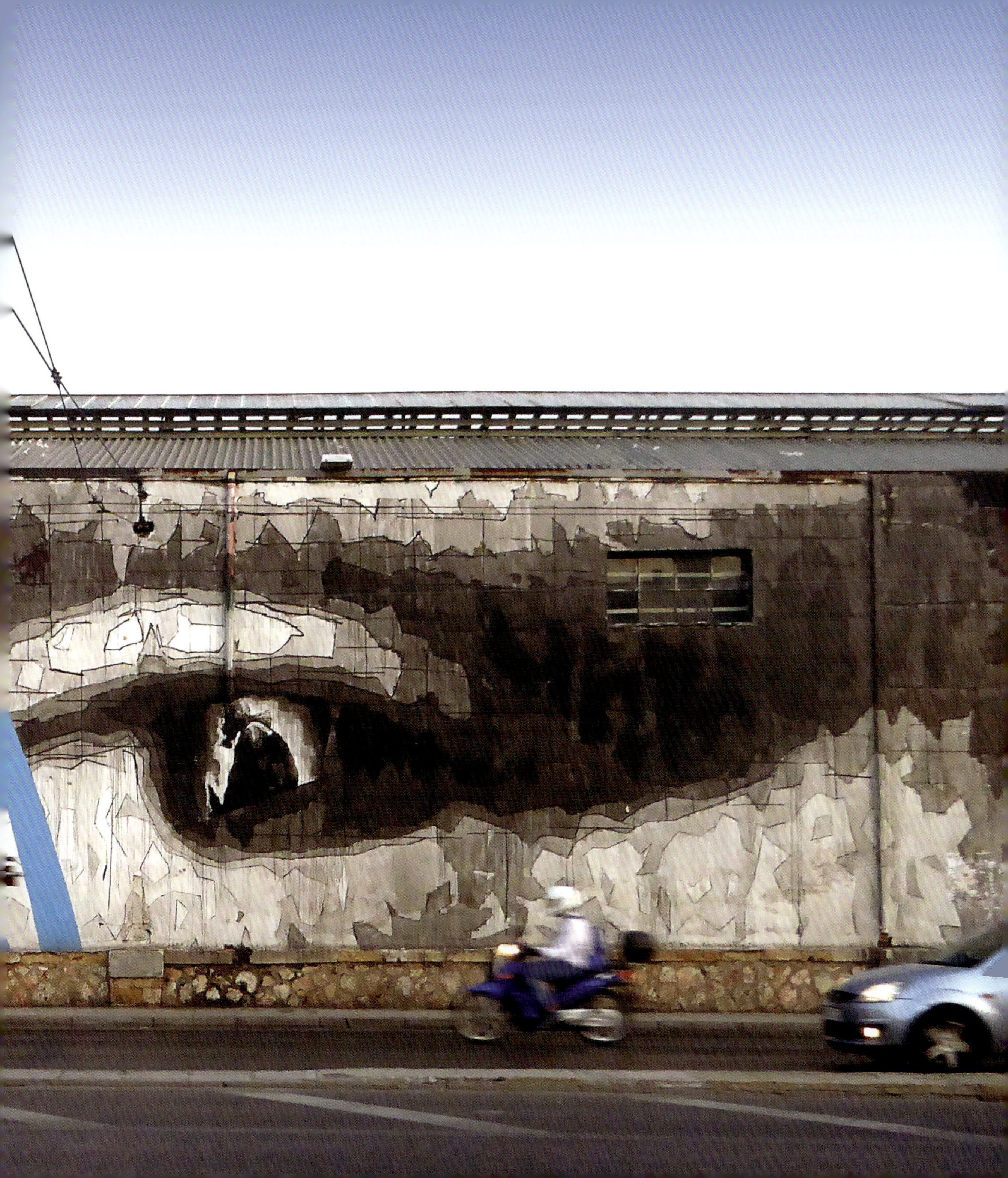

GAZI—TECHNOPOLIS

Today, the factory has been transformed into a large art center known as "Technopolis" and dedicated to the memory of composer Manos Xatzidakis. Exhibitions, concerts, seminars, and theatrical performances take place on its grounds, and numerous bars and clubs are a major attraction for the young. Walking through the factory's grounds is to be literally transformed into nineteenth-century industrial Athens. Old boilers, brick chimneys, and refineries add a haunting feel reminiscent more of a concentration camp than a factory.

Yet, as the sun sets behind Aigaleo Mountain, the factory is transformed into a place of wonderment. It makes one consider, if at moments like this, the workers removed their caps, marveling at how such beauty and ugliness could coexist side by side.

Nights in Technopolis are magical. Lit up in blue, green, and red beams of light, the factory, visible from a great distance, soars up to the sky. Music pours out from everywhere as people drink and dance late into the night. A gentle reminder, or rather a plea: if you find yourself here, raise your glass in a toast to all those who worked and died on these grounds.

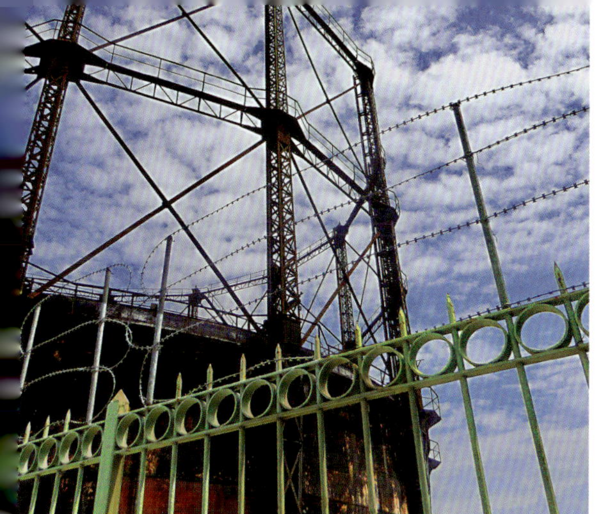

Previous pages: *Gioconda by INO, large mural on Pireos Street across the Gas Factory*

Top: *Gas Factory grounds exhibit and museum*

Right: *Clockwork Man by INO on Gazi Square*

Following pages: *Workers' houses with brick chimneys used today as exhibit spaces*

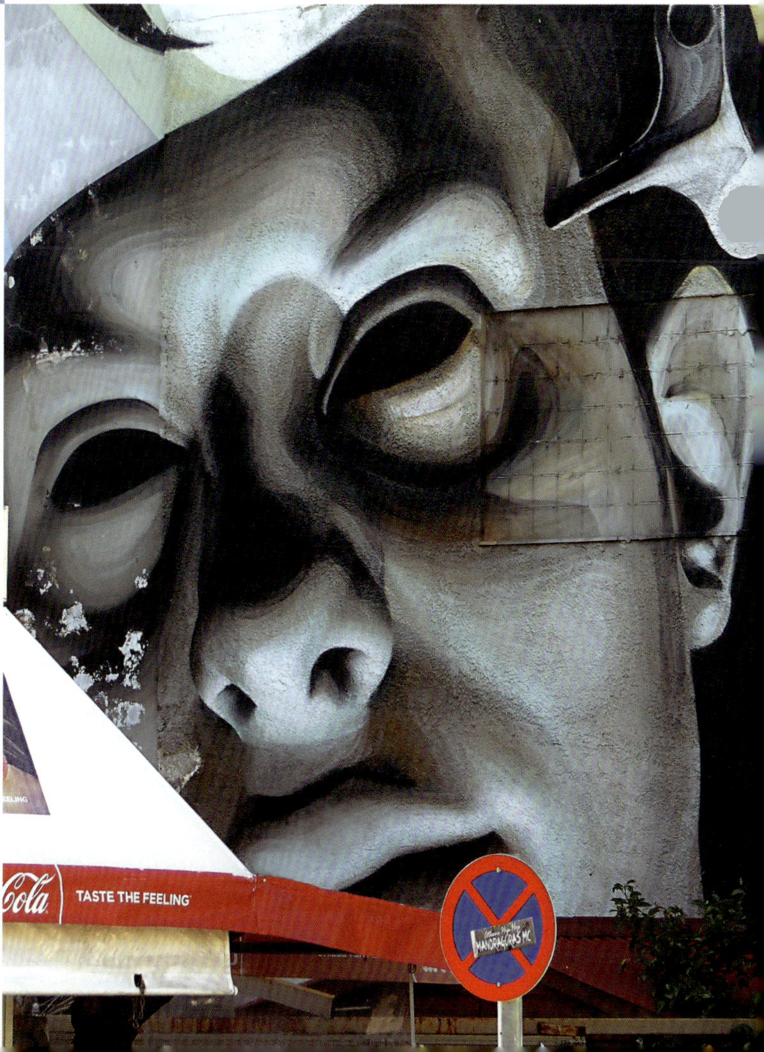

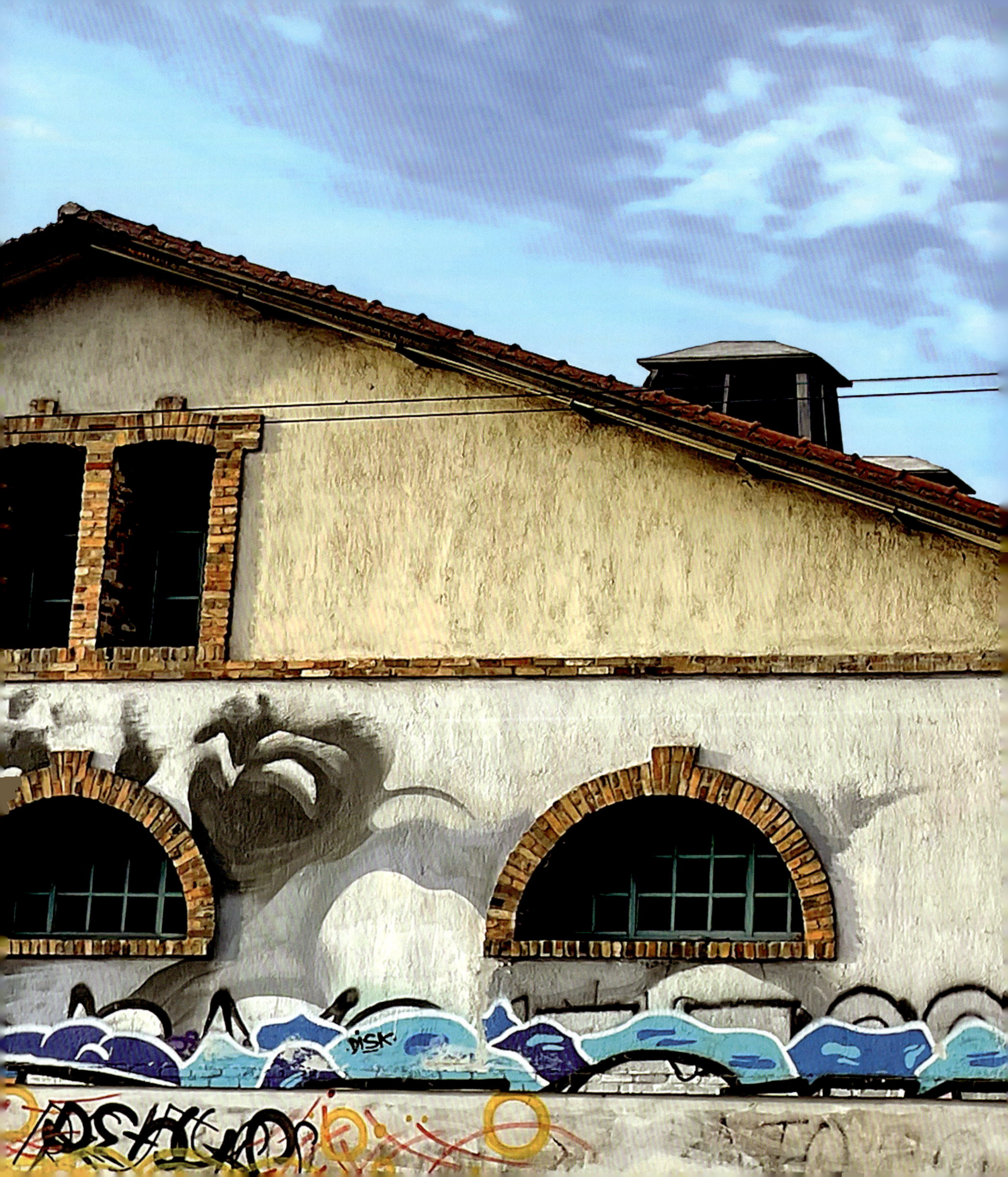
DISK

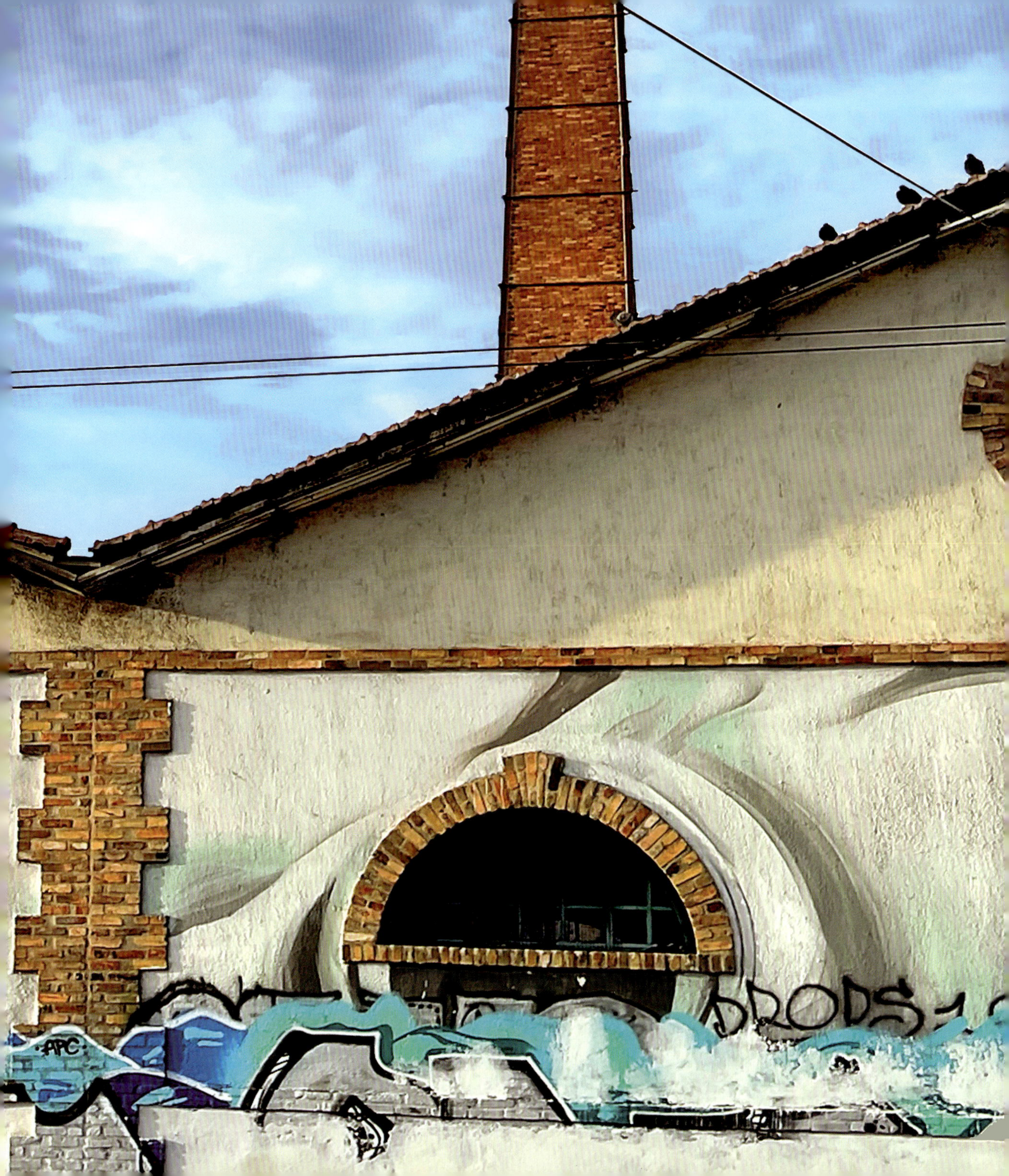

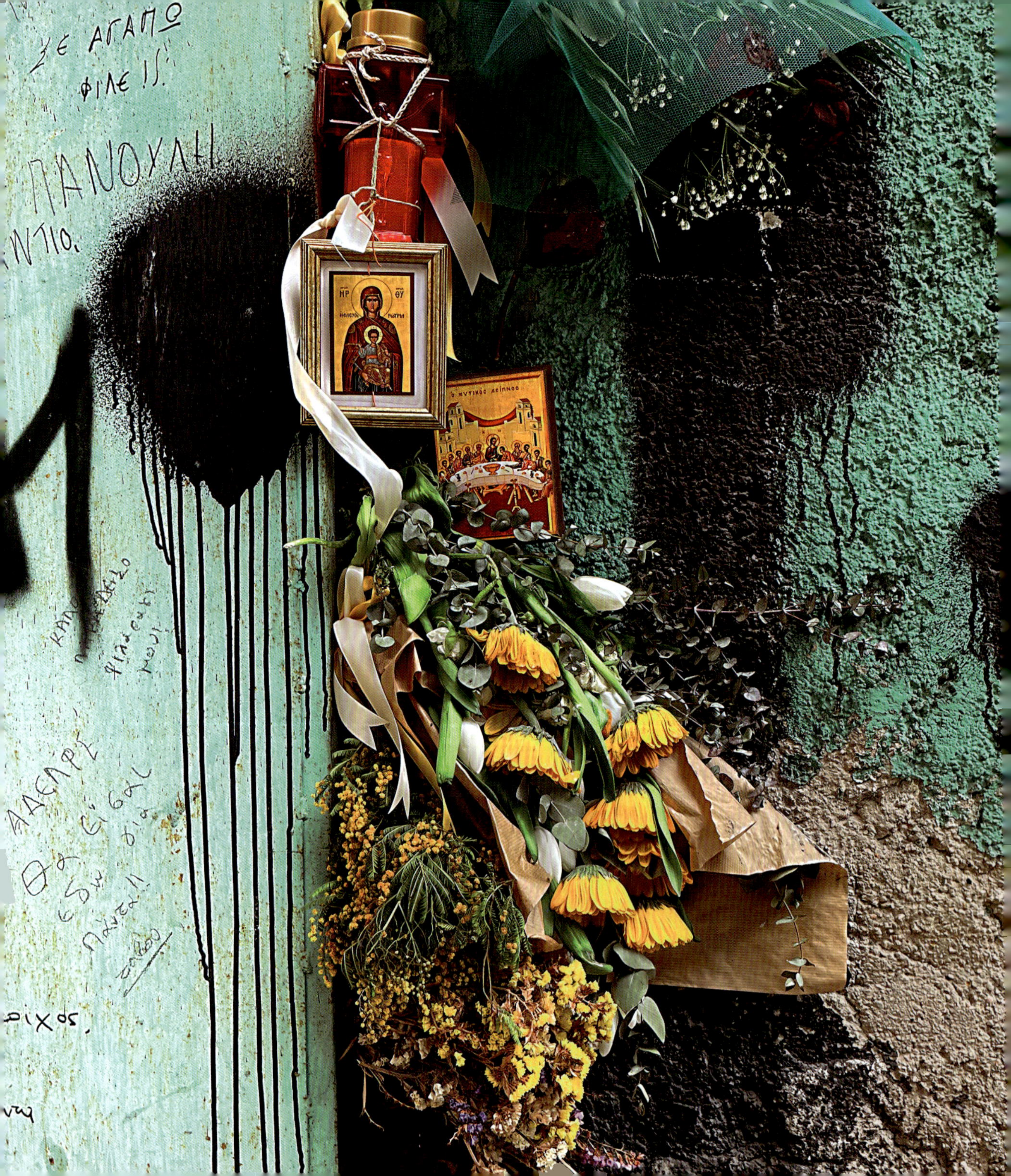
ΣΕ ΑΓΑΠΩ
ΦΙΛΕ !!
ΠΑΝΟΥΛΗ

KOLONOS

Arriving at Kolonos Street is like delving into the belly of the beast. A world where abandonment and decay are felt everywhere. There's something foreboding in this place, almost dangerous. The people look tired, filled with suspicion, afraid and aggressive, always on the lookout, guarding their flanks at the sight of an outsider. Most residents are illegal aliens, but there are also very poor Greeks, struggling to make sense of the world around them.

This is a not a safe area to visit and one should be cautious. Humble neoclassical buildings are juxtaposed with modern apartment buildings, burned down hotels, and brothels. "Welcome" signs for cheap sex are seen everywhere, leading to narrow corridors, where human and drug trafficking reign supreme.

The women working here are mostly held illegally by their pimps, their passports taken and their identification papers burned. A visit is about ten euros, and a session lasts about eight minutes. Precautions are rarely taken, and often the women end up in the hospital.

Kolonos Street, *memorial for slain young man, named Pavlos*

KOLONOS

Everything in this neighborhood is in flux. Users shoot up in abandoned buildings and then collapse on the pavement. Young men belonging to different gangs, stroll the streets looking for a fight. Frustration and despair run rampant. Knives are drawn, and people are stabbed. This is not the life they imagined. It's a nightmare that nobody knows how to wake up from.

So why come here? Because it matters, and because people should see what takes place here and speak out, but also because the street has a haunted feeling, even a charm, that will stay with you for a very long time.

It's morning now and the neon sex signs are turned off. The first Chinese stores raise their gates to reveal women dusting off plastic flowers and men arranging clothes and handbags into piles. A nearby coffee shop welcomes their first customers, two builders heading to a construction site. The street is quiet, almost tranquil. I hope that the working women find some peace, a place of solace before their nightmare begins all over again.

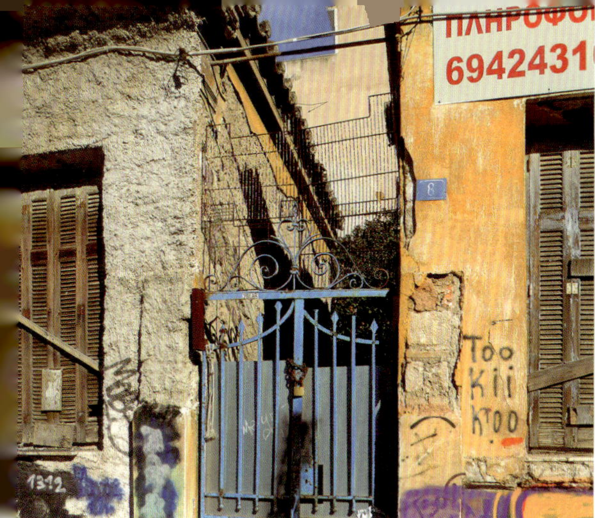

Top: *Working class neoclassical home for sale*

Right: *Abandoned headquarters of the Greek Communist Party, Metaxourgeio Division*

Following pages: *Beautiful neoclassical home in Kolonos red light district*

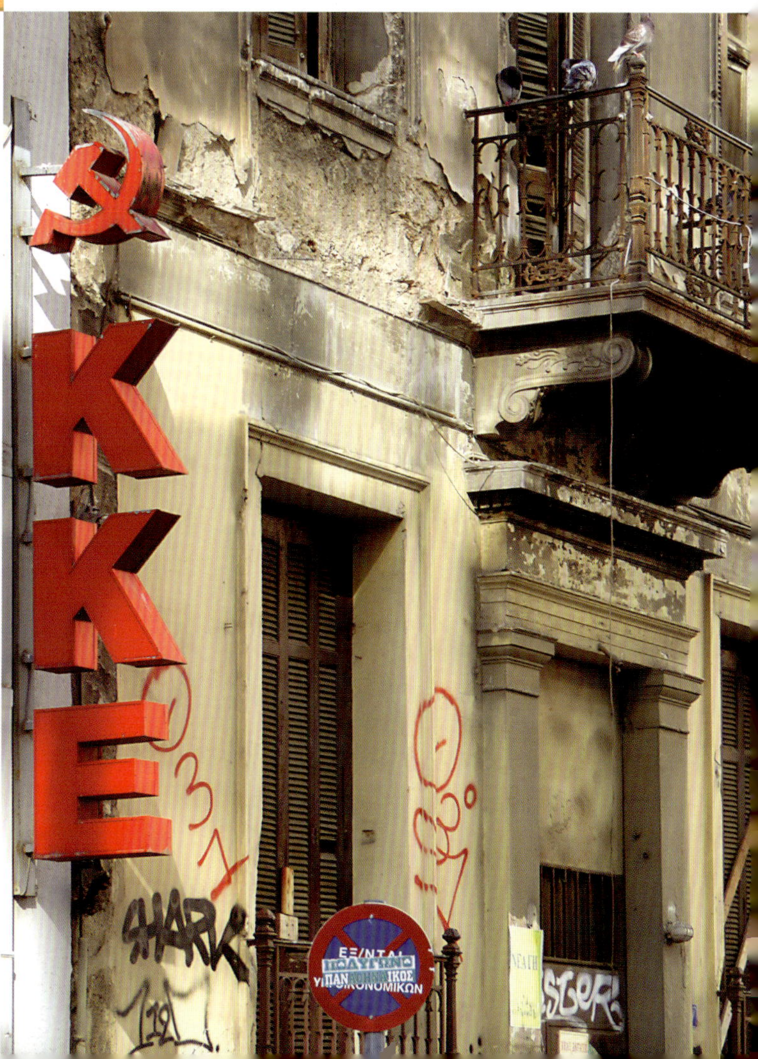

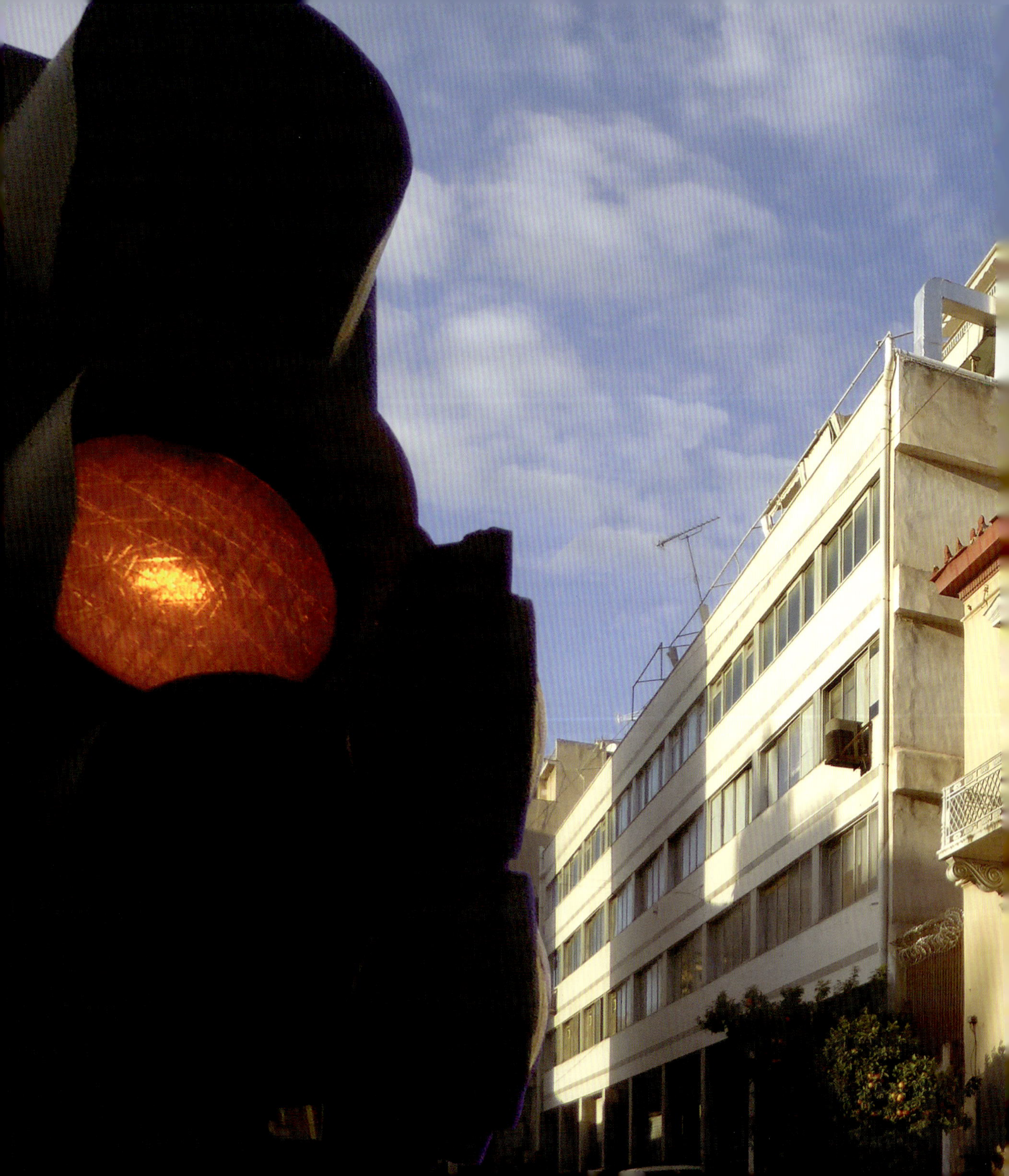

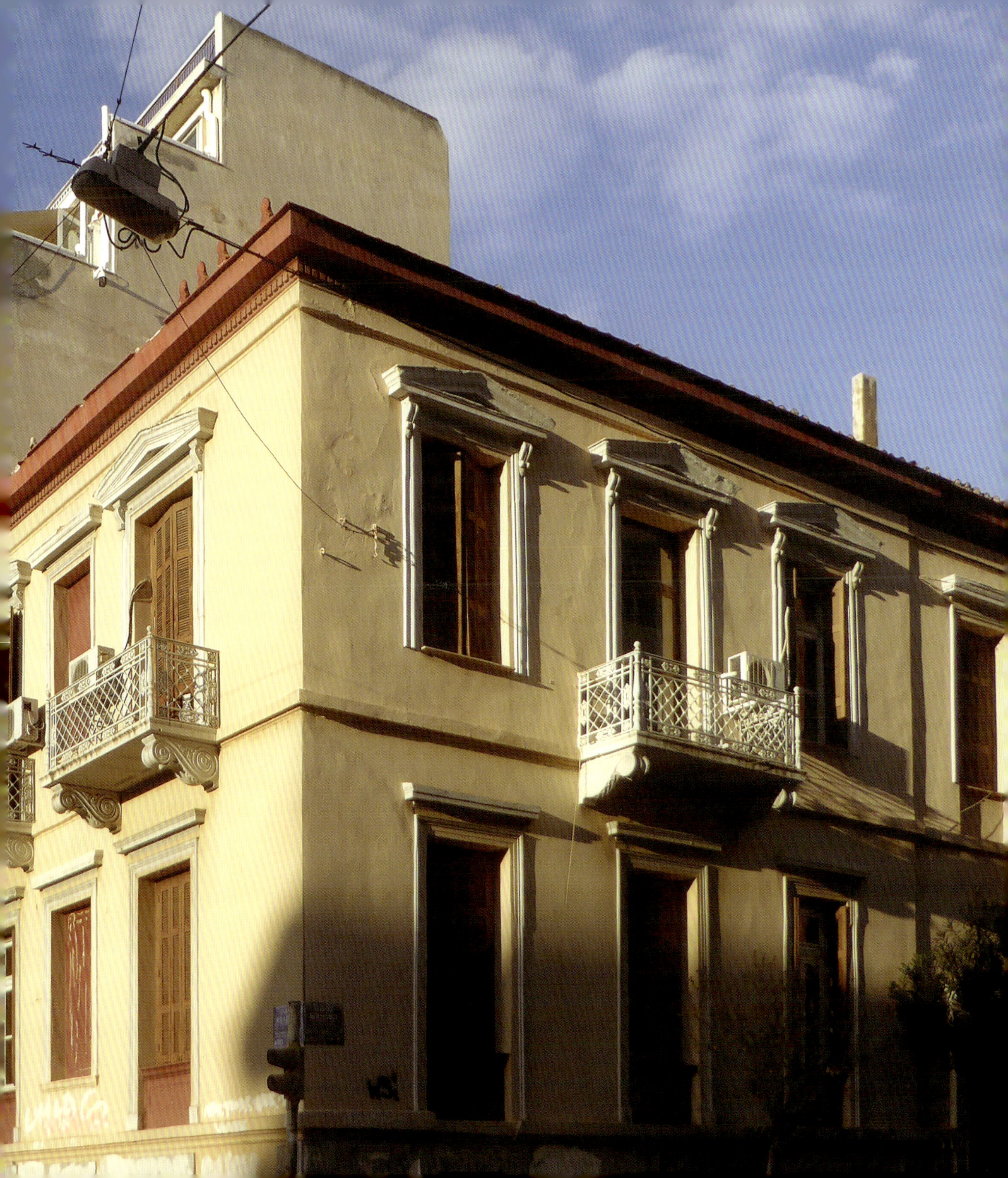

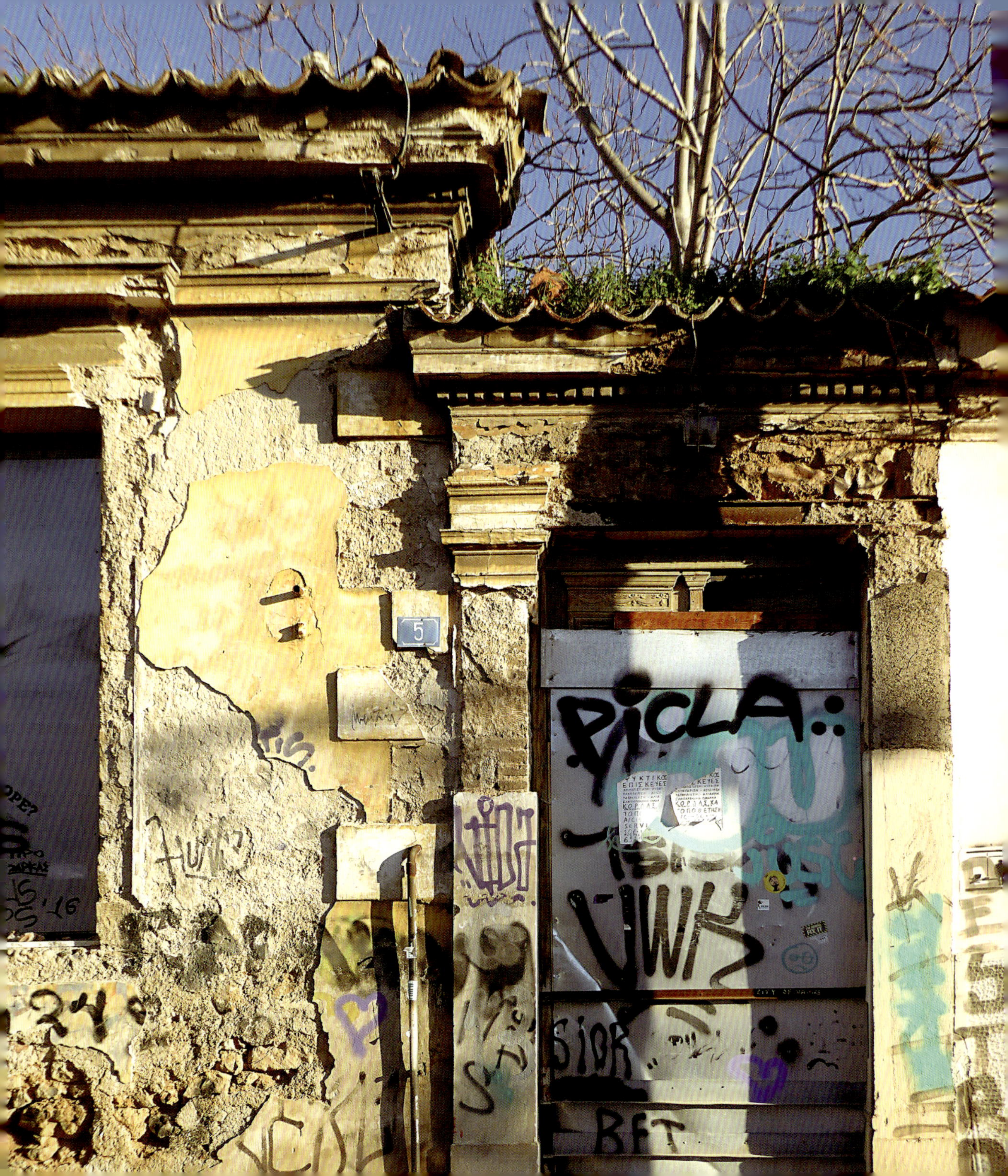
5
PICLA

IERA ODOS

The high priest raises his torch, and the initiates bow deeply to the ground. Lavender and jasmine fill the air mixed with burning wax. Dawn is nearing and the procession is about to begin. It's a long march from Athens to Salamis to attend the Eleusinian mysteries and pay homage to the great goddess, Demeter. The crowd undulates left and right, whispering hymns. They purify their bodies in the nearby spring, pouring libations to the dead, and so, they begin.

They walk in silence past tombs of distinguished men and well-to-do citizens and past small sanctuaries and temples. They cross the ancient olive grove and the Kifissos plain with eyes always focused to the west. The distance is long, and they do not delay.

A taxi driver honks his horn and raises his fist at a truck driver, and in turn, the truck driver showers him back with every possible expletive. A motorist swerves around a pedestrian, as a bus pulls away from its stop, almost hitting them both. Other than that, the street is deserted. There are very few people walking about, and those who are seem tired

Iera Odos, *meaning "Sacred Way," modest neoclassical home under luminous sunlight*

IERA ODOS

and listless. This street, that is only alive at night and where the ancient tombs once stood, is now a sanctuary of Athenian entertainment.

"Iera Odos," meaning "Sacred Way," hosts some of the most famous nightclubs in Athens. From "bouzoukia" to mainstream music, pop, techno, disco, and high-end strip clubs. The street undulates with life and some of the most important pop musicians and bands perform here. Hundreds of fans are willing to spend a small fortune on a bottle of whiskey or vodka.

Trying to navigate your way in a car is pure madness. Stretch limousines block the street, dropping off customers, as crowds spill in and out of the clubs, smoking, drinking, or simply idling. For those who really like to stay up late, street carts serving first rate coffee and a hefty breakfast line up on the street, making the experience worth it.

So, dress up in all your finery and be prepared for a night like no other.

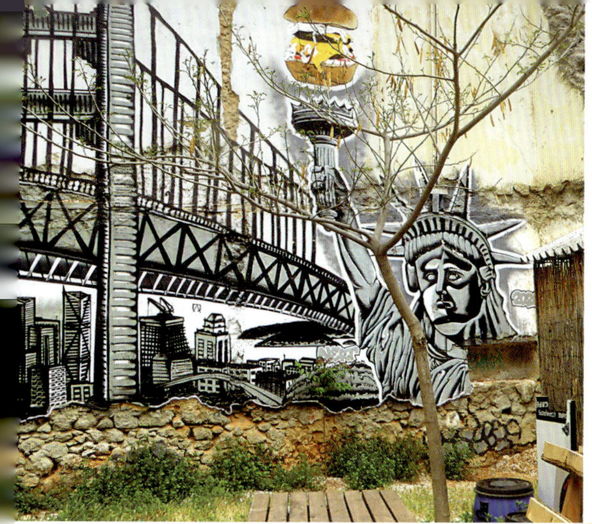

Top: *Holy Moly, outdoor kiosk serving burgers and coffee for late night patrons*

Right: *Art imitating nature*

Following pages: *Freedom for Sale by INO, 36 Iera Odos*

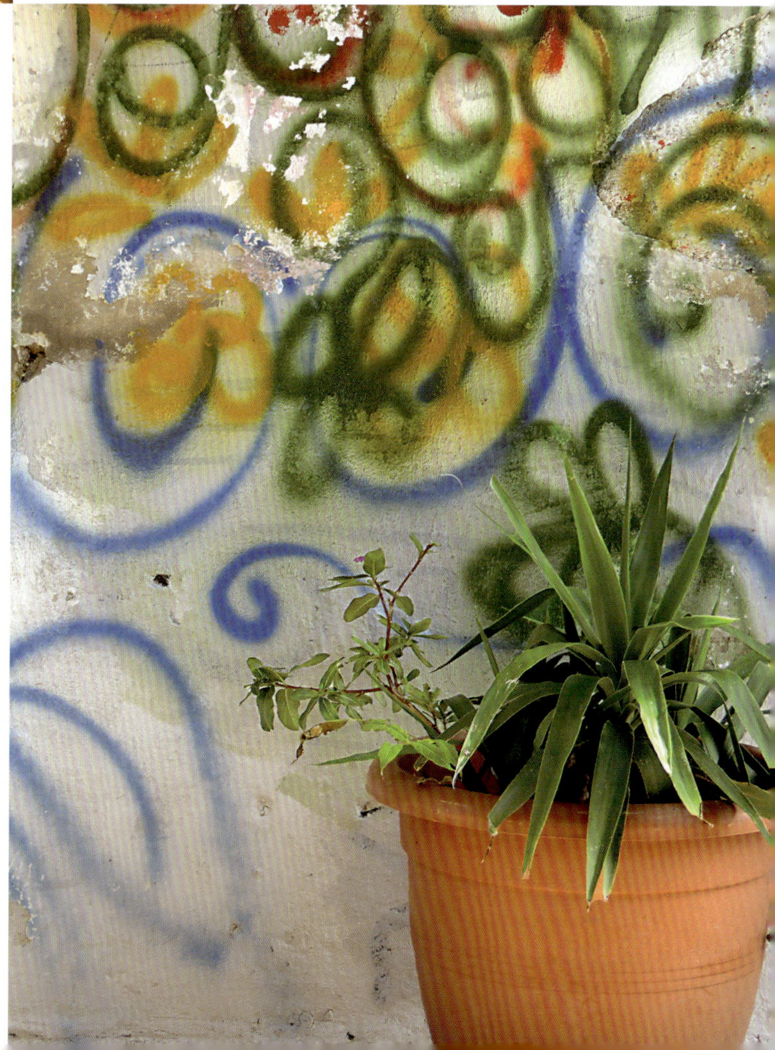

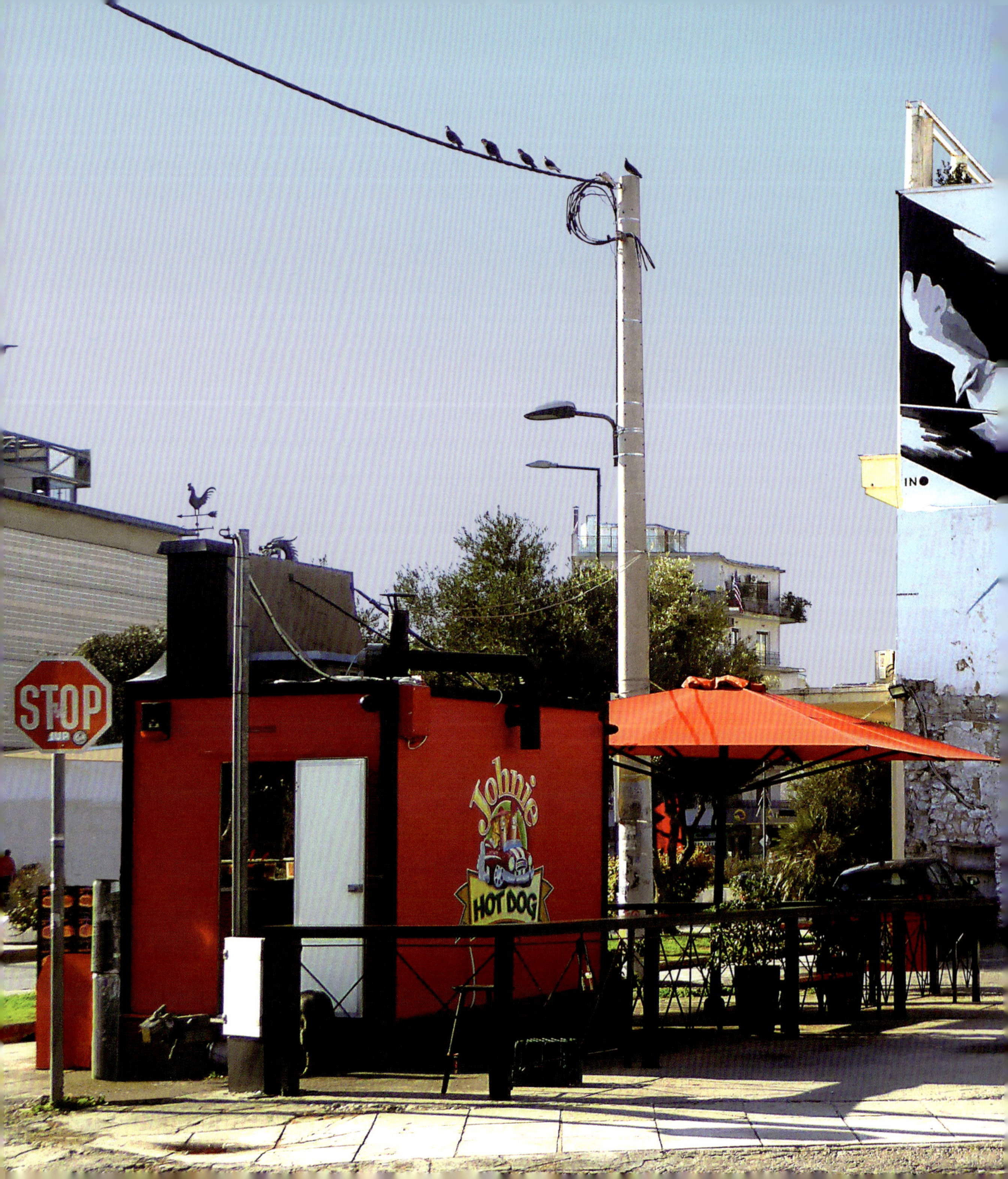
STOP
Johnie
HOT DOG

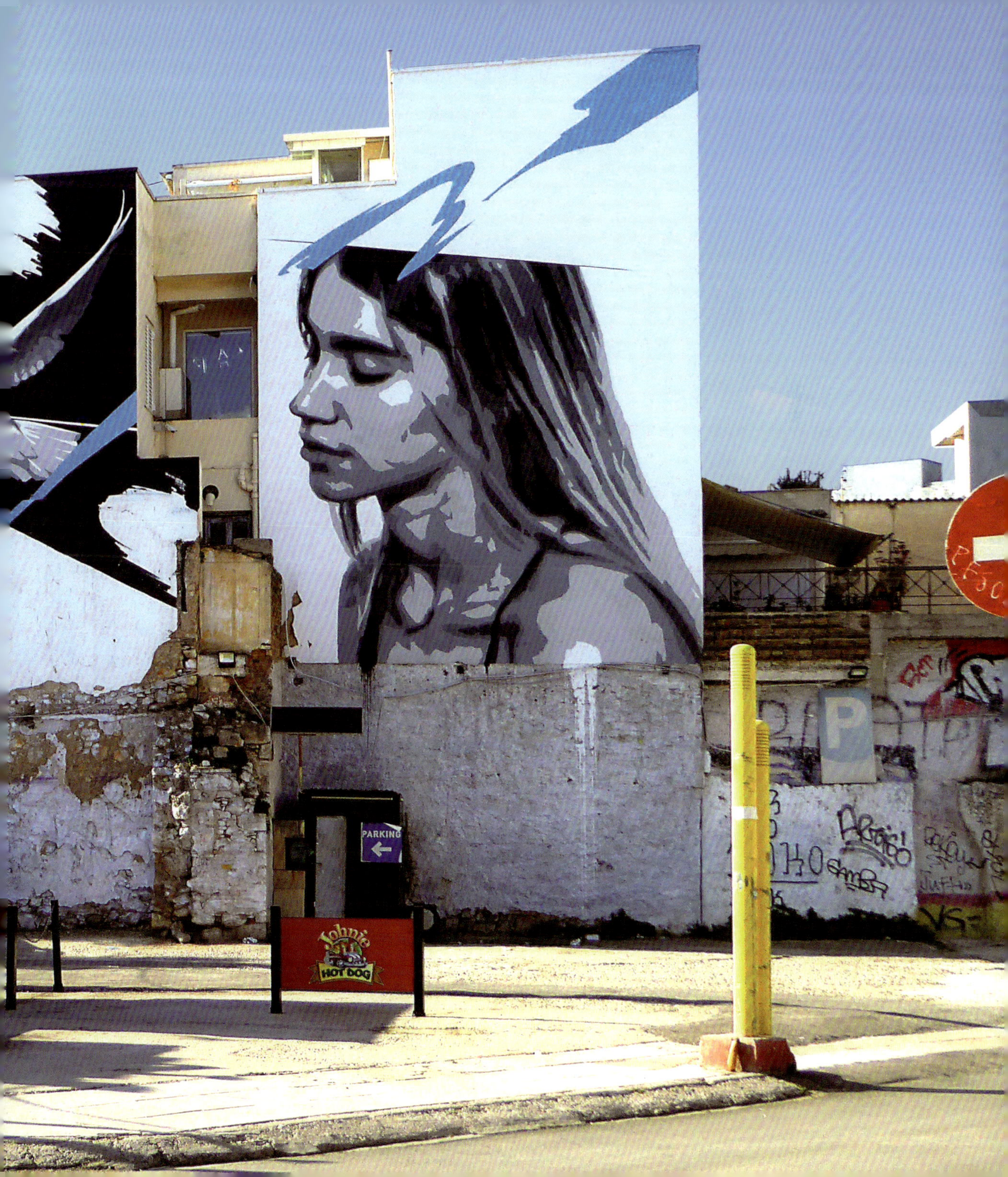
PARKING
P
Johnie
HOT DOG

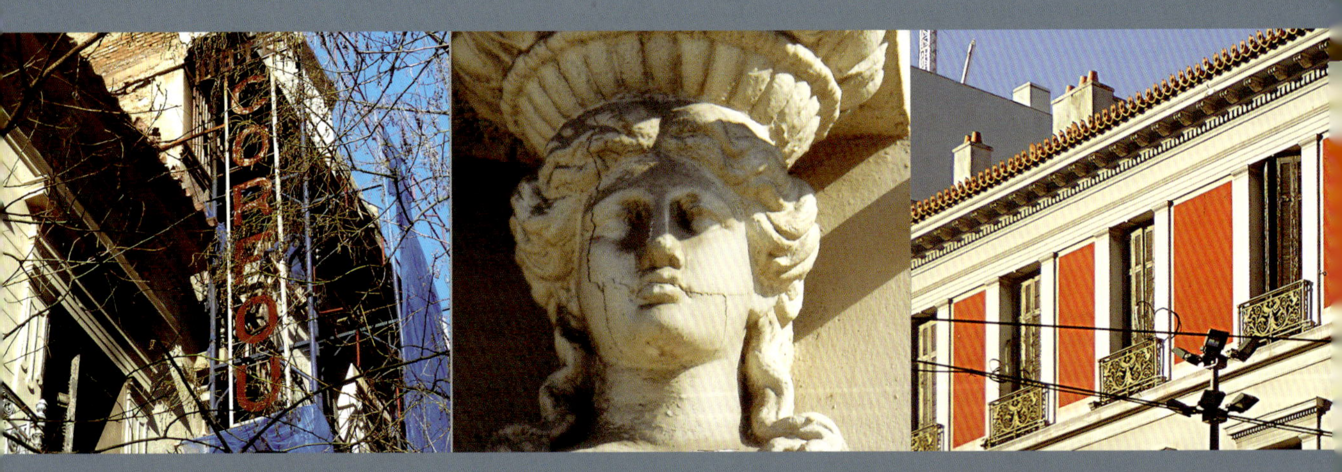
CORFOU

A LEAGUE OF THEIR OWN

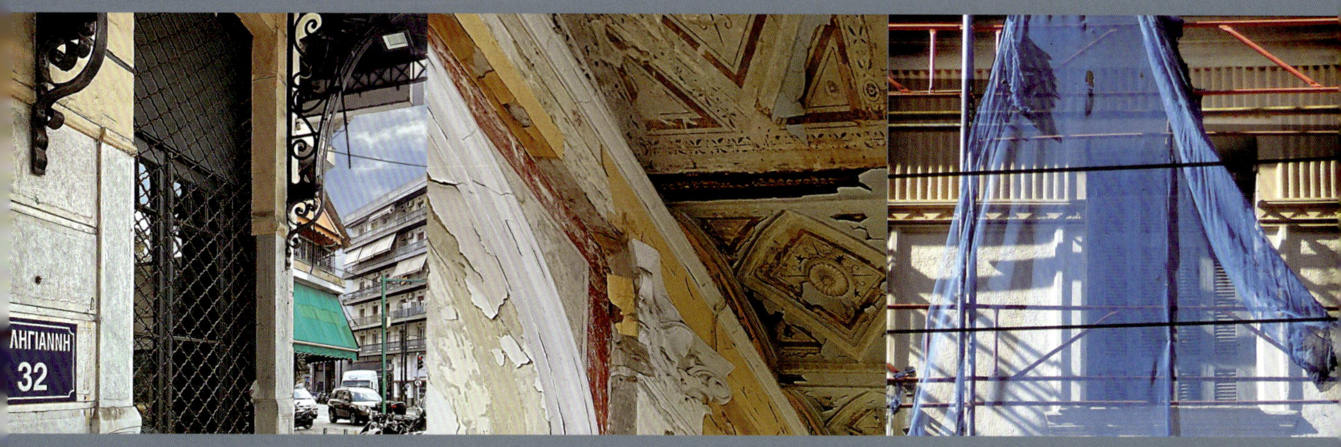

Growing up in Athens meant many things: visits to museums, walks in Plaka and Thissio, outdoor theaters, and book browsing. This was our world, our designated neighborhoods. I remember getting off at Omonoia Station, meandering through the smoke filled kafeneia and the run-down hotels, and hurrying up to Akademia's Street to my favorite bookstores.

Back then, Omonoia was a place to be avoided, an imposition of sorts that I had to pass through. Students, refugees, immigrants, retirees, everything and everyone could be seen there, as if eternally floating around the fountain. The small alleys behind the square always seemed lost in shadows no matter how bright the sky was. The smell of onions and grilled meat wafted out of souvlaki stands that were always packed no matter what time of day.

Omonoia Square and the nearby Vathis Square have not changed, and they're still not pretty places to visit. It's my perspective that has changed. What started as a simple project to photograph the neighborhoods led me into a world that I had been completely unaware of. Street after street, magnificent hotels stand in silence, waiting to be noticed, to be allowed to share their stories. It's heartbreaking, almost cruel to see these buildings standing abandoned, their only inhabitants pigeons, rats, and squatters. The few hotels still functioning are for casual sex or shelters for low-income people and refugees, a theme that occurs again and again in this western part of Athens that no one seems willing to address.

What I once saw as a place to avoid, I now see as a part of Athens that needs to be noticed. Finance is always a major issue and with so many other pending needs, it's apparent that the city has decided to abandon these areas to their fate. It shouldn't be this way. Athens has much more to offer and all it takes is to look around us.

The hotels presented in this section were mostly built at the turn of the twentieth century, but they are equally important to be mentioned before they follow the fate of so many other buildings. Recently, there was a movement by private investors to restore them and revamp the neighborhoods. Whatever this development brings, I hope that it's done with sensitivity and respect for all those who already live in the area.

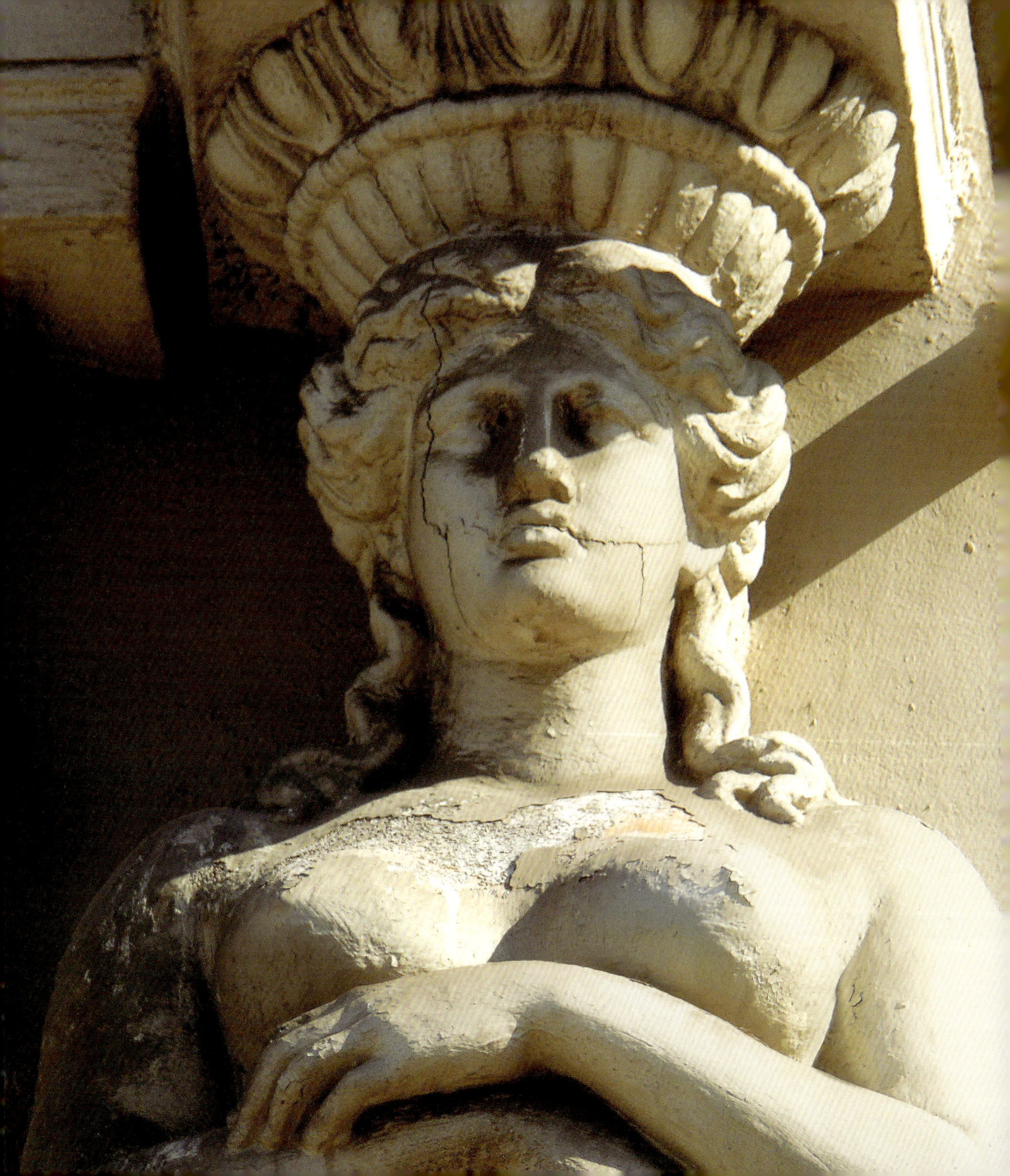

MEGAS ALEXANDROS & MPAGKEION HOTELS

Reaching Omonoia Square, one can't help but notice two magnificent hotels standing across from each other, like two siblings competing in grace. Megas Alexandros and Mpagkeion are two nineteenth-century gems, both the work of Ernst Ziller. Their construction was funded by Ioannis Mpagkas, a wheat merchant, who, while still alive, left his entire fortune to the Greek state, keeping only a small percentage for himself.

Perfect in symmetry, with ornate balconies, terracotta freezes, and Caryatids facades, the hotels hosted the elite and high-end merchants. With sixty-eight rooms each, plus salons, libraries, music rooms, and grand dining halls, they represent the mature neoclassical architecture of Athens.

Megas Alexandros was built in late 1880, and Mpakeion followed eight years later, adding an extra floor and a central, glass-roofed atrium. Centrally located, both hotels played an important role in the history of Athens. During The Second World War, Mpakeion was used as German headquarters, while Megas Alexandros' furniture was burned by the British for firewood.

Megas Alexandros Hotel, *Caryatid head, signature style of architect Ernst Ziller*

Two worlds, however, existed at the hotel. When the proper families retired to their rooms, another less savory society emerged. Located in the basement of Mpagkeion, "Café Santan," an infamous night club, entertained many Athenians and foreigners into the early morning hours. People from all classes gathered there to drink and enjoy the "plucked nightingales," foreign dancers who sang popular Italian operettas.

Several years later, the same place was transformed into a famous patisserie, and in the early 1920s became one of the most important literary gathering places in Athens. This transformation into a center of scholars and writers was due to the poet, essayist, and my beloved uncle, Mario Vagianos. Agras, Psathas, Zotos, Lapathiotis, Giofyllis, Varnalis, and Ritsos were only a few of the literary elite that found a home here.

Today, Mpagkeion functions as an art and performance center. It's worn-out floors, peeling ceilings, tall mirrors, and winding staircases add a layer of enchantment that push the performances outside the boundaries. Thinking of my uncle and the life he led, I can't help but feel a little wistful for being too young to truly understand his importance.

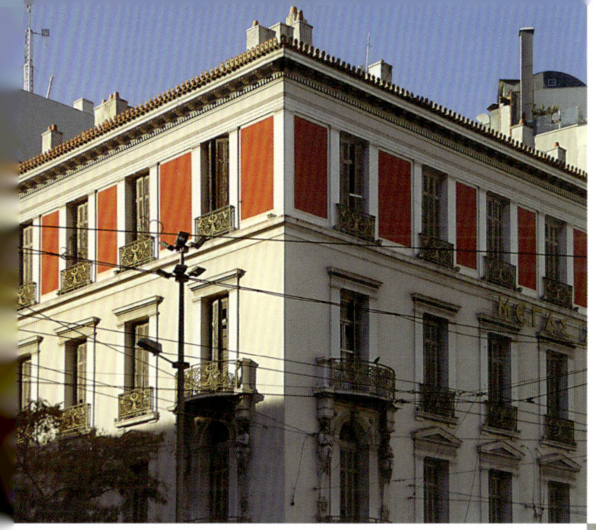

Top: *Megas Alexandros at sunset*

Right: *Interior of Mpagkeion Hotel, ceiling detail; work of Ernst Ziller, funded by Ioannis Mpagkas; currently used as an art center*

Following pages: *Majestic Megas Alexandros and Mpagkeion Hotels overlooking Omonoia Square*

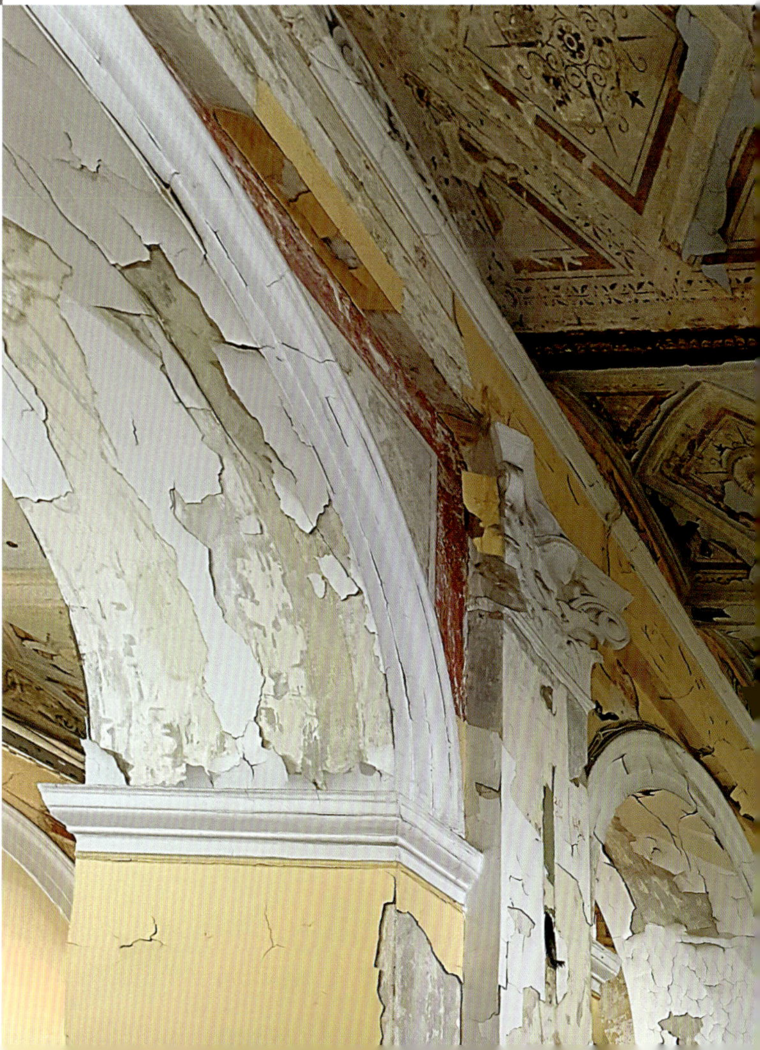

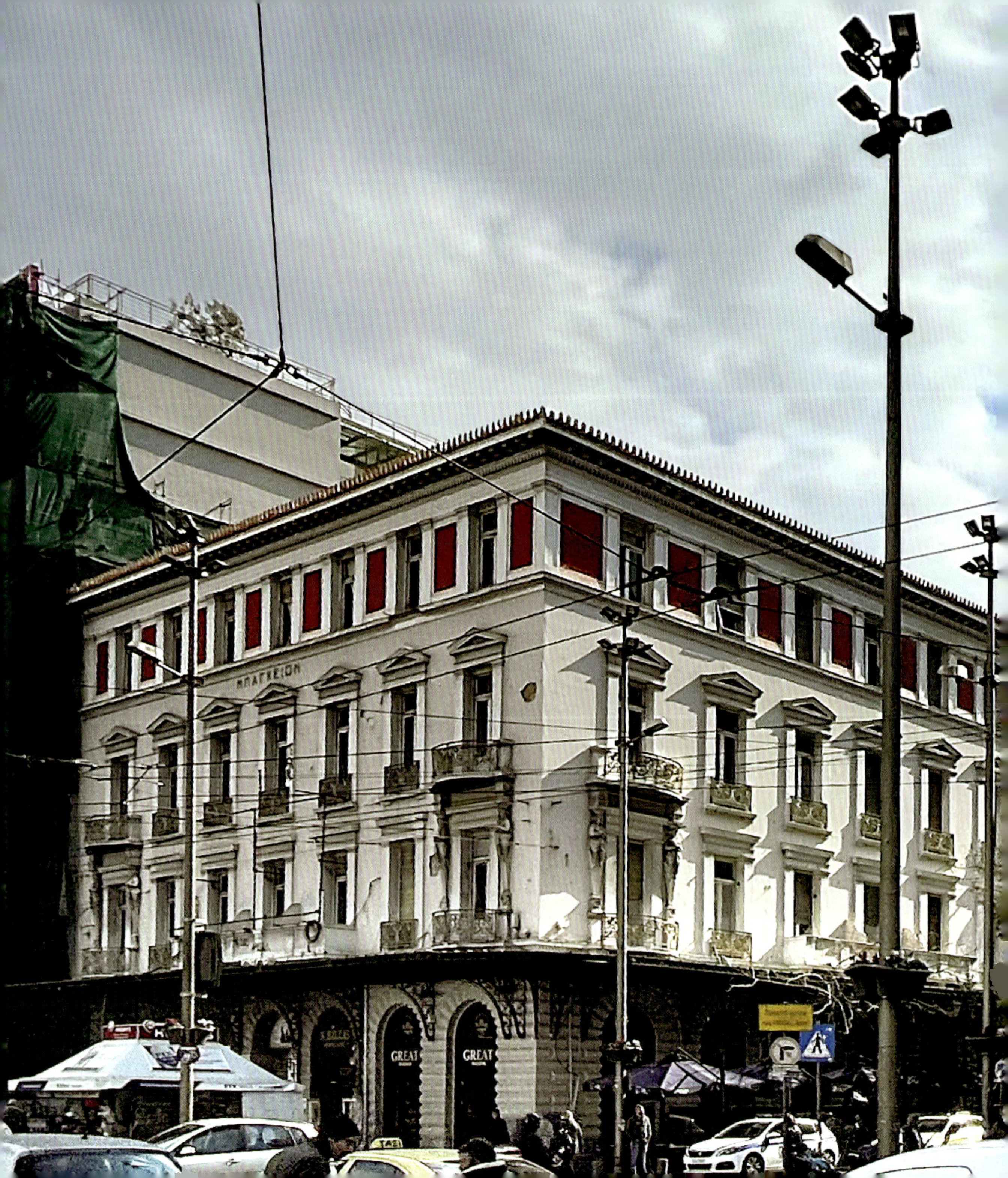
ΜΠΑΓΚΕΙΟΝ
GREAT
GREAT

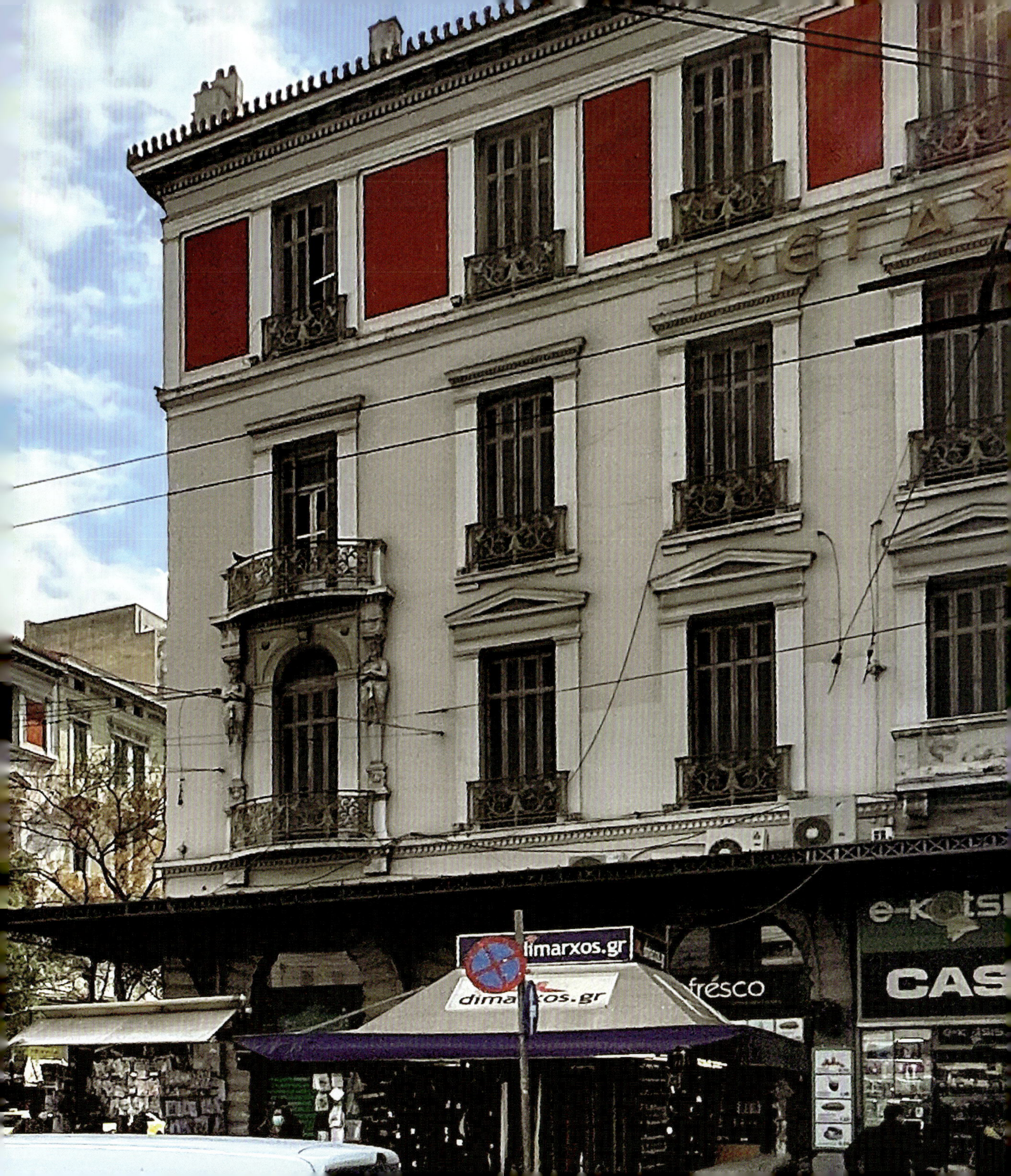
dimarxos.gr
dimarxos.gr
fresco

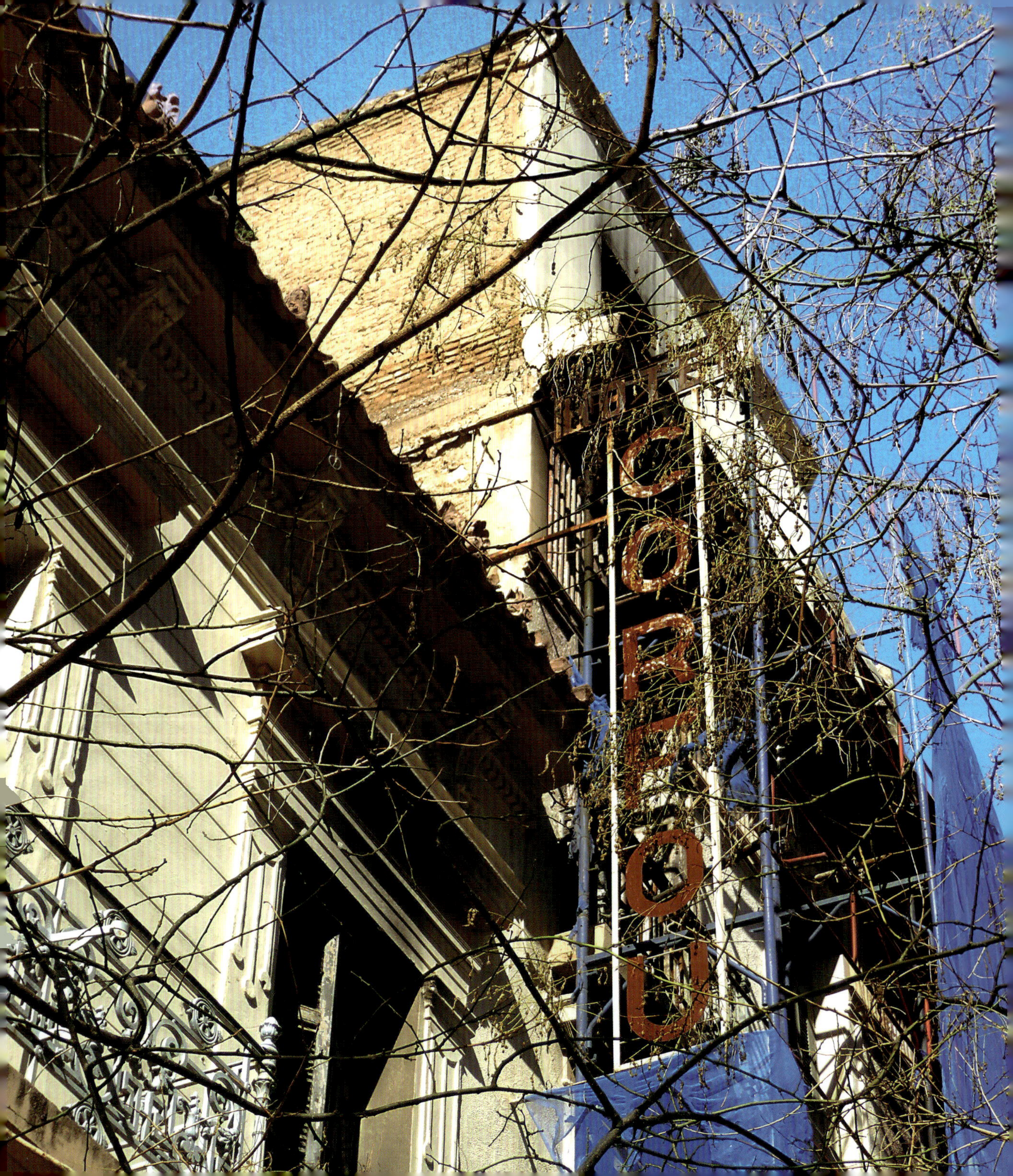
CORFOU

HOTEL CORFOU

Maybe it was the blue net draping the building, matching the sky above it, or the cast iron sign with the rusty letters, CORFOU, that caught my eye, but I stopped, unaware of the man running straight into me. His filthy clothes and heavily tattooed neck gave him a less than friendly appearance. The man cursed and scurried away.

The sight is a familiar one. Street after street, rows of abandoned hotels extending from Omonoia to Vathis Square have become centers for the homeless and addicts. The proximity of the hotels to Larissa rail station once made it an ideal location for development and a thriving hub for travelers. Different hotels serviced people from different geographical areas, creating a miniature Greece enclosed within a few streets.

Nearby Vathis Square, with its small cafés and shops, became a meeting place where people shared news and information. A willow tree shaded the square, adding some relief during the hot summer days.

Hotel Corfou *with early art deco sign*

HOTEL CORFOU

The name of the square was derived from the word "vathouloma," a deep indentation in the ground where the waters of the river Kyclobouros collected. Malaria and other communicative diseases were not uncommon.

Like so many other parts of western Athens, the area attracts many unsavory characters. The living conditions can be extremely dangerous. It was not so long ago that a mother and her two-year old child died in a fire in one of these sunless rooms.

Yet on this clear December morning, change is palatable. Iron beams and scaffolding are being raised, and signs of new construction are visible. Investment companies have committed themselves to renovating these hotels, cleaning up the area, and attracting much needed commerce and, hopefully, a better quality of life.

In the meantime, Hotel Corfou, under its blue veil, continues to stand unattended, its empty shell a poignant reminder that change may not come any time soon.

Opposite: *Hotel Corfou under blue construction net waiting to be restored*

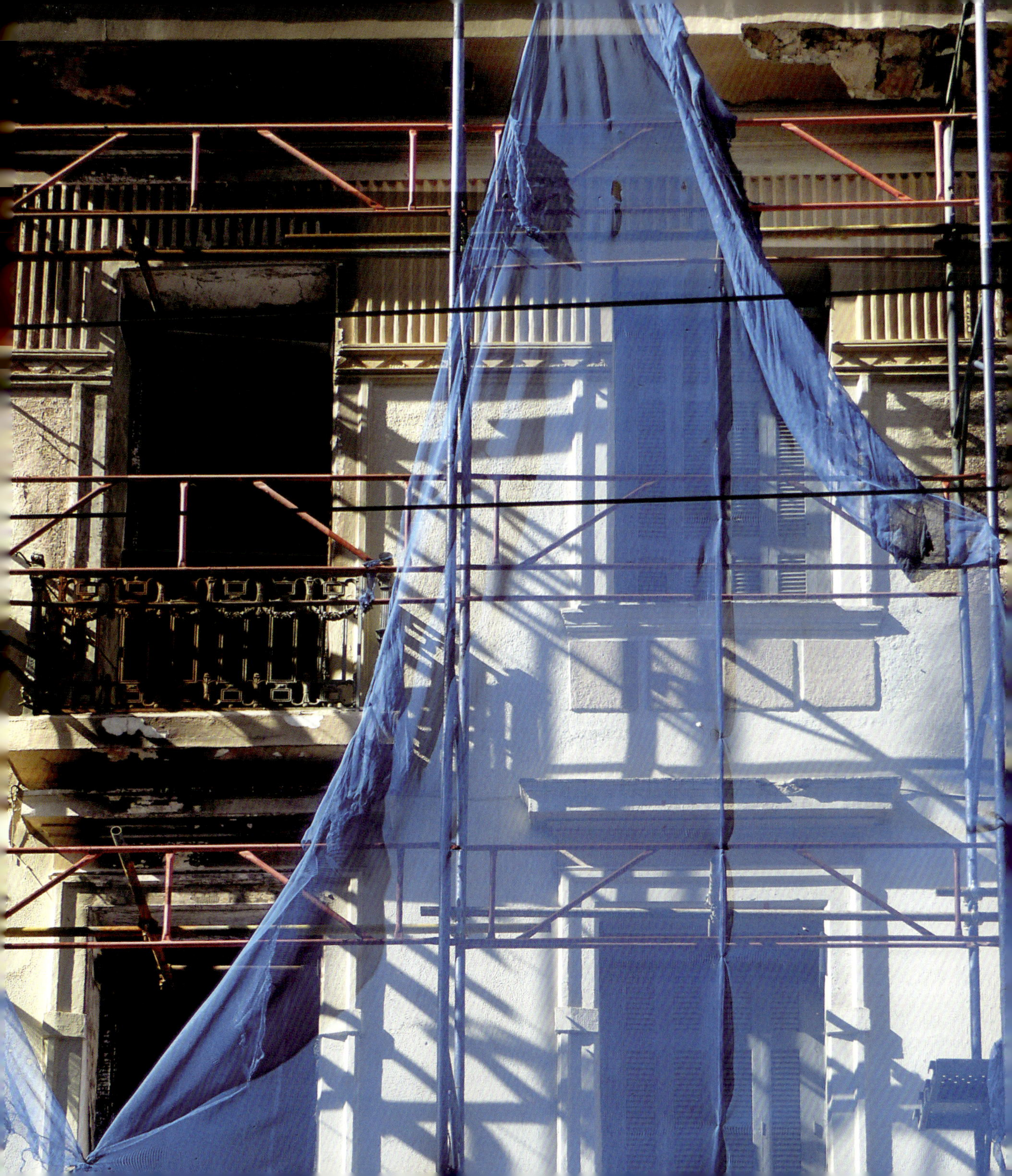

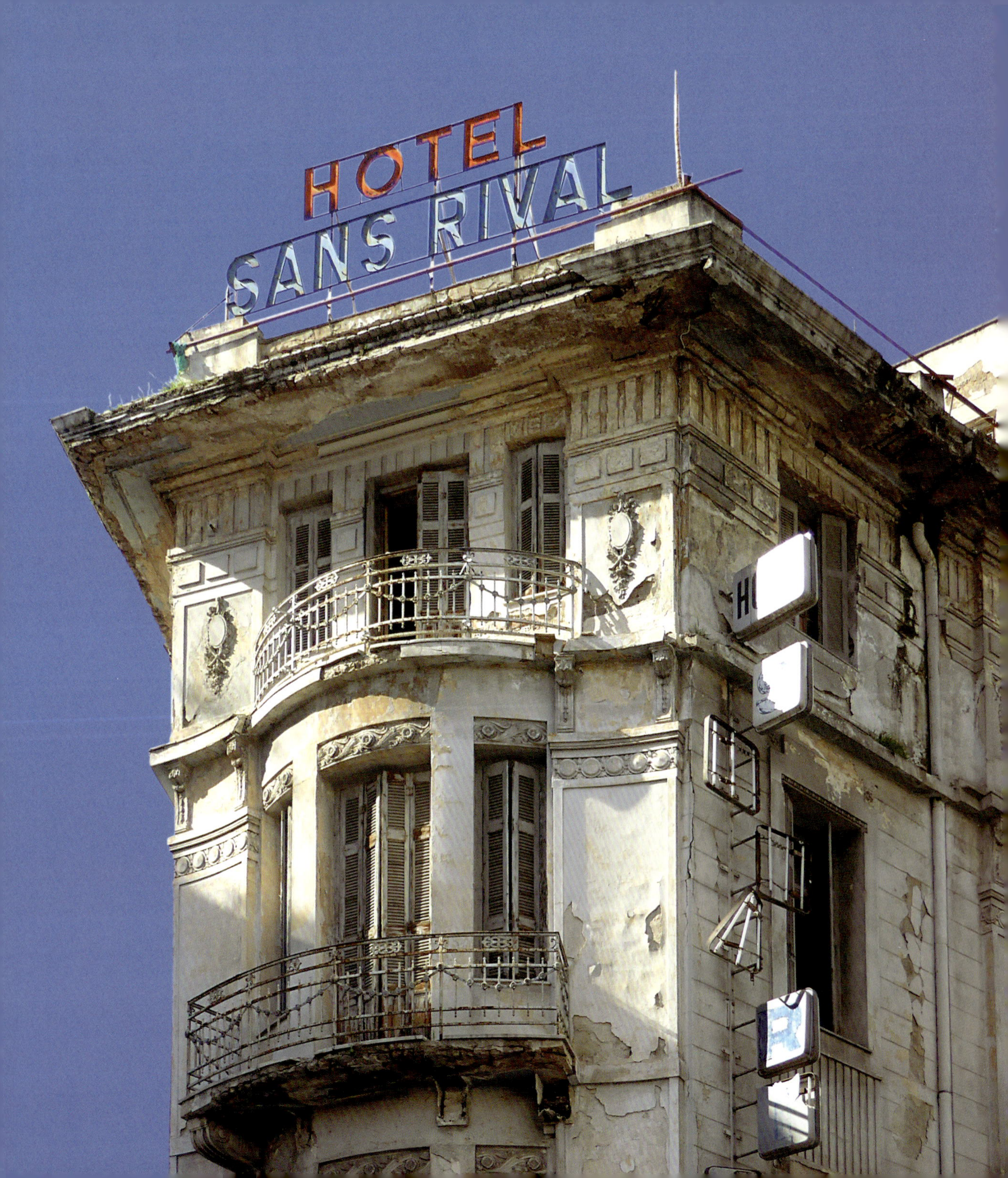
HOTEL
SANS RIVAL

HOTEL SANS RIVAL

Sans Rival is a stunning Art Nouveau, neoclassical building close to Omonoia and the Larissa train station. Alone, standing at the crossroads of Liosion and Konstantinos Paleologos Streets, it speaks of past grandeur but also of something unresolved that needs addressing.

The hotel is impressive no matter what time of the day you see it, but if you pass by it late at night you may capture its true essence. You may see people coming in and out dressed in tuxedos and silk dresses or hear piano music spilling into the night. You may see children, playing hide and seek in the vast corridors under their nanny's stern watch.

At other times, you may see suitcases stacked at the front entrance, or valets cleaning off hats and coats, and doormen bowing for one last time to the departing quests. You may see the concierge, still dressed in his elegant uniform, locking the guest book away. Cooks, chambermaids, bellboys, and upper management all gathered around the bar, sipping cognac. Come morning, these doors will be locked forever, the hotel left in its silence and memories.

Hotel Sans Rival, *"Unrivaled," art nouveau building on Liossion and Konstantinou Paleologou Streets*

HOTEL SANS RIVAL

Sans Rival is one of the oldest hotels in Athens and is a true architectural gem. It's been standing for almost a century, minutes away from the once popular Square Vathis, also known as Independence Square. Sans Rival means "Unrivaled," and to this day it carries its name with pride.

The hotel consisted of fifty rooms and was advertised as a "Mega Sleeping Hotel," equal to the finest hotels of Europe. It boasted running water and the prospect of a hot bath. Its reputation reached far and wide and at various times was visited by dignitaries, famous actors, and musicians.

Today, the hotel is closer than ever to revealing its secrets and freeing its ghosts. A contract has been signed for its restoration with the promise that every detail will remain in place. The hope is that other sleeping giants will be awakened and restored with care, bringing back the old splendor to a neighborhood that so desperately needs it.

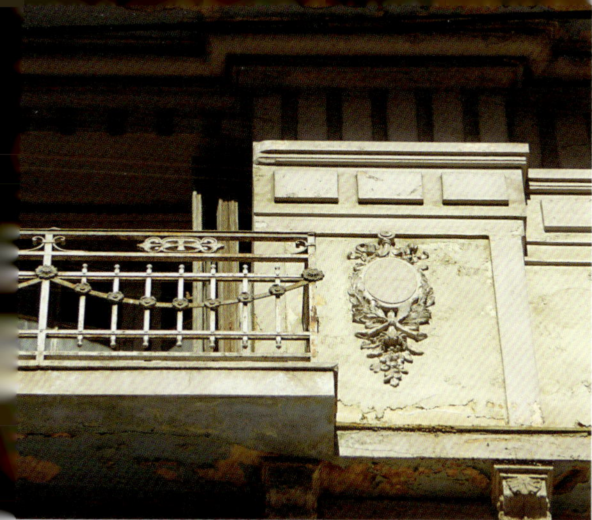

Top: *Detail of building's facade with cartouches*

Right: *Hotel's entrance under renovation*

Following pages: *Advertised as the "Mega Sleeping Hotel," Sans Rival boasted running water and the "possibility" of a hot bath*

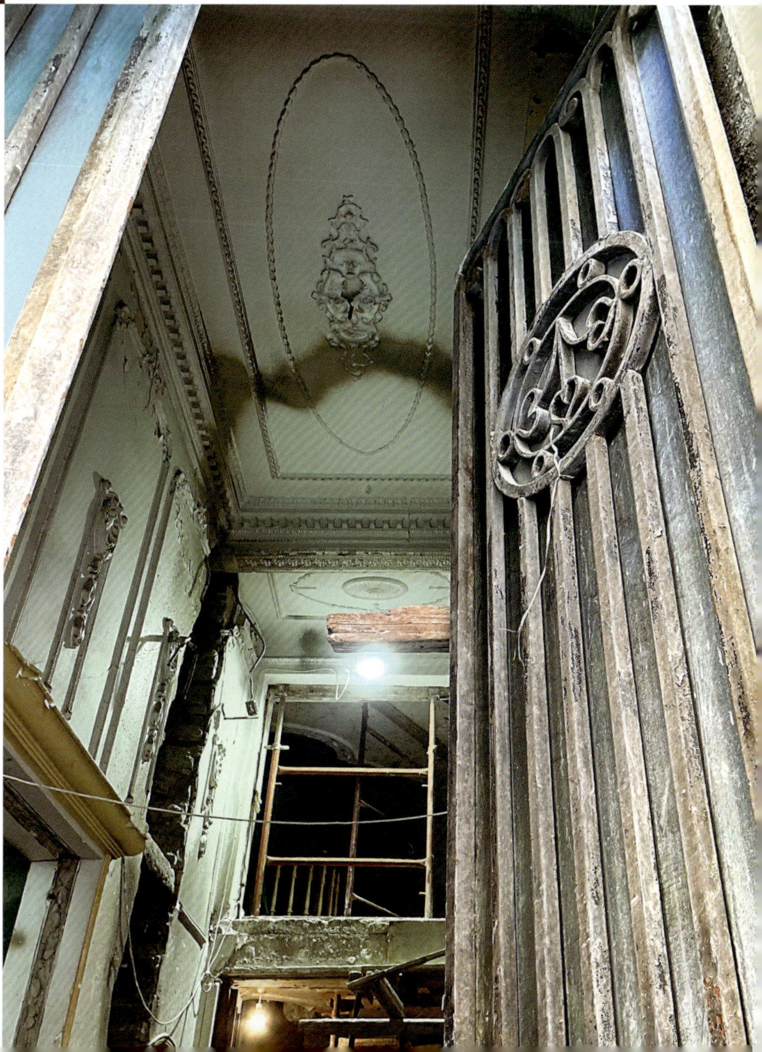

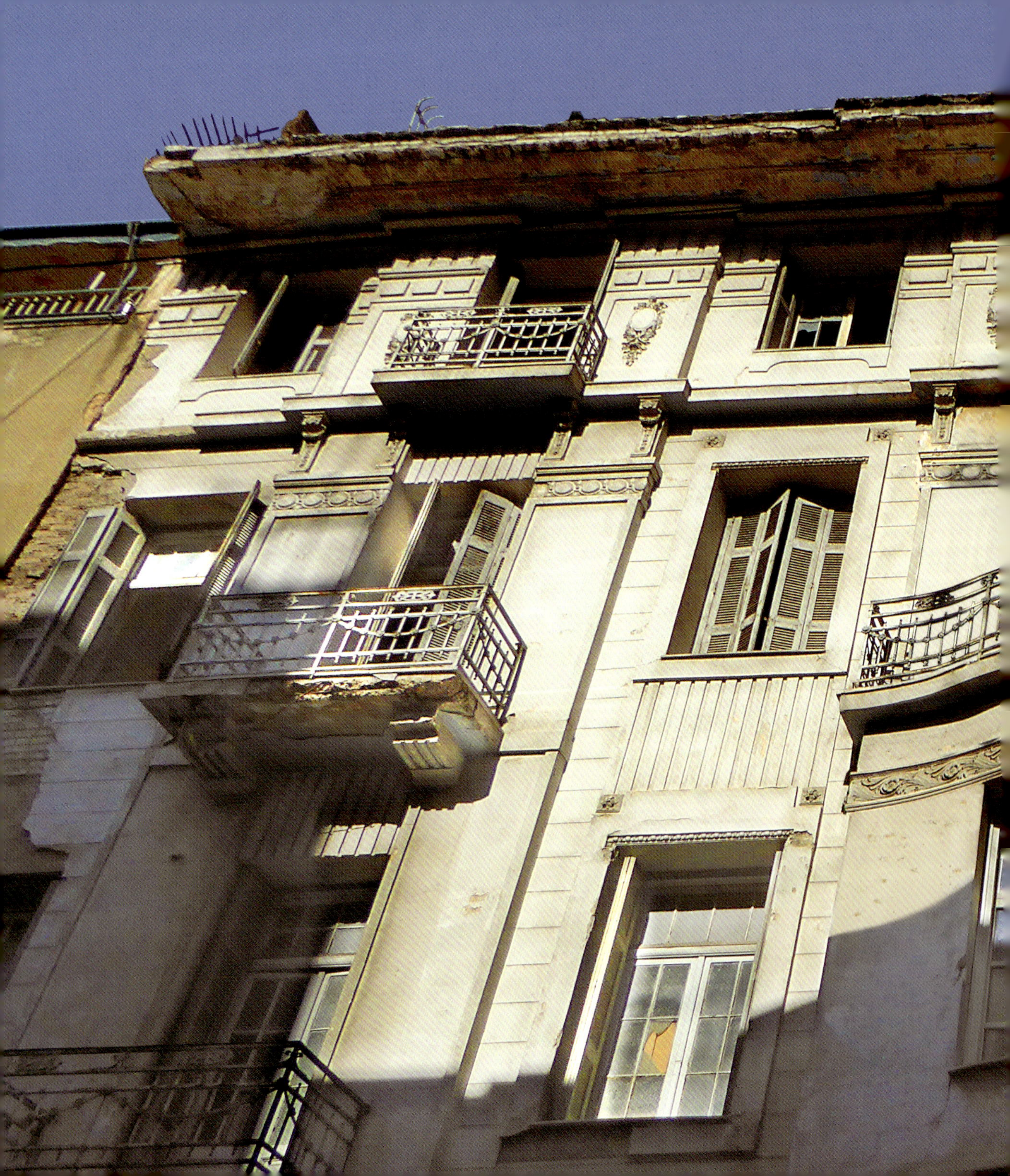

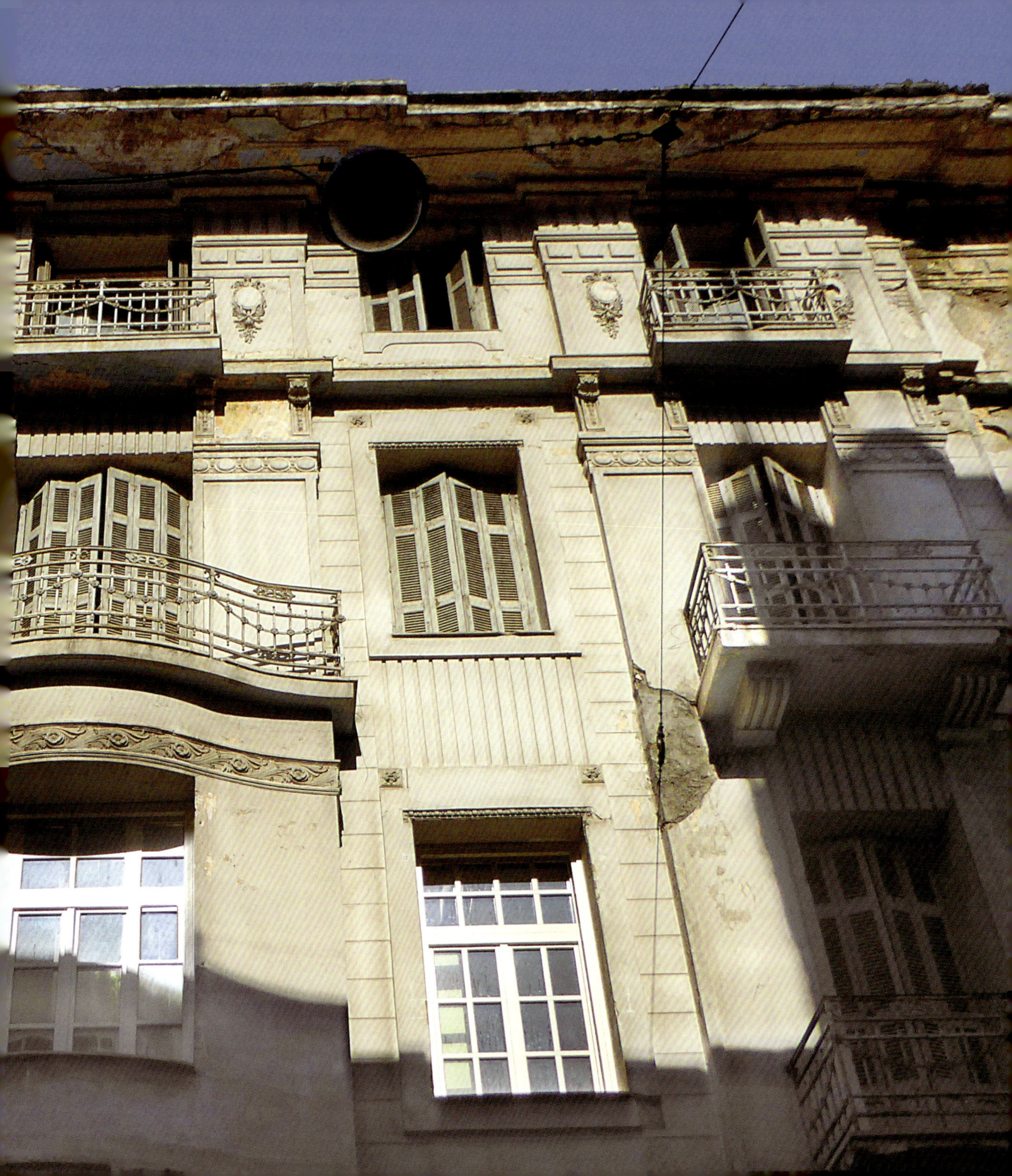

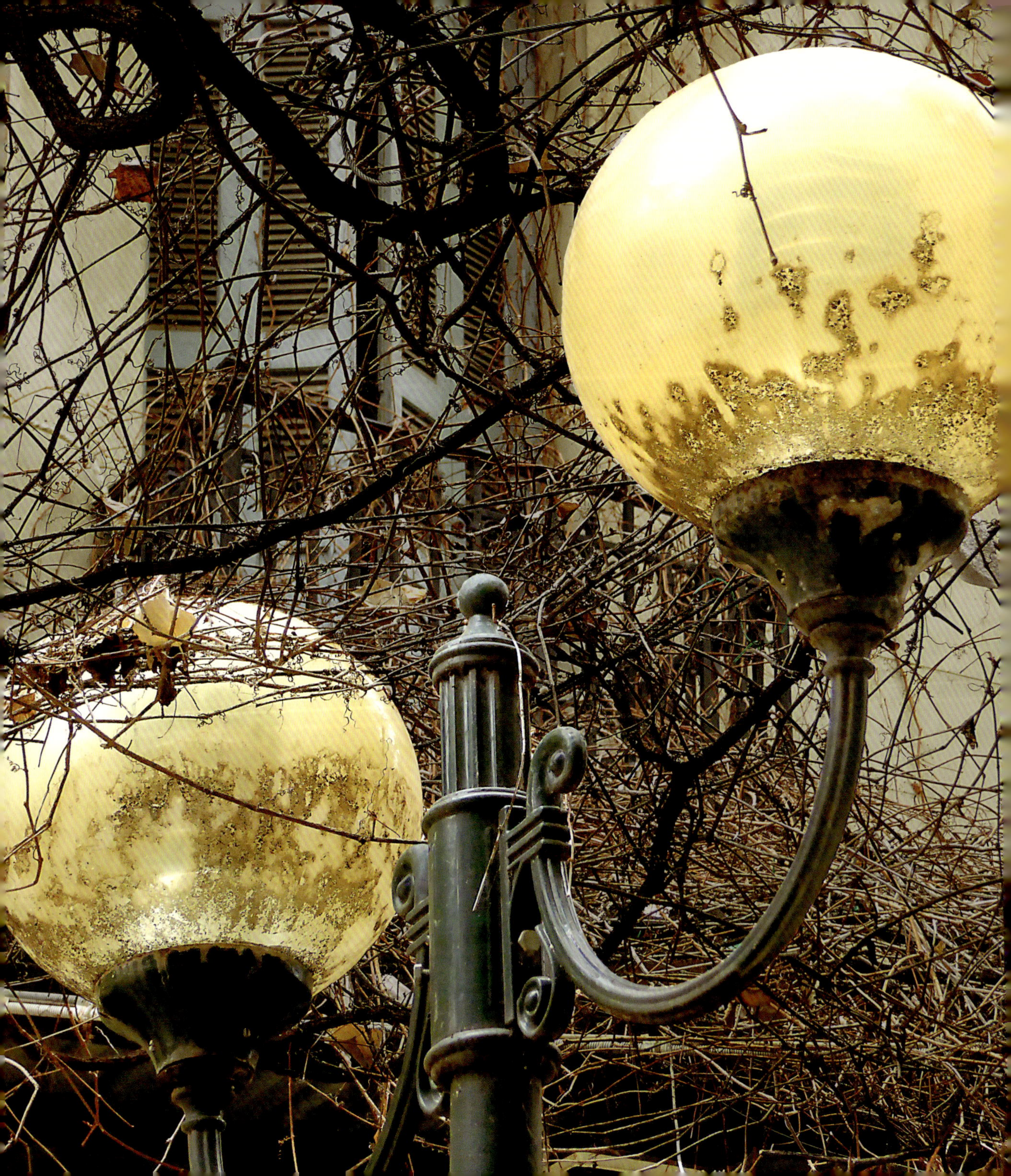

HOTEL ELIKON

A memory. I'm about sixteen years old, hurrying through Dorou Street looking over my shoulder. I'm anxious, but it's the fastest way to the train. I'm late, and I know that my parents will be worried. Right in front of the entrance to the Elikon Hotel, I drop my bag; books and pencils scatter everywhere.

A man standing below a broken light post makes an obscene gesture. Anger spills over me. I pick up a book and throw it at him, hitting him on the shoulder. The man curses and disappears into the darkness. From the first-floor balcony, someone is applauding. "Good for you," an elderly man shouts down at me. I smile. It's the first time I ever smiled on this street.

Walking past the Elikon Hotel today, I have mixed feelings. The hotel's run-down, blue color is now painted bright yellow. The windows are washed, and the sign painted in red and white. I've read somewhere that the hotel has been cleaned up and offers decent accommodations. I hope it's true, but the feeling of unease never leaves me.

Elikon Hotel, *3 Dorou Street, Omonoia*

HOTEL ELIKON

I turn the corner, still observing the building and its narrow entrance. I notice the pure neoclassical lines, the freshly painted green shutters, and the cast iron balconies. The place is far bigger than I remember it but maybe it's because I never took the time to "really" see it.

Next to it, Hotel Europa, stands enveloped in silence. The alley feels abandoned like in the old days. Some discarded clothes hang from the tree branches undulating in the wind. The light post with its art deco design still seems to be broken. Not much has changed after all.

Satovriandou Street, or "Hotel Strip," as this alley is often called, extends from Omonoia Square to the Larissa train station. Block after block, hotels, in various levels of decay, mark the street, remnants of an Athens founded in antithesis. Hotel signs, such as the "Mediterrannae," "Eptanissos," "Satobrian," "Aktiaon," speak of a different glory and affluence. Night after night, they patiently wait to be lit up and welcome their new customers. Will they ever arrive?

Opposite: *Hotel Elikon;* **Following pages:** *Clothes hanging from a tree branch on Satovriandou Street*

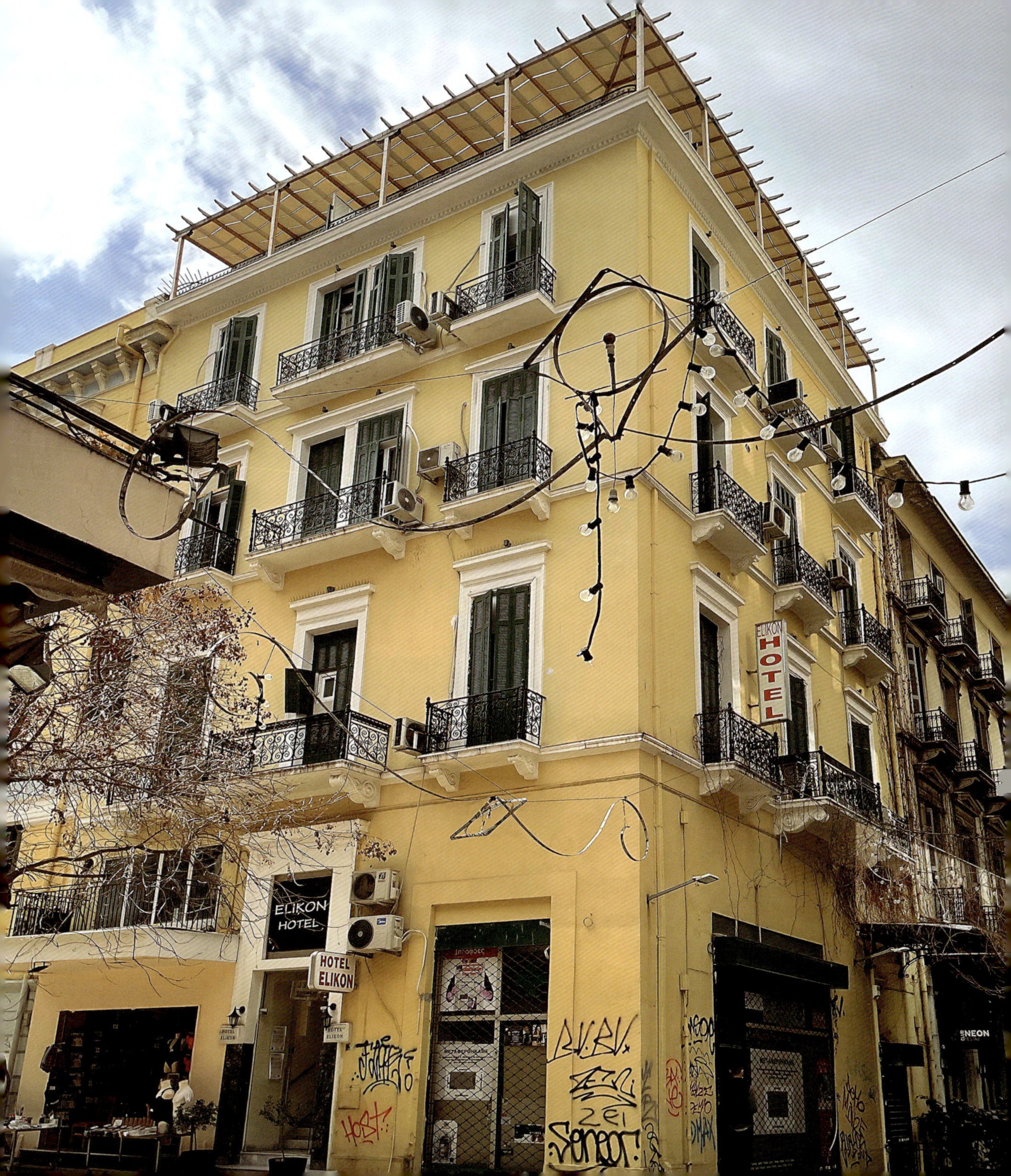
ELIKON
HOTEL
ELIKON
HOTEL
HOTEL
ELIKON
NEON

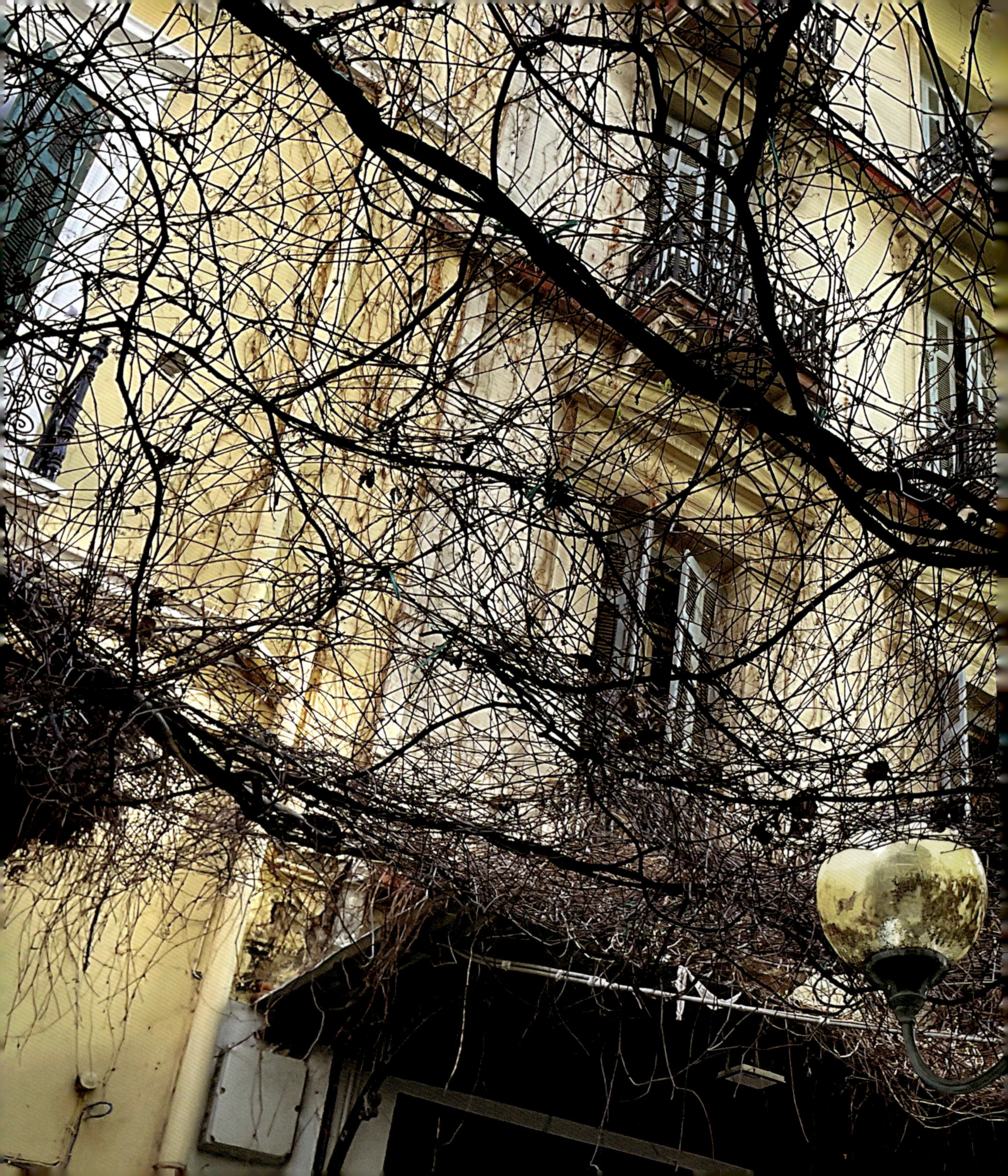

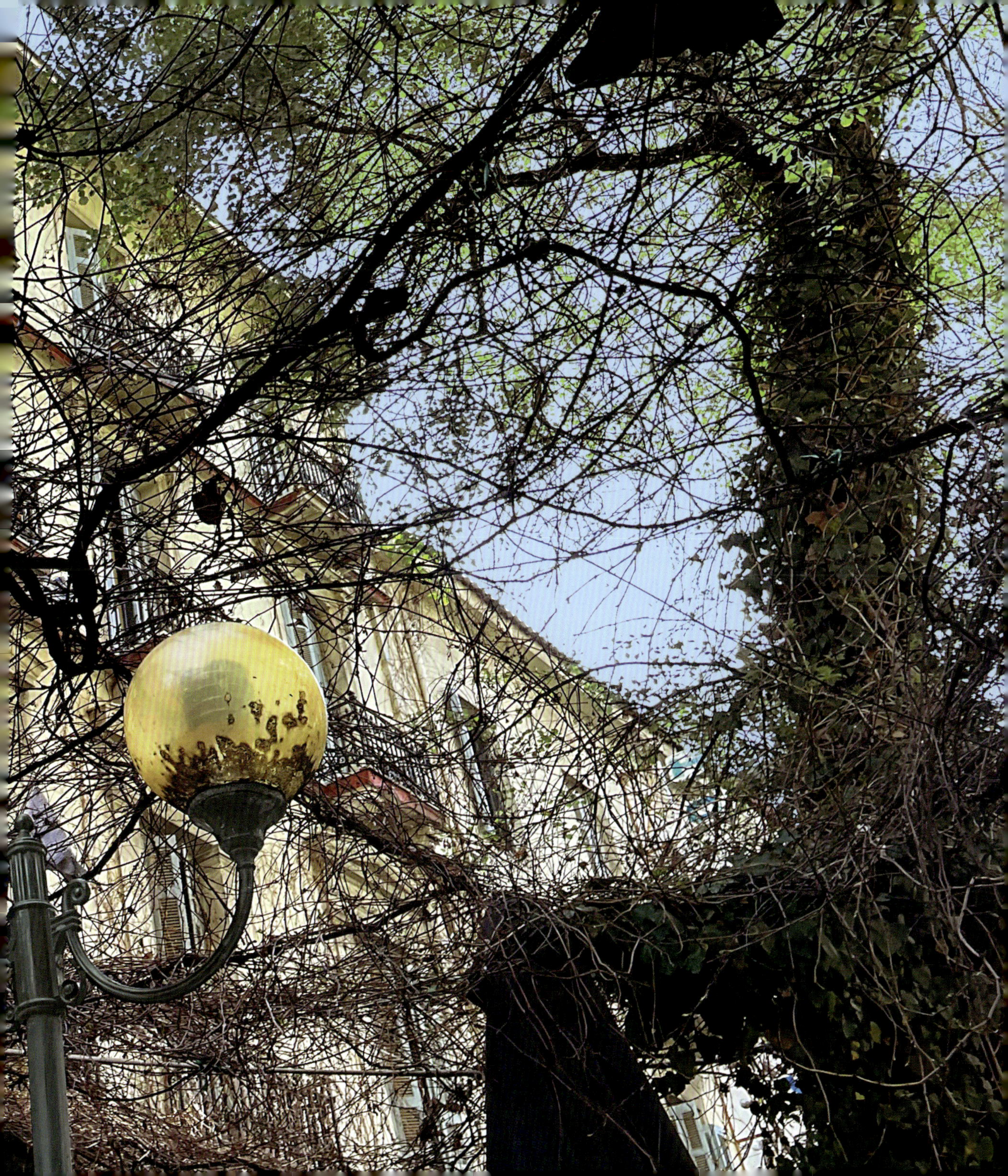

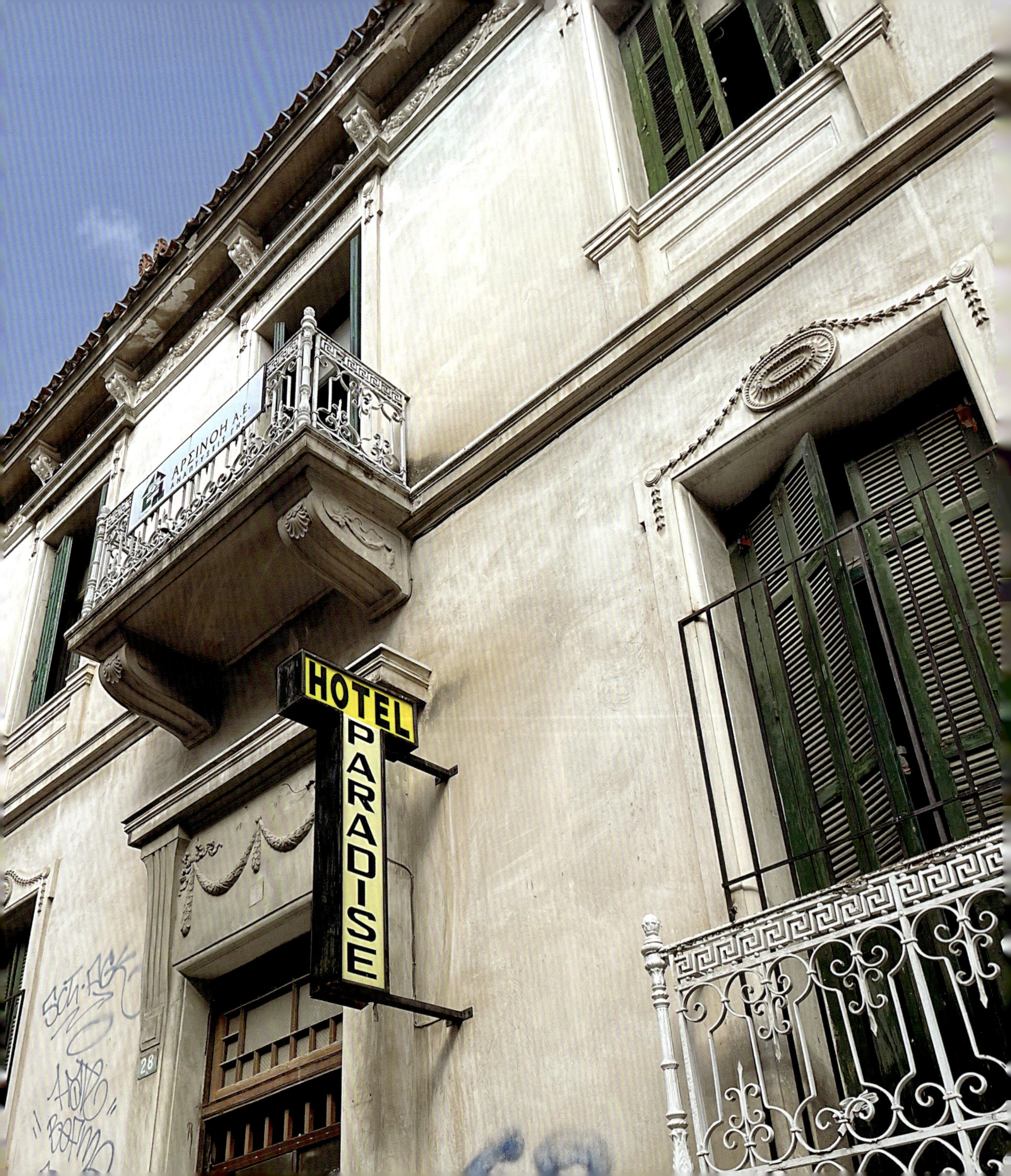
ΑΡΣΙΝΟΗ Α.Ε.
ΑΝΑΠΤΥΞΕΙΣ ΓΗΣ
HOTEL
PARADISE
28

HOTEL PARADISE

Two mothers stand outside the school's gates waiting for classes to be over. They talk about the new supermarket opening up in the neighborhood and wonder if the local grocery store will have to close. They seem to be split about what's best for the area, but they both agree that they need more shopping choices.

The neighborhood is so cut off from the rest of Athens, it might as well be in a different city. The sense of neglect is palatable. The buildings stand empty, as if, one day, most of the inhabitants decided to walk away en masse. Vanished. Those who remained don't seem to fare any better.

Mothers in dark colored hijabs push baby carriages in and out of neglected apartments, as men loiter on the stairs smoking cigarettes. Most of the apartments are on the ground floor or in basements with few windows and no sunlight. In winter, the walls absorb so much moisture, the temperature becomes frigid, and in summer, the heat is so intense, it makes it hard to breath.

Paradise Hotel, *corner of Fabrierou and Akominatou Streets*

HOTEL PARADISE

The streets always seem dark, even if there's sunlight, and the dumpsters overflow with uncollected garbage. The few stores sell the basics: milk, soft drinks, cigarettes and maybe some vegetables. Otherwise, one must wait for the street market that takes place once a week, but even then, the prices may be too high, leaving one empty handed.

When night falls people hurry into their apartments drawing their curtains. Those who lived in the area before the economic crisis speak of a friendly neighborhood where everybody knew each other and where children played in the streets without worry. Now they describe places where fifteen to twenty men share two rooms taking turns who is to sleep while the others search for work.

Hotel Paradise, across from the school, is a testament to this decay, its name adding an extra irony. Pigeons fly in and out of the windows, undeterred by the past or the future. Its shutters, half broken now and beaten up from the wind and the rain, seem to mock us, silent reminders of how ephemeral all things are.

Opposite: *Detail of sea shells, pomegranate garlands, meanders, and acanthus flowers on the building's facade, symbols of well being*

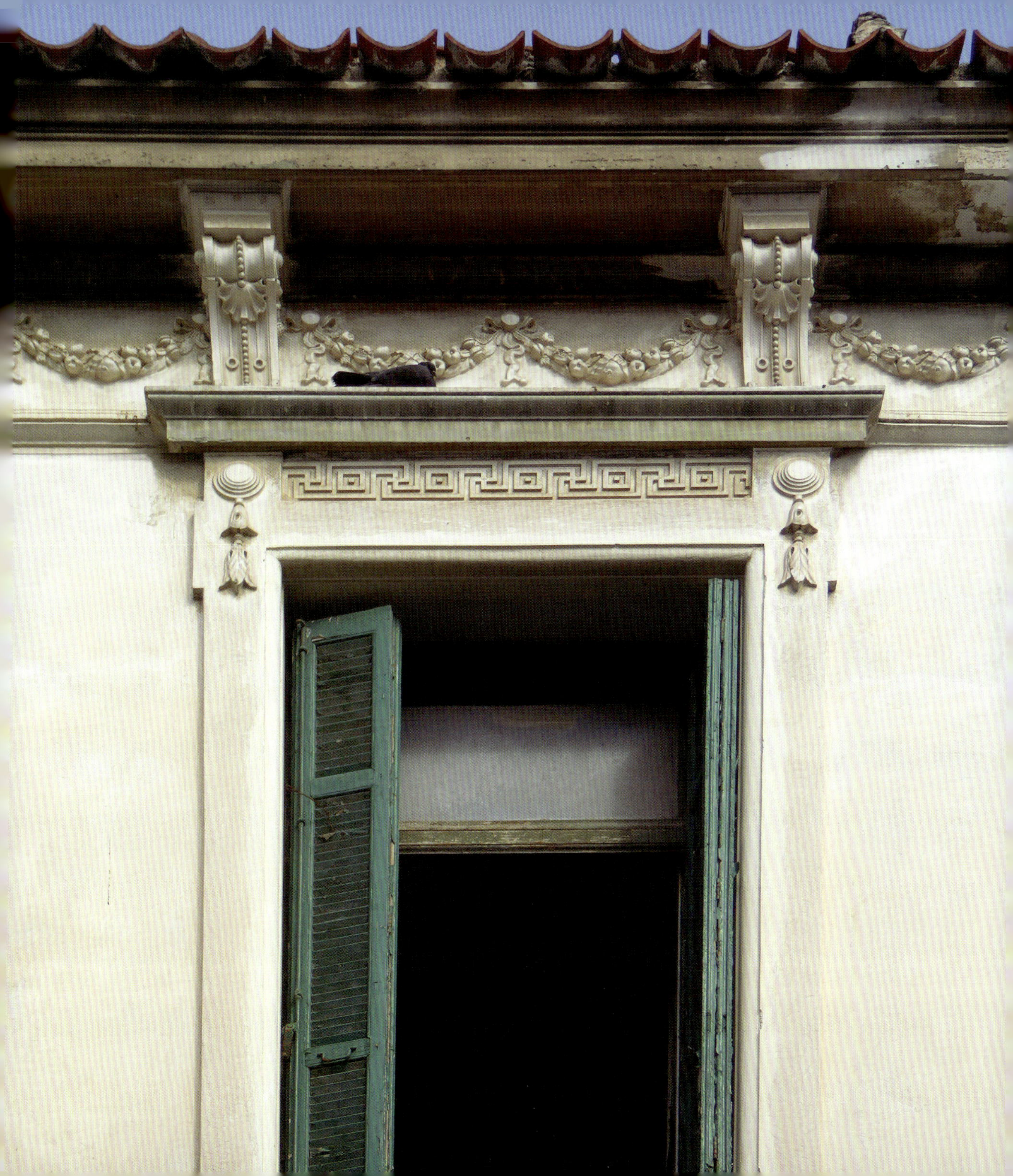

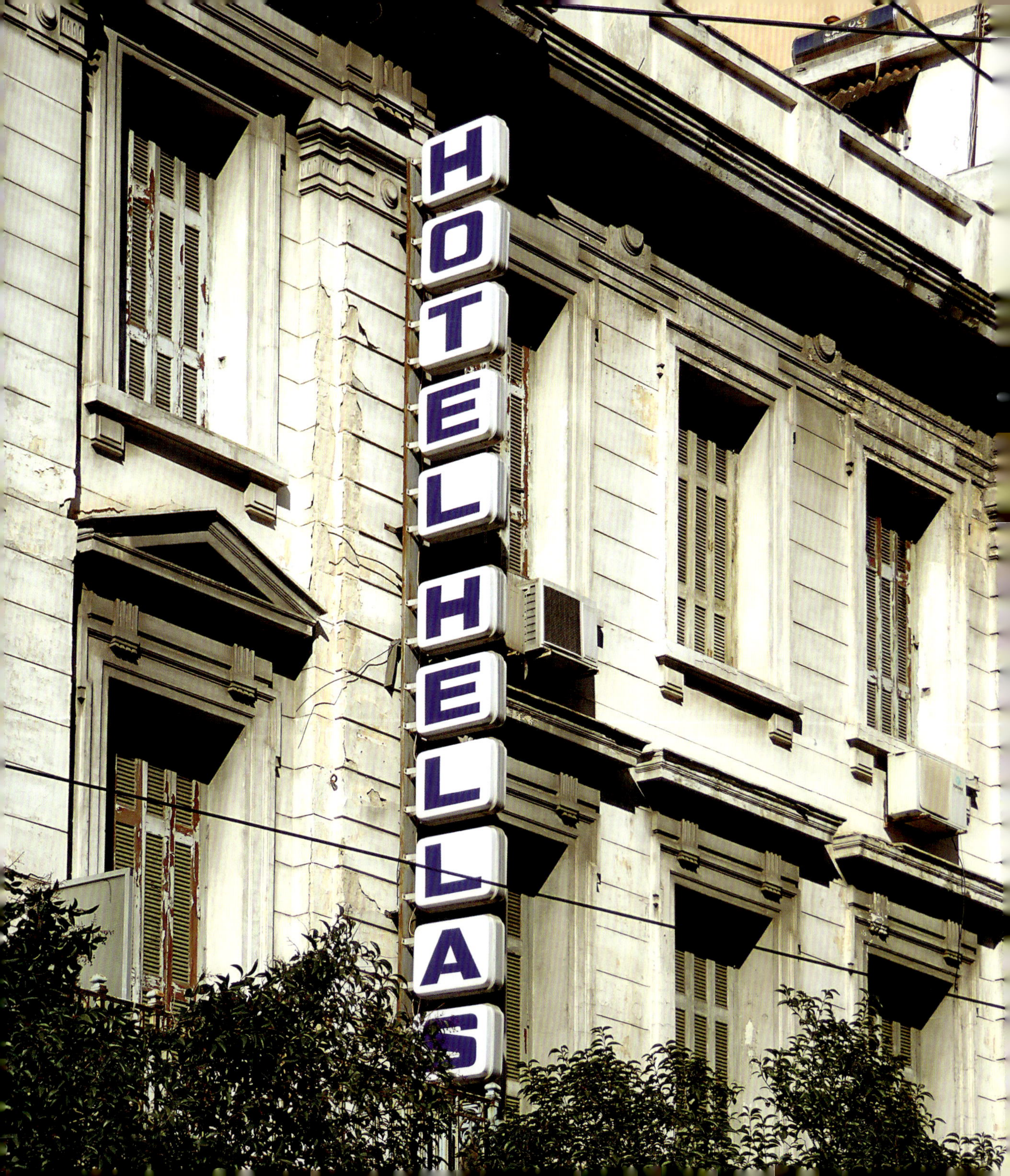
HOTEL HELLAS

HOTEL HELLAS

At the side street of Hotel Hellas, under the scaffolding, a user pulls a filthy blanket over his head. His partner, a woman of undetermined age, sucks hard on a cigarette butt and then tosses it away. Her eyes are glazed, and her hands shake. She scratches a scab, and it starts bleeding. A few feet away, a man shoots heroin in broad daylight. Containers of half-eaten food and dirty coffee cups are scattered everywhere. The stench of human waste is so unbearable, people hurry away.

Across the street, a store owner unloads some boxes. His expression is one of both pity and disgust. A squad of policemen on motorcycles soon arrive. They seem to know the users, because their manner is relaxed. The man who had just shot the heroin stands up but staggers back down. The store owner shakes his head. "Even if they cart them away, they'll be back by tonight," he says. The cops drive away.

Hotel Hellas, a working hotel until the 1990s, has seen many changes. Imposing, like so many of the other abandoned hotels in the area, it must

---

Hotel Hellas, *3 Septemvriou and Satovriandou Streets, Omonoia*

HOTEL HELLAS

have been a wonder to look at in its heyday. Built in the first decade of the twentieth century, it was considered one of the best and most frequented hotels in the area. Spacious, with an emblematic exterior, it once proudly carried its name, Hellas.

Today, the hotel looks as tired as everything else in this part of Athens. It's hard to ignore how unsavory and dangerous the area has become. However, like everything else, time passes, and things change. Who knows, maybe one day the hotel, like so many others in the area, will regain its former beauty. Neighborhoods change as different classes move in and out. It's inevitable that sooner or later these hotels will be restored, but the question remains for whom and at what cost?

In the meantime, people keep walking with heads bent, living in uncertainty and eager to erase images of such despair from their minds. As for the children, the moment the school bell rings, the mothers run into the courtyard, grabbing them by the hand, hurrying away.

Opposite: *Hotel signage in quintessential typographic treatment* ***Following pages:*** *Side view of the hotel, now a gathering place for squatters and the homeless*

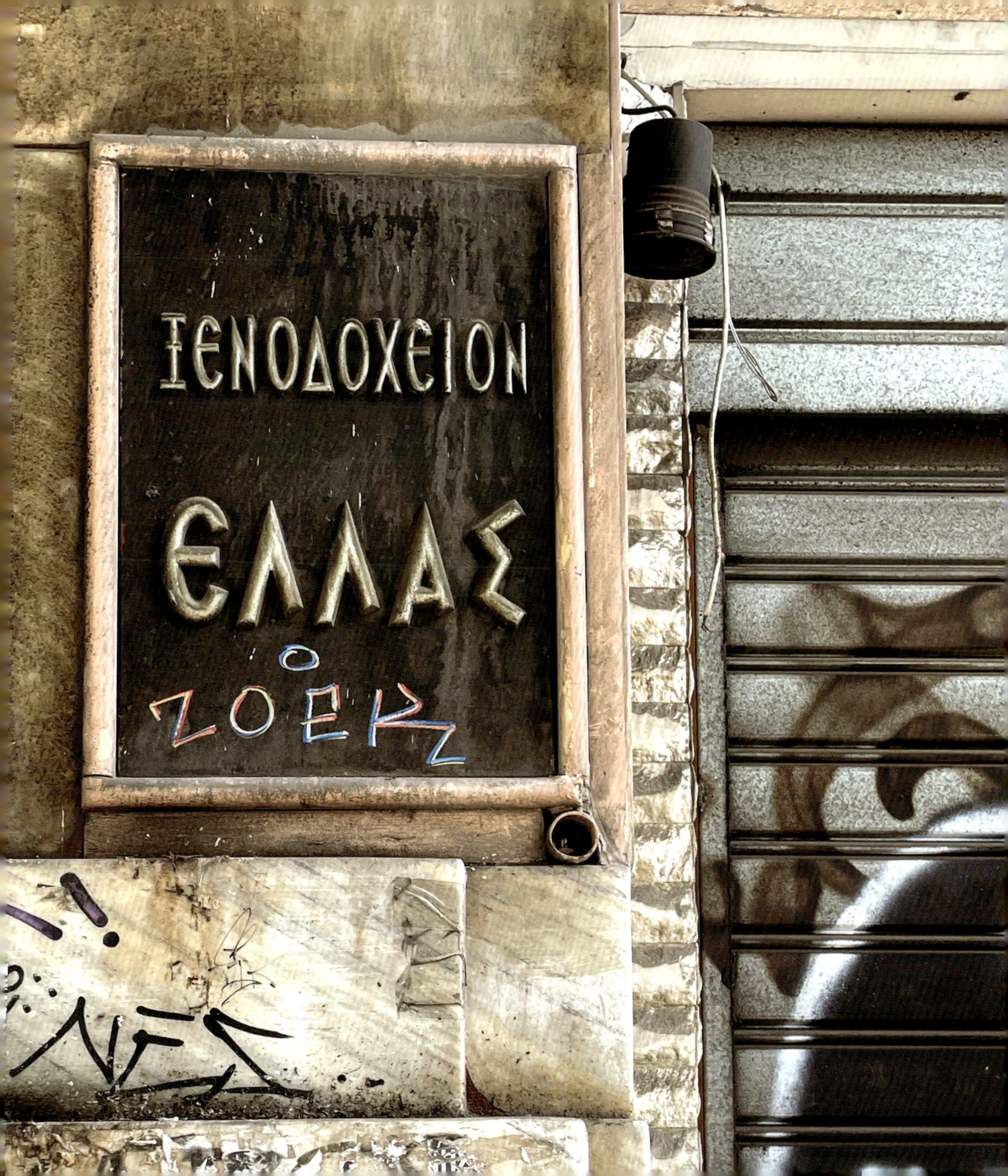
ΞΕΝΟΔΟΧΕΙΟΝ
ΕΛΛΑΣ

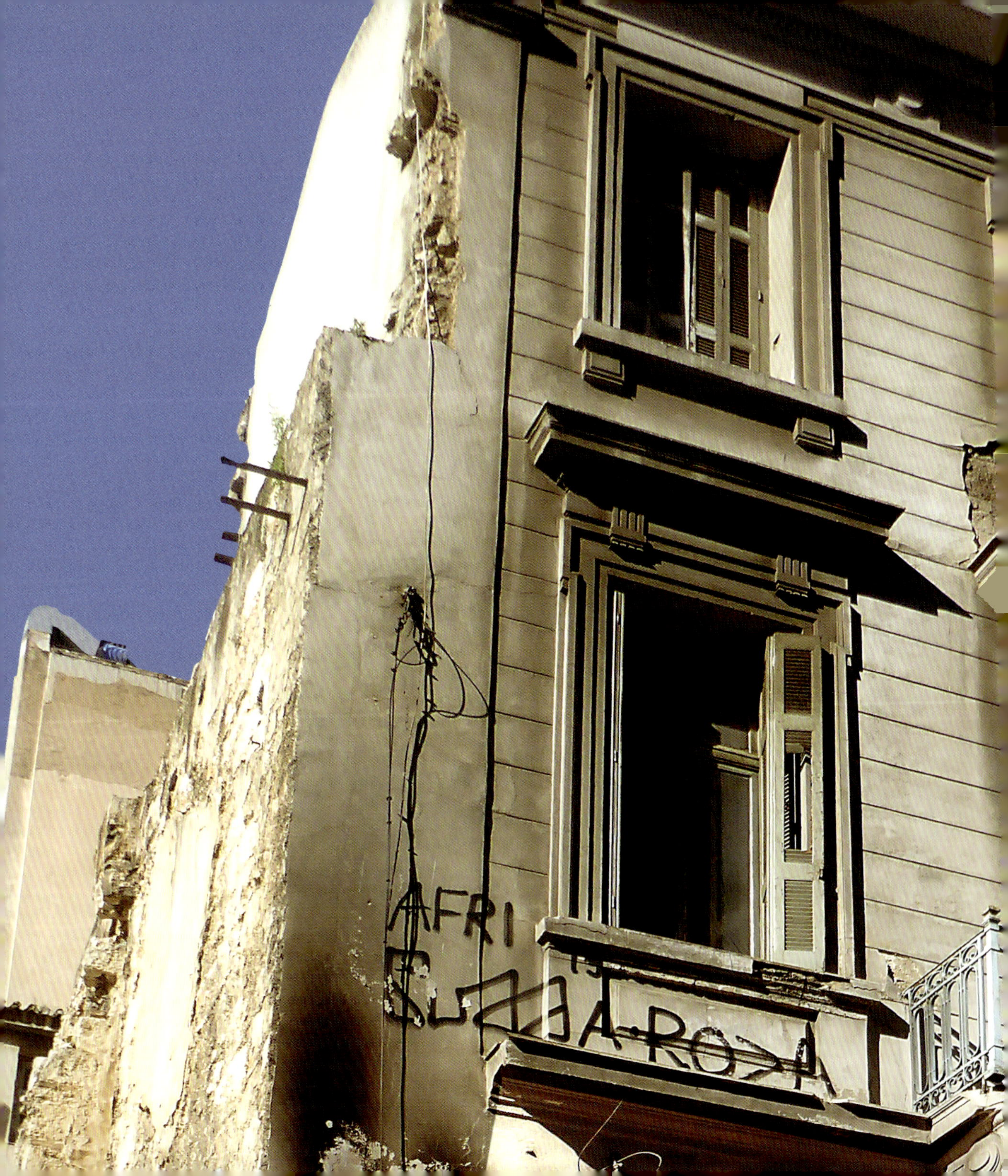
AFRI

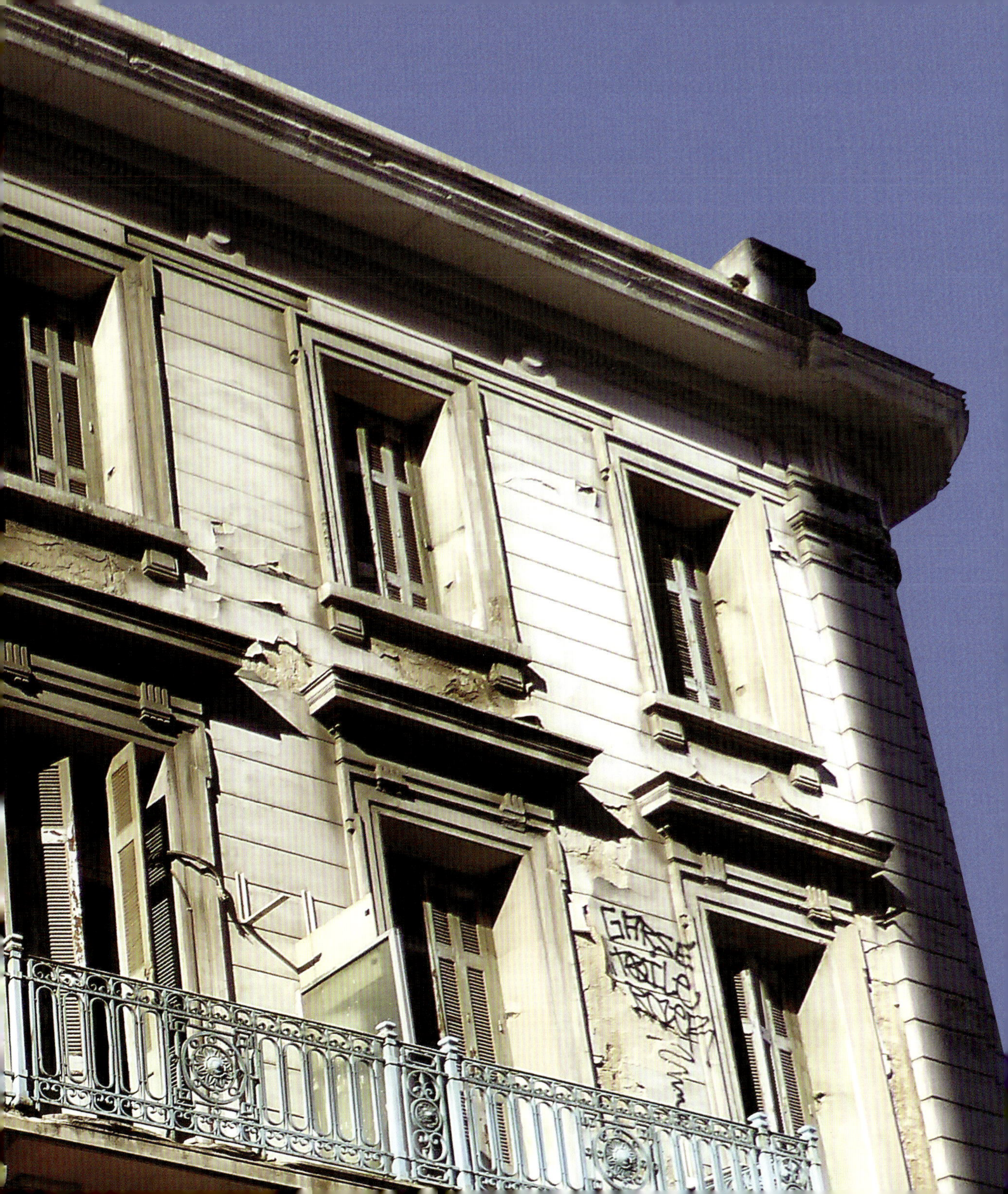

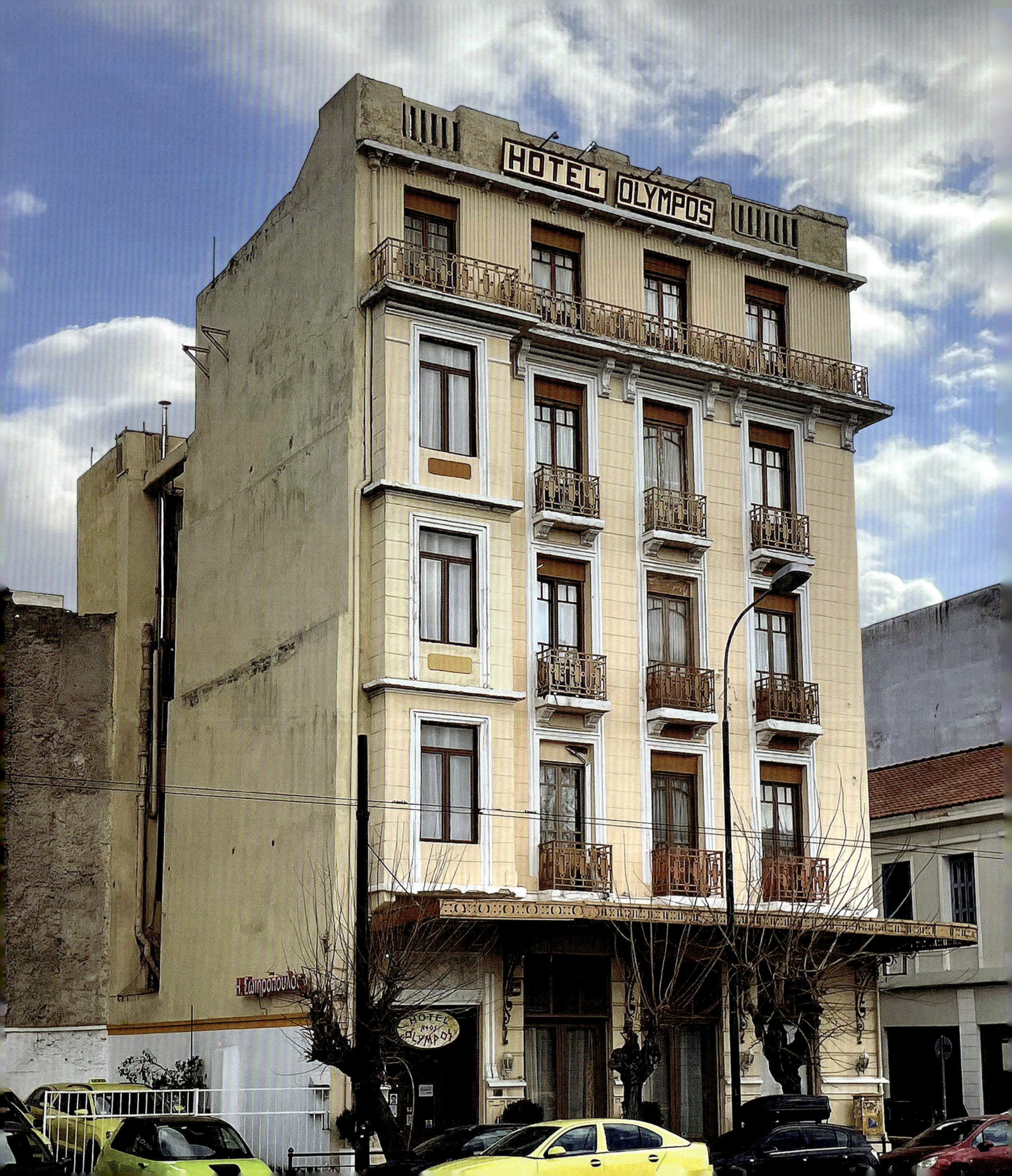
HOTEL
OLYMPOS

HOTEL NEOS OLYMPOS

Once abandoned and now used as a hostel, Hotel New Olympus stands at the very end of the old hotel strip. Another grand beauty for its time, it was one of the most frequented hotels, not only because of its proximity to the station, but also for its impeccable service. One glimpse at its exterior, and the exquisitely designed balconies, proves how stunning it must have looked in its time.

The hotel is located on Diligiannis Street, a major road and one of the gloomiest ones in the western part of Athens. Surrounded by brothels, auto repair shops, and light industries, it's a neighborhood that hardly any Athenians frequent, unless they absolutely have to.

No matter how isolated and marginal the area is, magnificent neoclassical buildings still manage to maintain some dignity. Alleys that lead to mysterious castle-like structures and empty lots with rising murals above the highway, makes one wonder what kind of neighborhood it used to be. It's difficult to discern the nationalities of the people living here, but the road to assimilation is a hard one.

Hotel New Olympus, *38 Theodore Diligiannis Avenue*

HOTEL NEOS OLYMPOS

A true conundrum of architectural styles and periods, the neighborhood attracts and appalls with no easy answers. Refugees, immigrants, and the poor have made this area their home, trying to live their lives as quietly as they can.

The abandoned Larissa railway station, sitting across from the hotel and surrounded by barbed wire and trash, is another architectural marvel. The main part of the station was built between 1884 and 1889, based on plans by a team of French engineers. Its final form, a combination of neoclassicism with art deco elements, was drawn from designs by Ernest Ziller, who added the dome-like roofs.

There's talk that the station may be converted into a railroad museum, but there's no indication of any work being done. Looking at the sunset spilling into the horizon and turning everything golden, one can't help but think that maybe this gloomiest of neighborhoods can be transformed into something Olympian.

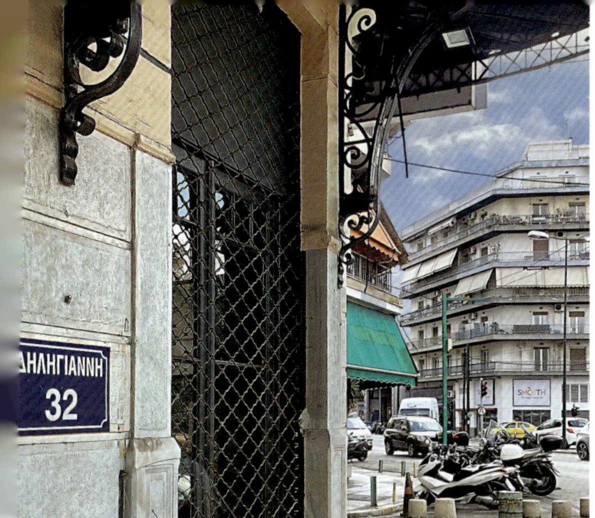

Top: *Diligiannis Street, a major industrial road of Athens*

Right: *Destroyed grounds of beautiful neoclassical building near Olympus Hotel*

Following pages: *Detail of exquisite cast iron work running around the hotel's perimeter*

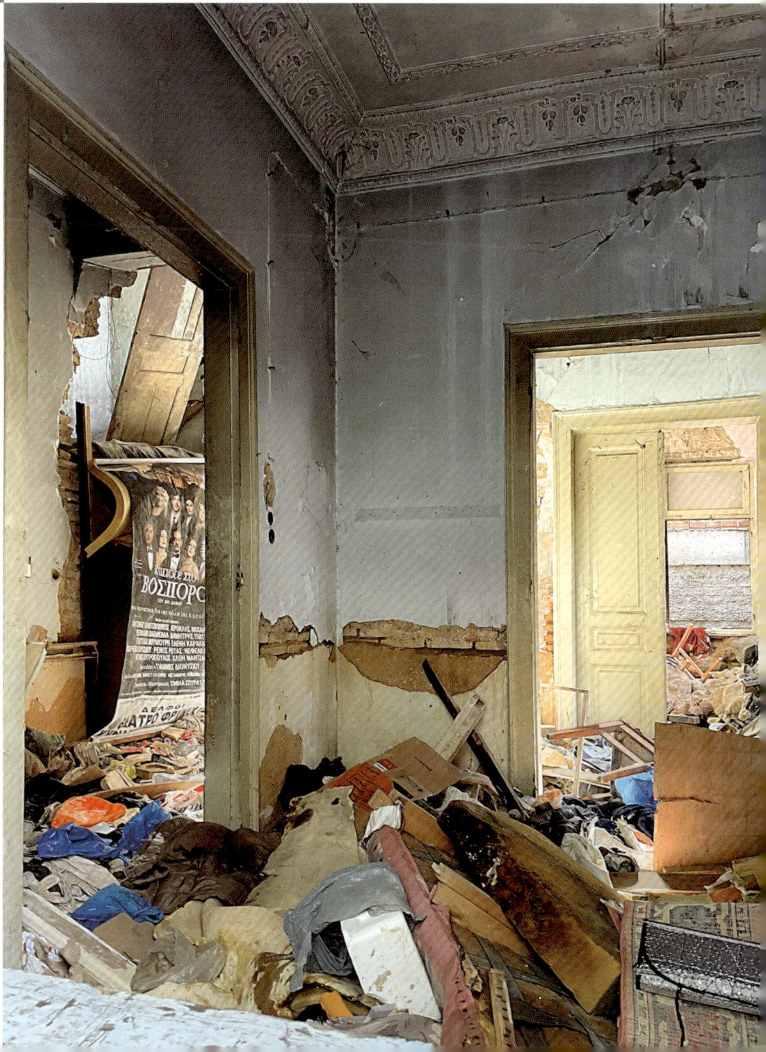

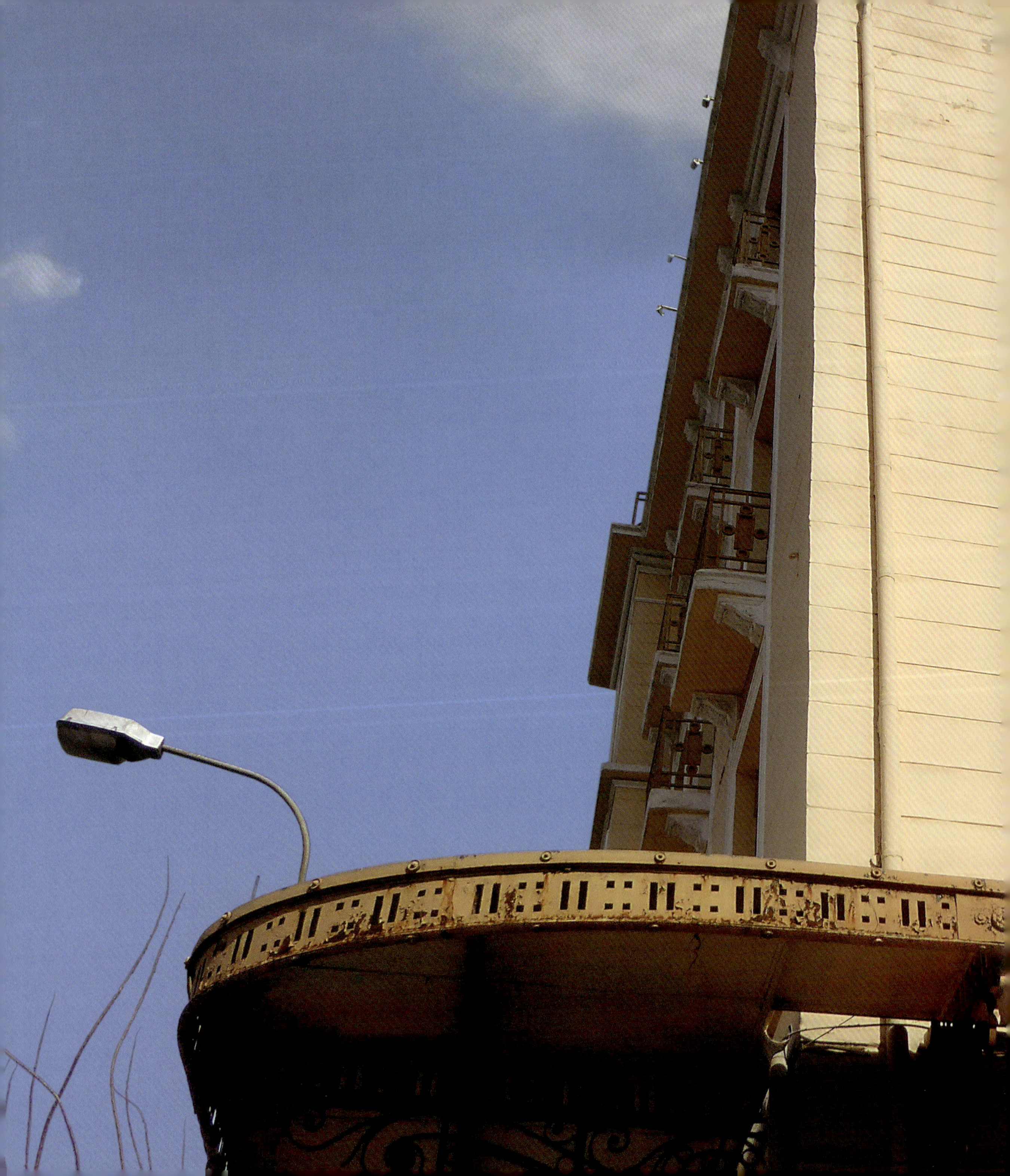

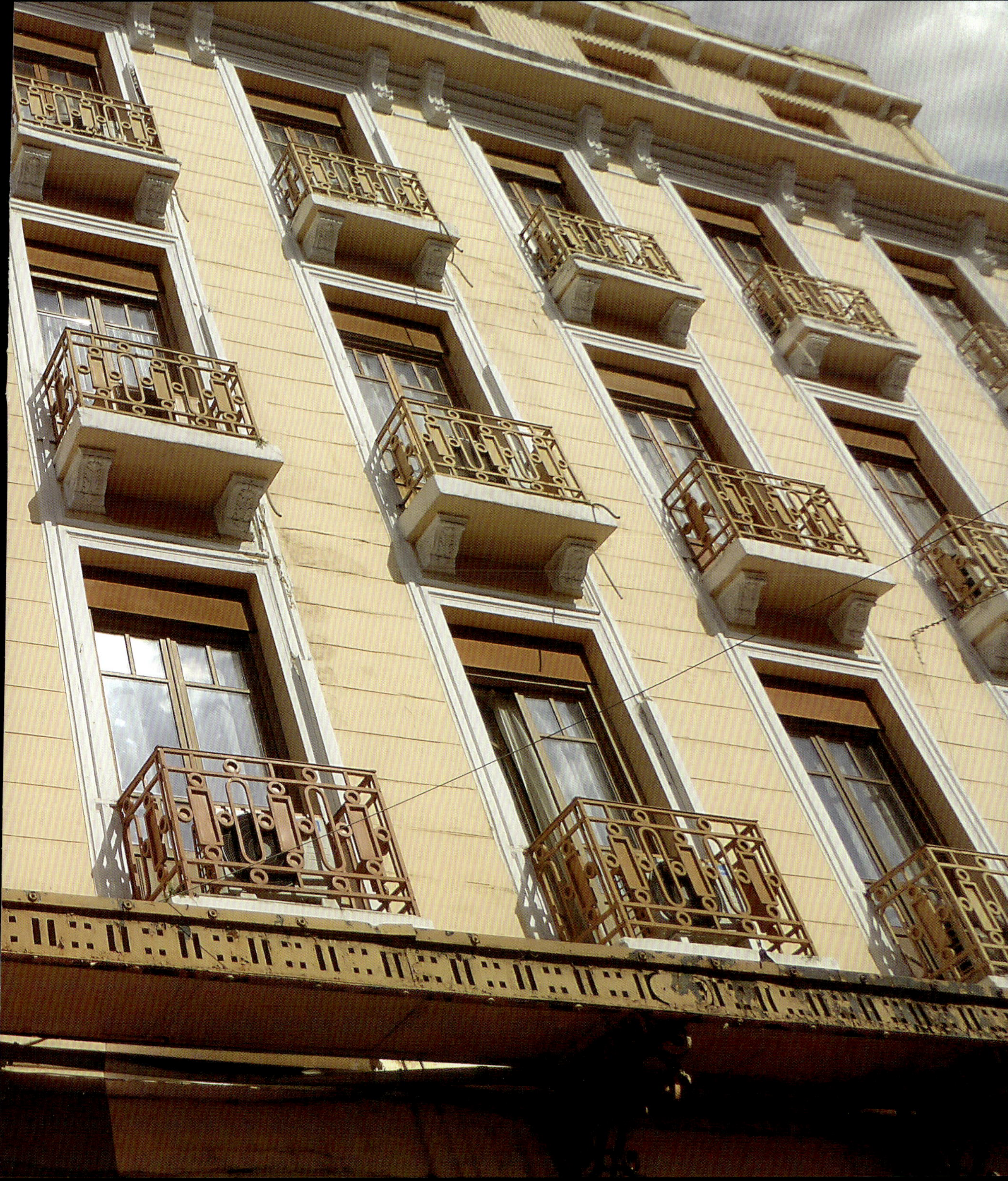

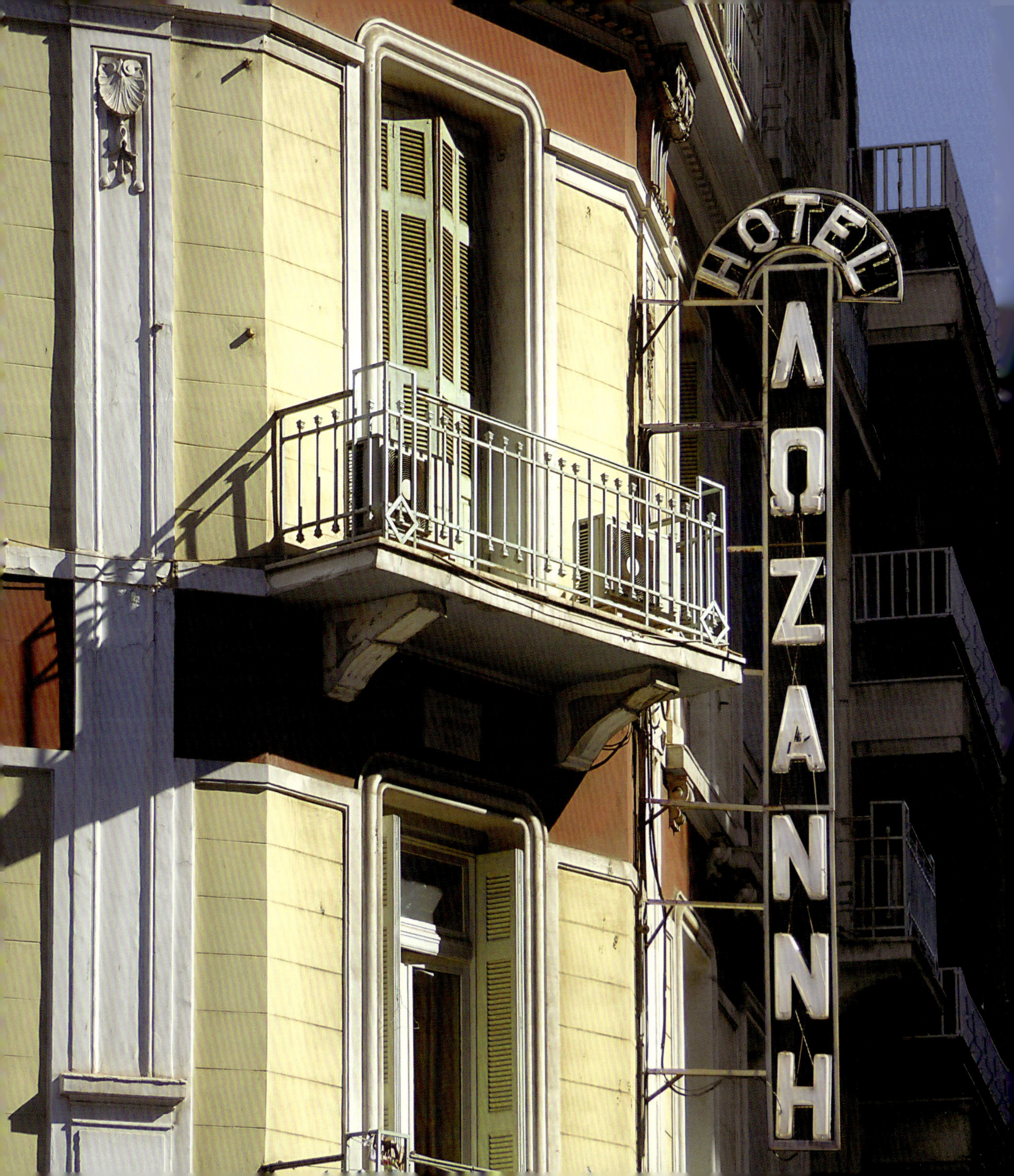
HOTEL
ΛΩΖΑΝΗ

HOTEL LAUSANNE

Hotel Lozanne, near Vathis Square, rises above the traffic like an aged mistress. Even from a distance the hotel exudes a melancholy that catches you unaware. Its Deco sign, with its elegant typography, speaks of summer resorts near the coast of southern France or Miami. You can almost feel the breeze as men in fresh linen suits and panama hats walk arm in arm with women under lace trimmed parasols. Suddenly a car passes, honking its horn, and the image vanishes. Reality sets in. What you're left with is a decayed street and the tired eyes of the small store vendors.

Hotel Lozanne is advertised as a hostel, although it looks more like a single room occupancy residence for men. Clothes hang on the balcony rails, and men gaze out from the windows smoking cigarettes. All around, small stores selling plastic houseware products and cheap clothes wait for someone to stop in. The customers are so few that someday the stores don't even bother opening. The plight of these hotels is obvious and raises questions. How did they get to this point of neglect?

Hotel Lausanne, *54 Kapodistriou Ioanni Street, near Vathis Square; early twentieth-century Art Deco sign*

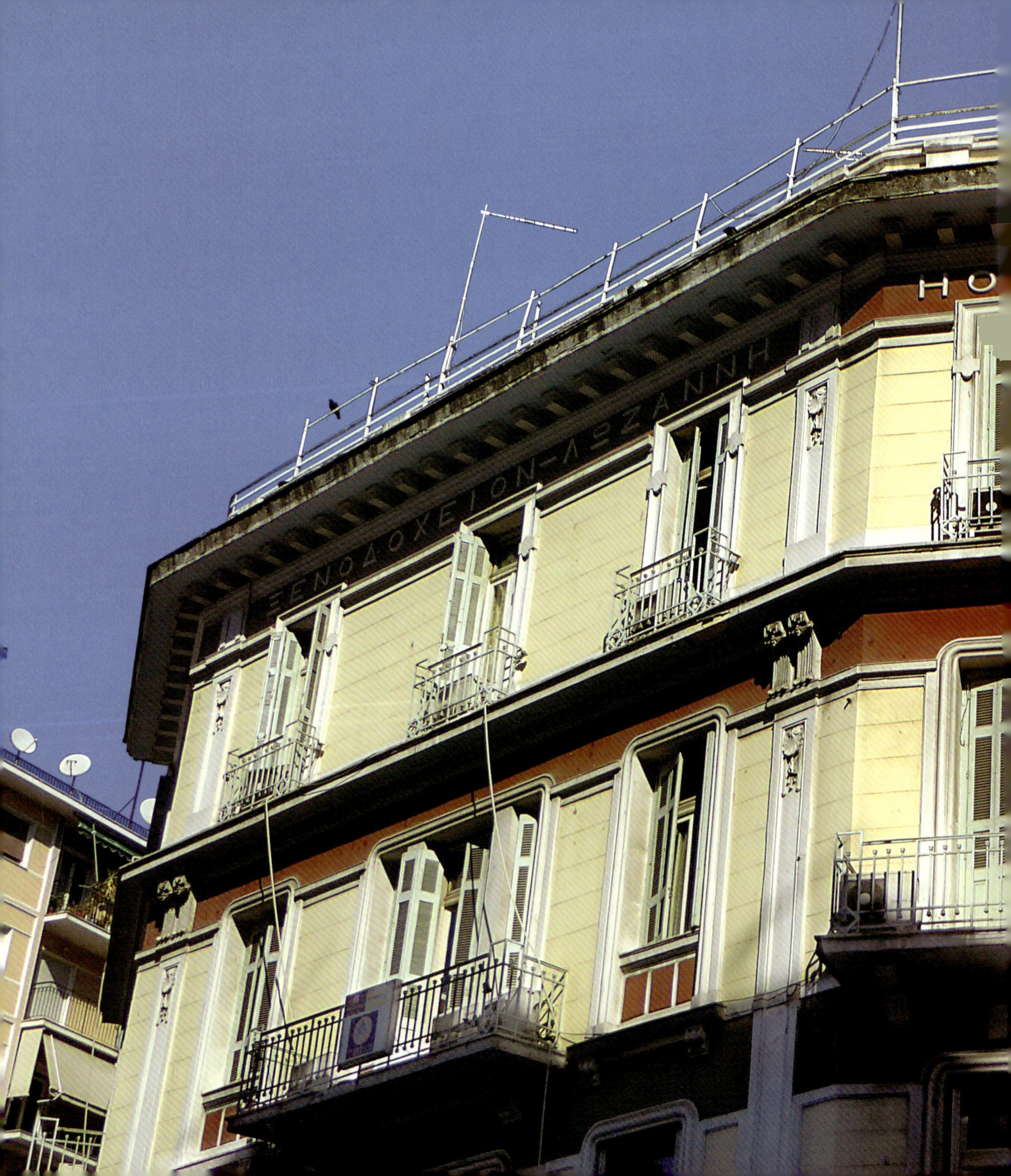
ΞΕΝΟΔΟΧΕΙΟΝ-ΛΩΖΑΝΝΗ

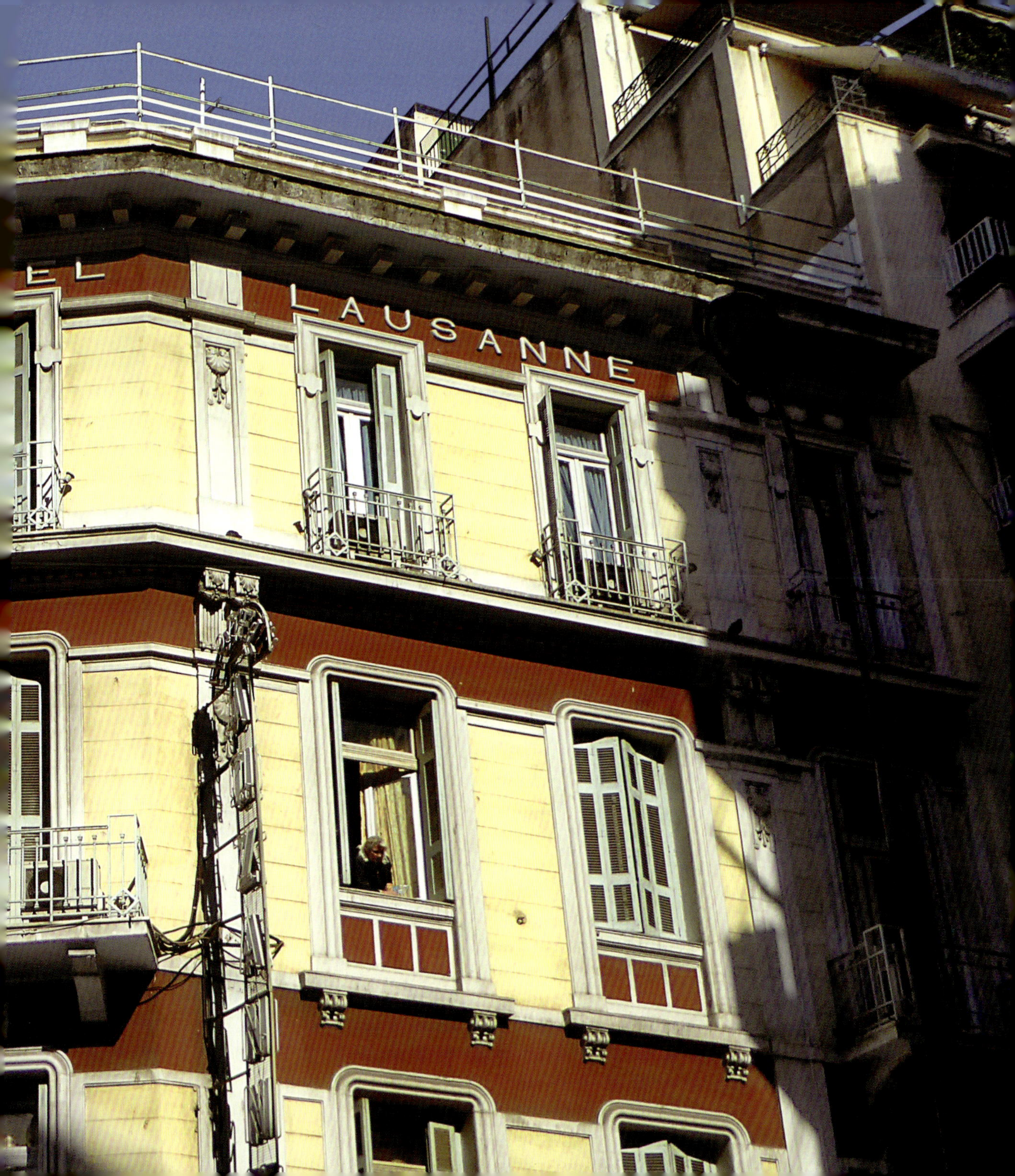
EL LAUSANNE

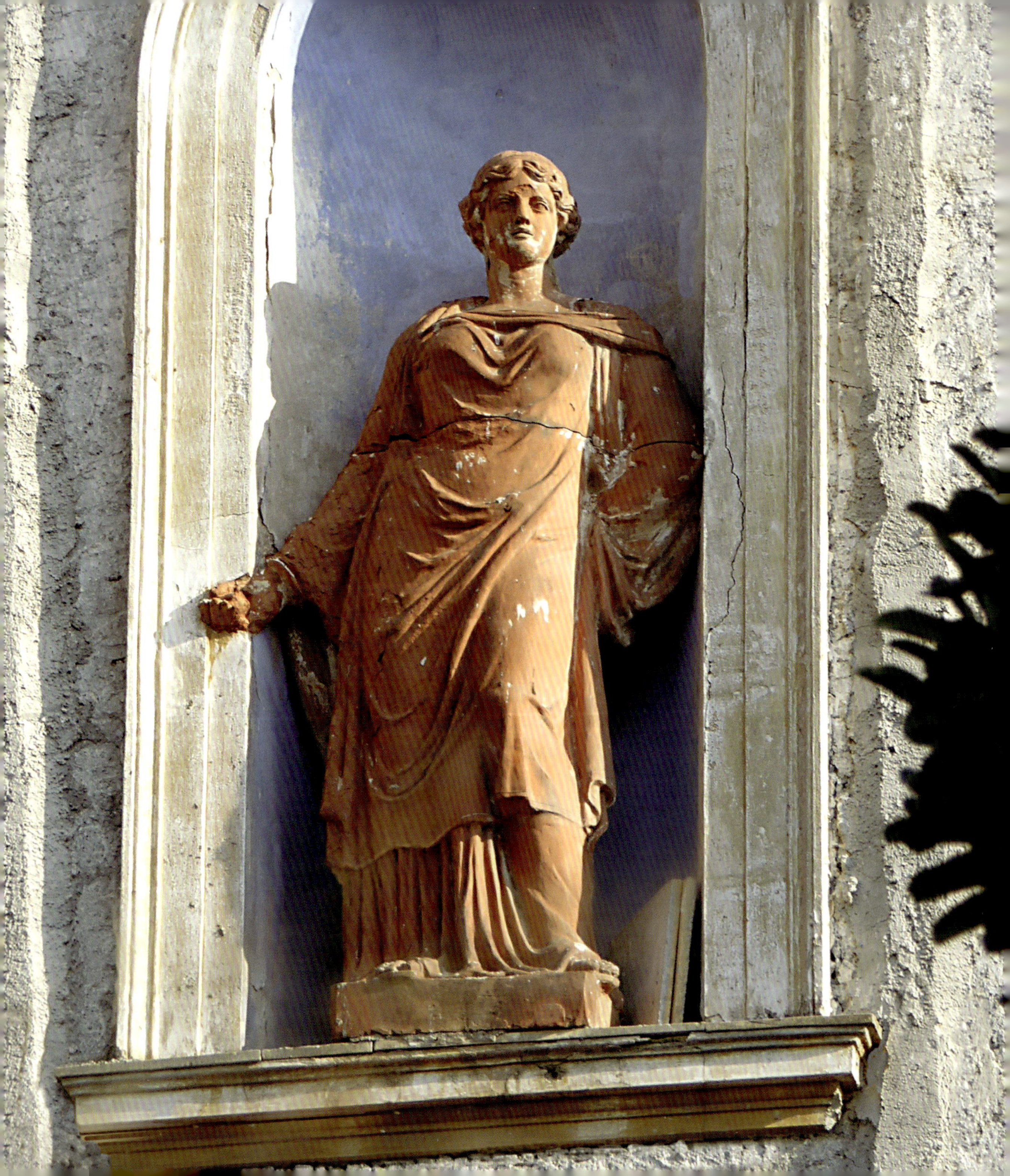

MUSEUM INDEX

Deciding which of the many museums to feature was not an easy process. Because of space limitations, I chose to showcase some of the lesser-known ones with the hope to bring awareness to these hidden treasures. Below is a full list of all museums in Athens, each one more fascinating than the other. For any omissions I sincerely apologize in advance.

Acropolis Museum
www.theacropolismuseum.gr
Dionysiou Areopagitou 15, Athens

Archeological Museum of Kerameikos
Ermou 148, Thission

Acropolis Research Center
Makrigianni 2-4, Athens

Athenais Cultural Center
Athinais.com.gr
Kastorias 36, Botanikos

Athens University History Museum
www. historymuseum.uoa.gr
Tholou 5, Plaka

Athens War Museum
www.warmuseum.gr
Leoforos Vasillisis Sofias and Rizari 2

Athens City Museum – Vourou Eutaxia
www.athenscitymuseum.gr
Ioannou Paparrigopoulou 5-7, Athens

Archeological Museum of Piraeus
www.piraeus.org/museum.html
Charilaou Trikoupi 31, Piraeus

Byzantine and Christian Museum
www.byzantinemuseum.gr
Vasilissis Sofias 22, Athens

Benaki Museum of Islamic Art
www.benaki.org
Agion Asomaton 22 and Dipilou 12, Psyrri

B. & M. Theocharakis Foundation for the Fine Arts & Music
www.thf.gr
Vasilissis Sofias 9 and Merlin 1, Sintagma

Opposite: *Standing woman, Kolettis mansion, Athens*

MUSEUM INDEX

Benaki Museum
www.benaki.gr
Koumpari 1 and Vasilissis Sofias

Benaki Museum – PIREOS 138
www.benaki.gr
Pireos 138 and Andronikou, Gazi

Centre for Popular Craft & Tradition "Aggeliki Xatzimichali
www.cityofathens.gr
Xatzimichali 6, Plaka

Dodekanisiako Museum
www.cityofathens.gr
Dodonis 19, Athens

DESTE Foundation for Contemporary Art
www.deste.gr
Filellinon 11, Nea Ionia

Engraving and Graphic Arts Museum
Navarchou Nikodimou 11, Athina

Electrical Railway Museum
Akti Kallimasioti 275, Piraeus

Epigraphic Museum
Tositsa 1, Athens

Eugenides Foundation – Planetarium
www.eef.edu.gr/
387 Syggrou Avenue, entrance at 11 Pentelis Street, Athens

Filio Haidemenou Museum of Asia Minor Greeks
Dekelias 153 and Attalias 2, Nea Filadelphia

Frissiras Museum of Modern European Art
www.frissirasmuseum.com
Monis Asteriou 3-7, Plaka

G. Gounaropoulos Museum
Gounaropoulou 6, Ilisia

Goulandris Museum of Natural History
www.gnhm.gr
Levidou 13, Kifisia

Hellenic Literary and Historical Archive (ELIA)
www.elia.org.gr
Agiou Andreou 5, Athens

Herakleidon Museum
www.herakleidon.org
Iraklidon 16, Athina

MUSEUM INDEX

Hellenic Children's Museum
www.hcm.gr
Kidathineon 14, Plaka

Hellenic World Foundation – Idrima Mizonos Politismou
www.ime.gr
Pireos 254, Tavros

Hellenic Motor Museum
www.hellenicmotormuseum.gr
3rd Septemvriou 74-78, Athens

Hellenic Maritime Museum
https://www.hmmuseum.gr/
Akti Themistokleous, Piraeus

Ilias Lalaounis Jewelry Museum
www.lalaounis-jewelrymuseum.gr
Kallisperi 12, Athens

Kouvoutsaki Art Institute
www.kouvoutsakis-pinakothiki.gr/
Levidou 11, Kifisia

Loverdos Museum – Ziller Mansion
www.loverdosmuseum-bma.gr
Mavromichali 6, Athina

Museum of Ancient Market
Stoa Attalou, Thission

Museum of Cycladic Art
www.cycladic.gr
Neofitou Douka 4, Athens

Museum of Criminology
Mikras Asias 75, Goudi

Museum of Greek Folk Art
Kidathineon 17, Plaka

Museum of Greek Folk Musical Instruments "Fivos Anoyanakis" – Centre for Ethnomusicology
Diogenous 1, Athens

Museum of European and Eastern Art
Euelpidon 1, Athens

Melina Mercuri Museum and Cultural Centre and Shadow Puppet Theater of Charidimos
Iraklidon 66 and Thessalonikis, Thissio

Municipal Gallery of Athens
Leonidiou Millerou, Metaxourgeio

MUSEUM INDEX

Megaron Athens Concert Hall
www.megaron.gr/en/
Vasilissis Sofias & Kokkali

Michalis Cacoyannis Foundation
www.mcf.gr/en/mcf/
Pireos 206, Tavros

Modern Ceramics Study Center
www.potterymuseum.gr/
Melidoni 4, Athina

MOMus – Museum Alex Mylona
www.momus.gr
Agion Asomaton Square 5, Athens

Museum of Technology "Phaeton"
www.phaetonmuseum.gr
Kalamos 360 klm. National Road Athens-Lamia

Museum of Hellenic Air Force
www.haf.gr
Athens Deikelia Air Base, Tatoi

Museum of the Anti-dictatorship Struggle – A/T VELOS
www.flisvosmarina.com/el/
www.velos.hellenicnavy.gr
Flisvos Marina, Paleo Faliro

Maritime Tradition Museum
www.maritime-museum.gr
Anapafseos, Perama

Museum of Anthropology, Athens University
www.anthropologymuseum.med.uoa.gr
Mikras Asias 75, Athens

Museum of Paleontology and Geology, Athens University
www.old.biol.uoa.gr/zoolmuseum/
Oulof Palme, Zografou

Museum of Mineralogy and Petrology, Athens University
https://www.uoa.gr/to_panepistimio/moyseia/oryktologias_kai_petrologias/
Zografou

Museum of Eleftherios Venizelos
www.cityofathens.gr
Christou Lada 2, Eleftherias Park

Museum of Greek Children's Art
www.childrensartmuseum.gr
Kodrou 9, Plaka

MUSEUM INDEX

Museum of the History of Greek Costume
Dimokritou 7, Athens

Marika Kotopouli Museum
Alekou Panagouli 14, Zografou

Mineralogical Museum of Lavrion
www.emel.gr/oryktologiko-mouseio
Plateia Iroon Politechniou, Lavrio

Museum of Political Exiles "Ai Stratis"
www.exile-museum.gr
Agion Asomaton 31, Keramikos

Museum of Emotions for Children & Teens
www.mce.gr
Karatza 7 and Tsami Karatasou, Filopappu

National Archeological Museum
www.namuseum.gr
Patision 44 and Tositsa, Athens

National Gallery -Museum of Alexandros Soutzos
www.nationalgallery.gr
Michalakopoulou 1 and Leoforos Vasileos Kostantinou 55

National Museum of Contemporary Art (EMST)
www.emst.gr
Former Fix Factory, Kallirrois Avenue. & Amvr. Frantzi Street, Athens

National Museum of Contemporary Art – New Wing, Athens Concert Hall
Vasilissis Sofias and P. Kokkali, Athens

Nikos Chatzikyriakos-Gikas Art Gallery – Benaki Museum
www.benaki.org
Kriezotou 3, Athens

National Garden Botanical Museum
Leoforos Vasilissis Sofias, Vasilissis Olgas Kiosk

National Historical Museum
www.nhmuseum.gr
Stadiou 13, Athens

National Bank of Greece Cultural Foundation
www.miet.gr
20 Aghiou Konstantinou & Menandrou Streets

MUSEUM INDEX

Numismatic Museum of Athens
www.nummus.gr
Panepistimiou 12, Athens

OTE Museum of Telecommunications
www.otegroupmuseum.gr
Proteos 25, New Kifisia

Onassis Stegi
www.onassis.org/onassis-stegi
Leoforos Andrea Siggrou 107, Athens

Pavlos and Alexandra Kanellopoulos Museum
camu.gr
Panos and Theoria 12, Athens

Piraeus Municipal Art Gallery
www.piraeus.gov.gr
Pireos 5, Piraeus

Perama Fisheries Museum
Dimokratias 210, Perama

Pottery Museum
www.potterymuseum.gr
Melidoni 6, Kerameikos

Panos Aravantinos Museum
Agiou Kostantinou2, Municipal Theater of Piraeus

Skironio Center – Kifissias Park of Contemporary Sculpture
www.skironio.gr
Georgiou Lira 73, Kifisia

Syggros Hospital Museum
www.syggros-hosp.gr/mouseio.htm
Dragoumi 5, Athens 5

Shadow Puppet Theater Museum "Evgenios Spatharis"
www.karagiozismuseum.gr
Mesogion and Boriou Ipirou 27, Kastalias Square, Marousi

Sketching Museum
Liosion 22, Athens

Sofia Laskaridou, Municipal Gallery of Kallithea
120 Laskaridou, Kallithea

Stavros Niarchos Foundation Cultural Center
https://www.snfcc.org/
Leoforos Siggrou 364, Kallithea

MUSEUM INDEX

Tourism Museum
www.tourismmuseum.gr
Kleomenous 2, Athens

The Philatelic and Postal Museum
www.ftmuseum.gr
Plateia Stadiou 5 and Fokianou 2

The Jewish Museum of Greece
www.jewishmuseum.gr
Nikis 39, Athens

Theater Museum of Athens
www.theatermuseum.gr
Akademias 50, Athens

Tactual Museum of Athens
www.tactualmuseum.gr
Doiranis 198, Kallithea

Technopolis City of Athens
www.athens-technopolis.gr
Pireos Street

The Greek Film Archive Foundation
Iera Odos 48, Kerameikos

The Angelos' and Leto's Katakouzenos House Museum
www.katakouzenos.gr
Leoforos Amalias 4, Sintagma

The Aikaterini Laskaridis Foundation
www.laskaridisfountation.org
Praxitelous 169 and Mpoumpoulinas, Piraeus

Vorres Museum NPID
vorresmuseum.gr
Diadochou Konstantinou 1, Peania

Yannis Tsarouchis Foundation Museum
www.tsarouchis.gr
Ploutarchou 28, Marousi

Zygomalas Folk Museum
Aulona, Athens

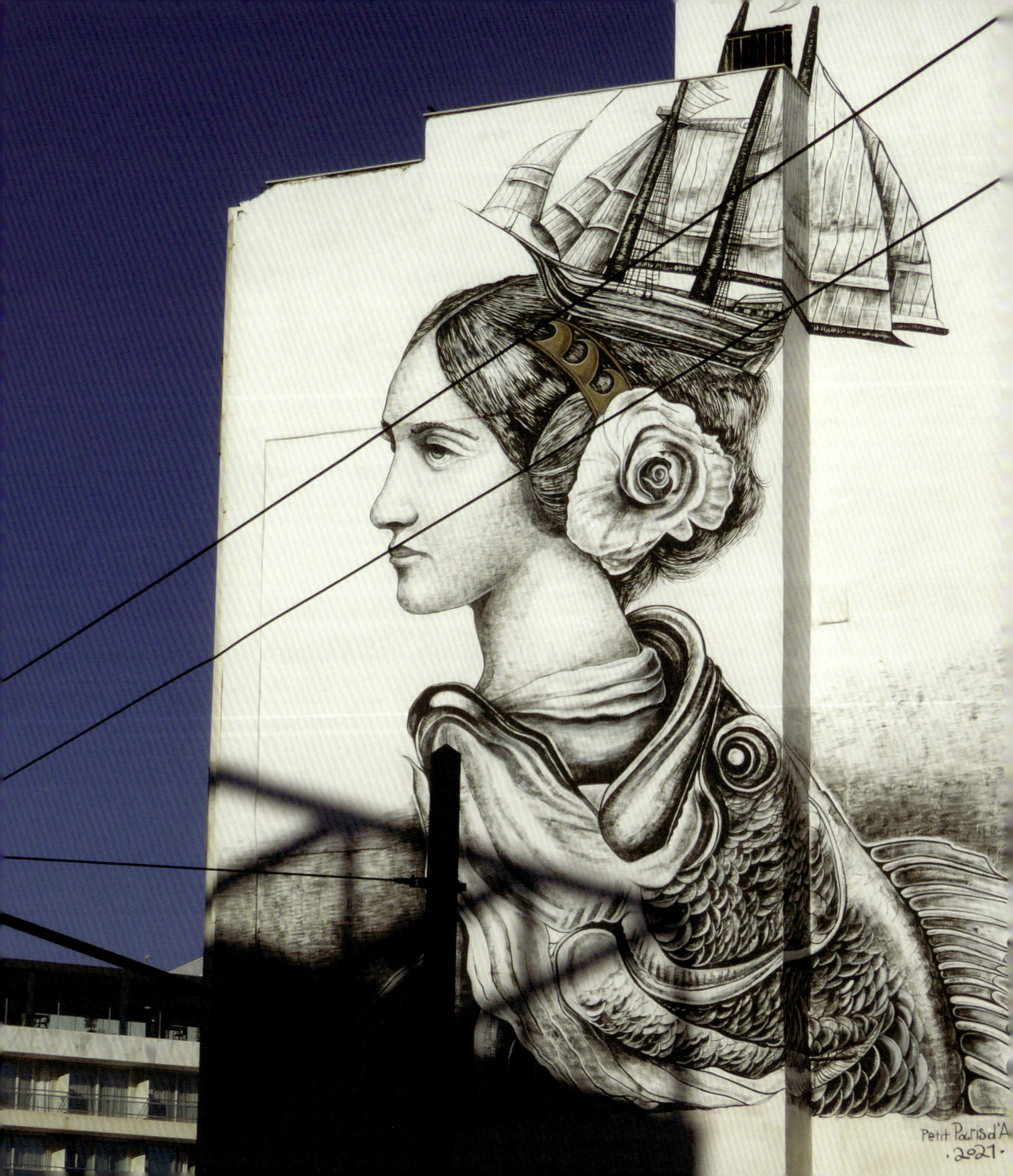
Petit Paris d'A
·2021·

STREET ARTISTS

On my many walks I was fortunate to encounter the work of some astonishing muralists whose empathy, insightfulness and humor opened my mind and taught me how to "see better." Greece is experiencing a renaissance in street art with numerous artists creating thought provoking murals. The list below is a small representation of these artists. I'm certain that I've overlooked some. My sincere hope is that one day, I'll be able to complete the list.

Achilles

Alex Kataras

Alex Martinez

Alexandros Vasmoulakis aka Vasmou

Anna Dimitriou

Apset

Artemios

Ashos

Atek

Bane

Beebs

Bibbito

Bilos

Blaze

Blu

Cacao Rocks

Caze

Chrysolie

Cleo43

Coins

Dask

Dimitris Dokos

Dimitris Taxis

Elato-Twis

Fikos

Gera

Goin

Gonzalo Borondo

Gospel

Greg Papagrigoriou

Gregos

Ino

Insane 51

Ioye

Jasone

Opposite: *Ode 2 the Big Sea, mural by Leonidas Giannakopoulos, Agiou Konstantinou Street, Athens*

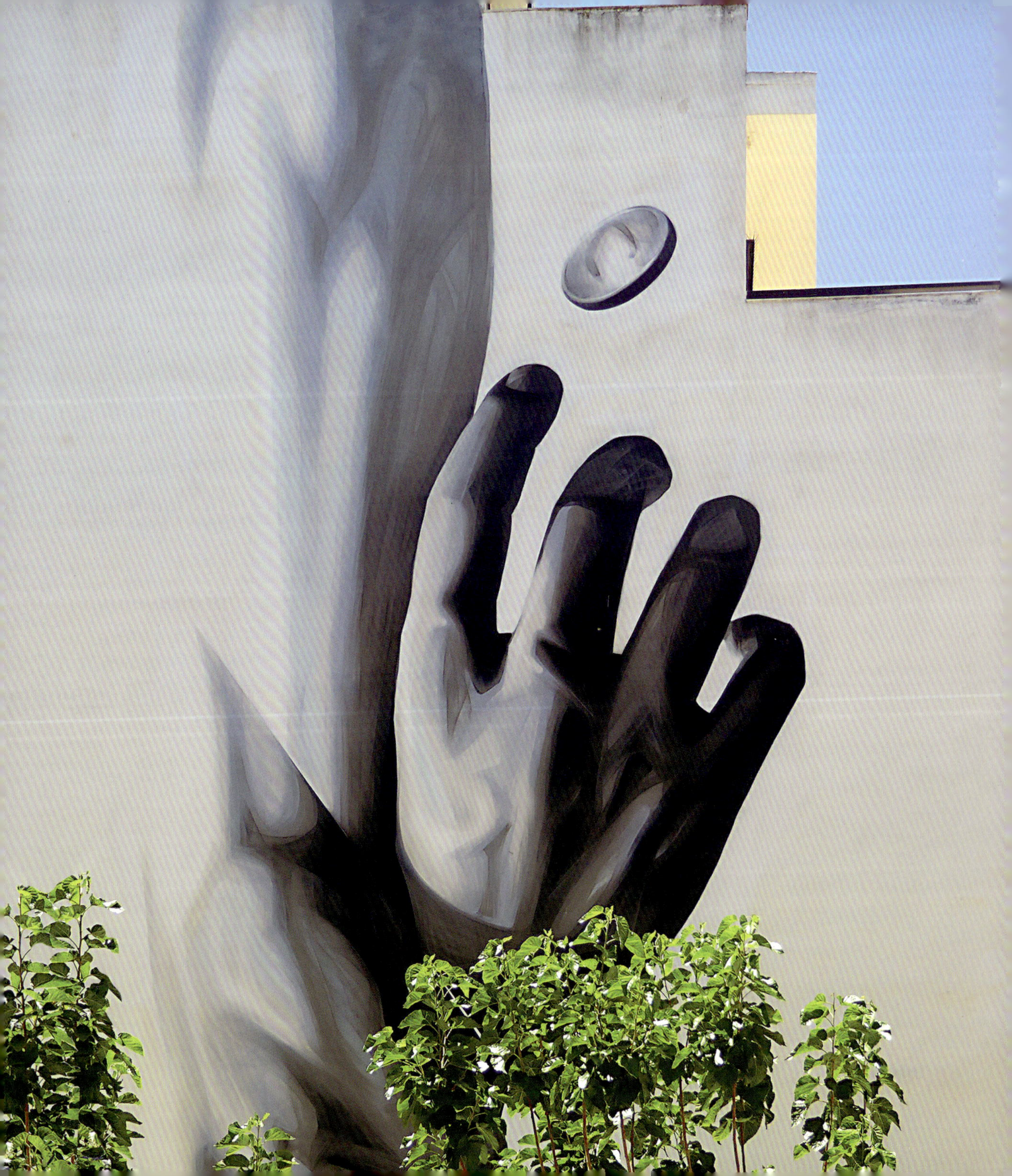

STREET ARTISTS

Jola
Ketz
Kouka Ntadi
Leonidas Giannakopoulos
Liakada
Live2
Lune
MamboAthens
Manolis Anastasakos
Manomatic
Mariana Cute
Marios Simopoulos
MrDada
Nastwo
Nikos Tsounakas
Nique
Nozo1
OneBran
Oré
Orgi
Os Gemeos
Pavlos Tsankonas
Poiztwo
Rimon
Rtmone
Ruin
Same84
Senor
Sidren
Simek
Simoni Fontana
Simple G
Sinke
Sive, aka Stamatis Laskaris
Snuz
Sonke Wia
Soteur
Sotiris Fen
Spent
Stamatis Liaskos
Stmts
Taish
Tam
Think
Vasmou
WD (Wild Drawings)
Woozy
Yiakou
Yoker

Opposite: *Wake Up, mural by INO, Exarcheia*

It's my belief that nothing occurs in a vacuum and that every encounter, action, and reaction serves the purpose of awakening the mind. This experience is unique and personal for every individual but when shared with others, it becomes miraculous.

I've been fortunate to be represented by ORO Editions, a publishing house that allows me to bring forth my vision, no matter how small or large it is. For this, I want to thank Gordon Goff for his trust, Kirby Anderson for being such an exceptional project manager and Brooke Biro for going above and beyond to share the book with a larger audience.

I want to thank TJ Gemignani for not only being such a brilliant photo editor and for bringing my photographs to life, but also for his constant support and encouragement; my sister, Titika Angelidakis for answering my late-night calls and reviving my flagging confidence, and my mother, Irini Angelidakis for providing me with the most nutritious foods keeping me healthy.

I also want to thank the many talented artists I discovered in my wanderings who allowed me to see Athens through their eyes, as well as my friends

ACKNOWLEDGMENT

in New York and Athens who always stand by me: Chara A., Eileen B., Greg A. J., Fran L., Elisa S., Jack A.S., Lynette S., Nick T., and Tiffany E.W. You are truly the best.

Thanasis Giochalas' and Tonia Kafetzaki's book, *Athena, Tracing the City with History and Literature as a Guide* (*Αθήνα, ιχνηλατώντας την πόλη με οδηγό την ιστορία και τη λογοτεχνία*), has been an invaluable source of inspiration and knowledge, and so have the many compelling articles from the publications of *Michani tou Xronou, Kathimerini Newspaper, LiFO* Magazine, and *Athens Voice*.

Finally, I'd like to thank Athens, this magical city with its vast history, contradictions, and tenacious spirit, that never ceases to inspire and amaze me. Walking around the small streets and alleys filled me with a profound love for its people and their stories, sometimes exhilarating and other times painful, but never losing sight of what's important.

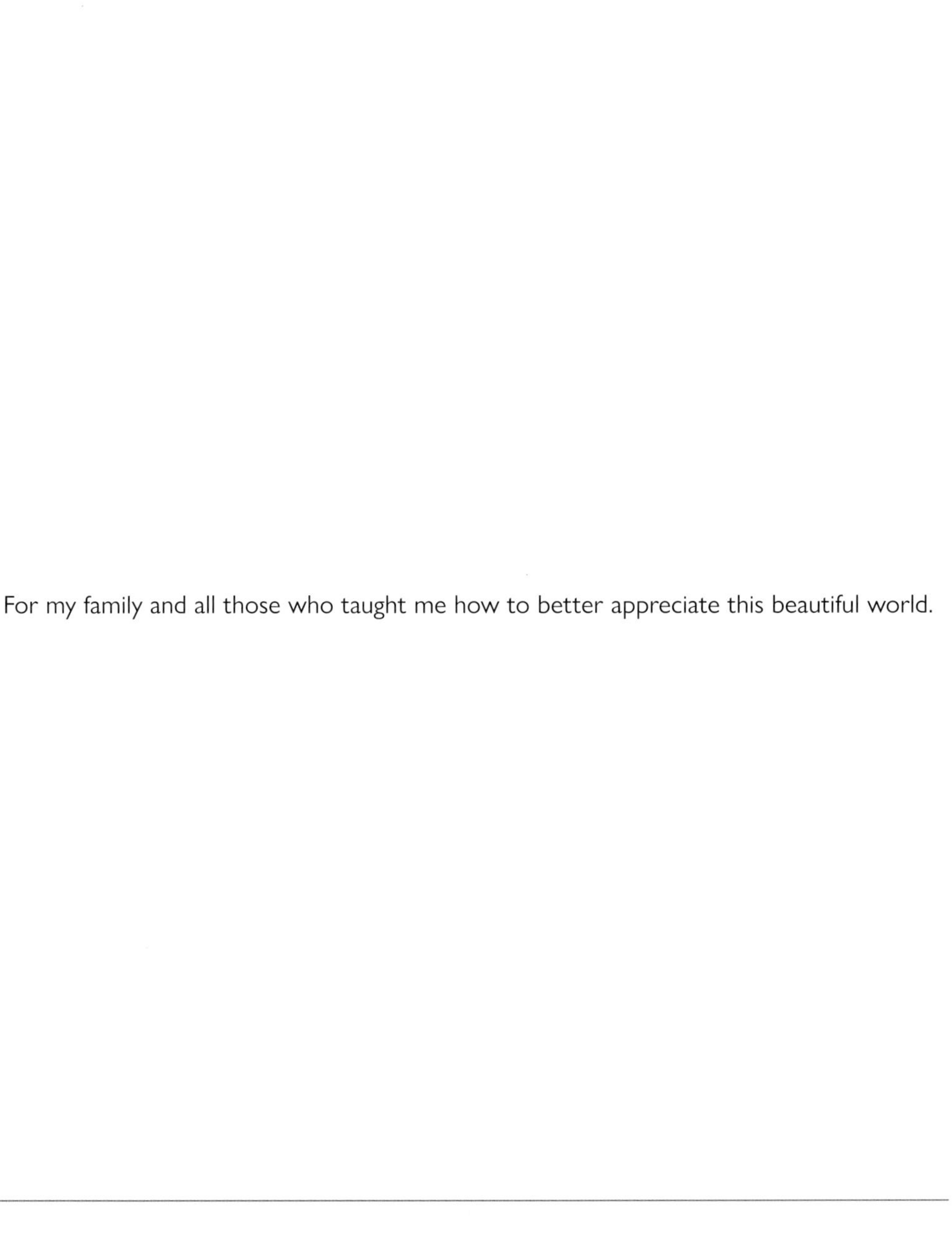

For my family and all those who taught me how to better appreciate this beautiful world.

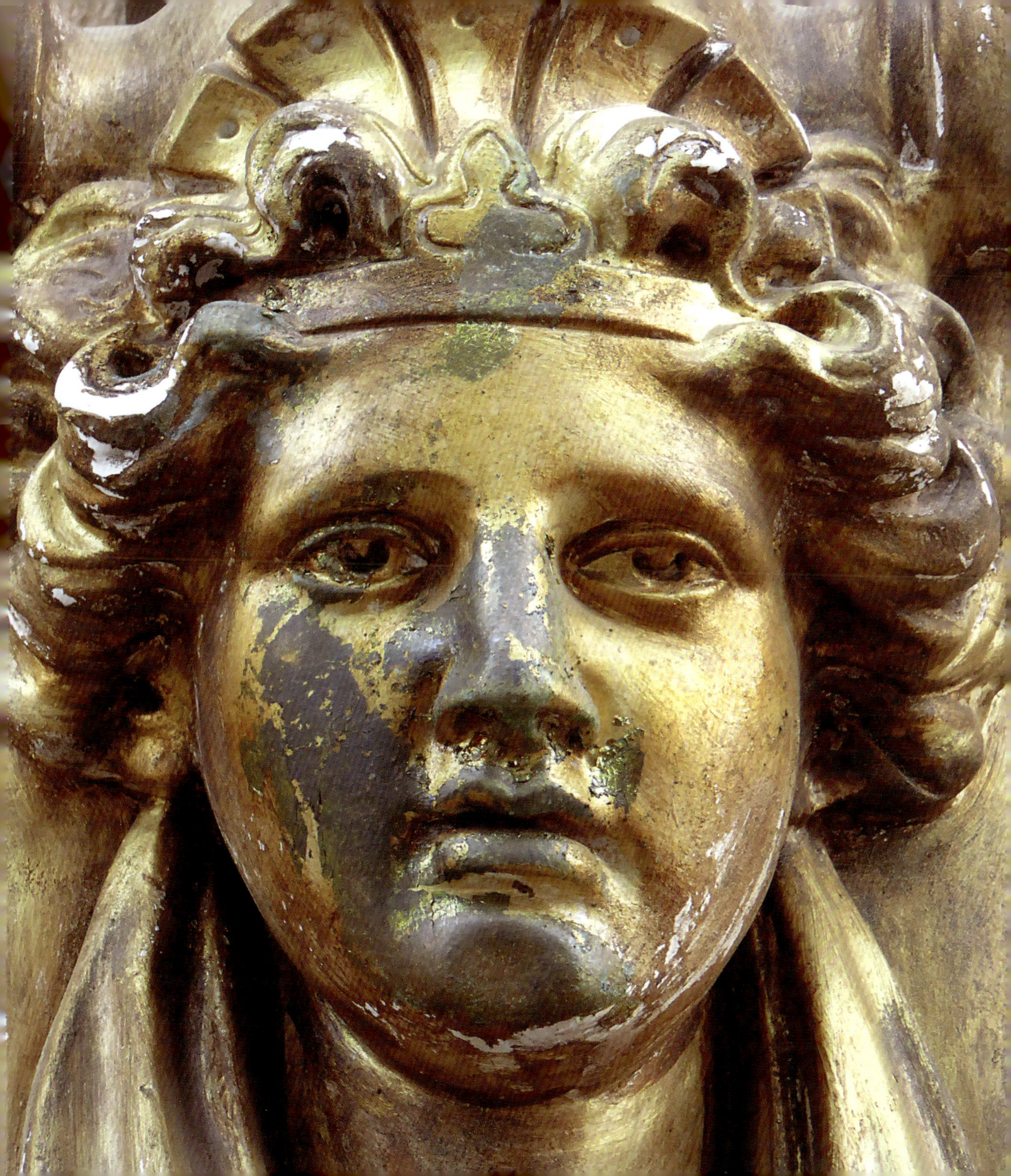